"Insightful, forward-thinking, and practical. As technology becomes increasingly integrated into our lives, balancing it with human judgment is emerging as a crucial skill for the future. The book looks into the dilemma of how much control we should allow technology in our lives. It offers a clear framework for thoughtful decision-making, helping readers navigate the intersection of innovation and ethics, leading them toward a deeper understanding of responsible technological advancement. A valuable guide for shaping thoughtful responses to the challenges ahead."
Emilia Wietrak, *Professor of People Management and Organization, ESADE Business School, Spain*

"Artificial intelligence is transforming the way we live, becoming increasingly significant and intrusive in all human activities. In this context, it is essential to ensure that AI augments human abilities rather than replacing them. This book serves precisely this purpose, providing readers with a clear framework for leveraging data, AI systems, and human judgment. A highly readable and extremely engaging work, born from interactions with 150 experts from 50 different nations and written by an author whose professional and personal life embodies the spirit of 'augmentation', intended as the relentless pursuit of new challenges and opportunities, adaptability in shifting contexts, and innovation through cross-cultural exchange."
Francesco Villante, *Professor of Nuclear and Subnuclear Physics, University of L'Aquila, Italy*

"Giulio Toscani is a business school professor with a unique profile: he combines his executive experience in high-tech companies with his expertise in managing cross-cultural teams and his passion for teaching management at global business schools. Giulio is a true Renaissance man with a profound humanistic component, who has managed to produce solid research work at the intersection of big data, AI systems, and human judgment to illuminate this 21st-century management masterpiece. *PrAIority* is a fascinating book that examines the interaction between cutting-edge technology and the leadership imperative to bring a human perspective to the new world of AI. An essential read."
Xavier Ferràs, *MBA, PhD, Professor of Innovation, Operations and Data Sciences at ESADE Business School, Spain*

"Giulio Toscani provides a compelling case for how artificial intelligence will enhance human abilities rather than replace them. The intersection of data, AI systems, and human judgment is where managers, decision makers, and business leaders have the most to gain from AI. This book explains how. With a strong emphasis on human-AI collaboration, ethical considerations, and the role of critical thinking, this book provides a comprehensive framework for understanding how AI will add value to various fields. It is an invaluable resource for professionals seeking to enhance their skills and stay ahead in the AI-driven future."
Marco Tortoriello, *Professor of Strategy and Organizations at Bocconi University, Italy*

"Amid the daily flood of AI-generated statements, opinions, and assertions about human thinking, it is refreshing—and grounding—to read some truly human thought about AI."
Luis Palencia, *Professor in the Department of Accounting and Control, IESE Business School, Spain*

Augmented

In a world where artificial intelligence is reshaping industries, how can we ensure that AI enhances human skills rather than replacing them? This book offers readers an accessible and insightful guide to the positive potential of AI for human augmentation.

Drawing from consultations with 150 AI experts from across 50 countries, *Augmented* introduces the concept of "prAIority", which connects three essential pillars: data, AI systems, and human judgment. It examines how data fuels innovation, the intricacies of designing and refining AI systems, and the critical role of human expertise in harnessing AI's strengths. Breaking down complex ideas, this book equips readers with the knowledge to understand how AI can be integrated into their decision-making processes, ultimately empowering them to achieve better outcomes in diverse fields such as healthcare, design, and business.

With a focus throughout on human–AI collaboration rather than automation and on seamless integration—for smarter, faster decisions, and innovation—this is a must-read book for professionals looking to enhance their skills and stay ahead in the AI-driven future as well as curious beginners seeking a clear framework.

Augmented

prAIority to Enhance Human Judgment through Data and AI

Giulio Toscani

CRC Press
Taylor & Francis Group
Boca Raton London New York

CRC Press is an imprint of the
Taylor & Francis Group, an **informa** business

Designed cover image: Giulio Toscani

First edition published 2025
by CRC Press
2385 NW Executive Center Drive, Suite 320, Boca Raton FL 33431

and by CRC Press
4 Park Square, Milton Park, Abingdon, Oxon, OX14 4RN

CRC Press is an imprint of Taylor & Francis Group, LLC

© 2025 Giulio Toscani

ISBN: 978-1-032-87534-7 (hbk)
ISBN: 978-1-032-86493-8 (pbk)
ISBN: 978-1-003-53316-0 (ebk)

DOI: 10.1201/9781003533160

Typeset in Times
by Newgen Publishing UK

Contents

About the Author

Giulio Toscani is a dynamic thought leader in digital strategy with more than 20 years of global experience spanning academia and industry. He earned a PhD at the KTH Royal Institute of Technology, Sweden, and has served as an Adjunct Professor at ESADE, Spain. Currently, he shares his expertise at renowned institutions such as Stockholm University, Politecnico Milano, and NUCB, Japan. As an advisor and investor, Dr. Toscani is actively involved with Navozyme in Singapore and Muns in Spain, having also worked with multinationals such as Telefonica, General Electric, Nike, and PWC on their digital transformations.

1 prAIority

Technology is by far weaker than necessity.

Eschilo, *Prometheus Bound.*

1.1 INTRODUCTION TO PRAIORITY

prAIority is an emerging skill that integrates data, Artificial Intelligence (AI) systems, and human judgment to enhance human capabilities rather than replace them. Inspired by Aristotle's *Nicomachean Ethics*,[1] it draws on the virtues of *episteme* (knowledge), *phronesis* (practical wisdom), and *techne* (craft) to create a balanced approach to AI use. First, it emphasizes the importance of high-quality data (episteme) as the foundation for AI, addressing challenges such as data silos and ensuring data integrity. Second, AI systems (techne) should be designed to augment human decision-making, not simply automate tasks, while prioritizing ethical considerations like privacy and bias. Finally, human judgment (phronesis) remains crucial, guiding AI applications with practical wisdom to ensure they align with ethical standards and societal values. prAIority advocates for AI that serves as a tool for human empowerment, balancing technological innovation with ethical responsibility and human oversight. prAIority, inspired by Aristotle's ethics, is a concept that has evolved through my extensive work interviewing data scientists worldwide, spending countless hours understanding their challenges with data, AI systems, and human judgment. These in-depth discussions revealed common struggles, from data management and privacy concerns to the complexities of integrating AI into real-world scenarios. Throughout the book, you will find numerous references to this research, shaped into various papers and articles. Key topics include Tacit Knowledge, exploring how unwritten, experiential insights influence AI development, and a cross-disciplinary approach that emphasizes the value of blending expertise from diverse fields. Data privacy is another critical theme, addressing how data scientists navigate the delicate balance between leveraging data and maintaining user trust. The book also explores the realities of working with AI, contrasting the McDonaldization of AI—where efficiency and standardization dominate—with the potential for AI augmentation that enhances humans rather than replacing them. Additionally, I explore the multiple dimensions of time in coding, examining how time pressures, deadlines, and the pace of technological change affect AI development. prAIority aims to offer a balanced approach, advocating for AI that augments human capabilities while respecting ethical standards and societal values. This approach emphasizes that AI should not just automate tasks but should be thoughtfully integrated into human decision-making processes, guided by practical wisdom and ethical responsibility.

DOI: 10.1201/9781003533160-1

1.1.1 HCI Human–Computer Interaction

Human–computer interaction (HCI) is a field of study that focuses on the design and use of computer technology, emphasizing the interfaces between people (users) and computers.[2] Throughout this book, we will explore why the role of HCI is important in prAIority, in both user engagement and technology development. HCI principles help design interfaces that are easy to use, making technology accessible to a broader audience and leading to higher user satisfaction through intuitive and enjoyable experiences. It ensures accessibility for all, including those with disabilities, by incorporating features such as screen readers and alternative input methods. On the technology development side, HCI drives innovation by exploring new ways for humans to interact with technology, such as touch screens, voice recognition, and gesture controls. Efficient HCI design streamlines processes, reduces the time and effort required to complete tasks, minimizes errors, and improves the reliability of technology. Additionally, user-friendly interfaces increase the likelihood of technology adoption, making it easier for new technologies to gain traction in the market. In our digital age, HCI ensures technology is intuitive and user-friendly, shaping how we engage with devices like smartphones. This chapter explores HCI's role in managing digital density and enhancing user experiences, while also examining how augmenting technologies combine human decision-making with machine intelligence for improved outcomes.

Human factors is a science and engineering field that focuses on human abilities, limitations, and performance. It aims to design systems that are efficient, safe, comfortable, and enjoyable for users. It also involves creativity, allowing practitioners to apply their skills in innovative ways. When we talk about human factors in the context of computing, it becomes HCI. HCI is a specialized area within human factors, focusing specifically on how people interact with computers and technology. Essentially, HCI is about understanding and improving the way humans use computing systems.[3]

Technology shapes how we live, work, and communicate, with HCI playing a key role. HCI determines how we engage with computers, software, and digital devices, making it crucial for both users and developers. Consider smartphones. For users, HCI ensures devices are user-friendly and efficient, with intuitive gestures and easy navigation enhancing satisfaction. For developers, HCI principles guide the creation of apps that meet user expectations, promoting engagement and reducing frustration. Product managers and decision-makers also benefit from HCI insights. Tools like Google Maps use HCI principles to provide real-time, efficient guidance, improving our driving experience.[4] Similarly, HCI-informed tools like ChatGPT streamline tasks, freeing up time for more critical activities. HCI's impact extends to innovation and entrepreneurship. Voice-activated assistants like Siri and Alexa, developed through HCI research, have revolutionized our interaction with technology. However, HCI must balance efficiency with human adaptability to future changes. Incorporating critical thinking and tacit knowledge—personal, experience-based insights—enhances HCI. Designers and developers draw on critical thinking and tacit knowledge to create natural, intuitive user experiences, as we will see in Chapter 2. This deep, experiential knowledge, gained through practice, anticipates user needs in ways explicit knowledge cannot. For decision-makers, valuing certain features like critical thinking and tacit knowledge fosters innovation and agility within organizations. It leads to better strategic choices and more responsive products and services. HCI enriches tools making them more user-friendly and effective.

1.1.2 prAIority Three Pillars: Data, AI Systems, and Human Judgment

In today's world, HCI has gained immense significance, but the introduction of AI is reshaping this landscape at an accelerated pace. With the increasing reliance on AI systems across industries, "prAIority"—the skill of strategically focusing on how data, AI systems, and human judgment can augment our potential—has never been more crucial. By harnessing these three pillars, organizations and individuals can unlock new opportunities for growth and innovation, ensuring they remain competitive in this rapidly evolving environment. However, the concept of prAIority is not entirely new; it has deep roots in ancient philosophy, particularly Aristotle's *Nicomachean Ethics*, where three key intellectual virtues are emphasized: "*episteme*", "*phronesis*", and "*techne*". Aristotle established a clear distinction between *technê* and *epistêmê*, differentiating between a contingent reality and a necessary one. *Technê* is typically translated as craft or art, while *epistêmê*, often interpreted as knowledge, is more precisely understood here as scientific knowledge. Additionally, *phronesis* is translated as practical wisdom.[5] These virtues, when applied to modern AI systems, provide a framework for the skill of prAIority, which balances the integration of data (episteme), human judgment (phronesis), and AI systems (techne). To fully develop the skill of prAIority, it is necessary to recognize the importance of these three elements and how they interact with each other. Each plays a vital role, and without balance, the potential benefits of AI technology may not be fully realized. Let's explore how episteme, phronesis, and techne translate into the three pillars of prAIory and why this balance is essential for maximizing human augmentation. In Aristotle's philosophy, episteme refers to scientific knowledge—knowledge that is universal, objective, and verifiable. In the context of prAIority, episteme can be understood as the pillar of data, big data.[6] Data, much like scientific knowledge, is the foundation upon which AI systems are built and is necessary for creating effective solutions. Imagine building a strong house. To do this, you need a solid foundation—like concrete or bricks. In the same way, data acts as the foundation for AI systems.[7] For example, consider a simple AI that recommends movies. If the AI is trained on a dataset of movie ratings, genres, and user preferences, it learns what types of films people enjoy. Just as scientific knowledge helps us understand the world, high-quality data helps the AI understand patterns and make accurate suggestions.[8] Without enough good data, the AI might recommend movies that don't match what users like, much like a house built on a weak foundation might collapse. So, data is essential for creating effective AI solutions that meet user needs. The vast amounts of data available today provide unprecedented opportunities for AI to uncover insights that would otherwise remain hidden. However, for data to truly drive innovation, it must be structured, accurate, and integrated across systems, free from the isolation of silos. An excellent example of how episteme—or data—drives prAIority can be seen in the transport sector. Consider the development of AI-driven traffic management systems that optimize urban mobility. These systems rely on massive datasets, including real-time traffic flow, accident reports, and historical travel patterns, to predict congestion and suggest alternative routes.[9] The accuracy and effectiveness of these systems are directly tied to the quality and completeness of the data they are trained on. If the data is incomplete or outdated, the AI's ability to manage traffic efficiently will diminish.[10] Therefore, understanding the role of data, or episteme, is critical to prAIority, as it ensures that AI operates from a robust and up-to-date knowledge base. While data and AI tools provide incredible computational power, they are not sufficient on their own. Aristotle's concept of phronesis, or practical wisdom, highlights the importance of human judgment in decision-making. Phronesis is the capacity to make wise choices in specific situations, taking into account not just facts, but also ethical considerations, context, and experience. In the realm of prAIority, "phronesis" represents the human element—the ability to apply human judgment and empathy when working alongside AI systems.[11] Aristotle regarded phronesis as the greatest of intellectual virtues. It involves the complex interplay between theoretical understanding and practical judgment.[12] An example of phronesis in action is the use of AI in autonomous vehicles. While AI systems can process data in real time to navigate roads, they lack the moral and ethical reasoning that humans possess. In a situation where a self-driving car must decide between two harmful outcomes, such as avoiding one obstacle, but potentially hitting another, human judgment is needed to weigh the ethical implications of the decision. This is where phronesis plays a role in prAIority: humans must remain in control of AI systems to guide them in making decisions that align with societal values and ethical norms.

THE DARK FOREST OF EXISTENCE: EXPLORING THE POSSIBILITIES OF HUMAN EXTINCTION AND SIMULATION

An example of the absence of human judgment can be found in Nick Bostrom's 2003 hypothesis, which posits that at least one of the following statements must be true: (1) the human species is very likely to go extinct before reaching a "posthuman" stage, (2) any posthuman civilization is extremely unlikely to conduct a significant number of simulations of their evolutionary history, or (3) we are almost certainly living in a computer simulation. This suggests that the belief in a substantial chance of becoming posthumans who create ancestor simulations is likely false unless we are already in a simulation. To clarify, if (1) is true, we will almost certainly go extinct before achieving posthumanity. If (2) holds, it implies a strong uniformity among advanced civilizations, meaning very few would have wealthy individuals interested in running ancestor simulations. If (3) is accurate, it indicates that we likely exist within a simulation. Given our current ignorance, it seems reasonable to distribute our beliefs fairly evenly among (1), (2), and (3).[13]

In the context of autonomous vehicles, this means that while the AI handles the technical aspects of driving,[14] humans are responsible for ensuring that the technology operates within ethical boundaries. Finally, Aristotle's *techne* refers to the art of making things, often associated with craftsmanship and technical knowledge. In modern terms, "techne" represents the AI systems themselves—the tools and technologies that allow us to augment our capabilities and solve complex problems. Techne is the pillar of prAIority that encompasses the technical infrastructure, algorithms, and machine learning models that drive AI innovation. It is through techne that AI systems can execute tasks with precision, speed, and scalability. A powerful example of techne in prAIority can be seen in public sector initiatives, such as predictive analytics used to optimize resource allocation. For example, some cities use AI to analyze data on traffic patterns, weather conditions, and emergency response times to predict where accidents or incidents are likely to occur.[15] This allows municipalities to allocate police, ambulances, or road maintenance crews more effectively, enhancing public safety. However, these AI-driven predictions are only as good as the algorithms and models that underpin them. In other words, techne plays a vital role in prAIority by ensuring that the AI systems themselves are well-designed, efficient, and capable of augmenting human decision-making processes. While episteme (data), phronesis (practical wisdom), and techne (AI systems) are each critical to prAIority, it is the balance between them that ensures AI serves to augment, rather than replace, human capabilities. Without sufficient data, AI systems lack the knowledge base to make informed decisions. Without human judgment, AI risks making decisions that are technically correct but ethically questionable or misaligned with human values. And without well-designed AI systems, even the best data and human wisdom cannot be effectively harnessed. Take, for instance, the challenges faced by public transportation systems. In some cities, AI systems have been implemented to optimize bus routes and schedules based on data about passenger volume, traffic patterns, and weather conditions. When these systems are integrated effectively—combining real-time data (episteme), human oversight to ensure that community needs are met (phronesis), and powerful algorithms to process the data (techne)—the result is a more efficient and responsive transportation system. However, in cities where these elements are not balanced, the results can be less successful. In cases where data is not shared across different departments or where human judgment is absent in the decision-making process, the AI systems may fail to account for important factors, such as the needs of underserved communities or the accessibility of routes. The skill of prAIority is built upon the harmonious integration of "episteme" (data), "phronesis" (human judgment), and "techne" (AI systems). Each element plays a vital role in ensuring that AI augments human capabilities rather than replacing them. Data provides the foundation of knowledge, human wisdom ensures that ethical and practical considerations are taken into account, and AI systems enable the efficient execution of tasks. By balancing these three pillars, we can fully harness the potential of AI to create a future where humans and machines work together to solve complex problems, innovate, and improve the quality of life across industries. The concept of prAIoritizing initiatives to effectively augment human capabilities hinges on understanding that not all AI developments hold equal value or potential. prAIority focuses on three key elements—data, AI applications, and human judgment—working together to unlock human potential. Data is the foundation, driving insights and enabling AI to make intelligent decisions. AI applications, in turn, process and analyze this data, automating tasks and optimizing outcomes. However, the human element remains crucial, as it's our creativity, intuition, and decision-making that guide AI and leverage its full capabilities. When these three components are aligned, they enhance one another, allowing us to innovate and solve complex challenges. By making prAIority a focus, we can harness technology to drive meaningful progress. Trust is the common elements between them, which is likely multifaceted. We may trust specific computations, but distrust them in certain contexts or for certain groups. For instance, marginalized individuals might need proof that the data, the AI system, and the skills of the developers are fair to them. In fact, data can be biased against them, the AI system could be tuned on profits instead of on equality, and the developers who designed it just focused on operational efficiency instead of minority fairness. As a result, people might perceive AI as producing biased outcomes, leading them to modify the data they provide or critically evaluate its results. Trust, like usability, is about the relationship between technology and its users, and varies across different users or communities.[16] By discerning which data, AI applications, and human judgment will most significantly enhance human abilities, we can focus our efforts and resources on those that promise the greatest benefit, ensuring that AI serves as a true partner in human progress. "prAIority" means carefully choosing which AI technologies to develop and use first, based on how well they can improve humans. This approach targets areas where AI can make a big difference, such as healthcare, education, creative industries, and decision-making. AI helps handle complex tasks by enhancing human thinking, while humans provide a more intuitive approach to uncertain situations. This concept supports the idea that AI should augment, not replace, human abilities.[17] Without prAIority, we risk spreading our efforts too thin, diluting the potential benefits and possibly even exacerbating existing challenges.

1.1.3 prAIority to Augment Human Abilities Rather Than Replace Them with Automation

The approach we take to implementing AI systems will determine whether that potential is realized in ways that truly benefit humanity. This is where prAIority becomes critical—a strategy focused on augmenting human abilities rather than outright replacing them with automation.

AI VS. RADIOLOGISTS: TASK MASTERY, NOT JOB REPLACEMENT

Geoffrey Hinton, Nobel Prize in Physics 2024[18] and a pioneer in the field of artificial intelligence, in 2016 compared the role of radiologists to Wile E. Coyote in the famous cartoon. "If you work as a radiologist, you're like Wile E. Coyote", Hinton remarked. "You've already run off the edge of the cliff, but you haven't realized there's no ground beneath you yet".[19] His metaphor reflects the rapid advancements in AI, particularly in deep-learning systems for medical imaging. Commercial applications in breast and heart imaging have already demonstrated the capabilities of AI in fields that were once the exclusive domain of highly trained professionals. Hinton predicted that within five years, deep learning systems would outperform radiologists, though he acknowledged it might take ten years. He shared this view at a hospital, where, unsurprisingly, it was not well received. Despite this bold claim, it is important to recognize that AI performs tasks, not entire jobs as OpenAI CEO Sam Altman testified at the U.S. Congress in 2023.[20] Hinton's argument emphasizes that AI excels at specific tasks within a profession, but replacing a job in its entirety is much more complex. The U.S. Department of Labor's ONET database (www.onetonline.org), which lists detailed descriptions of various jobs, provides insight into the reality of this challenge. For example, the role of a radiologist is composed of around 30 different tasks, ranging from diagnosing illnesses through imaging to consulting with other doctors. AI may be able to fully automate one or two of these tasks, such as image interpretation, but the vast majority of responsibilities still require human expertise, judgment, and interaction. Ultimately, AI's role in the workplace should be seen as augmenting human capabilities, not replacing them wholesale. Like the internet or other transformative technologies, AI enhances the way tasks are performed, but jobs themselves encompass a wide array of activities that machines alone cannot replicate. While AI can significantly improve efficiency in areas like radiology, the profession as a whole involves a level of complexity and human insight that remains beyond the reach of current technology.

At its core, prAIority seeks to blend the strengths of AI systems with human expertise, decision-making, and creativity. The goal is not to automate jobs, rather difficult, but to automate some tasks to empower humans to do more, better. Augmentation[21] through AI enables humans to remain in control, making critical decisions, innovating, and applying empathy, all while leveraging AI to process vast data sets or handle routine tasks. In contrast, when automation becomes the goal in and of itself, we risk losing human ingenuity and creating systems that, while efficient, lack flexibility and understanding. Why is prAIority essential? First, it ensures that technology serves as an enhancement rather than a replacement. When AI augments human capabilities, people are freed from repetitive, low-value tasks and given the bandwidth to focus on higher-level strategic work. This leads to smarter, more effective outcomes in fields like medicine, engineering, education, and beyond. Humans can be unpredictable, emotional, irrational, and biased in ways that often appear counterproductive. Our impulsive and self-centered tendencies sometimes seem like they might lead to our own undoing. This raises the question of whether removing humans from certain aspects of life might actually be beneficial. However, in his 1930 essay, Economic Possibilities for Our Grandchildren, economist John Maynard Keynes envisioned a future where humans would work just 15 hours per week by the 21st century, effectively creating a five-day weekend. Keynes believed this would present humanity with a new challenge: "For the first time since his creation, man will be faced with his real, his permanent problem—how to occupy the leisure".[22] While our irrational tendencies might seem like weaknesses, many of these traits have evolved to serve us well. Our emotional responses, shaped over millennia, are often designed to provide the best means of handling various situations, including the challenge of filling increased leisure time. Rather than liabilities, these emotional and instinctive behaviors may help us adapt to the changing demands of the future.[23] Like in these examples.

CHATBOTS TO THE RESCUE: HOW AI IS REVOLUTIONIZING CUSTOMER SERVICE FOR LEADING BRANDS[24]

Many companies turned to AI to automate customer service tasks, introducing chatbots that promised efficiency. While automation sped up response times, it failed to provide the empathy and nuance required in more complex customer interactions. Without human oversight or involvement, these AI systems led to customer frustration, unresolved issues, and brand damage. In this case, automating customer service without augmenting human agents led to a breakdown in trust. A prAIority approach would have combined AI's speed in handling routine queries with human agents' ability to solve complex problems and offer personalized care. Here are examples of companies leveraging AI chatbots to enhance their customer service:

Eye-oo:

Eye-oo, a multi-brand eyewear e-commerce platform, relies on excellent customer service to support its collection of popular fashion brands and designer eyewear, including handmade limited edition pieces. To improve response times and reduce the burden on support agents dealing with frequently asked questions, Eye-oo implemented Tidio's AI-powered customer service solution. By incorporating automation while maintaining personalization, they saw a 25% increase in sales, a fivefold boost in conversions, and a 30-second reduction in average response times. Chatbots successfully handled 82% of support conversations, leading to significant lead generation and sales growth.

H&M: H&M, a global fashion retailer, introduced the H&M Virtual Assistant, an AI-powered chatbot designed to offer round-the-clock support. This virtual assistant helps customers with product information, sizing, availability, delivery options, and returns. By engaging users through style-related questions and personalized outfit suggestions, the chatbot has improved the shopping experience. H&M's AI efforts led to a 70% reduction in response times and the introduction of voice search in their mobile app, which enhanced both customer satisfaction and operational efficiency.

Bella Santé: Bella Santé, a prominent med spa in the Greater Boston area, transitioned from traditional call centers to AI-powered customer service. By integrating Tidio's live chat and FAQ chatbots, the company automated 75% of customer conversations. Within six months, Bella Santé gathered over 450 new leads and boosted sales by $66,000, all while personalizing the customer experience. Human agents were alerted to step in when needed, ensuring that customers received timely assistance with complex issues.

However, the lack of prAIority can lead to negative consequences. Since 2019, Tesla's Autopilot has been involved in 736 crashes in the United States, including 17 fatal accidents, with 11 fatalities occurring since May 2022. Between June 2021 and May 15, Tesla vehicles were implicated in nearly 70% of reported crashes involving advanced driver-assist systems, totaling 273 incidents.[25] When crashes involve Tesla's Autopilot, they raise complex legal and ethical issues. Legally, it is difficult to determine who is at fault: the driver, the company, or the technology itself. These incidents challenge existing laws regarding responsibility and technology. Ethically, there is ongoing debate about the extent to which we should rely on machines for critical tasks like driving. It is essential to ensure that these technologies are both safe and reliable before they become widespread.[26] Balancing innovation with safety and ethical considerations is crucial. Beyond preventing these pitfalls, prAIority prevents a more subtle, but equally dangerous risk: spreading efforts too thin. Without clear priorities, organizations might invest in a multitude of AI projects that do not provide tangible benefits, diluting focus and resources. When we fail to prioritize the right AI interventions—those that empower humans rather than displace them—we risk exacerbating existing challenges, such as economic inequality or job displacement. By focusing on AI systems that augment human strengths, we ensure that our efforts are concentrated where they can deliver the most value. prAIority is a vital approach in the age of AI. By concentrating efforts on augmenting human abilities rather than automating tasks, we avoid many of the pitfalls of automation and ensure that AI serves as a tool for human empowerment. This strategy not only yields better outcomes, but also allows us to focus our resources effectively, ensuring that AI truly enhances the world in which we live and work.

1.2 DATA: THE FOUNDATION OF PRAIORITY

1.2.1 Discuss the Critical Role of Data in prAIorization and How It Drives AI's Ability to Create and Predict

prAIority starts with recognizing the areas where AI can most significantly enhance human activity. It involves prioritizing the development and application of AI technologies based on their potential to elevate humans. Central to this concept is the importance of data—AI thrives on data to unlock its full potential.[27] In every sector AI can transform decision-making and innovation by analyzing vast datasets. For example, in healthcare, AI processes large volumes of medical data to detect patterns that doctors might miss, enabling earlier diagnoses and more tailored treatments. However this only suggests the idea that AI should complement, not replace, human abilities, as we will see later. Notable examples of AI in healthcare are its ability to classify eight diabetes complications with 97% accuracy and predict complications and poor blood sugar control with up to 90% accuracy.[28] This combination of AI's data processing power and doctors' clinical expertise leads to better patient outcomes and more efficient healthcare delivery. In education, AI can create tailored learning experiences that adapt to the unique needs and pace of each student, fostering a more inclusive and effective learning environment.[29] By focusing on such high-impact areas, we can leverage AI's strengths to address some of humanity's most pressing challenges. prAIority initiatives requires a thoughtful consideration of both immediate needs and long-term goals. As International Grandmaster Savielly Tartakower famously stated, "Tactics is knowing what to do when there's something to do. Strategy is knowing what to do when there's nothing to do".[30] This captures the essence of short-term action versus long-term vision, highlighting the contrast between iteration and true innovation.[31] While some AI applications can deliver quick wins, such as automating routine tasks to free up human time and energy, others may require more sustained investment, but offer transformative potential. For instance, developing AI systems that enhance creativity can lead to groundbreaking innovations in art, music, and literature, enriching our cultural landscape and expanding the horizons of human expression. For example the recent rise of generative AI is transforming music creation, with synthetic media[32] poised to revolutionize production, consumption, and distribution. This marks the third phase of media evolution, following old and new media. AI-generated music is democratizing content creation, shifting the focus from technology to data availability. Research links deep immersion in music with heightened emotional experiences,[33] a trend now driven by platforms like TikTok, where user engagement enhances immersion. AI's impact is evident in projects like Holly+ by Holly Herndon[34] and Sir Paul McCartney's use of AI[35] to extract John Lennon's vocals, showcasing AI's growing role in music production. This is just the beginning. Throughout the chapter on generative AI, and indeed across the entire book, we will explore how data is set to play an entirely new and transformative role.

1.2.2 Digital Density: How High-Quality, Diverse Data Can Improve AI Outcomes and Provide Meaningful Insights of How Technology Shapes Daily Life

Over the centuries, technological advancements have increasingly distanced us from nature, culminating in the invention of computers in the 1940s. However, it was not until the 1980s that these machines began to significantly impact the daily lives of ordinary people. Between the 1940s and 1980s, only specialists used computers. These machines were too valuable and complicated for the average person. During this period, computers were highly protected and respected, setting the stage for the interactive era that came later.[36] For this reason, in 1977 Ken Olsen, President of Digital Equipment Corporation (DEC), famously said "There is No Reason for Any Individual To

Have a Computer in Their Home".[37] Many years later, in today's world, computers have become central to how we live, work, and communicate. At the core of this technological advancement is the evolving field of HCI, which shapes how individuals engage with digital devices, software, and computers. And data plays a crucial role in this. Understanding the complexities of HCI is not just important—it's transformative for anyone involved in technology. To grasp its significance, let's take the example of the ubiquitous smartphone, an essential tool for many. From a user's perspective, HCI ensures the device is user-friendly, efficient, and responsive to their needs. This involves intuitive gestures, navigable menus, and smooth interaction—all powered by data and constant connectivity. A well-designed interface, grounded in HCI principles, allows users to send messages, browse the internet, or access apps effortlessly, enhancing their experience. From a developer's point of view, HCI, driven by data, is just as crucial. It helps create apps that meet user expectations and needs. Every app is fueled by data. For instance, by applying HCI principles, a developer can design a social media platform that encourages meaningful engagement while reducing user fatigue. In contrast, overlooking HCI can result in poor app design, leading to decreased usage, frustration, and user abandonment. One of the earliest examples of successful HCI was the Apple Macintosh, released in 1984, which revolutionized personal computing with its graphical user interface (GUI). This device set new standards for how people interact with computers, highlighting the power of user-friendly technology rooted in data.

Digital density[38] refers to the abundance of digital data, connectivity, and interactions within a specific space or context. Environments with high digital density need advanced HCI designs to help users make sense of the overwhelming amount of data and interactions. In such settings, users require intuitive interfaces to navigate complex data sets and complete tasks efficiently. Key challenges in these environments include managing information overload, ensuring data privacy, and maintaining seamless connectivity. To address these, systems must adapt to the user's context, offering relevant information and actions based on location, time, and activity. Interfaces that change according to user behavior and preferences can greatly enhance usability and efficiency. Effective data visualization techniques are essential for making sense of large volumes of data, allowing users to quickly interpret and act on information. Interactive design is also crucial, ensuring users can engage with digital systems through intuitive methods like gestures, voice commands, and touch interfaces. Moreover, an increasing number of individuals involved in product management and decision-making roles are recognizing the pivotal role that HCI plays in their day-to-day work. Understanding HCI principles can be a game-changer in terms of product development, resource allocation, and overall efficiency. Consider the example of using Google Maps to navigate through familiar traffic-congested roads. While you are still responsible for driving, Google Maps, based on HCI principles, provides you with real-time, efficient guidance, allowing you to reach your destination faster and with less stress. Similarly, when utilizing a tool like ChatGPT to draft a speech, you can rely on HCI-informed design to streamline the writing process, leaving you with more time to focus on perfecting the final version and delivering the speech effectively. This strategic approach can make the difference between a successful, stress-free experience and a time-consuming, error-prone endeavor. It can also determine which products excel in the market and which fall short. HCI is not limited to its role in making individual interactions with technology more efficient and user-friendly; it also has a significant impact on innovation and entrepreneurship as we will see in Chapter 7 and 8. Consider the creators of voice-activated digital assistants like Siri and Alexa. These entrepreneurs leveraged HCI research to develop revolutionary products that understand and respond to human voice commands. As a result, they fundamentally changed the way we interact with technology. The significance of HCI in this context is undeniable. However, it prompts us to question whether HCI, in its quest for efficiency, is potentially diminishing the role of human beings and their adaptability to future changes.

THE TRANSFORMATIVE IMPACT OF CHATGPT ON WRITING AND THOUGHT

In the modern digital landscape, ChatGPT and similar AI language models are rapidly changing how we interact with technology and each other. These models offer remarkable assistance in drafting emails, writing essays, generating code, and much more. However, as these tools become more integrated into our daily routines, important questions arise about their impact on our cognitive abilities, particularly in terms of writing and thought structuring. The decline of handwriting skills has been evident for years, exacerbated by the prevalence of keyboards and touchscreens. While this shift has streamlined many aspects of communication and work, it has also sparked concerns about the broader implications for cognitive development and fine motor skills. Handwriting engages different parts of the brain compared to typing, fostering better memory retention and deeper understanding. With handwriting becoming less common, there is a risk of losing these cognitive benefits. The advent of AI tools like ChatGPT raises further concerns about the erosion of writing skills. When students and professionals rely heavily on AI to generate text, they may not develop or maintain the ability to articulate their thoughts independently. Writing is a complex skill that involves not just linguistic knowledge but also critical thinking and creativity. If these processes are outsourced to AI, individuals might find their ability to express themselves clearly and originally diminished. Noam Chomsky's theory posits that language is intrinsic to human thought.[39] According to Chomsky, language transcends its role as a mere communication tool and stands as a cornerstone of human cognition. This perspective aligns with Humboldt's[40] assertion, contrasting Kant's[41] view that language is simply a tool for thought rather than a co-producer of thoughts. Language profoundly shapes how we conceptualize and understand the world. If, as Chomsky suggests, language is central to structuring thought, the role of AI in generating language becomes particularly significant. As AI models like ChatGPT become more adept at generating coherent and contextually appropriate text, they increasingly take on the role of structuring our thoughts. This shift can be beneficial, offering clarity and precision in communication. However, it also raises concerns about over-reliance on AI for cognitive tasks that are essential to intellectual development. If AI starts to structure our thoughts by providing ready-made responses and frameworks, we might begin to lose the ability to engage in deep, reflective thinking. The process of writing is often a journey of discovery, where ideas evolve through the act of articulation. By bypassing this process, we risk superficiality in our thinking and a lack of originality in our ideas.

The challenge, then, is to find a balance between leveraging AI's capabilities and maintaining our cognitive skills. AI can be a powerful tool for enhancing productivity and creativity, but it should not replace the fundamental human processes of thinking and writing. Achieving a balance between AI and human roles can be approached by using AI as a supplement rather than a replacement. For instance, AI can handle repetitive tasks like grammar checks or formatting, allowing humans to focus on the creative and critical aspects of writing. In education, AI should be integrated in ways that encourage independent thinking. AI can illustrate concepts or provide examples, but students should still engage in the primary cognitive work. At the Georgia Institute of Technology, this approach was exemplified by Jill Watson, an AI teaching assistant in a master's-level AI course. Many students were unaware that Jill, who was named after IBM's Watson, wasn't human. The class of around 300 students generated roughly 10,000 messages on an online forum each semester—an overwhelming volume for a human assistant, as reported by The Wall Street Journal. Professor Ashok Goel explained that while student numbers might increase, the variety of questions remains relatively stable. To manage repetitive inquiries, Goel and his team developed Jill Watson, equipping her with thousands of past questions and answers. Jill was highly effective, answering questions with a 97% success rate according to Slate. She could understand the context of queries and respond accurately. However, her success didn't replace human teaching assistants. Jill couldn't handle all questions, and more importantly, she couldn't motivate students or provide guidance on coursework. Instead, her role allowed human assistants to focus on more meaningful tasks. Jill exemplified how AI can enhance human capabilities: "Where humans cannot go, Jill will go. And what humans do not want to do, Jill can automate".[42] However, more creative goals can be to be mindful of the long-term impact of AI on cognitive abilities. Encourage practices that foster deep thinking, such as journaling, debate, and handwritten note-taking.[43] As AI continues to evolve, its role in shaping human thought will likely become even more pronounced. It is essential to navigate this evolution thoughtfully, ensuring that AI enhances rather than diminishes our cognitive capabilities. The future may involve a symbiotic relationship where AI and human intelligence complement each other, each playing to its strengths. For instance, AI can process vast amounts of information quickly, identifying patterns and insights that might elude human analysts, like in Georgia State University where they used an AI chatbot named Pounce to reduce "summer melt" by 22 percent, meaning 324 more students attended their first day of fall classes. "Summer melt" occurs when students who enroll in spring drop out before fall. Pounce's success came from targeted text messaging, particularly benefiting low-income, first-generation students who often need personalized support. Georgia State partnered with AdmitHub, an education technology company specializing in conversational AI, to tackle common barriers to enrollment, like financial aid, placement exams, and class registration. Pounce provided 24/7 answers to student queries via text, addressing confusion over forms and campus offices. In its first summer trial in 2016, Pounce delivered over 200,000 responses, handling a volume of questions that would have required 10 additional full-time staff members. Scott Burke, assistant vice president of undergraduate admissions, highlighted that each interaction was customized to the student's enrollment needs. Due to its success, Georgia State continues to use Pounce, expanding its role in other student success initiatives.[44] Meanwhile, humans can provide the nuanced understanding and ethical considerations necessary for meaningful and responsible application of these insights. ChatGPT and other AI language models are undeniably transforming our approach to writing and thinking. While these tools offer significant benefits in terms of efficiency and clarity, they also pose challenges to our cognitive independence and creativity. By consciously balancing the use of AI with the development and maintenance of our cognitive skills, we can harness the power of AI without sacrificing our intellectual autonomy. Ultimately, the key lies in using AI to augment our capabilities, not to replace them.[45] As we continue to integrate AI into our lives, we must remain vigilant about its impact on our cognitive processes, ensuring that we remain active participants in our own intellectual development. This approach will help us navigate the complex interplay between technology and thought, fostering a future where both AI and human intelligence thrive. In the digital age, where technology profoundly influences our lives, HCI serves as the cornerstone of our interactions with this technology. It not only facilitates seamless user experiences but also encourages continuous learning and adaptability. It empowers developers to create user-friendly products and equips individuals to tackle future challenges. For decision-makers, HCI provides critical insights that inform strategic choices and prepare them for the future. For innovators, it offers a rich palette of options for pioneering groundbreaking advancements. HCI, in essence, serves as a tool for everyone to enhance their humanity, rather than merely seeking comfort. As a result, an appreciation of HCI is not just beneficial, but essential in the technologically driven world we inhabit. It bridges the gap between human potential and technological progress, ultimately determining the success and well-being of individuals and society as a whole.

1.2.3 Highlight the Challenges of Data Integration and the Impact of Isolated Data Silos on AI Effectiveness

The first pillar of prAIority—data—plays a foundational role in the success of any AI-driven initiative. Data integration, however, is not without its challenges. One of the most significant obstacles to effective AI deployment is the persistence of isolated data silos. These silos, where data is trapped within specific departments, organizations, or systems, prevent the free flow of information and hinder AI's ability to deliver meaningful insights. Data silos lead to fragmentation and inefficiency. In many organizations, departments generate and store data independently, making it difficult to access a holistic view of the information. For AI systems to be effective, they must be fed with comprehensive, high-quality, and diverse datasets. When data is isolated, AI models cannot learn from the full spectrum of available knowledge, limiting their potential and accuracy. This fragmentation can impact industries as diverse as healthcare, transport, and the public sector, where integrated data is essential for AI to provide actionable solutions. A positive example of overcoming data integration challenges can be seen in London's Transport for London (TfL) system.[46] TfL integrated data across its bus, subway, and rail networks to provide seamless, real-time updates for commuters. By breaking down data silos between different transportation departments, TfL created an AI system that improves route planning, reduces congestion, and enhances customer experience. For instance, the system's ability to predict train delays or suggest alternative routes has significantly improved commuter efficiency, demonstrating the power of data integration in transport. In contrast, data silos can cripple transport systems. Take the case of some older public transportation networks in the United States. In certain cities, bus, metro, and train systems operate in isolation, with separate datasets that aren't shared across platforms.[47] This lack of integration leads to poor AI-enabled tools for route optimization, creating frustration for commuters who struggle to access real-time updates or plan efficient routes. Moreover, without integrated data, transport authorities cannot predict demand spikes or proactively address bottlenecks, resulting in inefficiencies and delays. A success story from the public sector comes from Estonia, one of the world's most digitally integrated governments.[48] Estonia's X-Road system seamlessly connects multiple government databases, allowing citizens and government officials to access various services through a single digital platform. By integrating these data sources, Estonia has reduced administrative overhead and improved service delivery through AI-enabled solutions. Citizens can file taxes, access healthcare records, or apply for government assistance without redundant paperwork, thanks to data integration. The AI systems built on top of this integrated data ecosystem offer faster processing times and more personalized services, proving the benefits of breaking down silos. On the negative side, many countries struggle with data silos in the public sector, particularly in areas like education and transportation. For instance, in some regions, student records and performance data are stored in isolated systems across different schools and educational institutions. This fragmentation prevents educators from accessing a complete view of a student's academic history, which can hinder the effectiveness of AI-driven tools designed to personalize learning and identify students who need additional support. Similarly, in transportation, data related to traffic management, public transit schedules, and infrastructure maintenance is often scattered across various agencies. This lack of integration can result in inefficient traffic management and delayed responses to infrastructure issues. For example, AI systems designed to optimize traffic flow or predict maintenance needs are less effective when they don't have access to comprehensive, unified datasets. The result is missed opportunities for improving efficiency and safety in transportation systems.

DATA SILOS EXPOSED: HOW EQUIFAX'S FRAGMENTED SYSTEMS FUELED A MAJOR BREACH

The consequences of data silos extend beyond isolated inefficiencies. A well-known example of data silos causing problems is the 2017 Equifax data breach. Equifax, one of the largest credit reporting agencies, suffered a massive breach that exposed the personal information of approximately 147 million people. The breach was exacerbated by data silos within the company. Equifax had multiple databases and systems that were not well-integrated, leading to fragmented and inconsistent data management practices. When the breach occurred, the lack of centralized, coherent data made it difficult for the company to fully assess the scope of the breach and respond effectively. The siloed data also complicated efforts to notify affected individuals and mitigate the damage. The result: Equifax was obliged to compensate affected customer with $425 million.[49] The incident highlighted how poor data integration and management can lead to severe consequences, including compromised customer security and trust, and emphasized the need for better data consolidation and security practices.

Overcoming data silos is essential for the success of prAIority. Transport systems like TfL, public sector models like Estonia's X-Road or avoiding another Equifax data breach, demonstrate the power of integrated data in enabling AI to augment human abilities and provide more efficient, personalized services. On the other hand, examples of fragmented systems highlight the potential downsides of isolated data, from misdiagnoses in healthcare to inefficient public transportation. Addressing the challenge of data silos is the first step toward ensuring that AI systems are effective, equitable, and able to deliver on their promises of enhancing human capabilities.

1.3 AI SYSTEMS: DESIGNING FOR AUGMENTATION

1.3.1 THE SECOND PILLAR OF prAIority: AI SYSTEMS. EXPLORE THE DEVELOPMENT AND DEPLOYMENT OF AI SYSTEMS TAILORED TO ENHANCE HUMANS

Humans have existed for a long time, bound by the limitations set by nature. However, when Prometheus, he who predicts or the clairvoyant, ("methéos" who think and "pro" in advance), taught human beings the art of Techne, they were transformed into rational beings, gaining the ability to transcend those natural boundaries.[50] Balancing short-term gains with long-term aspirations ensures that our AI efforts are both impactful and sustainable. Therefore, second pillar of prAIority revolves around techne: AI systems—smart tools that are designed not to replace humans, but to enhance their skills, amplify their potential, and elevate decision-making processes.[51] In this approach, AI isn't positioned as the ultimate decision-maker, but rather as a strategic partner, working alongside humans to tackle complex tasks with precision, speed, and innovation. When implemented effectively, AI systems can help unlock new possibilities, making workflows smoother, jobs more fulfilling, and outcomes more reliable. However, if poorly designed or deployed, these systems can also cause disruption, frustration, and even outright failure. To understand this dynamic, let's take a closer look at two examples from the manufacturing industry—one where AI empowers workers, and another where its misuse led to negative consequences. Manufacturing is a sector that has rapidly embraced AI to improve productivity and streamline operations. One standout example is the rise of smart factories,[52] where AI systems and humans collaborate to produce goods more efficiently than ever before. In these settings, AI systems process vast amounts of real-time data from sensors embedded throughout the factory floor. By continuously monitoring variables like machine performance, material flow, and even worker safety, AI can predict potential issues before they cause delays or malfunctions. This enables human operators to focus on higher-level decision-making rather than spending time on routine monitoring tasks. Take Siemens' Amberg Electronics Plant, one of the world's most advanced smart factories.[53] The Amberg factory is a glimpse into a larger trend reshaping manufacturing worldwide. Across industries, digital twins are transforming how products are designed and produced. Automakers, for instance, once relied on physical prototypes for new models, but now they use digital replicas that mimic real-world behavior. These virtual models can be test-driven, put through wind tunnels, or even crash-tested—and rebuilt in moments. Supermarkets simulate their stores to optimize shelf layouts and aisle designs, while chemical plants use digital twins to make their operations more sustainable and energy-efficient. At Amberg, AI-driven systems handle nearly 75% of the production process, yet humans maintain control. These AI systems streamline production schedules, minimize waste, and predict machine maintenance with precision, freeing up workers to focus on creative problem-solving and product innovation. Rather than replacing humans, AI enhances their roles, allowing them to make more strategic decisions that improve both efficiency and quality. AI serves as a skill-boosting partner, elevating the work experience and driving productivity. And this is just the start. Siemens has incorporated augmented reality (AR) into its suite of data-driven manufacturing tools, enabling managers to visualize products in physical space. Looking ahead, AR will likely revolutionize the entire manufacturing process, allowing factory managers and designers to immerse themselves in virtual production environments, much like how gamers use AR, to experience and interact with machinery and production lines in unprecedented ways. However, not all AI applications in manufacturing have been successful. The balance between enhancing human capabilities and replacing them is delicate, and crossing that line can lead to unintended negative consequences. A well-known example is Tesla's early efforts to over-automate its production lines. In an attempt to accelerate electric vehicle production and increase output, Tesla relied heavily on AI-powered robotics to automate nearly every stage of the manufacturing process. While the aim was to streamline operations and reduce human involvement, the outcome was far from ideal. Instead of improving efficiency, the over-reliance on automation caused major production bottlenecks. Even Tesla's CEO, Elon Musk, acknowledged that automation was hampering the production of the Model 3 and that human intervention was needed.[54] While the AI systems performed well in specific tasks, they struggled to handle the complexities of real-world manufacturing, where unforeseen issues often require human intuition and adaptability. The machines frequently broke down, and the AI lacked the flexibility to quickly adjust to unexpected problems—something humans are naturally equipped to do. In the end, Tesla had to bring back human workers to address and manage the challenges that the automated systems could not overcome. This is a prime example of AI being deployed not to enhance humans, but to replace them—and failing to do so. Instead of serving as a partner to the human workforce, AI systems were asked to take over tasks that required human creativity and problem-solving. The result was a more inefficient, frustrating, and error-prone process. The contrast between these two examples highlights a crucial principle of prAIority: AI systems should be designed and deployed to enhance humans, not to supplant them. When AI systems are seen as collaborators—supporting human workers by automating the tedious, analyzing the complex, and predicting the uncertain—they become powerful tools for progress. But when they are used to replace human intuition, judgment, and adaptability, they can often fail to meet expectations, causing disruptions rather than improvements. By complementing humans with the strengths of AI—such as its capacity to analyze data, process information at incredible speeds, and make predictions—we can unlock the full potential of both human intelligence and machine learning. In this symbiotic relationship, humans remain at the center, steering AI's power toward innovation and progress. Another critical aspect of prAIority is ensuring that the deployment of AI technologies is equitable and inclusive. As we develop AI systems, it is imperative to consider who benefits from these technologies and who might be left behind. For example, in workplaces, using AI to enhance one person's skills can negatively impact others, making their tasks obsolete or less important. This is called shift-right intelligence-augmentation (SRIA). It underscores the need for careful planning, thorough training, and reskilling programs to manage changes in employee roles and skills.[55] prAIority promotes social good and bridge existing gaps can help create a more just and equitable society. For example, AI-driven tools that improve accessibility for people with disabilities, can significantly enhance their quality of life and enable fuller participation in various aspects of society. AI tools that improve accessibility for people with disabilities can greatly enhance their quality of life and help them participate more fully in society. However, since resources are limited, decisions must be made about who benefits most from these tools unless, like in the case of touchless technology, it becomes available at a cheaper costs. The debate over whether to focus on comfort or necessity is complex and ongoing, with no easy answer.

TOUCHLESS TECHNOLOGY, A LUXURY OR A NECESSITY?

Touchless technology has driven the shift to Zero UI, which became more important due to the COVID-19 pandemic and hygiene concerns. Zero UI allows users to interact with technology through voice, gestures, eye tracking, and biometrics like facial recognition, avoiding physical contact. This technology is increasingly used in smart devices, IoT sensors, smart appliances, and consumer robotics.

Touchscreens and shared devices are common but raise hygiene concerns post-pandemic. Touchless solutions, including voice control, biometric recognition, and gesture control, offer a hygienic alternative. Advances in image recognition and natural language processing have accelerated Zero UI from a luxury to a necessity.

Key Takeaways:

- Zero UI enables hygienic interactions through voice, gestures, and biometrics.
- The pandemic has accelerated the adoption of touchless technology, making it essential for everyday life.

However, while countries like Canada, Israel, and Iceland had credit card ownership exceeding 74 percent, many third-world countries, such as Bangladesh and Morocco, had credit card penetration of around just 1% in 2021. This highlights that touchless technology is not only a luxury in these regions but even credit card usage is limited. In such contexts, priorities might shift toward more fundamental needs. So, in places like Morocco or Bangladesh, should the focus in prAIoritizing be on advancing touchless technology, expanding credit card access, or…. addressing basic healthcare needs?[56]

Before examining the augmenting concept in the next paragraph of human judgment, it's essential to grasp also the other three more types: assisting, arresting and automating, called the four conjoined agencies.[57]

1. Assisting technologies amplify human capabilities by providing tools and artifacts that humans use without the ability to independently develop protocols or select actions. Examples include cardiac surgery machines, virtual collaboration tools, PowerPoint, and Excel spreadsheets. These technologies introduce new information, reshape advice networks, and facilitate organizational change by establishing new routines. However, humans often resist or modify these technologies to uphold existing practices. For instance, studies on enterprise resource planning systems reveal initial resistance followed by adaptation to circumvent constraints. *The Economist*, in 2019 had significantly increased its website traffic through newsletters, more than doubling the previous figures. This growth was driven by strategic redesigns and content updates. The publisher, which

relies more on revenue from print and digital subscribers than advertising compared to others, started to actively refining its digital platforms such as the website, apps, and newsletters.[58]

2. Arresting technologies can execute actions, but lack the ability to develop protocols. They operate autonomously when specific conditions are met, reducing human intervention. A prominent example is blockchain-based smart contracts, which automatically perform actions upon condition fulfillment, ensuring security and consistency in transactions. In organizational settings, they authenticate materials in supply chains and automate payment releases. For instance, at Navozyme, A deeptech company in the maritime sector, they offer Blockchain-based Maritime Certificates, ensuring all certificates and their data can be verified in real-time, without intermediaries. This enables seamless data exchange between shipping companies and port authorities, ensuring secure operations and reducing the risk of online fraud.

3. Automating technologies both develop protocols and execute actions independently. Unstructured machine learning programs like neural networks exemplify this capability, learning from diverse data sets and autonomously performing tasks. Examples include automated trading, fraud detection systems, traffic management systems, and email spam, all without human involvement. However, these technologies can develop flawed protocols, as seen with algorithms mistakenly identifying items based on irrelevant correlations. They adapt protocols rapidly based on situational factors, which, if not monitored, can lead to undesirable outcomes.

1.3.2 AI SYSTEMS CAN PROCESS AND ANALYZE DATA TO SUPPORT COMPLEX TASKS, PROVIDING EXAMPLES FROM VARIOUS INDUSTRIES

AI systems have emerged as powerful tools for processing and analyzing vast amounts of data, enabling them to support complex tasks across various industries. By leveraging advanced algorithms, machine learning models, and data-driven insights, AI has the potential to revolutionize decision-making processes. However, the design of these systems plays a critical role in determining whether they complement human decision-making or inadvertently undermine it. Here we will explore how AI systems process data to tackle intricate challenges, providing examples from diverse industries, and emphasize the need for a human-centered approach in AI design. We'll also examine the aviation industry to illustrate both successful and negative applications of AI in decision-making. At the heart of AI's ability to support complex tasks is its capacity to process and analyze large datasets efficiently. In many industries, data is generated at an unprecedented scale, and manually analyzing this information is often impossible. AI systems bridge this gap by applying algorithms that can detect patterns, make predictions, and provide actionable insights based on the data they process. For instance, AI models such as neural networks and decision trees can analyze historical data to identify trends and forecast future outcomes. LLM (Large Language models) enables AI systems to understand and generate human language, making it possible to analyze unstructured data such as text or speech. Computer vision allows AI to analyze images and videos, transforming fields like healthcare, transportation, and security. However, it's essential to recognize that AI systems, while powerful, must be designed to complement human decision-making rather than replace it. Human expertise and judgment remain invaluable in interpreting AI-driven insights and making nuanced decisions in complex environments. AI systems excel at pattern recognition, data analysis, and automating routine tasks, but humans bring creativity, empathy, and ethical reasoning to the decision-making process. The financial industry is a sector where AI is reshaping decision-making processes.[59] Financial institutions rely on AI to manage risk, detect fraudulent transactions, and optimize investment strategies. For example, AI-powered algorithms can analyze market data in real-time, identifying trends and anomalies that might indicate potential risks or opportunities.[60] These systems use historical data to make predictions about market movements, enabling investors to make informed decisions. One area where AI has had a transformative impact is algorithmic trading. AI systems analyze vast amounts of financial data to execute trades at high speeds, identifying market inefficiencies that human traders might overlook. While algorithmic trading has proven highly effective, it also highlights the importance of designing AI systems that complement human oversight. In cases where AI-driven trading algorithms have operated without human intervention, markets have experienced sudden, unexplained crashes known as "flash crashes".[61] These events underscore the need for human supervision to ensure AI operates within ethical and safe boundaries. In this context, AI systems can process complex financial data and make recommendations, but human traders and analysts are crucial for interpreting these insights and making strategic decisions that account for broader market factors. The aviation industry is highly complex, requiring precision, quick decision-making, and a deep understanding of safety protocols. AI has become an integral part of modern aviation, from optimizing flight routes to enhancing safety through predictive maintenance. However, the design and implementation of AI in aviation provide both positive and negative examples of how AI can complement or undermine human decision-making. One of the most successful applications of AI in aviation is predictive maintenance. AI systems analyze data from aircraft sensors, identifying patterns that indicate potential mechanical failures before they occur. For instance, General Electric (GE) was the first to develop AI-powered systems that process terabytes of data generated by aircraft engines during flights.[62] By analyzing this data, AI can predict when components are likely to fail and schedule maintenance accordingly, reducing downtime and enhancing safety. In this case, AI complements human decision-making by providing real-time insights that help maintenance teams address issues proactively. Rather than waiting for a part to fail, engineers can replace or repair components based on data-driven predictions. This reduces the likelihood of unexpected mechanical failures and enhances overall operational efficiency. A stark contrast to the success of AI in predictive maintenance is the tragic case of the Boeing 737 MAX aircraft, where an AI-driven system known as the Maneuvering Characteristics Augmentation System (MCAS) played a role in two fatal crashes in 2018 and 2019. The MCAS system was designed to prevent the aircraft from stalling by automatically adjusting the plane's nose downward in certain situations.[63] However, the system's reliance on a single angle-of-attack sensor, combined with insufficient pilot training, led to catastrophic consequences. In both crashes, the MCAS system received incorrect data from the sensor, which caused it to push the nose of the plane down repeatedly, despite the pilots' efforts to regain control. The pilots were unaware of how to override the system, as they had not been adequately trained on its functionality. This example highlights the dangers of designing AI systems that undermine human decision-making. In this case, the AI system took control away from the pilots, operating autonomously based on faulty data. The lack of transparency and insufficient pilot training in using the system prevented the crew from intervening effectively. The lesson here is clear: AI systems in aviation, or any industry, must be designed to assist human operators, not replace them, especially in critical situations where human judgment is vital. These examples underscore the importance of designing AI systems that complement human decision-making rather than replace it. AI excels in processing large datasets and providing actionable insights, but it should never be the sole decision-maker, particularly in high-stakes environments like aviation or healthcare. Human expertise, intuition, and ethical reasoning are irreplaceable components of the decision-making process. For AI to function effectively in complex tasks, it must be transparent, interpretable, and designed with the end-user in mind. This includes providing users with the necessary training and information to understand how the AI system operates, as well as ensuring that the system can be overridden when necessary. AI systems have the potential to transform industries by processing and analyzing vast amounts of data, enabling them to support complex tasks. However, the true power of AI lies in its ability to complement human decision-making. By designing AI systems that empower rather than replace human expertise, we can unlock new possibilities for innovation, efficiency, and safety across sectors such as healthcare, finance, and aviation. The aviation industry, in particular, provides a powerful reminder of the need for careful, human-centered AI design, where collaboration between human and machine is essential for success.

1.4 PRAIORITY: INTEGRATING WITH HUMANS

1.4.1 THE THIRDS PILLAR OF PRAIORITY: HUMAN JUDGMENT

Ethical considerations also play a pivotal role in AI prioritization. As AI becomes increasingly integrated into our daily lives, questions about privacy, bias, and accountability become more pressing. Prioritizing ethical AI development means investing in technologies and practices that uphold these principles, such as developing transparent algorithms that can be audited for fairness and ensuring that AI systems are designed to respect user privacy. By foregrounding ethics in our prAIority efforts, we can build AI systems that are not only powerful but also trustworthy and aligned with our values. In the realm of decision-making, AI has the potential to augment human judgment by providing data-driven insights and reducing cognitive biases. However, the effectiveness of AI in this domain depends on our ability to prioritize the development of systems that are not only accurate but also interpretable and transparent.

TECHNOLOGY DIPLOMACY TO PRAIORITIZE[64]

AI's profound impact demands stronger global cooperation on policy, governance, and ethics. Technology diplomacy is essential to align AI policies, prevent misuse, and enhance human welfare globally for the following three reasons:

1. AI is likely to have more profound impacts on our lives than other recent technologies, necessitating stronger cooperation to address broader policy and governance challenges beyond regulatory and technological issues.
2. In a time of significant global challenges, international policy coordination is crucial to address the ethical, cultural, economic, and political implications of AI. Technology diplomacy can facilitate the global alignment of AI policy and governance, creating a robust AI innovation system and preventing malicious uses of AI.
3. Technology diplomacy promotes dialogue, fostering shared understanding and coordinated efforts to use AI for the benefit of humanity. This requires sustained efforts to develop mutually beneficial approaches and strong common interests across jurisdictions, recognizing the complexity of this task.

Decision-makers need to understand how AI reaches its conclusions to trust and effectively use these tools. Prioritizing the development of XAI (Explainable AI, as we will see in Chapter 5, ensures that human-AI collaboration is grounded in mutual understanding and trust. The prioritization of AI initiatives is not just about selecting the most promising technologies, but also about creating a supportive ecosystem for AI development and deployment. This involves fostering interdisciplinary collaboration, investing in education and training programs to equip people with the necessary skills, and building robust regulatory frameworks that guide the ethical use of AI. To implement trustworthy AI systems, it's important to define how these systems should be held accountable under the law through regular audits. We introduce the idea of a "responsible AI system", which is essential and can be achieved through such auditing processes, despite challenges like regulatory sandboxes. Trustworthy AI requires a broad perspective, and reaching a consensus on regulation is key.[65] Unfortunately, different regions, like China, the EU, and the United States, have varying approaches to regulation, as discussed in Chapter 4. Ultimately, the goal of prioritizing AI initiatives is to harness the power of AI to enhance human capabilities in meaningful ways. This requires a clear understanding of both the potential and limitations of AI, as well as a commitment to using AI responsibly and ethically.

GLOBAL THREATS, UNIFIED RESPONSE AGAINST THE "COMMON ENEMY": CRAFTING AI REGULATIONS

To strategically prioritize our AI efforts beyond borders, we need to focus on maximizing AI's positive impact globally. This involves using AI to tackle complex problems, create new opportunities, and improve quality of life everywhere. A powerful way to unite diverse groups is by addressing common challenges or "common enemies".[66] In the past, the "common enemy" effect brought together countries that were otherwise at odds. For example, during World War II, nations with significant ideological differences, like the United States, the Soviet Union, and the United Kingdom, united to fight the Axis Powers (Germany, Italy, and Japan). Despite deep mistrust and conflicting interests, they worked together in military operations, intelligence sharing, and strategic planning to defeat their common enemy.[67] Another instance is the Global Coalition Against ISIS. In recent years, countries that often have conflicting political agendas, such as the United States, Russia, and various Middle Eastern nations, formed coalitions to combat ISIS. Despite regional conflicts and differences, these governments coordinated military efforts, shared intelligence, and supported local forces to counter ISIS, aiming to disrupt the terrorist organization's operations and reduce its influence globally.[68]

For governments, such challenges include terrorism and money laundering. For instance, combating these issues requires banks to scrutinize transactions closely, which can lead to ethical and legal concerns, including significant fines. To prevent illegal activities, banks often rely on highly sensitive alert systems that generate 95–99% false positives, requiring expert review. This common regulatory challenge can encourage international collaboration and innovation in AI, as countries work together to improve and harmonize these systems.[69] By addressing such shared concerns, we can foster cooperation and develop AI solutions that benefit everyone. This approach not only strengthens global partnerships but also drives the creation of regulations and technologies that enhance societal welfare and ensure AI is used responsibly.

The concept of prAIority initiatives to effectively augment human capabilities is a guiding principle for navigating the rapidly evolving landscape of AI technology. It emphasizes the importance of focusing our efforts on high-impact areas, balancing immediate needs with long-term goals, ensuring equity and inclusivity, upholding ethical standards, and creating a supportive ecosystem for AI development. Through strategic prioritization, we can unlock the full potential of AI as a force for good, transforming our world and enriching the human experience in ways that were once unimaginable. By thoughtfully selecting areas where AI can be most beneficial, we ensure that this powerful technology enhances human capabilities rather than disrupts them. The primary goal is to use AI to augment human intelligence and creativity, enabling us to solve complex problems, innovate in ways previously unimaginable, and improve our overall quality of life.

AI-GENERATED VS. HUMAN MCDONALDIZED MUSIC: GANGNAM STYLE CASE[70]

AI-generated content introduces significant challenges, such as reduced creativity and media fragmentation.[71] However, human behaviors, like McDonaldization, can impose even greater constraints. The case study of "Gangnam Style" shows that Western music's transformation is often driven by human automation rather than AI, emphasizing a shift in the industry rather than mere commodification. For example, just as eating a hamburger quickly satisfies hunger, the success of songs is often measured by sales and downloads. "Gangnam Style" earned

$6.01 million in digital revenue by December 21, 2012, despite not receiving critical acclaim.[72] Unlike AI, which aims to change paradigms rather than streamline processes,[73] human-driven efficiency in music can be seen in the use of simple, repetitive structures. For instance, the art piece "Corpus Nil" uses bio-signals to create complex experiences, demonstrating AI's potential for innovation.[74] McDonaldized calculability, or the ease of measuring time, has contributed to the decline in physical music sales. Predictability, seen in standardized hotel rooms and Hollywood sequels, also affects music, pushing compositions to follow popular trends. "Gangnam Style" reflects this with its simple, replicable instrumental layers and measurable aspects, now reproducible by AI. Control, exercised through repetitive tasks in McDonald's, parallels the music industry, where "Gangnam Style" used technology and basic melodies performed by a computer, eliminating the need for traditional musicians. TikTok's success with addictive video content highlights the extensive data available on AI-generated images.[75] This paper focuses on music, noting that advancements in image generation surpass those in music because pixels are simpler to encode digitally compared to the complex variables in sound.[76]

prAIority in AI deployment begins with identifying sectors where AI can have the most significant positive impact. This includes personalized shopping experience, where AI is transforming the retail industry by creating highly personalized shopping experiences for customers. By analyzing vast amounts of data, including purchase history, browsing behavior, and social media activity, AI can recommend products that align with individual preferences and trends.[77] This enhances customer satisfaction and increases sales. For instance, AI-driven recommendation engines used by companies like Amazon and Netflix analyze user data to suggest products or content that the user is likely to enjoy, leading to higher engagement and conversion rates.[78] Another example is AI predictive maintenance for equipment, in the energy sector, where AI can significantly enhance operational efficiency through predictive maintenance. By analyzing data from sensors and equipment in real-time, AI can predict when a piece of equipment is likely to fail or require maintenance.[79] This allows for proactive maintenance scheduling, reducing downtime and avoiding costly repairs. For example, energy companies use AI to monitor the condition of wind turbines and predict potential failures before they occur, ensuring continuous and efficient energy production while reducing maintenance costs.[80] However, effective maintenance extends beyond reducing downtime. The rapid growth of industrial automation, IoT, cheaper data storage, and AI/ML advancements offer multidimensional value. However, maintenance organizations struggle to fully leverage these technologies beyond pilot projects. Driving efficiency in maintenance maximizes asset usage and keeps operations moving, benefiting both facility-based and field assets. Ultimately, the business value of effective maintenance is greater than just asset uptime, as Deloitte stated in predictive maintenance report.[81] Therefore the main barriers to predictive maintenance include difficulties in data collection and management, security and privacy concerns, immature technologies, high costs, and unclear economic benefits. Additionally, there are challenges in technical skills, data literacy, internal change management, and employee resistance.[82] Predictive maintenance by AI is not here yet, since it's a multidimensional challenge that goes beyond just data issues. By applying prAIority in multidimensional critical areas, we ensure that AI development addresses real-world challenges and contributes to the greater good. prAIority involves also a deep understanding of the ethical implications of AI deployment. By prioritizing ethics in AI development, we build trust and ensure AI benefits everyone equally. Trust is multidimensional (FIGURE 1.1), comprising cognitive and emotional trust. Cognitive trust relies on AI's transparency, reliability, and tangible benefits.[83] Emotional trust involves AI's human-like qualities, which is why humanoid robots are more accepted emotionally. This emphasizes the importance of AI "skills" and transparency, as discussed in Chapter 5.

In addition to ethical considerations, prioritizing the development of AI skills and knowledge across the workforce is crucial. As AI continues to evolve, the demand for professionals who

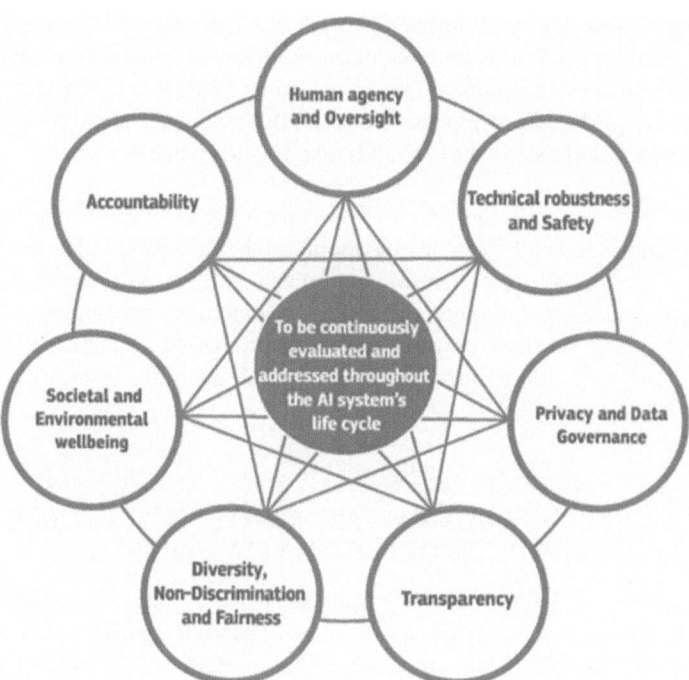

FIGURE 1.1 Interrelationship of the seven requirements: all are of equal importance, support each other, and should be implemented and evaluated throughout the AI system's lifecycle. (https://ec.europa.eu/futurium/en/ai-alliance-consultation/guidelines/1.html.)

understand and can work with AI technologies will grow, as we have seen for AI predictive maintenance. Investing in education and training programs that equip people with the necessary skills ensures that we have a workforce ready to harness the power of AI. This not only boosts economic growth but also reduces the risk of job loss due to automation. For example, Annie Evans, a coal miner, transitioned to becoming a data miner.

FROM COAL DUST TO CODE: ANNIE EVANS' JOURNEY[84]

Annie Evans used to stand in the pouring rain at 3 a.m., fixing broken coal mine equipment in Elgin, Texas. As a heavy maintenance superintendent, each minute of downtime could cost her company up to $170. Now, the third-generation coal miner finds her adrenaline rush fixing code in a soft swivel chair. At 33, she's a data scientist in a paid residency at Galvanize in Austin. Evans's career switch is rare, especially as coal mining jobs decline. In 2015, U.S. coal mining jobs dropped by 59% from 1980. Despite political promises, low natural gas prices, green energy, and automation threaten the industry more. Evans witnessed her employer's struggles with regulations and low profits. Her family has deep roots in coal mining—her grandfather, father, and cousin all worked in the industry. Despite this, Evans discovered a talent for programming. She taught herself to code in Visual Basic, automating tedious tasks at her job. For five years, she coded in her spare time, realizing it was the happiest part of her week.

Moreover, prAIority development involves balancing innovation with societal values. Encouraging AI research can lead to groundbreaking discoveries, but it's also crucial to consider the societal impact of these innovations. By involving diverse stakeholders, like policymakers, industry leaders, and the public, we can ensure AI development aligns with societal needs. For example, MIT faculty collaborated with educators in Kentucky to help coal miners, like Annie Evans, transition to careers in coding, demonstrating a balanced approach to technological and societal progress.[85] Another critical aspect of prAIority is addressing the digital divide. Ensuring that AI benefits are accessible to all, regardless of socio-economic status, location, or background, is imperative. This involves investing in infrastructure, such as internet connectivity and computing resources, in underserved areas. By making AI technologies accessible to a broader population, we democratize the benefits of AI and promote inclusive growth as we have seen for coal miners. Additionally, prioritizing AI deployment involves anticipating and mitigating potential risks. This includes developing robust cybersecurity measures to protect against AI-driven threats and ensuring that AI systems are resilient to manipulation or bias. By proactively addressing these risks, we safeguard the integrity and reliability of AI technologies.

CYBERSECURITY IS ABOUT "WHEN" NOT "IF". BUT IT COULD BE A GROWTH OPPORTUNITY FOR SME.

The proportion of firms with fewer than 10 employees experiencing cyberattacks has risen from 23% to 36% over the past three years, according to Hiscox's annual report. In Switzerland, half of large companies have been cyberattack victims. Payment diversion fraud is the most common type, affecting one in three businesses last year. These attacks divert or steal payments intended for legitimate recipients. Ransomware attacks continue, such as the 2017 Wannacry attack.[86] Data theft is also prevalent, with confidential business data and intellectual property being frequent targets. The average attack costs €15,000, but some businesses have suffered losses exceeding €238,000. One in five businesses reported that the attack threatened their viability. Beyond financial losses, cyberattacks can damage a brand and erode consumer trust. For instance, in 2020, the U.S. cybersecurity firm FireEye was hacked, losing a sophisticated toolkit, likely to a nation-state. To prevent attacks, businesses should install modern anti-virus technology with endpoint detection and response (EDR), use multifactor identification, and properly back up data. Online training and cybersecurity audits are also crucial. Human error is a significant vulnerability, so educating employees on best practices is essential.[87]

However, businesses could also view cybersecurity as a growth opportunity. Effective cybersecurity strategies build trust, encouraging customers to engage with companies that use technology and data responsibly. While technologies like cloud and AI can be costly, managing these costs is vital. Government policies and industry collaboration can help bridge the cybersecurity skills gap. Promoting cyber skills from an early age and including people from diverse educational backgrounds can expand the talent pool. Corporate Social Responsibility funds from large companies can support cybersecurity skill development, improving overall security for SMEs and their customers.[88]

prAIority also extends to collaboration and partnership. The complexity and scale of AI deployment require the triple helix collaboration between governments, academia, industry, and civil society[89] that we have seen in Chapter 4. By working together, these stakeholders can share knowledge, resources, and expertise, accelerating AI development and ensuring its responsible use. International cooperation is vital for addressing global challenges like climate change, pandemics, and cybersecurity. By combining resources, countries can maximize AI's potential to solve these critical issues. Data plays a key role also in international politics, providing advantages in economic growth, national security, and global influence. Effective data use helps governments make informed decisions, manage crises like pandemics, and shape public opinion through platforms like social media. AI, fueled by data, is reshaping global geopolitics. It enhances intelligence gathering and military technology, raising concerns about an AI arms race that could threaten global security. Economically, nations leading in AI will gain a competitive edge, as seen in the U.S.-China rivalry for AI dominance. However, the use of AI in politics also raises ethical concerns, such as spreading disinformation and manipulating public opinion, requiring global cooperation to establish standards for AI governance.[90] Moreover, prAIority involves continuously evaluating and adapting AI deployment strategies. The fast-paced nature of technological advancements means that strategies must be not just be responsive, as we mentioned in the STAR model, but also flexible to change. Regular assessment of AI initiatives is crucial to ensure they stay aligned with evolving goals and societal needs. However, due to human influence, it is essential to establish standardized assessment criteria, particularly to address and limit data heterogeneity.[91] When data from various sources is inconsistent or lacks alignment, it becomes challenging to pinpoint where AI can add the most value. Without a clear and structured approach to managing data diversity, it is difficult to strategically plan for the implementation of AI in a way that maximizes its impact.[92] Standardized data practices not only enhance the reliability of AI outcomes, but also support informed decision-making by creating a unified foundation upon which AI systems can operate effectively. Ensuring data consistency enables AI initiatives to focus on areas where they can drive the most meaningful results. prAIority encompasses fostering a culture of continuous learning and adaptation. As AI technologies and their applications evolve, it is crucial for individuals, organizations, and societies to remain agile and open to change. This involves promoting a mindset that embraces innovation, experimentation, and lifelong learning. By cultivating this culture, we can ensure that we are well-prepared to navigate the dynamic landscape of AI and leverage its full potential. In conclusion, the importance of prAIority lies in its ability to guide the development and application of AI technologies in a manner that maximizes benefits while minimizing risks. By focusing on key areas such as ethics, education, innovation, accessibility, risk management, collaboration, and continuous evaluation, we can ensure that AI serves as a powerful tool to augment human capabilities and address some of the most pressing challenges of our time. This thoughtful and deliberate approach to AI deployment not only enhances individual and collective potential but also paves the way for a future where AI and humanity coexist harmoniously, driving progress and prosperity for all.

1.4.2 EXAMPLES OF AI APPLICATIONS THAT SUPPORT AND AUGMENT HUMAN EXPERTISE IN FIELDS LIKE HEALTHCARE AND EDUCATION

prAIority, refers to the seamless collaboration between humans and machines, where machines learn from data and identify patterns based on their own algorithms.[93] However, the ultimate decision-making authority, or agency, remains firmly in human hands. A compelling illustration of this concept is the application of deep learning in detecting skin cancer. In one notable instance, an algorithm grouped images of a specific type of skin cancer based on the lighting conditions of the photographs rather than the characteristics of the disease. In fact, when this model was tested on images captured by various smartphones in different lighting conditions and distances, it struggled to maintain diagnostic accuracy.[94] This example underscores the indispensable role of human oversight in interpreting and acting upon machine-generated insights.

Augmenting technologies[95] develop protocols by analyzing data and offering predictive insights but rely on humans to make final decisions and select actions. Structured machine learning algorithms illustrate this by identifying patterns and recommending actions for human consideration. These algorithms are employed in courtrooms to predict recidivism rates and in police departments for predictive policing. Online retailers use them to suggest products based on consumer behavior. In a news outlet, a structured machine learning algorithm could analyze data to suggest cover story articles, uncovering patterns that editors might overlook. Although valuable, human judgment is critical as over-reliance on technology suggestions, devoid of contextual understanding, can lead to suboptimal decisions. These forms of conjoined agency—assisting, arresting, augmenting, and automating—shift the locus of agency in distinct ways. Assisting technologies enhance human capabilities without enabling independent decision-making. Arresting technologies execute predefined tasks autonomously, limiting human intervention. Automating technologies operate independently, developing and executing protocols autonomously. Augmenting technologies offer data-driven insights, leaving final decisions to humans. Effective integration of these technologies into organizational routines hinges on understanding these dynamics to ensure they complement rather than restrict human agency. When we discuss augmenting, it is crucial to consider the unique interplay of machine intelligence and human distinctiveness. Take, for instance, the comparison between pigs and dogs: despite pigs being more intelligent (at least when manipulating a joystick),[96] societal norms dictate that we treat these animals differently, often consuming bacon despite acknowledging the pig's intelligence. This brings to mind the philosophical insights of Arnold Gehlen[97] who posited that we humans are distinct not just because of our cognitive abilities, but also due to our physical embodiment. Unlike animals, driven by instinct, humans must actively engage with and dominate nature to survive, a necessity arising from our lack of instinctual guidance. There is deep interdependence of physical embodiment and cognitive processes:[98] intelligence cannot be fully comprehended or developed without acknowledging the role of the body. This perspective emphasizes the profound differences between human actions, which involve conscious decision-making and mastery over our environment, and animal reactions, which are primarily instinctual. In the context of augmentation, it is this human capacity for agency and deliberate action that enables us to effectively collaborate with and harness machine intelligence. Augmenting is a dynamic partnership where machines and humans each play crucial roles. Machines excel at mapping, coordinating and controlling, while humans bring initiation, development and realization to the table.[99] This collaboration allows for more accurate, reliable, and contextually aware outcomes, reinforcing the indispensable value of human oversight and decision-making in an increasingly automated world.

AUGMENTING TECHNOLOGIES

Augmented Reality (AR): AR overlays digital information on the real world, enhancing user perception and interaction with their environment.

Examples include AR apps like Briteyellow's indoor navigation, still much safer than the outdoor one.[100] It digitizes indoor spaces, enabling precise location, tracking, and guidance of customers and staff. Using AR and VR wayfinding apps, it enhances customer experience and attracts more visitors. Its indoor tracking sensors monitor well-being, boosting efficiency and reducing costs.

A well-known example of AR gaming is Pokemon Go, a 2016 AR mobile game by Niantic, part of the Pokémon franchise. Players use GPS to locate, capture, and battle virtual Pokémon in real-world locations. Free-to-play, it offers in-app purchases and started with 150 Pokémon, growing to 800 by 2024.[101] The app cleverly directed players to specific locations, creating a unique business model. This approach led to partnerships like the one with McDonald's,[102] where the game featured special characters at their restaurants, drawing more customers to their premises. AR in education goes from GeoGebra AR by letting students explore and interact with various regions and landscapes in real time.

Virtual Reality (VR): VR immerses users in a completely digital environment, used for applications like training simulations or virtual tours like the virtual reconstruction of the Iranian Archeological site of Persepolis.[103]

Mixed Reality (MR): MR combines elements of both AR and VR, allowing digital and physical objects to interact in real-time.

Wearable technology, such as smart glasses, smartwatches, and fitness trackers, enhances user experiences by delivering real-time data and interactive features. A recent example is the collaboration between Ray-Ban and Meta, resulting in smart glasses that seamlessly combine advanced technology with classic design.[104] Enhanced Interaction: Augmenting technologies provide new ways for users to interact with digital information, making interfaces more engaging and intuitive.

Improved Accessibility: These technologies can offer assistive features for users with disabilities, such as enhanced vision or hearing aids.

Personalization: Augmenting technologies can offer personalized experiences based on user preferences and behaviors.

Training and education benefit greatly from AR and VR, which offer immersive learning experiences through realistic simulations. These technologies enable safe and effective training, such as for firefighters, who can practice dealing with extreme heat without facing real-world dangers like toxic gases.[105]

1.5 THE DARK SIDE OF DIGITAL DENSITY

The concept of digital density, with its concentration of data and interactions within digital spaces, brings remarkable benefits and transformative possibilities. However, it also casts a significant shadow, particularly in the realm of privacy. As our lives become increasingly intertwined with digital technologies, the sheer volume of data generated and collected can create serious privacy concerns, posing risks to individuals, communities, and society as a whole.[106] Every action we take online—whether browsing websites, using social media, shopping, or even just carrying our smartphones—produces a stream of data. This data is not merely a record of our actions, but a detailed map of our choices, preferences, and even our thoughts.[107] The digital footprints we leave behind can reveal intimate details about our lives, from our daily routines and personal interests to our health issues and financial status. As digital density grows, so does the amount of data collected, and with it, the potential for misuse like the 2018 case of Cambridge Analytics.[108] One of the most significant concerns is the erosion of personal privacy. Companies, governments, and malicious actors can exploit the vast amounts of data generated in high digital density environments. Businesses often collect data to personalize services and target advertisements, but this can lead to intrusive profiling and the manipulation of consumer behavior. The practice of tracking and analyzing every click, like, and purchase creates detailed profiles that can predict and influence future actions. This level of surveillance can make individuals feel constantly monitored and reduce their sense of autonomy and control.[109] Governments, too, can harness digital density to enhance surveillance and control over citizens. While surveillance technologies can improve security and efficiency, they can also be used to suppress dissent and infringe upon civil liberties. In countries with less stringent privacy protections, as we are going to see in Chapter 4 with the China approach to data privacy, extensive data collection by the state can lead to the monitoring of political activities, the stifling of free speech, and the targeting of marginalized groups. The balance between security and privacy becomes precarious, and the potential for abuse grows as digital density increases.[110] Moreover, the aggregation of personal data poses significant security risks. Large databases of sensitive information become attractive targets for cybercriminals. Data breaches and cyberattacks can result in the exposure of personal information, financial loss, and identity theft. The more data that is collected and stored, the greater the risk that it could fall into the wrong hands. The consequences of such breaches can be devastating, affecting millions of people and leading to a loss of trust in digital systems like the Wannacry ramsomware in 2017.[111] Another dark side of digital density is the potential for discrimination and bias. Data-driven systems, including AI and machine learning algorithms, rely on vast amounts of data to function. However, if this data reflects existing biases or inequalities, these systems can perpetuate and even exacerbate discrimination. For example, predictive policing algorithms can target certain communities disproportionately, leading to over-policing and unjust treatment. Similarly, biased data in hiring algorithms can result in unfair employment practices.[112] As digital density increases, ensuring that data collection and analysis are fair and equitable becomes more challenging yet more critical. The pervasive nature of data collection also raises ethical concerns about consent and transparency. Often, individuals are unaware of how much data is being collected about them and how it is being used. Privacy policies are frequently opaque and difficult to understand, and consent is often obtained through long, convoluted agreements that few people read. This lack of transparency undermines informed consent and leaves individuals vulnerable to privacy invasions without their knowledge or understanding.[113]

DIGITAL VULNERABILITY: HOW OVERSHARING CAN THREATEN YOUR SAFETY AND CAREER[114]

Exposing personal data on social media can impact your employability, make you vulnerable to cybercrime, or even put your life at risk. Recent incidents, such as the death of former Russian submarine captain Stanislav Rzhitsky, highlight the importance of rethinking privacy in our lives. Rzhitsky was tracked and killed by a gunman while running in a Krasnodar park, using the fitness app Strava. While most people aren't former submarine captains, this event underscores the broader implications of sharing personal data. Apps like Strava can inadvertently expose sensitive information. Cyclists who post their routes and bike details could attract thieves, while military personnel who share running activities near secret locations, like Helmand Province in Afghanistan, risk revealing critical security data. Despite efforts to anonymize users' data, vulnerabilities persist, as seen in incidents involving security personnel at Israeli bases who were unknowingly exposed. The misuse of fitness apps raises the question: how can we balance sharing progress for motivation with maintaining privacy? Cybersecurity is a growing concern, not a matter of "if" but "when", as highlighted by past incidents like the 2017 Wannacry ransomware attack, which disrupted global systems, including the UK NHS. While security measures have since improved, individual vulnerabilities remain. Even casual browsing on social media can result in data misuse. A 2018 CareerBuilder survey found that over 50% of employers encountered social media content that discouraged them from hiring candidates, and around 70% use social media to screen potential hires. This highlights how digital footprints can negatively impact personal and professional lives. As someone who avoids most social media but maintains a LinkedIn profile, I recognize the dilemma of balancing privacy with the need for a digital presence. While it's crucial to maintain some online visibility, it's equally important to be mindful of the data we share. Even if you have nothing to hide, approach sharing personal information with caution, especially details about your daily life and activities.

Furthermore, the pressure to participate in digital spaces can make opting out of data collection impractical or impossible. For example, many essential services, from banking to healthcare to education, have digital components that require data sharing. The digital divide can exacerbate this issue, as those without access to technology or the skills to use it are left behind, while those who participate are often compelled to surrender their privacy in exchange for access. The increasing digital density creates an environment where individuals must navigate complex privacy landscapes to maintain some semblance of control over their personal information.[115] As we grapple with the dark side of digital density, it is crucial to consider and implement robust privacy protections. Stricter regulations, such as the General Data Protection Regulation (GDPR) in the European Union, are steps in the right direction, providing individuals with more control over their data and requiring companies to be transparent about their data practices.[116] However, legislation alone is not enough. There must be a broader cultural shift toward valuing and protecting privacy. This includes developing technologies that prioritize privacy by design, such as encryption and decentralized data storage, and fostering a public dialogue about the importance of privacy in the digital age.[117] Individuals also play a role in protecting their privacy. Being aware of the data we share, using privacy-enhancing tools, and advocating for stronger privacy protections can help mitigate some of the risks associated with digital density. Education and awareness are key to empowering individuals to take control of their digital lives and make informed choices about their privacy, as in 2010 when thousands of Germans opted out from google street view.[118] While digital density brings undeniable benefits and opportunities, it also presents significant privacy challenges. The vast amounts of data generated in dense digital environments can be exploited by businesses, governments, and cybercriminals, leading to the erosion of personal privacy, security risks, discrimination, and ethical concerns. Addressing these issues requires a multifaceted approach, including stronger regulations, technological innovations, and greater public awareness. As we navigate the complexities of the digital age, it is essential to prioritize privacy and ensure that the benefits of digital density do not come at the expense of our fundamental rights and freedoms.

THE RISE AND FALL OF BABYLON HEALTH: HYPE, MISSTEPS, AND THE CLASH WITH HEALTHCARE REALITY[119]

Babylon Health, valued at over $4 billion when it went public in 2021, declared bankruptcy just months later, failing to live up to its hype. Founded in London in 2013 by Ali Parsa, a former banker, Babylon aimed to revolutionize healthcare by making it as accessible as Google made information. Despite attracting tens of millions in venture capital by 2016, the company had only developed a video call app for patients to speak with doctors, with the promise of an AI-powered symptom checker on the horizon. Employees were dazzled by the company's potential, but their enthusiasm waned once they saw that Babylon's so-called AI was little more than decision trees in Excel spreadsheets, created by junior doctors. Despite this, Babylon continued to secure major contracts, including with the NHS and investors like China's Tencent and Saudi Arabia's sovereign wealth fund. However, by the time it went public, its financial losses were skyrocketing, and the company soon faced bankruptcy. Former employees attribute Babylon's failure to an obsession with "blitzscaling" and poor leadership, leading to inefficiencies and overlapping projects. Teams worked on different, incompatible versions of its key symptom checker, and onboarding was chaotic. Leadership turnover and extravagant retreats added to the dysfunction. The company struggled to finish products in time, resorting to mock-ups for demonstrations.

While Parsa claimed Babylon's AI could outperform doctors in diagnosing patients, the system was flawed. NHS consultant David Watkins, tweeting as @DrMurphy11, exposed the bot's failures, such as missing heart attack symptoms and asking irrelevant questions. Despite expanding globally, including to Canada and the U.S., Babylon couldn't compete in the crowded telemedicine market. Ultimately, Babylon's rapid tech-driven growth clashed with the complex, careful nature of healthcare.

1.6 CONCLUSIONS OF HCI, DIGITAL DENSITY, AND AUGMENTING

In the digital era, the synergy between technology and human interaction defines our evolving landscape. HCI stands at the forefront, shaping how individuals engage with computers and digital devices, profoundly influencing daily life, work environments, and communication dynamics. The significance of HCI transcends mere usability; it encompasses user satisfaction, efficiency, and the very essence of technological evolution as we will see in the next chapters.

HCI ensures that our interactions with devices like smartphones are intuitive, seamless, and responsive to human needs. Whether through touch gestures on a screen or voice commands to a digital assistant, HCI principles underpin the design of these technologies, enhancing user experiences and promoting widespread adoption. Consider the transformative impact of the Apple Macintosh in 1984, which introduced the GUI to personal computing. This innovation marked a pivotal moment where HCI principles significantly influenced the accessibility and usability of computers, setting new standards for user-friendly technology. From a developer's perspective, HCI knowledge is equally crucial. It guides the creation of apps and software that not only meet user expectations but also foster engagement and productivity. However, as technology advances, there arises a critical consideration: the balance between efficiency and human adaptability. While HCI optimizes usability and efficiency, it also prompts reflection on whether technology is potentially eclipsing human agency and adaptability. This concern is particularly relevant in the context of augmenting technologies—those that analyze data, provide insights, and recommend actions, but ultimately rely on human judgment for decision-making. Augmenting exemplifies the symbiotic relationship between humans and machines, where each contributes distinct strengths. Machines excel in processing data, identifying patterns, and executing tasks with speed and precision. For example, machine learning algorithms can analyze vast datasets to suggest optimal courses of action, such as predicting consumer behavior or identifying potential risks in supply chains. However, the ultimate authority in decision-making remains vested in human judgment, which provides critical context, ethical considerations, and the ability to adapt to unforeseen circumstances. This dynamic interplay between human oversight and machine intelligence underscores the essential role of human agency in guiding technological progress responsibly. It ensures that technology remains aligned with human values and ethical standards while harnessing the potential of AI and automation to enhance productivity and innovation. The integration of data, AI systems and human judgment not only improves user experiences but also fosters a deeper understanding of how technology can complement human capabilities rather than replace them. prAIority stands as a cornerstone of modern technological progress, bridging the gap between human potential and the capabilities of digital systems. Its application ensures that technology remains human-centered, intuitive, and supportive of diverse user needs and preferences. As we navigate the complexities of a digitally dense world, prAIority continues to evolve, guiding us toward a future where technological advancements enhance rather than diminish our humanity. Embracing prAIority principles in design, development, and decision-making empowers us to harness the transformative power of technology while safeguarding the unique attributes that define us as human beings.

NOTES

1 Massingham, P. (2019). An Aristotelian interpretation of practical wisdom: The case of retirees. *Palgrave Communications*, 5, 123.
2 MacKenzie, I. S. (2024). *Human–computer interaction: An empirical research perspective*. Elsevier.
3 MacKenzie, *Human–computer interaction*.
4 Ben-Elia, E. (2021). An exploratory real-world wayfinding experiment: A comparison of drivers' spatial learning with a paper map vs. turn-by-turn audiovisual route guidance. *Transportation Research Interdisciplinary Perspectives*, 9, 100280.
5 Episteme and Techne. https://plato.stanford.edu/entries/episteme-techne/#Aris
6 Toscani, G. (under review). Cold chain simplicity: How basic data powers human-focused solutions.
7 11 must-know AI terms explained – the ultimate construction analogy guide. www.donato.ai/press/11-must-know-ai-terms-explained-the-ultimate-construction-analogy-guide

8 Xu, Y., Liu, X., Cao, X., Huang, C., Liu, E., Qian, S., ... & Zhang, J. (2021). Artificial intelligence: A powerful paradigm for scientific research. *The Innovation*, 2(4), 100179.

9 Elassy, M., Al-Hattab, M., Takruri, M., & Badawi, S. (2024). Intelligent transportation systems for sustainable smart cities. *Transportation Engineering*, *16*, 100252.

10 Chan, R. K. C., Lim, J. M. Y., & Parthiban, R. (2021). A neural network approach for traffic prediction and routing with missing data imputation for intelligent transportation system. *Expert Systems with Applications*, *171*, 114573.

11 Leading successful AI projects in three words: Group, relevant, and empathetic. https://dobetter.esade.edu/en/successful-ai-projects?_gl=11ecq64w_upMQ.._gaNzgyMDIwODUwLjE3MjYwMzkwNjU._ga_S41Q3C9XT0MTcyNjAzOTA2NC4xLjAuMTcyNjAzOTA2NC4wLjAuMTgxMzE4MDg2NA

12 Massingham, Aristotelian interpretation of practical wisdom.

13 Bostrom, N. (2003). Are we living in a computer simulation? *The Philosophical Quarterly*, *53*(211), 243–255.

14 Chen, L., Lin, S., Lu, X., Cao, D., Wu, H., Guo, C., ... & Wang, F. Y. (2021). Deep neural network based vehicle and pedestrian detection for autonomous driving: A survey. *IEEE Transactions on Intelligent Transportation Systems*, *22*(6), 3234–3246.

15 Berhanu, Y., Schröder, D., Wodajo, B. T., & Alemayehu, E. (2024). Machine learning for predictions of road traffic accidents and spatial network analysis for safe routing on accident and congestion-prone road networks. *Results in Engineering*, *23*, 102737.

16 Augmenting human intelligence – the IBM point of view. www.ibm.com/downloads/cas/2ZDOY697

17 Jarrahi, M. H. (2018). Artificial intelligence and the future of work: Human-AI symbiosis in organizational decision making. *Business Horizons*, *61*(4), 577–586.

18 The Nobel Prize in Physics. (2024). www.nobelprize.org/prizes/physics/2024/press-release/

19 A.I. versus M.D. www.newyorker.com/magazine/2017/04/03/ai-versus-md

20 OpenAI CEO Sam Altman testifies at Senate artificial intelligence hearing. www.youtube.com/watch?v=TO0J2Yw7usM

21 Murray, A., Rhymer, J., & Sirmon, D. G. (2020). Humans and technology: Forms of conjoined agency in organizations. *Academy of Management Review*, *46*(3), 552–571.

22 Workism is making americans miserable. www.theatlantic.com/ideas/archive/2019/02/religion-workism-making-americans-miserable/583441/

23 Eliminating the human. www.technologyreview.com/2017/08/15/149854/eliminating-the-human/

24 10 companies using AI for customer service (and thriving). www.tidio.com/blog/companies-using-ai-for-customer-service/

25 Teslas running Autopilot involved in 273 crashes reported. www.washingtonpost.com/technology/2022/06/15/tesla-autopilot-crashes/

26 Car crashes involving Tesla's autopilot. https://jgwinterlaw.com/car-crash-tesla-autopilot/

27 Henke, N., & Jacques Bughin, L. (2016). *The age of analytics: Competing in a data-driven world*. McKinsey Global Institute.

28 Maleki Varnosfaderani, S., & Forouzanfar, M. (2024). The role of AI in hospitals and clinics: Transforming healthcare in the 21st century. *Bioengineering*, *11*(4), 337.

29 Gligorea, I., Cioca, M., Oancea, R., Gorski, A. T., Gorski, H., & Tudorache, P. (2023). Adaptive learning using artificial intelligence in e-learning: A literature review. *Education Sciences*, *13*(12), 1216.

30 Savielly Tartakower. www.goodreads.com/author/quotes/363694.Savielly_Tartakower

31 The paradox of doing more with less while driving business growth; opportunity vs. opportunity cost. www.forbes.com/sites/briansolis/2023/02/02/beyond-when-and-where-doing-more-with-less-and-driving-growth-through-investments-in-iteration-and-innovation/

32 Sinthetic Media Landascape. (2023). www.syntheticmedialandscape.com/. Accessed on January 4, 2023.

33 Lowis, M. J. (2010). Emotional responses to music listening: A review of some previous research and an original, five-phase study. *Journal of Applied Arts and Health*, *1*(1), 81–92.

34 Barshad, A. (2022). This singer deepfaked her own voice—and thinks you should too. www.wired.co.uk/article/holly-herndon-ai-deepfakes-music. Accessed on December 2023.

35 Savage, M. (2023). Sir Paul McCartney says artificial intelligence has enabled a "final" Beatles song. www.bbc.com/news/entertainment-arts-65881813

36 MacKenzie, *Human–computer interaction*.

37 Cerf, C., & Navasky, V. (1984). *The Experts Speak: The Definitive Compendium of Authoritative Misinformation*. Quote Page 209 and 338, Pantheon Books.

38 Digital strategy does not equal IT strategy. https://hbr.org/2012/11/digital-strategy-does-not-equa

39 Chomsky, N. (2002). *On nature and language*. Cambridge University Press.

40 Von Humboldt, W. (1839). *Über die Kawi-Sprache auf der Insel Java: Nebst einer Einleitung über die Verschiedenheit des menschlichen Sprachbaues und ihren Einfluss auf die geistige Entwickelung des Menschengeschlechts. Südsee-Sprache, als östlicher Zweig des Malayischen Sprachstammes* (Vol. 3). Dümmler.

41 Kant, I. (1983). *Anthropologie in pragmatischer Hinsicht* (1798). Literarische Anthropologie, 39.

42 Neelakantan, S. (2020). Successful AI examples in higher education that can inspire our future. Data-powered AI tools help universities drive enrollment and streamline operations but scaling up their use and training is a challenge.

43 WEF. www.weforum.org/agenda/2020/10/top-10-work-skills-of-tomorrow-how-long-it-takes-to-learn-them/

44 Neelakantan, Successful AI examples.

45 Murray et al., Humans and technology.

46 Stone, M., & Aravopoulou, E. (2018). Improving journeys by opening data: The case of Transport for London (TfL). *The Bottom Line*, *31*(1), 2–15.

47 America's public transit doesn't have to be this way. It can learn lessons from abroad. www.weforum.org/agenda/2023/11/americas-public-transit-doesnt-have-to-be-this-way-it-can-learn-lessons-from-abroad/

48 Estonian e-government ecosystem: Foundation, applications, outcomes. https://thedocs.worldbank.org/en/doc/165711456838073531-0050022016/original/WDR16BPEstonianeGovecosystemVassil.pdf

49 Equifax data breach settlement. www.ftc.gov/enforcement/refunds/equifax-data-breach-settlement

50 Galimberti, U. (2008). *Psiche e techne: l'uomo nell'età della tecnica (Vol. 12)*. Feltrinelli Editore.

51 AI won't take your job if you know about IA. www.gse.harvard.edu/ideas/news/24/02/ai-wont-take-your-job-if-you-know-about-ia

52 Anumbe, N., Saidy, C., & Harik, R. (2022). A primer on the factories of the future. *Sensors*, *22*(15), 5834.

53 Revolution on the factory floor. www.forbes.com/sites/insights-teradata/2019/07/08/revolution-on-the-siemens-factory-floor/

54 Elon Musk drafts in humans after robots slow down Tesla Model 3 production. www.theguardian.com/technology/2018/apr/16/elon-musk-humans-robots-slow-down-tesla-model-3-production

55 Augmenting human intelligence – The IBM point of view www.ibm.com/downloads/cas/2ZDOY697

56 Credit cards worldwide—Statistics & facts. www.statista.com/topics/8212/credit-cards-worldwide/#topicOverview

57 Murray et al., Humans and technology.

58 Media Managers Club. (n.d.). "Every week there are some sort of experiments going on": How *The Economist* grows revenue by improving the digital experience. http://mediamanagersclub.org/%E2%80%9Cevery-week-there-are-some-sort-experiments-going-on%E2%80%9D-how-economist-grows-revenue-improving-digital

59 How artificial intelligence is reshaping the financial services industry. www.ey.com/en_gr/financial-services/how-artificial-intelligence-is-reshaping-the-financial-services-industry

60 Javaid, H. A. (2024). AI-driven predictive analytics in finance: Transforming risk assessment and decision-making. *Advances in Computer Sciences*, *7*(1).

61 Bao, T., Nekrasova, E., Neugebauer, T., & Riyanto, Y. E. (2022). Algorithmic trading in experimental markets with human traders: A literature survey. Sascha Füllbrunn and Ernan Haruvy (Eds.), *Handbook of Experimental Finance* (pp. 302–322) Edward Elgar.

62 How AI and machine learning are helping drive the GE digital transformation. www.forbes.com/sites/ciocentral/2017/06/07/how-ai-and-machine-learning-are-helping-drive-the-ge-digital-transformation/

63 Herkert, J., Borenstein, J., & Miller, K. (2020). The Boeing 737 MAX: Lessons for engineering ethics. *Science and Engineering Ethics*, *26*, 2957–2974.

64 Feijóo, C., Kwon, Y., Bauer, J. M., Bohlin, E., Howell, B., Jain, R., ... & Xia, J. (2020). Harnessing AI to increase wellbeing for all: The case for a new technology diplomacy. *Telecommunications Policy*, *44*(6), 101988.

65 Díaz-Rodríguez, N., Del Ser, J., Coeckelbergh, M., de Prado, M. L., Herrera-Viedma, E., & Herrera, F. (2023). Connecting the dots in trustworthy Artificial Intelligence: From AI principles, ethics, and key requirements to responsible AI systems and regulation. *Information Fusion*, *99*, 101896.

66 De Jaegher, K. (2021). Common-enemy effects: Multidisciplinary antecedents and economic perspectives. *Journal of Economic Surveys*, *35*(1), 3–33.

67 Stoler, M. (2022). *Allies in war: Britain and America against the Axis powers, 1940–1945*. Plunkett Lake Press.

68 McInnis, K. J. (2016, August). *Coalition contributions to countering the Islamic State*. Washington, DC: Congressional Research Service, the Library of Congress.

69 Augmenting human intelligence—The IBM point of view. www.ibm.com/downloads/cas/2ZDOY697

70 Toscani G., & Grant, P. (under review). AI harmony vs. human mcdonaldization: Unveiling music's contemporary constraints.

71 Fehér, K., Vicsek, L. M., & Deuze, M. (2024). Modeling AI trust for 2050. AI and society. *The Journal of Human-Centered Systems and Machine Intelligence*.

72 Gruger, W. (2012) "PSY's 'Gangnam style' video hits 1 billion views, unprecedented milestone". *Billboard Magazine*. Retrieved from www.billboard.com/biz/articles/news/1483733/psys-gangnam-style-video-hits-1-billion-views-unprecedented-milestone

73 Wei, J., Karuppiah, M., & Prathik, A. (2022). College music education and teaching based on AI techniques. *Computers and Electrical Engineering*, *100*, 107851.

74 Ghislaine, B. (2021). The internet of bodies—Alive, connected and collective: The virtual physical future of our bodies and our senses. *AI and Society*.

75 Qin, Y., Omar, B., & Musetti, A. (2022). The addiction behavior of short-form video app TikTok: The information quality and system quality perspective. *Frontiers in Psychology*, *13*, 932805.

76 Kim, D., & Lee, J. (2022). Predictive evaluation of spectrogram-based vehicle sound quality via data augmentation and explainable artificial Intelligence: Image color adjustment with brightness and contrast. *Mechanical Systems and Signal Processing*, *179*, 109363.

77 Personalize your customer's shopping experience with AI. https://hbr.org/sponsored/2024/05/personalize-your-customers-shopping-experience-with-ai

78 Lad, A., Butala, S., & Bide, P. (2019, November). A comparative analysis of over-the-top platforms: Amazon Prime Video and Netflix. In *International conference on communication and intelligent systems* (pp. 283–299), Bansal, J. C., Gupta, M. K., Sharma, H., & Agarwal, B. (eds). Springer.

79 Hamdan, A., Ibekwe, K. I., Ilojianya, V. I., Sonko, S., & Etukudoh, E. A. (2024). AI in renewable energy: A review of predictive maintenance and energy optimization. *International Journal of Science and Research Archive*, *11*(1), 718–729.

80 Chatterjee, J., & Dethlefs, N. (2021). Scientometric review of artificial intelligence for operations & maintenance of wind turbines: The past, present and future. *Renewable and Sustainable Energy Reviews*, *144*, 111051.

81 Using AI in predictive maintenance to forecast the future. www2.deloitte.com/us/en/pages/consulting/articles/using-ai-in-predictive-maintenance.html

82 Giada, C. V., & Rossella, P. (2021). Barriers to predictive maintenance implementation in the Italian machinery industry. *IFAC-PapersOnLine*, *54*(1), 1266–1271.

83 Glikson, E., & Woolley, A. W. (2020). Human trust in artificial intelligence: Review of empirical research. *Academy of Management Annals*, *14*(2), 627–660.

84 The coal miner who became a data miner. https://money.cnn.com/2017/05/17/technology/coal-miner-data-miner/index.html

85 From coal mining to data mining? www.csail.mit.edu/news/coal-mining-data-mining

86 The WannaCry attack is a wake-up call. www.ft.com/content/f6cd3e38-388a-11e7-821a-6027b8a20f23

87 A matter of when not if': Why is it crucial for businesses to protect themselves from cyberattacks? www.euronews.com/business/2023/10/17/a-matter-of-when-not-if-why-is-it-crucial-for-businesses-to-protect-themselves-from-cybera

88 MEs can turn cybersecurity risk into opportunity. Here's how. www.weforum.org/agenda/2024/07/smes-can-turn-cybersecurity-risk-into-opportunity-heres-how/

89 Ranga, M., & Etzkowitz, H. (2015). Triple helix systems: An analytical framework for innovation policy and practice in the knowledge society. *Entrepreneurship and Knowledge Exchange*, 117–158.

90 Marwala, T. (2023). *Artificial intelligence, game theory and mechanism design in politics*. Springer Nature.

91   Toscani (under review). Cold chain simplicity.
92   Toscani (under review). Cold chain simplicity.
93   Murray et al., Humans and technology.
94   Goyal, M., Knackstedt, T., Yan, S., & Hassanpour, S. (2020). Artificial intelligence-based image classi-
     fication methods for diagnosis of skin cancer: Challenges and opportunities. *Computers in Biology and
     Medicine*, *127*, 104065.
95   Murray et al., Humans and technology.
96   Croney, C. C. (1999). Cognitive abilities of domestic pigs. Thesis in Animal Science. The Pennsylvania
     State University, College of Agricultural Sciences (pp. 1–105).
97   Gehlen, A. (1988). *Man, his nature and place in the world* (Vol. 3). Columbia University Press.
98   Whang, O. (2023). Can intelligence be separated from the body? Some researchers question whether AI
     can be truly intelligent without a body to interact with and learn from the physical world. *New York Times*,
     April 11.
99   Broekhuizen, T., Dekker, H., de Faria, P., Firk, S., Nguyen, D. K., & Sofka, W. (2023). AI for managing
     open innovation: Opportunities, challenges, and a research agenda. *Journal of Business Research*, *167*,
     114196.
100 What is augmented reality indoor navigation. www.briteyellow.com/what-is-augmented-reality-indoor-
     navigation/
101 Pokémon Go. https://en.wikipedia.org/wiki/Pokémon_Go
102 Pokémon GO's McDonald's partnership points to a promising business model. www.forbes.com/sites/
     parmyolson/2016/07/20/pokemon-go-mcdonalds-japan-nintendo-revenue/
103 Almasooudi, M. F. (2024). The possibility of applying metaverse in cultural heritage tourism: A case
     study on the ancient city of Babylon. *Tourism and Hospitality Research*, *0*(0).
104 Meta.com. Smart Glasses. www.meta.com/es/en/smart-glasses/
105 AR FightAR webpage. http://fight-ar.com/
106 Véliz, C. (2021). *Privacy is power*. Melville House.
107 Kosinski, M., Stillwell, D., & Graepel, T. (2013). Private traits and attributes are predictable from digital
     records of human behavior. *Proceedings of the National Academy of Sciences*, *110*(15), 5802–5805.
108 Cambridge Analytica and Facebook: The scandal and the fallout so far. www.nytimes.com/2018/04/04/
     us/politics/cambridge-analytica-scandal-fallout.html
109 Zuboff, S. (2023). The age of surveillance capitalism. In *Social theory re-wired* (pp. 203–213), Winchester,
     D. & Longhofer, W. (eds). Routledge.
110 China's "social credit" scheme involves cajolery and sanctions. www.economist.com/china/2019/03/28/
     chinas-social-credit-scheme-involves-cajolery-and-sanctions
111 The WannaCry attack is a wake-up call. www.ft.com/content/f6cd3e38-388a-11e7-821a-6027b8a20f23
112 Predictive policing algorithms are racist. They need to be dismantled. www.technologyreview.com/
     2020/07/17/1005396/predictive-policing-algorithms-racist-dismantled-machine-learning-bias-criminal-
     justice/
113 AI and human rights. www.europarl.europa.eu/RegData/etudes/IDAN/2024/754450/EXPO_IDA
     (2024)754450_EN.pdf
114 Strava and beyond: What fitness apps teach us about the value of privacy. https://dobetter.esade.edu/
     en/strava-fitness-apps-teach-privacy-value?_gl=1*148p963*_up*MQ..*_ga*MTAzOTAzNzU0MS4xN
     zI2NzM0MjU1*_ga_S41Q3C9XT0*MTcyNjczNDI1NC4xLjAuMTcyNjczNDI1NC4wLjAuOTIzN
     TYwMDEy
115 Right to be forgotten on the internet. https://eur-lex.europa.eu/EN/legal-content/summary/right-to-be-
     forgotten-on-the-internet.html
116 The General Data Protection Regulation (GDPR). www.consilium.europa.eu/en/policies/data-protect
     ion/data-protection-regulation/
117 Your data and privacy. www.washingtonpost.com/personal-tech/data-privacy/
118 Thousands of Germans opt out of Google Street View. www.bbc.com/news/technology-11595495
119 The fall of Babylon is a warning for AI unicorns. www.wired.com/story/babylon-health-warning-ai-
     unicorns/

2 Human Judgment in prAIority

Critical Thinking and Tacit Knowledge

Fatti non foste a viver come bruti, Ma per seguir virtute e conoscenza. (You were not made to live as brutes, but to follow virtue and knowledge.)

Dante Alighieri
Divina Commedia "Inferno" canto 26, l. 118.

This chapter examines the role of two features of the human judgment of prAIorization: critical thinking and tacit knowledge. It emphasizes how intuitive, experience-based understanding complements objective analysis in technology use. By integrating tacit knowledge with critical thinking, AI professionals can create more intuitive interfaces and better address user needs. The interface of Sutherland's Sketchpad, Xerox's Dynabook concept, and the computer mouse from the 1960s were early examples of humans interacting with computers. However, widespread development didn't occur until the late 1970s with products like the VIC-20 by Commodore Business Machines, which brought computing into people's homes. Unfortunately, the user interface was often poor, with these systems typically using a command-line interface. The simple operating system had a BASIC-language interpreter and a console prompt. I still remember my VIC-20, programming my own video games in BASIC, controlled with the arrow keys on the keyboard and saved onto a cassette tape using a tape recorder. These early personal computers lacked the intuitive interfaces we are familiar with today, making them less user-friendly and accessible to the average person.[1]

However, since the VIC-20 excelled at addressing small HCI issues, the larger, more complex questions began to emerge: why do people make errors, forget tasks, or struggle with technology installations? Why is driving while talking challenging? Why do social media platforms captivate us? Understanding human behavior is crucial for designing interactive systems that meet user needs. Unlike animals, humans can persist in unsuccessful actions, fostering deeper insights and innovative thinking through the freedom to learn from disappointment, as it sparks imagination that outstrips reality.[2] This involves analyzing critical thinking and tacit knowledge, which helps developers to design system that can then allow humans to think autonomously and beyond the immediate reality.

2.1 CRITICAL THINKING

2.1.1 CRITICAL THINKING AND PROBLEM FORMULATION

Critical thinking, a process of actively and skillfully analyzing, evaluating, and synthesizing information to guide decision-making and problem-solving, plays a pivotal role in effective problem formulation.[3] It involves questioning assumptions, considering alternative perspectives, and systematically

DOI: 10.1201/9781003533160-2

assessing evidence. Two notable examples where critical thinking significantly aided problem formulation are the development of the Polio vaccine[4] and the resolution of the Watergate scandal[5] in United States, while two instances where it fell short include the early handling of the COVID-19 pandemic[6] and the failure of the Mars Climate Orbiter mission.[7] The development of the Polio vaccine in the mid-20th century is a prime example of critical thinking facilitating problem formulation. In the 1950s, polio was a devastating disease with no known cure, and its eradication seemed nearly impossible. Dr. Jonas Salk approached this problem with a critical mindset, scrutinizing existing research and experimenting with various vaccine formulations. He evaluated the potential effectiveness and safety of his vaccine through rigorous testing, ultimately developing a successful vaccine that was both safe and effective. His approach required analyzing vast amounts of data, questioning established practices, and continually adapting his methodology based on new information. This critical thinking process led to a groundbreaking solution that significantly reduced polio incidence worldwide.[8] Similarly, critical thinking was essential in resolving the Watergate scandal of the 1970s. Investigative journalists Bob Woodward and Carl Bernstein, along with other critical thinkers in the media and government, employed a methodical approach to uncover the details of the scandal. They questioned official statements, meticulously examined evidence, and considered alternative explanations. Their critical analysis revealed the extent of the cover-up and led to a broader investigation, which ultimately resulted in the resignation of President Richard Nixon. Their ability to dissect complex information, challenge assumptions, and synthesize new insights was crucial in formulating a comprehensive understanding of the scandal and addressing the problem effectively.[9] Unfortunately, the early response to the COVID-19 pandemic illustrates the limitation of critical thinking: is not always a panacea for problem formulation. Despite initial warnings from the scientific community on COVID-19, critical thinking was undermined by a lack of coordinated response and mismanagement at various levels. Decision-makers struggled to formulate effective strategies due to conflicting information, political pressures, and inadequate resources. This resulted in delayed responses and inconsistent public health measures, highlighting how critical thinking alone was insufficient without proper implementation and communication.[10] Another example of critical thinking falling short is the failure of NASA's Mars Climate Orbiter mission in 1999. The mission's objective was to study the Martian climate, but it failed due to a fundamental error in unit conversion between the teams involved. The critical thinking process should have included thorough verification of all assumptions and data formats to prevent such errors. Unfortunately, the lack of rigorous cross-checking and attention to detail led to the mission's loss. This case demonstrates that critical thinking can be compromised by procedural oversights and inadequate attention to practical details, ultimately leading to failure in problem formulation and execution.[11] While critical thinking can profoundly enhance problem formulation, as seen in the successful development of the Polio vaccine and the Watergate investigations, it is not infallible. The early COVID-19 response and the Mars Climate Orbiter mission failures illustrate how critical thinking can be undermined by external factors and procedural errors. In the second part of this chapter, we will explore how effective problem formulation goes beyond critical thinking; it also involves tacit knowledge and learning derived from planning, precise execution, and adaptability to achieve successful outcomes.

2.1.2   CULTURAL APPROACH TO CRITICAL THINKING

Critical thinking helps individuals and organizations to identify the root causes of problems, assess potential solutions, and make well-informed decisions. Without critical thinking, problem formulation can become haphazard and inefficient, leading to inadequate or misaligned solutions.[12] Why do we continue to avoid critical thinking, even though its importance has been known since the time of ancient Greek philosophers? My research, which involved interviewing data scientists, revealed specific behaviors that hinder critical thinking.[13] One common issue is the persistence of false expectations; for example, managers often demand the rapid deployment of AI models without data or considering the time needed to ensure accuracy, simply because "it's AI". This rush undermines the quality of work and critical analysis. Another challenge is the comfort zone, especially prevalent among senior professionals, but not limited to them. Many interviewees admitted to falling into routines that prioritize doing tasks automatically over learning new skills. This avoidance of innovative challenges restricts growth and stifles critical thinking. Toxic practices within companies, often driven by ego, hierarchy, or power dynamics, further impede critical thinking.[14] These negative behaviors create an environment where questioning the status quo or proposing new ideas is discouraged, making it difficult for innovation to thrive. Lastly, unreliability plays a significant role; when professionals lose trust in their work environment, they disengage and stop contributing critically. Without trust in the system, the willingness to think deeply and question processes diminishes, leading to a stagnant work culture where critical thinking is sidelined. These patterns of behavior show that critical thinking is often hindered by systemic issues and personal comfort, rather than a lack of awareness of its importance.[15] Critical thinking is crucial for data scientists when addressing complex problems, as it enables them to deconstruct issues, question assumptions, and consider multiple perspectives. This method goes beyond superficial analysis, resulting in more thoughtful and well-rounded solutions. For instance, in new product development, critical thinking prompts data scientists to ask key questions about market needs, target audiences, and the strengths and weaknesses of existing solutions.[16] This line of questioning informs decisions on which features to prioritize and identifies gaps in the market that need to be filled. However, various factors can impede this process. False expectations, comfort zones, negative practices, and unreliability significantly affect how problems are framed and tackled. Lewis's cross-cultural model[17] underscores that problem-solving approaches differ widely across cultures, categorized as linear, multi-active, or reactive, each shaped by distinct norms and values. These cultural differences influence how data scientists formulate problems and implement solutions, often leading to diverse strategies that reflect their cultural context. Anticipating challenges is another key element of critical thinking. Data scientists must identify potential hurdles, such as technical constraints, market changes, or shifts in customer behavior, and develop strategies that are proactive and adaptable. This thorough approach ensures problems are accurately defined and solutions are tailored to specific needs rather than generic fixes. Despite its importance, critical thinking can be compromised by common barriers. False expectations can set teams on unrealistic paths, comfort zones can stifle creativity and innovation, and negative practices like rushed decisions or groupthink can weaken analytical rigor. Unreliable data and assumptions further cloud judgment, leading to flawed outcomes. Organizations can cultivate critical thinking by fostering an environment that encourages questioning and continuous evaluation of assumptions. By promoting a culture of scrutiny, companies enhance their problem-solving and decision-making capabilities, leading to more precise and effective solutions. This mindset not only improves product development but also strengthens an organization's resilience in a rapidly changing world. Understanding the impact of cultural differences on problem formulation and solution-seeking, as highlighted by Lewis's model, further enriches this approach, making it adaptable and inclusive of diverse perspectives.[18] Linear cultures, such as the Germans, typically exhibit a straightforward approach to problem-solving. They prefer a methodical and sequential process, moving directly from problem identification to solution implementation. In these cultures, efficiency and clarity are paramount, and solutions are sought through structured analysis and step-by-step procedures. For instance, a German team facing a production issue might quickly convene to identify the problem, conduct a detailed analysis, and implement a solution without much deviation from the planned process.[19] This direct approach ensures that problems are addressed efficiently, but it may sometimes overlook the need for flexibility or creative input. In contrast, nonlinear cultures, such as Italians, often integrate more flexible and relational elements into their problem-solving processes. These cultures may incorporate social or ritualistic activities, such as enjoying a pasta meal or engaging in informal discussions, as part of their approach to problem formulation. For example, an Italian team dealing with a complex issue might find that informal gatherings, like cooking pasta together, and social interactions help stimulate creative thinking and foster collaborative solutions.[20] The inclusion of such cultural practices can provide valuable opportunities for brainstorming and relationship-building, which are essential for generating innovative ideas. Consensus cultures, such as those found in China and Japan, often emphasize collective agreement and harmony in problem-solving.[21] In these cultures, there may be a tendency for group denial or avoidance of conflict, where the problem is not explicitly acknowledged if it disrupts group cohesion. For instance, a Chinese or Japanese team might collectively agree to downplay or avoid discussing a problem to maintain harmony, potentially delaying the identification of effective solutions. This approach underscores the cultural preference for maintaining social harmony over addressing issues directly, which can impact the problem-solving process.

CULTURAL PERCEPTIONS AND THE LIMITS OF CRITICAL THINKING: MY TRAVELER PERSONAL REFLECTION

I have been over 100 countries for work, travel or living and still find myself immersed in various cultures due to my frequent travels, and each culture offers unique insights into the human mind and its capacity for critical thinking. For instance, I am accustomed to running every morning, typically in a pair of shorts and a comfortable t-shirt. However, in different cultural contexts, I adapt my attire. In Pakistan, for example, I run in a shalwar kameez, a traditional dress that blends me with the local environment. One day, while staying at a hotel, I noticed an interesting event that highlighted the intersection of critical thinking and cultural perceptions. After returning from my morning run, dressed in a shalwar, I was met with a rather perplexed hotel guard. The night before, he had seen a man dressed in shalwar running in the hotel and disappearing into it. The guard, unfamiliar with foreigners wearing shalwar, failed to recognize me as a guest, and became alarmed. His concern grew to the point that he even checked each room, including mine, yet only found my wife while I was having shower, and he didn't think to ask if anyone else might be present. The next morning, the guard approached me, visibly upset, and explained how my change of attire had caused confusion and fear. I pointed out four key lapses in his actions: he had failed to memorize me when I left the hotel, wasn't vigilant enough to stop me upon reentry, didn't respond quickly enough to catch me, and conducted an incomplete room check. Despite these observations, the guard remained steadfast in his belief that my choice to run in shalwar was the root of the problem, not his actions. As the hotel manager and other staff joined the conversation, it became evident that the guard's reaction was not just a result of cultural misunderstanding, but also a lack of critical thinking. Critical thinking requires one to analyze situations, recognize errors, and learn from them, all of which were missing in the guard's response. Instead of reflecting on his mistakes, the guard became more defensive and angrier, failing to see how his assumptions and actions led to the situation. This incident underscored how critical thinking is often shaped by cultural contexts and how challenging it can be to step outside of those contexts to reassess and learn. Cultural norms and values influence the way individuals perceive and respond to situations, sometimes at the expense of critical thinking. In the guard's case, his cultural conditioning made it difficult for him to process the situation objectively. His inability to adapt or question his assumptions shows how deeply ingrained cultural perceptions can be, often clouding judgment and preventing learning. This experience serves as a reminder that critical thinking is not just about individual intelligence or reasoning skills; it is also about the willingness to step outside of one's cultural comfort zone, question preconceived notions, and embrace different perspectives. This is why the second concept of tacit knowledge will be introduced later. Without it, critical thinking can be hindered, resulting in missed opportunities for growth and deeper understanding.

2.1.3   Critical Thinking Advantages

Critical thinking is an essential skill when it comes to understanding and leveraging the intersection of humans and digital systems like AI. Before exploring the connection between thoughts and AI, let's understand the significance of thought in humans and HCI. Thought achieves autonomy by detaching from sensory input, inhibiting instinctual processes, and enabling internal reflection as per the quote of Dante Alighieri distinguishing humans from animals (brutes) *"You were not made to live as brutes, but to follow virtue and knowledge"*. This "folding back" enables virtual experimentation, making actions more practical as technology advances.[22] Shifting toward AI in personal, industrial, and social spheres requires a seamless blend of innovation and adaptability.[23] First, personal level: individuals should embrace lifelong learning and develop strong digital skills, moving beyond just the privacy concerns discussed in Chapter 1, to effectively incorporate AI tools into their everyday lives. This approach fosters a mindset that values curiosity and adaptability, allowing people to fully leverage new technologies to boost their productivity, creativity, and overall well-being. Second, industrially: businesses and organizations aiming to cultivate a culture of innovation and flexibility should invest in research and development, enhance employee skills, and embrace the latest technologies. These efforts can drive efficiency and competitiveness, which will be discussed further in Chapter 3 under the principle of "Usability". By harnessing advancements like artificial intelligence, automation, and data analytics, companies can streamline their operations, cut costs, and unlock new growth opportunities. This transformation calls for forward-thinking leadership that can manage the complexities of technology adoption and inspire a shared dedication to progress. Third, socially: the adoption of new technology must be inclusive and equitable, ensuring that all members of society benefit from advancements. This entails creating policies like General Data Protection Regulation (GDPR)[24] and frameworks that support digital inclusion, bridging the digital divide, and providing access to technology for underserved communities. Public awareness campaigns, educational programs, and community initiatives can play pivotal roles in fostering a societal shift toward technology. By promoting digital literacy and encouraging responsible use of technology, we can cultivate a society that is not only technologically adept, but also mindful of the ethical implications and social impact of these advancements.[25]

CRITICAL THINKING: NETFLIX

Consider a recommendation algorithm used by streaming services like Netflix. These systems analyze viewing habits to suggest content, enhancing user engagement. However, critical thinking compels us to question how these algorithms shape our choices and behaviors. For instance, why did Netflix decide to replace its numerical rating system with a nonrated list of movies? This shift aims to avoid creating expectations, prompting us to engage with content more openly and without preconceived notions.[26] Are the recommendations genuinely enhancing our experience, or are they reinforcing existing preferences and limiting exposure to new ideas? By scrutinizing these aspects, we can better understand the balance between personalization and diversity in AI-driven recommendations.

Critical thinking in this context involves evaluating how AI systems operate at personal, industrial, and social level and their implications for user experience. Similarly, when designing AI systems, critical thinking helps ensure that these systems are not only functional, but also ethically sound and user-centered. For example, consider the design of a voice-activated assistant. While the technology aims to simplify tasks through voice commands, critical thinking must address issues like privacy and user consent. How is user data being collected and used? Are users fully aware of what information they are sharing? Ensuring transparency and respect for user privacy are critical considerations that must be addressed to build trust and enhance the overall user experience.[27] Another aspect where critical thinking plays a crucial role is in evaluating the limitations and biases inherent in AI systems. AI algorithms are inherently dependent on the quality of the data used to train them. If this data contains biases or inaccuracies, the AI's outputs can not only reflect, but also amplify these issues. A notable example is Microsoft's chatbot, Tay, designed for Twitter (now X). Tay learned from inappropriate tweets and began replicating these biases, resulting in offensive tweets about gender groups and minorities.[28] By critically assessing the data and the algorithm's performance, we can work toward more equitable and effective AI systems. To develop the prAIority skill, critical thinking involves understanding the diverse needs of users and designing interfaces that address those needs. Social progress has shown us that it's not just about making technology easier to use, but also about ensuring accessibility and inclusivity. A crucial part of this process is defining what exclusion means, as demonstrated by Microsoft's approach.[29] This means considering users with varying abilities and preferences, and ensuring that design choices do not inadvertently exclude or disadvantage certain groups. Critical thinking helps designers ask important questions: does the interface work well for users with visual or motor impairments? Are there multiple ways for users to interact with the system to accommodate different preferences? Critical thinking helps bridge the gap between AI's technical capabilities and HCI's focus on user experience. It involves questioning assumptions, analyzing the impact of technology on users, and striving for ethical and inclusive solutions. As AI continues to advance and integrate into our daily lives, applying critical thinking ensures that these technologies enhance rather than hinder our interactions, fostering a more thoughtful and human-centered approach to technological innovation. By doing so, we can harness the full potential of AI and prAIority to create systems that are not only powerful, but also respectful and beneficial to users.

2.1.4 CRITICAL THINKING DISADVANTAGES

Critical thinking, while a valuable skill, can sometimes present challenges when applied to HCI. At its core, critical thinking involves evaluating information, questioning assumptions, and making reasoned judgments. In the context of HCI, it is meant to enhance the design and usability of technology by ensuring that user interactions are thoughtful and well-considered. However, this approach can also have its drawbacks, particularly when it comes to balancing theoretical analysis with practical application. One of the primary disadvantages is that critical thinking can lead to overcomplication in design processes. HCI professionals might become so absorbed in evaluating every possible scenario, questioning each design choice, and analyzing every potential outcome that they lose sight of practical implementation. This can result in designs that are overly complex or convoluted, as the constant scrutiny can delay decision-making and lead to endless revisions.

> ### DANIEL KAHNEMAN ON PARALYSIS
>
> Nobel laureate Daniel Kahneman suggested to solve this paralysis by querying the source of information: "The worst danger for many organizations is that toward the end, when it becomes very critical to check on a decision, everybody has to be on board. So how to manage dissent without paralysis is the name of the game? My key advice is to keep track of the process… and querying the sources of information is well worth doing".[30]

While it is essential to consider user needs and potential issues, excessive critical thinking can stifle creativity and hinder the development of straightforward, effective solutions. Another challenge is that critical thinking can sometimes overshadow user-centered design principles. HCI is fundamentally about creating technology that works well for users, and this often requires a focus on simplicity and usability. However, an overemphasis on critical analysis might lead to designs that are theoretically sound but practically difficult for users to navigate. For instance, designers might prioritize theoretical models or sophisticated features that, while innovative, can complicate the user experience. This misalignment between theoretical ideals and practical usability can result in interfaces that are difficult for users to interact with effectively. Critical thinking also runs the risk of creating a barrier to innovation. When designers are deeply engrossed in analyzing and questioning every aspect of their designs, they may become hesitant to experiment with new ideas or approaches. This cautious approach, while well-intentioned, can lead to a lack of bold innovation and a reluctance to push boundaries. The fear of making mistakes or failing to meet every critical standard can suppress the creativity needed to explore novel and transformative technologies.

JAPAN INNOVATION AND CRITICAL THINKING

In the 1980s and 1990s, Japan was seen as a hub of innovation, with nearly every household product being made in Japan.[31] However, in recent years, Japan's overemphasis on critical thinking has stifled innovation. This slow adaptation to changes in customer needs, a reluctance to invest openly in research and development, a focus on short-term goals, limited mobility of people and financial resources, and isolation from the global network have all contributed to this decline.[32]

Thus, critical thinking, in its quest for perfection, might inadvertently limit the scope of innovative design. Additionally, critical thinking can lead to paralysis by analysis. When faced with complex design problems, designers might spend excessive time analyzing data, researching alternatives, and contemplating every possible outcome. This thorough examination, while important, can result in decision-making delays and inefficiencies. In fast-paced technological environments, where timely responses and adaptability are crucial, this over-analysis can be a significant hindrance. The inability to make quick decisions due to an overabundance of critical evaluation can slow down the development process and impact a product's market readiness. There is also the issue of subjectivity in critical thinking. While critical thinking aims to be objective, it is influenced by personal biases, experiences, and perspectives. This subjectivity can lead to inconsistent or biased design choices. For example, a designer's own experiences and assumptions might shape their evaluation of usability, leading to designs that cater to their preferences rather than a diverse range of user needs. This can result in a lack of inclusivity and accessibility, as the design may not account for the varied requirements of different user groups. Furthermore, critical thinking, while aligning with the "lean" methodology's principle of focusing on the problem rather than the solution,[33] can at times result in an excessive emphasis on identifying problems rather than developing solutions. When the focus is on identifying potential issues and flaws, there is a risk that the design process becomes overly problem-centric. This can detract from a solution-oriented mindset, where the goal is to create effective and user-friendly technology. By dwelling too much on what could go wrong, designers might miss opportunities to develop positive, user-centered solutions and innovations. Critical thinking can also create communication challenges within multidisciplinary teams. AI projects often involve collaboration between designers, developers, psychologists, and other experts. If critical thinking leads to constant questioning and detailed analyses, it can create friction and misunderstandings among team members.[34] Different disciplines might have varying approaches and perspectives, and excessive critical evaluation can lead to conflicts or difficulties in reaching consensus. This can impede collaboration and slow down the progress of the project, as team members struggle to align their diverse viewpoints. While critical thinking is a valuable asset, it can lead to overcomplication and complexity in design, overshadow user-centered principles, suppress innovation, cause paralysis by analysis, introduce subjectivity, focus too much on problems, and create communication challenges within teams. Balancing critical thinking with practical usability and innovation is essential for creating effective and user-friendly technology. Recognizing these challenges can help professionals navigate the complexities of design and ensure that critical thinking enhances rather than hinders their work.

2.2   TACIT KNOWLEDGE: DEFINITION AND SIGNIFICANCE OF TACIT KNOWLEDGE

We know more than we can tell.[35]

—Polany

To truly understand the powerful influence of critical thinking on prAIority, it's important to recognize the value of human tacit knowledge in this field. Tacit knowledge, previously introduced within the Aristotelian phronesis—although knowledge has to do more with episteme—combines theoretical insights and hands-on experience. In organizational studies, this includes formal education (e.g., university degrees) and knowledge gained through professional practice.[36] Balancing critical thinking with practical usability and innovation driven by tacit knowledge is key to developing effective and user-friendly technology.[37] Tacit knowledge, unlike explicit knowledge that can be easily articulated and documented, is personal, context-specific, and often acquired through experience and practice. It includes insights, intuitions, and hunches that individuals develop over time, which are crucial for mastering complex skills and tasks.[38] In the realm of prAIority, tacit knowledge plays a pivotal role in shaping user experiences and guiding design principles. When developers and designers draw on their tacit knowledge, they are able to create interfaces and interactions that feel natural and intuitive to users, especially when supported by Generative AI[39] as we will see later. Tacit knowledge includes a deep understanding of human behavior, preferences, and cognitive processes that is challenging to formalize. However, it is valuable and powerful, allowing for quick, expert-level decisions in various situations. Despite its usefulness, tacit knowledge is often highly context-specific and tends to spread slowly and in a limited manner across individuals, organizations, locations, and time periods.[40] To offer personalized products that cater to customers on an individual level, the value of tacit knowledge inherent in individuals has become increasingly recognized as a crucial element of product design.[41] Take the example of a smartphone interface: while explicit knowledge, such as design principles like color theory and typography, plays a vital role, it is the designer's tacit knowledge—acquired through extensive experience working with users and refining designs—that often results in truly outstanding user experiences. A designer's capacity to foresee user needs and preferences, and to develop features that feel intuitively right, is often rooted in this deep, experiential knowledge. Similarly, from a developer's perspective, tacit knowledge is invaluable when creating software that meets user expectations. Developers who have spent significant time interacting with users and observing their behaviors can intuitively understand what features are needed and how to implement them in a way that feels seamless and intuitive. Capturing this type of insight can be challenging, yet it is essential for creating software that genuinely connects with users. Tacit knowledge, however, poses several challenges: the absence of a clear, unified definition, the presence of vast, diverse data, difficulties in verifying authenticity and completeness, uncertainties in linking tacit knowledge management with personalized design, and a lack of effective tools for practical knowledge sharing and inheritance.[42] For decision-makers, acknowledging the importance of tacit knowledge can result in more informed strategic choices. For instance, if tacit knowledge is not considered in the design of a website, users may be reduced to passive observers.[43] By cultivating environments where tacit knowledge is valued and shared, organizations can unlock the deep, often unspoken insights of their teams. This approach can lead to the development of more innovative products and services, as well as a more agile and responsive organization, driven by knowledge circulation, customer co-creation, and innovation in mass personalized design.[44]

BEYOND ALGORITHMS: HOW TACIT KNOWLEDGE SHAPES TOOLS LIKE GOOGLE MAPS AND CHATGPT

Tacit knowledge also enhances the effectiveness of tools like Google Maps or ChatGPT. For example, the real-time guidance offered by Google Maps results not only from advanced algorithms but also from the accumulated insights into how people navigate and interact with maps. In fact, humans utilize two types of representations: internal and external. Google Maps must comprehend how people acquire knowledge about their environment and how they apply this stored knowledge in conjunction with the navigational information provided by maps or other tools.[45] Similarly, the user-friendly design of ChatGPT reflects an understanding of how people interact with conversational agents, which has been honed through extensive user testing and feedback.[46]

Tacit knowledge, vital yet often intangible, requires daily cultivation, and remote working appears to pose a significant challenge to this nurturing process.[47] Numerous studies have begun to question whether the remote work environment hinders the development and sharing of tacit knowledge. This limitation potentially stifles creativity,[48] diminishes employees' sense of belonging to their company, and complicates the onboarding process for new hires.[49] For example, knowledge workers, endowed with exceptional expertise, education, and experience, thrive when well-designed information systems and robust social networks are in place. These elements not only enhance their processes and productivity, but also empower them to actively consume, produce, and share knowledge. However, challenges frequently emerge due to human factors and resistance to change, whether in management practices or the adoption of new systems, such as remote working, where tacit knowledge often appears to diminish.[50] Organizations that foster a culture of learning and support open dialogue and experimentation enable their knowledge workers to express themselves fully and adapt more readily to change.[51] Regrettably, the commodification of tacit knowledge has reduced it to just another marketing tool. Numerous examples online illustrate how the acquisition of this profound, nuanced knowledge is often trivialized, being framed merely as a means to enhance marketing, customer service, and sales. This approach undermines the true essence of tacit knowledge, which demands a deep understanding, rich experience, and the investment of considerable time to cultivate properly.[52]

2.3   CASE STUDIES OF TACIT KNOWLEDGE IN ACTION

Blending tacit knowledge with prAIority principles creates technology that's not only efficient but also finely tuned to human needs and behaviors. However, when explicit knowledge overshadows practical experience and interactive learning, IT systems fail to deliver lasting competitive advantages, leading to knowledge mismanagement. To solve this, companies must craft robust knowledge strategies that enhance design and development, resulting in products that are intuitive, responsive, and truly satisfying.[53] By embracing tacit knowledge, we ensure technological progress stays cutting-edge and deeply human-centered—a critical component in today's tech landscape, as shown by these four examples. First, understanding customer challenges uncovers new technological applications, such as in visual intelligence systems, where customers often struggle to express their needs. AI has driven this forward through innovations like ML visualization, visual analytics, visual-enabled machine learning, natural language processing, and multidimensional visualization, highlighting the shift toward visual knowledge discovery.[54] This approach requires every layer of an organization to be deeply customer-focused. Obsession, in this context, means a constant focus on the customer, a mindset that leading organizations embrace as it permeates their every decision.[55] Second, in additive manufacturing (AM) for medical devices, tacit knowledge is crucial for training employees to accurately capture images when a product fails during testing, enabling instant feedback. Despite numerous advances in AM, users still require substantial prior knowledge of the process to succeed.[56] Third, companies automating forensic operations depend on tacit knowledge to ensure precise placement of DNA samples into small containers. The automation team works closely with forensic labs to understand their workflow and behavior before offering a solution. Even within the structured, explicit protocols of a forensic science organization's quality management system, tacit knowledge remains essential. A baseline of acceptable performance is enhanced by team interactions and individual reasoning, adding a layer of expertise beyond the written processes.[57] Finally, production conglomerates are harnessing tacit knowledge to shift from the current practice of extensive documentation to more dynamic idea enactment, fostering innovation and efficiency.[58]

2.4   CRITICAL THINKING AND TACIT KNOWLEDGE: TOOLS AND METHODS FOR EVALUATING TECHNOLOGY

Tacit knowledge and critical thinking are closely connected. For example, tacit knowledge can enhance training sessions by creating a space for participants to discuss shared work challenges. In fact, designing training that encourages reflection on tacit knowledge can selectively build this expertise, improving the ability to learn from experience.[59] These discussions enable individuals to share their knowledge and experiences, thereby increasing the training's value and contributing to their own reservoir of experience-based insights. This exchange is particularly crucial for developers and designers as they thoroughly examine how users interact with technology, ensuring the experiences are seamless, efficient, and satisfying.[60] Critical thinking and tacit knowledge are essential in usability testing, a key method for evaluating digital interactions by observing real users as they navigate a website or application. While usability testing reveals where users struggle, understanding the reasons behind their frustration requires more than just observation.[61] Tacit knowledge—gained through experience—helps developers intuitively grasp users' unspoken challenges.[62] Critical thinking allows them to analyze and interpret these challenges effectively, leading to deeper insights into user behavior.[63] Together, these skills enable developers to identify and address the underlying issues, ultimately improving the overall user experience. Critical thinking and tacit knowledge are essential in identifying and addressing usability issues, such as when users repeatedly click a nonfunctional button or struggle to complete a task. These skills help reveal areas for improvement and offer insights into user expectations.

Usability testing, rooted in tacit knowledge, highlights usability issues, while analytics software provides a quantitative layer by tracking metrics like page views and click-through rates. For example, high checkout abandonment rates can point to a design flaw. Heatmaps further assist by showing areas of frequent user interaction, guiding the optimal placement of key elements to enhance the user experience. Alongside these tools, user surveys and feedback forms offer qualitative insights by directly capturing user experiences, preferences, and challenges. Surveys can uncover subjective aspects of user interactions that may not be visible through metrics alone—such as user frustration with features that are technically sound. Understanding these subjective experiences is crucial for creating user-centric designs. These examples confirm that both "learning by doing"—gaining knowledge through practical experience—and "learning by interaction"—acquiring knowledge through collaboration—promote knowledge sharing and drive innovation in processes and products or services. Efforts to manage informal, autonomous, and context-specific tacit knowledge are essential, as they create a capacity for competitive advantage. However, these practices must be framed within a national context, as it significantly influences tacit knowledge acquisition, shaped by factors like risk acceptance. In certain countries like the United States, a culture of "learning by doing" dominates, reflecting a preference for experiential learning. Conversely, in some European countries, "learning by interaction" and critical thinking are more common, highlighting the importance of dialogue and analytical thinking in knowledge development.[64] A more advanced technique involves A/B testing (now, with Generative AI easily expanded to A/B/C/D ... testing[65]), where two versions of a digital interface are compared to see which performs better. By testing different design variations on distinct user groups—whose differences must be clearly assessed—developers can identify which version yields better outcomes, such as increased engagement or higher conversion rates. This approach supports data-driven decision-making and iterative refinements based on real user feedback. Eye-tracking technology enhances this process by monitoring users' focus on the screen, revealing attention patterns and preferences. However, without critical thinking and contextual knowledge, eye-tracking data alone is insufficient. For instance, while eye-tracking can show frequent attention to a button, it does not explain why users might hesitate to click it, nor does it ensure compliance with privacy standards.[66] The deeper reasoning behind user actions, shaped by experience and subconscious factors, requires more than just visual data and technology. Aristotle's concept of phronesis human judgment(and practical wisdom)—one of the pillars of prAIority—are vital for interpreting results and making meaningful improvements to user experience. While feedback from UX experts and heuristic evaluations can refine digital interactions, this process relies on tacit knowledge, critical thinking, and a willingness to question assumptions and explore varied cases. UX experts assess usability using established principles, but these "best practices" can vary across contexts and organizations. Expert judgment complements quantitative data, providing a holistic view of technology's effectiveness. It's not about elevating human judgment above AI, but integrating it with data and AI capabilities.

THE FAILURE OF THE RECIDIVISM ALGORITHM IN THE U.S. LEGAL SYSTEM

A notable failure highlighting the limitations of relying solely on data is the COMPAS Recidivism Algorithm used in the U.S. legal system. Trained primarily on biased historical data, the tool wrongly flagged African American defendants as high risk twice as often as white defendants, demonstrating that ignoring systemic biases perpetuates injustice. This case underscores the importance of integrating diverse perspectives and critically evaluating data sources.[67] Analyzing digital interactions involves a blend of quantitative and qualitative methods, including usability testing, analytics, heatmaps, surveys, A/B testing, eye-tracking, and expert evaluations. These methods collectively help create digital experiences that are functional, intuitive, and engaging.

2.5 SOCIETAL IMPLICATIONS: UNDERSTANDING THE BROADER IMPACT OF TECHNOLOGY

We all agree that technology wields a profound influence on nearly every aspect of our lives, but the way it shapes our society can be visible, or, instead, subtle. From the moment we wake up to the buzzing of our alarms to the time we spend scrolling through social media before bed, technology intricately weaves itself into the fabric of our daily routines. Its impact extends beyond convenience, touching on deeper societal dimensions, such as how we interact with each other, how we work, and even how we perceive our own identities. The rise of digital platforms has transformed communication, making it easier to connect with others across vast distances. However, this shift comes with complexities. While technology fosters global connectivity, it also raises concerns about the erosion of face-to-face interactions and the potential loss of nuanced human connection.[68] The widespread use of online platforms often leads individuals to present idealized versions of themselves, fostering unrealistic comparisons and impacting mental well-being. This phenomenon contributes to issues such as burnout pandemic,[69] radical indifference,[70] and sexual problems linked to online pornography addiction.[71] Moreover, technology's influence on the workplace has been transformative. Automation and digital tools have revolutionized industries, increasing efficiency and creating new job opportunities. Yet, this shift also brings challenges, such as job displacement and the need for continual reskilling. As machines take on more tasks (not jobs, yet) traditionally performed by humans, there is an urgent need to address how society supports those whose roles are diminished or made obsolete. This includes rethinking education and training to better prepare individuals for a rapidly changing job market. The widespread adoption of technology also prompts significant ethical and privacy concerns. With the increasing collection and analysis of personal data, issues of consent and data security become paramount. How much of our personal information is too much? And how is it being used? These questions highlight the need for robust regulations and ethical standards to ensure that technology serves society in a way that respects individual rights and fosters trust. Another critical aspect is the digital divide. While technology has the potential to democratize access to information and resources, disparities in access between different socioeconomic groups can exacerbate existing inequalities. Bridging this divide is crucial for ensuring that technological advancements benefit everyone and do not widen the gap between the privileged and the underserved. This involves not only improving access to technology but also ensuring that digital literacy and support are available to all. In terms of cultural impact, technology has altered how we create, share, and consume content. The democratization of media production and distribution means that diverse voices can be heard, but it also raises questions about the quality and accuracy of information. The prevalence of misinformation and the echo chamber effect in online environments challenge our ability to discern truth from falsehood and engage in meaningful discourse. Ultimately, understanding the broader impact of technology requires a holistic view that considers its benefits and challenges. Technology holds immense potential to improve lives, enhance communication, and drive innovation. However, it also necessitates thoughtful consideration of its societal implications, from privacy concerns and ethical considerations to job displacement and digital inequality. As we navigate this ever-evolving landscape, it is essential to foster a balanced approach that leverages technology's strengths while addressing its potential downsides. By doing so, we can strive to create a future where technology enriches our lives, supports our well-being, and promotes a more equitable and connected society.

2.6 CONCLUSIONS

In our current digital world, critical thinking and tacit knowledge play vital roles across various practical applications, demonstrating their profound impact on both technology and daily life. In the realm of software development, critical thinking and tacit knowledge are indispensable. Critical thinking plays when experienced developers rely on their deep, often subconscious understanding of coding practices and system design to troubleshoot issues and optimize performance. When faced with a problem, such as a software bug that does not have a straightforward solution, their ability to think critically—drawing on past experiences and intuitions—enables them to devise creative fixes that might not be immediately apparent through a purely analytical approach. This process often involves recognizing patterns from previous projects, adapting solutions to the current context, and foreseeing potential future issues. Similarly, tacit knowledge, which encompasses the intuitive, experience-based insights that individuals gain over time, enriches how we interact with digital tools and navigate complex situations. For instance, consider the way seasoned data analysts approach large datasets. While algorithms can process and analyze data, it is the analysts' tacit knowledge—gained through years of experience—that allows them to identify subtle trends and anomalies that might elude purely quantitative methods. They use their intuition to interpret data contextually, making decisions that go beyond what the numbers alone suggest. In biology, the integration of tacit knowledge and critical thinking is evident in the work of experienced professionals. While advanced tools provide valuable data, it's the biologist's ability to leverage their experiential insights and critical reasoning that leads to effective solutions. For instance, a biologist might draw on their tacit knowledge to interpret complex results. This concept can also be illustrated through the behavior of scout bees, which search a large area for potential sites and then engage in a closed-loop system to select a location. Each bee influences the group's collective decision through body vibrations that convey information about the direction and distance to possible colony sites, along with the level of support for those sites. Stop signals further inhibit other dancers. This real-time negotiation continues until a quorum forms around a favored site, resulting in optimal decisions over 80% of the time. Recent advancements in interface design, networking, and AI processing enable us to replicate the decision-making process of honey bees and facilitate human collaboration. Such software allows individuals to explore options collectively within a decision space, while the AI engine processes input and behavioral data in real-time. This creates an intelligent system of networked participants, where each individual contributes their unique knowledge. Working in parallel, they reach decisions that optimize outcomes for the group as a whole. This nuanced understanding is essential for making informed decisions that significantly influence solution outcomes.[72] The field of digital marketing also highlights the practical value of tacit knowledge and critical thinking. Marketers rely on their deep understanding of consumer behavior—acquired through experience and observation—to craft campaigns that resonate with target audiences. When analyzing engagement metrics and feedback, their critical thinking skills enable them to discern patterns and adjust strategies in real-time, ensuring that marketing efforts remain relevant and effective. Furthermore, in user experience (UX) design, tacit knowledge is critical in creating intuitive interfaces. Designers, through hands-on experience and user feedback, develop an intuitive sense of what works well and what does not. This knowledge helps them design interfaces that align with user expectations and needs, often drawing on subtle, implicit insights rather than explicit data alone. Their ability to think critically about how users interact with digital products ensures that designs are not only aesthetically pleasing but also functional and user-friendly. In education, educators use their tacit knowledge to adapt teaching methods to the diverse needs of students. While digital tools and educational technologies provide a wealth of resources, it is the educators' ability to critically assess and apply these tools in ways that best support individual learning styles that enhances educational outcomes. Their experience helps them to intuitively understand how to leverage technology to address specific challenges, fostering a more engaging and effective learning environment. In summary, the integration of tacit knowledge and critical thinking in our digital world enables more nuanced, effective, and adaptive interactions with technology. From data analysis and software development to healthcare, marketing, UX design, and education, these cognitive skills enrich our ability to navigate complex scenarios and make informed decisions, demonstrating their indispensable value in both professional and personal contexts.

NOTES

1 Davenport, T. H. (2005). *Thinking for a living*. Harvard Business School Publishing.

2 Gehlen, A. (1988). *Man, his nature and place in the world* (Vol. 3). Columbia University Press.

3 Defining critical thinking. www.criticalthinking.org/pages/defining-critical-thinking/766

4 Meldrum, M. (1998). "A calculated risk": The Salk polio vaccine field trials of 1954. *British Medical Journal, 317*(7167), 1233–1236.

5 Olson, K. W. (2016). *Watergate: The presidential scandal that shook America*. University Press of Kansas.

6 Halpern, D. F., & Dunn, D. S. (2021). Critical thinking: A model of intelligence for solving real-world problems. *Journal of Intelligence, 9*(2), 22.

7 The failures of the Mars Climate Orbiter and Mars Polar lander: A perspective of the people involved. http://web.mit.edu/16.070/www/readings/Failures_MCO_MPL.pdf

8 History of polio. https://polioeradication.org/polio-today/history-of-polio/

9 Cohen, E. D. (2009). *Critical thinking unleashed*. Rowman & Littlefield Publishers.

10 Weible, C. M., Nohrstedt, D., Cairney, P., Carter, D. P., Crow, D. A., Durnová, A. P., ... & Stone, D. (2020). COVID-19 and the policy sciences: Initial reactions and perspectives. *Policy Sciences*, *53*, 225–241.

11 Deficiencies in Mission Critical Software Development for Mars Climate Orbiter. (1999). https://llis.nasa.gov/lesson/740

12 Facione, P. A. (2011). Critical thinking: What it is and why it counts. *Insight Assessment*, *1*(1), 1–23.

13 Toscani, G. (2025). From code to context: The impact of organizational problem framing on machine learning success.

14 Toscani, From code to context.

15 Toscani, From code to context.

16 Product interview questions for data scientists. (2024 Update). www.interviewquery.com/p/product-data-science-interview

17 Lewis, R. (2010). *When cultures collide* (pp. 171–211). Nicholas Brealey Publishing.

18 Lewis, *When cultures collide*.

19 Lewis, *When cultures collide*.

20 Lewis, *When cultures collide*.

21 Lewis, *When cultures collide*.

22 Galimberti, U. (2008). *Psiche e techne: l'uomo nell'età della tecnica (Vol. 12)*. Feltrinelli Editore.

23 Kelly, S., Kaye, S. A., & Oviedo-Trespalacios, O. (2023). What factors contribute to the acceptance of artificial intelligence? A systematic review. *Telematics and Informatics*, *77*, 101925.

24 The General Data Protection Regulation. (GDPR). www.consilium.europa.eu/en/policies/data-protection/data-protection-regulation/

25 Kelly, S., Kaye, S. A., & Oviedo-Trespalacios, O. (2023). What factors contribute to the acceptance of artificial intelligence? A systematic review. *Telematics and Informatics*, *77*, 101925.

26 Gomez-Uribe, C. A., & Hunt, N. (2015). The netflix recommender system: Algorithms, business value, and innovation. *ACM Transactions on Management Information Systems (TMIS)*, *6*(4), 1–19.

27 Cahn, S. M., & Véliz, C. (Eds.). (2023). *Privacy*. John Wiley & Sons.

28 Lee, S. E., Ju, N., & Lee, K. H. (2023). Service chatbot: Co-citation and big data analysis toward a review and research agenda. *Technological Forecasting and Social Change*, *194*, 122722.

29 Chou, J., Ibars, R. & Murillo, O. In pursuit of inclusive AI. https://query.prod.cms.rt.microsoft.com/cms/api/am/binary/RWEmS3

30 What we learned about effective decision making from Nobel laureate Daniel Kahneman. www.weforum.org/agenda/2024/03/what-we-learned-from-nobel-winner-daniel-kahneman/

31 Komiya, R., & Irino, M. (1992). Japan's economic and industrial policy in the 1980's. In *Keynes and the economic policies of the 1980s. Central issues in contemporary economic theory and policy* (pp. 137–174), Baldassarri, M. (ed). Palgrave Macmillan.

32 Kitagawa, F. (2005). Regionalization of innovation policies: The case of Japan. *European Planning Studies*, *13*(4), 601–618.

33 Maurya, A. (2016). *Scaling lean: Mastering the key metrics for startup growth*. Penguin.

34 Malone, T. & Crowston, K. (1994) The interdisciplinary study of coordination. *ACM Computing Surveys*, *26*(1), 87–119. https://dl.acm.org/doi/10.1145/174666.174668

35 Polanyi, M. (1966). The tacit dimension. Routledge and Kegan Paul.

36 Higgs, J. (2012). Realising practical wisdom from the pursuit of wise practice (Chapter 6). In *Phronesis as professional knowledge: Practical wisdom in the professions* (pp. 73–86). Pitman, A., & Kinsella, E. A. (eds). Sense Publishers.

37 Hadjimichael, D., & Tsoukas, H. (2019). Toward a better understanding of tacit knowledge in organizations: Taking stock and moving forward. *Academy of Management Annals*, *13*(2), 672–703.

38 Polanyi, *Tacit dimension*.

39 He, W., Xiao, Y., and Xie, Y. (2024). Revealing user tacit knowledge: Generative-image-AI helps create better design conversation. In *DRS2024: Boston* (pp. 23–28), Gray, C., Ciliotta Chehade, E., Hekkert, P., Forlano, L., Ciuccarelli, P., & Lloyd, P. (eds). Design Research Sociery. https://doi.org/10.21606/drs.2024.1329

40 Nissen, M. E., & Bordetsky, A. (2011). Leveraging mobile network technologies to accelerate tacit knowledge flows across organisations and distances. In *Technology and knowledge flow: The power of networks* (pp. 1–25), Trentin, G. (ed). Chandos Publishing.

41 Sun, X., Huang, R., Jiang, Z., Lu, J., & Yang, S. (2024). On tacit knowledge management in product design: Status, challenges, and trends. *Journal of Engineering Design*, 1–38.

42 Sun et al., On tacit knowledge management in product design.

43 Applen, J. D. (2002). Tacit knowledge, knowledge management, and active user participation in Web site navigation. *IEEE Transactions on Professional Communication*, *45*(4), 302–306.

44 Sun et al., On tacit knowledge management in product design.

45 Ishikawa, T. (2016). Maps in the head and tools in the hand: Wayfinding and navigation in a spatially enabled society. In *Community wayfinding: Pathways to understanding* (pp. 115–136), Hunter, R. H., Anderson, L. A., & Belza, B. L (eds). Springer.

46 Ali, O., Murray, P., Momin, M., & Al-Anzi, F. S. (2023). The knowledge and innovation challenges of ChatGPT: A scoping review. *Technology in Society*, 102402.

47 Toscani, G. (2023). The effects of the COVID-19 pandemic for artificial intelligence practitioners: The decrease in tacit knowledge sharing. *Journal of Knowledge Management*, *27*(7), 1871–1888.

48 Bhatti, S. H., Gavurova, B., Ahmed, A., Marcone, M. R., & Santoro, G. (2024). The impact of digital platforms on the creativity of remote workers through the mediating role of explicit and tacit knowledge sharing. *Journal of Knowledge Management*. https://doi.org/10.1108/jkm-08-2023-0682

49 Hadjimichael, D., & Tsoukas, H. (2019). Toward a better understanding of tacit knowledge in organizations: Taking stock and moving forward. *Academy of Management Annals*, *13*(2), 672–703.

50 Toscani, G. (2023). Cómo el trabajo en remoto está reduciendo el conocimiento implícito. *Harvard Deusto Business Review*, *331*, 74–82.

51 Davenport, T. H. (2005). *Thinking for a living*. Harvard Business School Publishing.

52 What is tacit knowledge? Examples, importance & best practices. https://medium.com/@HelpLook/what-is-tacit-knowledge-examples-importance-best-practices-8964b30e914c

53 Johannessen, J. A., Olaisen, J., & Olsen, B. (2001). Mismanagement of tacit knowledge: The importance of tacit knowledge, the danger of information technology, and what to do about it. *International Journal of Information Management*, *21*(1), 3–20.

54 Kovalerchuk, B., Andonie, R., Datia, N., Nazemi, K., & Banissi, E. (2022). Visual knowledge discovery with artificial intelligence: Challenges and future directions. In *Integrating artificial intelligence and visualization for visual knowledge discovery* (pp. 1–27), Kovalerchuk, B., Nazemi, K., Andonie, R., Datia, N., Banissi, E. (eds). Studies in Computational Intelligence, vol 1014. Springer.

55 Customer first. Customer obsessed. https://assets.kpmg.com/content/dam/kpmg/it/pdf/2020/01/Global-customer-experience-excellence-2019.pdf

56 Booth, J. W., Alperovich, J., Chawla, P., Ma, J., Reid, T. N., & Ramani, K. (August 30, 2017). The design for additive manufacturing worksheet. *ASME. Journal of Mechanical Design*. *139*(10), 100904.

57 Doak, S., & Assimakopoulos, D. (2010). Tacit knowledge: A needed addition to SOPs in a forensic science environment. *Forensic Science Policy & Management: An International Journal*, *1*(4), 171–177.

58 Søberg, P. V., & Chaudhuri, A. (2018). Technical knowledge creation: Enabling tacit knowledge use. *Knowledge and Process Management*, *25*(2), 88–96.

59 Matthew, C. T., & Sternberg, R. J. (2009). Developing experience-based (tacit) knowledge through reflection. *Learning and Individual Differences*, *19*(4), 530–540.

60 Taylor, T. Z., Prescott, R., Harrup, K., & Lee, C. (2021). Developing critical thinking skills among Transportation Security officers (TSOs) through sharing tacit knowledge. *Journal of Transportation Security*, *14*, 107–118.

61 Keenan, H. L. et al. (2022). Usability: An introduction to and literature review of usability testing for educational resources in radiation oncology. *Technical Innovations and Patient Support in Radiation Oncology*, *24*, 67–72.

62 Lejeune, M. (2011). Tacit knowledge: Revisiting the epistemology of knowledge. *McGill Journal of Education*, *46*(1), 91–105.

63 Facione, P. A. (2011). Critical thinking: What it is and why it counts. *Insight Assessment*, *1*(1), 1–23.

64 Kucharska, W., & Erickson, G. S. (2023). Tacit knowledge acquisition & sharing, and its influence on innovations: A Polish/US cross-country study. *International Journal of Information Management*, *71*, 102647.

65   Andrew, N. G. AI for everyone. www.coursera.org/learn/ai-for-everyone

66   Kim, J., Thomas, P., Sankaranarayana, R., Gedeon, T., & Yoon, H. J. (2015). Eye-tracking analysis of user behavior and performance in web search on large and small screens. *Journal of the Association for Information Science and Technology*, *66*(3), 526–544.

67   How we analyzed the COMPAS recidivism algorithm. www.propublica.org/article/how-we-analyzed-the-compas-recidivism-algorithm

68   Townsend, L., Wallace, C., Smart, A., & Norman, T. (2016). Building virtual bridges: How rural micro-enterprises develop social capital in online and face-to-face settings. *Sociologia Ruralis*, *56*(1), 29–47.

69   Han, B. C. (2015). *The burnout society*. Stanford University Press.

70   Zuboff, S. (2023). The age of surveillance capitalism. In *Social theory re-wired* (pp. 203–213), Longhofer, W. & Winchester, D. (eds). Routledge.

71   Jacobs, T., Geysemans, B., Van Hal, G., Glazemakers, I., Fog-Poulsen, K., Vermandel, A., ... & De Win, G. (2021). Associations between online pornography consumption and sexual dysfunction in young men: Multivariate analysis based on an international web-based survey. *JMIR Public Health and Surveillance*, *7*(10), e32542.

72   Metcalf, L., Askay, D. A., & Rosenberg, L. B. (2019). Keeping humans in the loop: Pooling knowledge through artificial swarm intelligence to improve business decision making. *California Management Review*, *61*(4), 84–109.

3 Usability and User Experience

It could have happened.
It had to happen.
It happened earlier. Later.
Nearer. Farther off.
It happened, but not to you.
You were saved because you were the first.
You were saved because you were the last.

Could Have—Wislawa Szymborska

3.1 IMPORTANCE OF PRAIORITY IN USABILITY AND USER EXPERIENCE

This chapter examines how usability in AI systems connects with prAIority, highlighting the need to understand user needs and go beyond basic functionality by identifying essential data and systems. It underscores the unpredictability of outcomes, where timing and circumstances dictate who is spared or affected. Usability is about achieving a delicate balance between design, timing, and human experience in AI. The right combination of these elements can greatly influence the user's experience and the overall impact of the technology, making thoughtful design choices crucial for meaningful interactions. Early computers, developed by engineers and scientists, often overlooked ease of use. Here, we explore applied psychology within the prAIority framework. The book's first section introduces key philosophical and psychological principles related to human senses, cognition, and motor skills—knowledge that became essential in the 1980s when computer science professionals were tasked with creating user-friendly interfaces,[1] especially with the rise of graphical user interfaces. The introduction of the model human processor (MHP), which depicted human sensory, cognitive, and motor functions akin to those used in interactions with computers.[2] A significant aspect of this work was integrating ideas from information processing models into HCI, adapting concepts like the Hick-Hyman law and Fitts' law to explain human behavior in interactive systems.[3] These models helped designers understand user interactions and make informed design decisions. Models should understand and predict user behavior demonstrating their utility in their design. However, by the 1980s, a transformation occurred. Computers became not only more powerful, but also user-friendly, making them accessible to a broader audience. For a computer to be successful, it must be both useful and enjoyable to use, as this makes it easier to encourage others to adopt it.[4] This shift moved computers from secure labs to desks in workplaces and homes. The emergence and progress of HCI played a crucial role in this transformation. HCI made computers usable by the average person, driving a dramatic change in how we interact with technology. Today,

DOI: 10.1201/9781003533160-3

this field continues to shape the way we use computers, making technology more accessible and integrated into our daily lives.[5]

3.2   UNDERSTANDING USABILITY: CORE PRINCIPLES AND BEST PRACTICES

The focus on usability and design has grown significantly. This isn't a modern trend; Nietzsche already highlights the importance of functionality, contrasting it with the pursuit of truth. He suggests a tension between life (functionality), which seeks stability and certainty, and knowledge (truth), which leads us into uncertain territory.[6] Even Plato recognized the importance of usability. He illustrated this with the example of a carpenter's beater for a weaving loom, a tool whose true value is best appreciated by the weaver.[7] Usability has always been crucial for creating effective and satisfying user experiences (UXs). Today, usability extends beyond physical products to digital environments, where we must consider how usability functions on a digital level. The prAIority skill involves identifying the best data (by asking what data aligns with your goal), the best AI systems (by considering which AI systems are most suitable for your objective), and applying human judgment (by assessing the challenges in achieving your goal). Understanding usability requires knowledge of design principles and psychology, though some psychological methods vary in effectiveness. For instance, participants preferred metaphors of human thinking (MOT) over cognitive walkthroughs (CW)[8] due to their broader scope, yet found MOT harder to grasp, while CW constrained their identification of usability issues. Participants discovered problems in diverse ways, not just through these techniques, highlighting differences in individual working styles. Best practices in usability ensure that digital products and systems are intuitive, efficient, and user-friendly.[9] Central to usability are five key principles: learnability, efficiency, memorability, error management, and satisfaction.[10] These principles guide the design and evaluation of user interfaces and interactions, ensuring that users can accomplish their tasks with ease and minimal frustration. **Learnability** refers to how easily new users can begin to use a system or product effectively. Humans are uniquely designed to learn, unlike other advanced mammals. They spend their first year of life outside the womb, reaching biological maturity through interaction with their environment. This learning is deeply intertwined with their biological development, unlike in animals. As a result, humans can adapt their sensory and motor abilities influenced by cultural surroundings. Thus, nature and culture are fundamentally interconnected, in contrast to the scientific method that separates them for experimentation.[11] In the context of prAIority, EndNote serves as a prime example of learnability. This comprehensive bibliographic software allows users to search online bibliographic databases, organize references, and automatically generate bibliographies in word processors. Despite its numerous features, EndNote requires users to adhere to a specific protocol, typically offering only one method to complete each task. This ease-of-use was a significant factor in its widespread adoption and success. By focusing on learnability, EndNote ensured that users could quickly become proficient, enhancing their overall experience and satisfaction.[12] **Efficiency** is the extent to which a product enables users to perform tasks quickly and effectively, therefore efficiency is the guiding principle for decision-making. Under these circumstances, personal judgments are supplanted by impersonal mechanisms shaped by cultural elements such as religions or schools of thought.[13] Effectiveness is more thoroughly explored than efficiency,[14] but when it comes to efficiency, consider Adani Green in India. They have introduced a new product, integrating various businesses, each with its distinct characteristics and importance. By streamlining existing tools like emails, Excel, SAP, and SAP Ariba into a cohesive workflow, they achieved complete purchase requisition tracking within just a month.[15] **Memorability** is crucial for products that users interact with intermittently. Making a product memorable simplifies the experience because having multiple memories associated with the same item allows for a consistent experience. In this way, experience shapes technology by creating a unified understanding from similar instances. Without this, technology can become a mere collection of unfulfilled hopes.[16] A system with high memorability allows users to return after a period of not using it and quickly re-establish proficiency. Consider the example of the Dropbox interface. Its straightforward drag-and-drop functionality and clear folder system ensure that users can easily remember how to use it, even after not accessing their accounts for a while. This memorability is essential for maintaining user satisfaction and reducing the cognitive load associated with relearning the system. **Error management** is about designing systems to prevent mistakes when possible and to assist users in recovering from them when they happen. The need to fix errors arises from the gap between human nature and the technological world, which can cause anxiety. It's not just the fast pace of life that's unsettling, but also the feeling of being overwhelmed by technology that seems beyond our control and understanding.[17] A good example of effective error management is Gmail's "Undo Send" feature. This allows users to retract an email shortly after sending it, avoiding the embarrassment of sending a message prematurely or to the wrong person. By incorporating such features, Gmail helps users feel more confident and in control, leading to a better overall experience. **Satisfaction** encompasses the overall pleasure and positive feelings that users derive from interacting with a product. User satisfaction is often the result of effectively applying the other four principles. For instance, the video conferencing tool Zoom has gained immense popularity due to its user-friendly design, reliability, and the seamless experience it offers. Features like one-click meeting entry, virtual backgrounds, and breakout rooms contribute to user satisfaction by making virtual meetings more engaging and less stressful.

FIVE EXAMPLES OF USABILITY[18]

ElectricFeel: Software for launching, growing, and scaling shared electric bike and moped fleets, including a mobile app for rentals and a system for managing fleet operations.

Shopify Experts Marketplace: Platform connecting Shopify merchants with skilled experts who provide high-quality services to help grow their businesses.

Movista: Workforce management software for retail and manufacturing suppliers, featuring a mobile app for coordinating and executing in-store and field tasks.

Trint: AI-powered speech-to-text platform that automatically transcribes audio and video files into editable, shareable transcripts.

Typeform: Online form and survey maker focused on design, providing a smooth, interactive experience for respondents, resulting in high completion rates.

Understanding and applying the core principles of usability—learnability, efficiency, memorability, error management, and satisfaction—are essential for designing user-centered AI systems. Real-world examples like the Electricfeel, Shopify, Movista, Trint, and Typeform illustrate how these principles can be effectively implemented to create products that not only meet users' needs but also enhance their overall experience. By prioritizing usability, designers and developers can unlock the full potential of human augmentation with AI, ensuring that technology serves to empower and enrich users' lives.

3.3   DESIGNING FOR THE USER: PRINCIPLES OF HUMAN-CENTERED DESIGN

Designing for the user is at the heart of human-centered design (HCD), a philosophy that emphasizes discovery, design, deliver, and measure to ensure technology meets real human needs.[19] HCD in actionable learning analytics focuses on three core principles: empowering teachers and stakeholders, aligning the learning design cycle with the analytics design process, and grounding solutions in educational theories. HCD principles help create solutions that are not just functional, but also intuitive and meaningful.[20] This approach emphasizes a deep understanding of users' contexts, challenges, and goals through direct interaction and observation. By centering on UXs, HCD ensures AI-driven technologies are accessible, effective, and enriching for those who use them. A key principle of HCD is discovery, grounded in empathy, which involves understanding users' lives and needs by stepping into their shoes.

DESIGNING THE UNEXPECTED: HOW IDEO TRANSFORMS THE SHOPPER EXPERIENCE THROUGH HUMAN INSIGHT[21]

IDEO adopted a HCD approach to revolutionize the shopping experience, emphasizing the importance of understanding customer behavior beyond surface-level changes. Through detailed observation and interviews, the team discovered that enhancing the in-store experience was not just about tweaking store layouts or changing signage colors. They realized that true engagement required capturing shoppers' attention in unexpected and meaningful ways. For instance, they explored integrating smartphones into the shopping journey, allowing for interactive and personalized experiences that would resonate with tech-savvy customers. Alternatively, they considered ways to encourage shoppers to disconnect from their devices, such as installing charging stations within shopping carts, providing a subtle nudge to be present and enjoy the in-store environment. These insights underscore the value of understanding the unspoken needs and behaviors of customers, demonstrating how design can bridge the gap between technology and human experience in retail

Similarly, in the AI field, empathy-driven design focuses on creating tools that truly support users, avoiding unnecessary complexity or irrelevant features. This marks a shift, as past AI dialogue systems often overlooked the importance of incorporating empathy, along with cultural and humor-based elements.[22] Another key principle is cocreation, where designers work closely with users throughout the development process. This iterative approach allows for ongoing feedback and refinement, resulting in solutions that align with users' real-world experiences. For instance, system designers face distinct challenges in developing mHealth systems. A contextualized codesign framework and established guidelines can serve as a common reference to guide mHealth system development and promote interdisciplinary collaboration between IT and health research. Notable examples of user cocreation include LEGO's Ideas platform and Philips Healthcare.

LEGO'S IDEAS PLATFORM OFFERS KEY INSIGHTS INTO THE POWER OF COCREATION AND CUSTOMER ENGAGEMENT[23]

Insight 1: Let Customers Find the Hits. LEGO allows fans to submit their designs for new sets, with the community voting on favorites. The winning designs become official LEGO products. However, predicting which ideas would garner the necessary 10,000 votes proved challenging. A large degree of randomness influenced which ideas advanced, with social influence playing a significant role in the selection process. While AI could theoretically help identify the most promising ideas, it's the organic, fan-driven approach that taps into user creativity and passion, leading to products that resonate deeply with LEGO enthusiasts.

Insight 2: Give Unhappiness an Outlet. Involving customers in product selection poses diplomatic challenges. From 2008 to 2019, 148 ideas reached the 10,000-vote milestone, but only 23 were developed by LEGO. Surprisingly, rejected ideas did not drive participants away from the platform. Instead, they became more engaged, although they expressed disappointment through increased negative feedback for a brief period. This short-lived reaction can be attributed to participants' loyalty to LEGO and the platform, as well as the personal connections they had built within the community. LEGO's design of the platform to foster individual relationships among fans has been key to maintaining this loyalty.

Insight 3: Share the Wealth. Although children are LEGO's primary audience, the company has expanded its reach by engaging adults through the BrickLink Designer Program (BDP). This program, where members can crowdfund their ideas, encourages not only creativity but also entrepreneurship. BrickLink, originally created by a fan in 2000, now hosts over 10,000 sellers in 70 countries, enabling enthusiasts to buy and sell bricks, sets, and original designs. By purchasing BrickLink, LEGO extended its relationship with adult fans and gained better control over the quality of ideas exchanged on the platform. The BDP has been a hit, with many designs reaching crowdfunding goals in minutes. Through this initiative, LEGO empowers creators by providing tools, support, and opportunities to monetize their work, strengthening its adult fan base while creating new revenue streams.

Philips Healthcare engages patients, doctors, and nurses in cocreation workshops to design new medical devices that meet real needs in healthcare. This collaborative approach results in more effective, user-friendly equipment. Unlike companies that merely digitize existing processes, Philips understood the need to fully reimagine its value proposition for the digital era. To achieve this, Philips has restructured its processes, systems, and data, focusing on integrated digital healthcare solutions. With a goal of improving three billion lives annually by 2025, Philips leverages technology across the healthcare spectrum, from prevention to home care, offering solutions like IntelliSpace and eICU to enhance patient outcomes.[24]

To deliver the final product, usability testing is another cornerstone of HCD, involving systematic evaluation of products by real users to identify issues and areas for improvement. Apple's development of the iPhone is a testament to the power of usability testing. Before the launch, Apple conducted extensive usability tests, observing how users interacted with the device and iterating based on their feedback. This rigorous process revealed critical insights, such as the need for a more responsive touchscreen and intuitive interface, which were crucial to the iPhone's success. By rigorously testing with users, Apple ensured the final product was not only innovative but also exceptionally user-friendly.[25] Accessibility and inclusivity are also fundamental to HCD, ensuring that it is possible to measure how technology is usable by people of all abilities and backgrounds. Microsoft's Inclusive Design Toolkit is a prime example of this principle in action. By involving people with diverse disabilities in the design process, Microsoft created tools and features that address a wide range of needs. For instance, the Xbox Adaptive Controller was developed in collaboration with gamers with disabilities, resulting in a highly customizable device that makes gaming accessible to everyone.[26] This commitment to inclusivity not only broadens the user base, but also enriches the overall UX.

FROM WALL DEVICE TO SMART INNOVATOR: THE EVOLUTION OF THE NEST LEARNING THERMOSTAT

HCD highlights the importance of context-aware solutions, where products are tailored to the specific environments they will be used in. A prime example is the Google Nest Learning Thermostat. By recognizing users' needs for both energy efficiency and comfort, Nest created a smart thermostat that adapts to individual schedules and preferences. When it launched in 2011, the Nest Learning Thermostat transformed the smart home industry, turning a basic wall device into an intelligent, user-friendly tool that helped save billions of kilowatt hours across millions of homes. In 2024, Nest has reimagined this innovation with the 4th generation model, their smartest and most elegant yet, now bundled with the redesigned Nest Temperature Sensor (second gen). Its ability to adjust settings based on user behavior and external conditions showcases the power of context-aware design in creating intuitive, efficient solutions.[27]

HCD principles are essential for creating AI-driven technologies that truly augment human capabilities. By prioritizing empathy, cocreation, usability testing, accessibility, and context-awareness, designers can develop solutions that are not only technologically advanced, but also deeply aligned with users' needs and experiences. Real-world examples, such as IDEO's shopping experience, Lego, Philips healthcare, Apple's iPhone, Microsoft's Inclusive Design Toolkit, and the Nest Learning Thermostat, illustrate the transformative impact of HCD in making technology more accessible, effective, and enriching for all users.

3.4   EVALUATING USER EXPERIENCE: METHODS AND METRICS

Evaluating UX is a critical aspect of developing effective and engaging AI-driven technologies, as it ensures that the end product meets user needs and expectations. The process involves various methods and metrics to gauge how users interact with a system, their satisfaction levels, and the overall usability of the product. Key methods for evaluating UX include usability testing, user surveys, analytics, and heuristic evaluations. Important metrics encompass task success rates, error frequencies, user satisfaction scores, and net promoter scores (NPS). The NPS has become popular for assessing customer loyalty and the likelihood of future use.[28] Usability testing, which dates back to the 1970s, is a fundamental method for evaluating UX. In this process, a user interacts with a product while verbalizing their thoughts, allowing observers to gain insights into the UX. While primarily used to guide design, usability testing can also be conducted independently of the design process.[29] This method involves observing real users as they interact with a product to identify usability issues and gather qualitative insights. For instance, during the development of Google Assistant, extensive usability testing was performed to enhance voice recognition and response accuracy. Testers completed tasks like setting reminders and searching for information while researchers noted any difficulties they encountered. These observations enabled Google to iteratively refine the Assistant, improving its intuitiveness and reliability for everyday use. They discovered that users' motivations affect their perceptions of voice AI assistants' roles. According to the "Computers Are Social Actors" (CASA) paradigm, users driven by social interaction often view a voice AI assistant as a social companion, while those focused on efficiency see it more as a functional tool. Conversely, users motivated by information tend to view it as technology, with less emphasis on social interaction.[30] The software engineering field has also seen the rise of AI programming assistants like GitHub Copilot, but developers often reject the initial suggestions from these tools, raising questions about their usability.[31] User surveys complement qualitative usability findings by capturing users' subjective experiences and satisfaction levels, providing valuable quantitative data.[32]

A notable example is Spotify's use of user data to refine its AI-driven music recommendation system. By continuously gathering data on the accuracy and relevance of its recommendations, Spotify gains valuable insights into user preferences and experiences. This feedback is instrumental in refining algorithms, ensuring the service evolves to better meet user tastes and expectations. Analytics are vital for understanding user interactions with the product over time. Popular features include "make your own playlist", "playlists made by Spotify", and "recommended songs". A study found a significant correlation between user satisfaction with "recommended songs" and their likelihood of adding these songs to their playlists. Nearly half of the time, users incorporate recommended songs into their playlists, highlighting the recommender system's influence on Spotify usage. Additionally, this satisfaction spans across different age groups and genders, indicating that recommendations are effective regardless of demographic factors.[33] For example, when Oneworld Alliance introduced its member benefits system, the alliance closely monitored user engagement metrics, such as how often travelers utilized the benefits and services offered. By analyzing these data points and focusing on strategic management, Oneworld was able to refine its rewards and benefits, enhancing user satisfaction and increasing overall engagement.[34] Heuristic evaluations involve experts assessing a product against established usability principles to identify potential issues. This method is frequently applied early in the design process to address usability concerns before they reach end-users. For instance, during the development of Marriott Bonvoy's new booking interface, usability experts conducted heuristic evaluations to ensure the interface met key usability standards, such as ease of navigation and clarity. This proactive approach helped Marriott address potential usability issues early, contributing to a smoother and more user-friendly booking experience.[35] Key metrics for evaluating UX include task success rates, which measure the percentage of users who can complete a task as intended, and error frequencies, which track how often users encounter problems. User satisfaction scores, often gathered through surveys, provide insights into users' overall impressions of the product. The NPS, which measures the likelihood of users recommending the product to others, is another critical metric that reflects overall user satisfaction and loyalty. Evaluating UX through a combination of methods and metrics is essential for the successful development of AI-driven technologies. By employing usability testing, user surveys, analytics, and heuristic evaluations, companies can gather comprehensive insights into how users interact with their products. Real-world examples from companies like Google, Spotify, Oneworld, and Marriott Bonvoy highlight the importance of these evaluations in refining AI systems to enhance usability and user satisfaction. This iterative process of evaluation and improvement ensures that AI-driven technologies not only meet but also exceed user expectations, ultimately leading to more effective and engaging UXs.

3.5   ENHANCING INTERACTIONS: ACCESSIBILITY AND INCLUSIVE DESIGN

In our journey to integrate AI with human abilities, it is essential to prioritize accessibility and inclusive design. Although we will delve into this topic in detail later, it's crucial to understand how these principles ensure technology benefits everyone, regardless of physical, cognitive, or situational challenges. Accessibility aims to make systems usable by people with diverse abilities, while inclusive design strives to create products that are naturally accessible to as many people as possible. By incorporating these principles into AI and digital interfaces, we foster a fairer technological world for all. Moreover, accessibility often enhances usability. For instance, easy-to-open packaging not only aids those with impairments but also offers convenience to all users. When a company adopts such designs, it demonstrates a commitment to understanding and meeting the needs of all consumers. One compelling example of accessibility and inclusive design in action in the digital world is Apple's VoiceOver screen reader. VoiceOver, integrated into all Apple devices, provides spoken descriptions of on-screen elements, allowing visually impaired users to navigate and interact with their devices independently.[36] This feature not only reads out text but also provides detailed descriptions of images using AI-powered image recognition, enabling users to understand the content of photos and graphics. VoiceOver's effectiveness is a testament to how accessibility can be seamlessly incorporated into mainstream technology, making digital interactions richer and more inclusive for visually impaired individuals. This free screen reader works smoothly with Apple's programs and provides strong support options, though mastering it can be complex. However, with the right training, it offers valuable access to today's digital world.[37]

BE MY EYES: LEVERAGING HUMAN KINDNESS AND TECHNOLOGY FOR EVERYDAY ACCESSIBILITY

A wonderful example is the Be My Eyes app, which connects visually impaired users with sighted volunteers through live video calls. This app takes advantage of the widespread use of smartphones and the kindness of volunteers to offer real-time help for tasks that need vision, like reading labels, navigating new places, or fixing technical problems. With its simple and user-friendly design, Be My Eyes embodies inclusive design principles, making it easy to use for both visually impaired individuals and volunteers. The app's success shows how prioritizing human empathy can enhance accessibility in everyday life for the visually impaired. Inclusive design also plays a vital role in creating educational technologies that cater to diverse learning needs.[38]

Microsoft's Immersive Reader is an AI-powered tool that supports students with dyslexia and other reading difficulties by offering features like text-to-speech, adjustable text spacing, and customizable color themes to improve readability. It simplifies complex words into syllables and provides visual aids, making reading more accessible for students with diverse learning challenges. By integrating these features into widely used platforms such as Microsoft Word and OneNote, Immersive Reader incorporates inclusive design into everyday educational tasks, creating a more inclusive learning environment. This approach not only benefits individuals with disabilities but also enhances the overall UX. However, if the feature is enabled at the account level, it overrides user preferences, rendering user settings ineffective. Additionally, Immersive Reader cannot read content from external tools embedded in the Rich Content Editor and does not appear on assignments involving external tools.[39] Voice-activated assistants like Amazon's Alexa and Google Assistant were initially developed to aid users with disabilities. However, their intuitive, hands-free operation has led to their broad adoption by the general public. These devices offer convenience in situations where manual interaction is challenging or unsafe, such as while cooking, driving, or multitasking. By prioritizing inclusive design, these technologies have become essential tools that enhance everyday life. Yet, their integration into daily routines raises privacy concerns, as these devices are always listening for voice commands and may inadvertently capture private conversations and sensitive information without explicit user consent. For instance, Amazon was found to have violated children's privacy laws by retaining kids' Alexa voice recordings indefinitely to improve its voice algorithms.[40] This underscores the urgent need for strong privacy safeguards and transparent data practices to protect users while maintaining the accessibility and convenience these technologies provide. Ultimately, enhancing interactions through accessibility and inclusive design ensures that technology advancements do not leave anyone behind. As AI continues to evolve, it is crucial to embed these principles into the fabric of technological development. By doing so, we not only create tools that are equitable and user-friendly but also drive innovation that considers the diverse needs of all users. Embracing accessibility and inclusive design in AI development is not just a technical necessity; it is a moral imperative that fosters a more inclusive and connected world.

3.6 USABILITY DISADVANTAGES: SKILL DEVELOPMENT AND CARBON FOOTPRINT

Focusing too heavily on usability, however, can paradoxically undermine users' skill development, even while creating more immediate and accessible experiences. Usability, which aims to make systems easy-to-learn and efficient-to-use, often simplifies complex tasks into straightforward, almost effortless actions, like making the digital identifiers in the United Kingdom more "palatable".[41] While this can benefit beginners or occasional users, it poses the risk of reducing the need for deeper understanding and skill development in long-term users. For instance, when software is designed to be highly intuitive, it often automates or conceals advanced features that could help users build their expertise. This can contribute to a decline in human effort, raise personal privacy and security concerns, and lead to diminished decision-making abilities due to AI's influence. Over-reliance on automation fosters a superficial interaction with others through technology, turning users into passive consumers instead of active problem-solvers. The potential loss of skills extends beyond technical abilities to include critical thinking and problem-solving.[42] When systems anticipate user needs and offer solutions with minimal input, users lose the chance to participate in meaningful decision-making processes. This can hinder creativity and innovation, as the challenge of navigating and mastering complex systems often sparks ingenuity. The opposite is evident in healthcare: actively involving patients in their care enhances health outcomes boosts satisfaction with the care experience, lowers costs, and even improves the clinician's experience.[43]

THE VICIOUS CYCLE OF SKILLS EROSION: HOW USABILITY AND AUTOMATION UNDERMINE HUMAN EXPERTISE

Prioritizing usability fosters an environment where users expect instant gratification, reducing their patience and persistence when faced with complex tasks, as we will later explore with the example of Amazon and its environmental implications. This shift in expectations is particularly harmful in educational and professional settings, where tackling challenging problems and developing advanced skills is vital. For instance, students who haven't spent enough time revising and consolidating key concepts due to external factors often show learning deficiencies—a trend now amplified by digital technology.[44] This phenomenon, known as the "vicious cycle of skills erosion", occurs when cognitive automation driven by advanced technologies increasingly automates knowledge work tasks. While this can lead to greater efficiency and lower costs, it also accelerates the erosion of skills and expertise in automated tasks. Although letting go of outdated skills is necessary to benefit from technology, the erosion of essential human expertise is problematic when workers are still responsible for tasks they no longer fully understand, leaving them unable to respond effectively if automation fails.

This can further lead to homogenized experiences, where unique and complex features of different systems are sacrificed for a standardized, streamlined interface, stifling diversity in design and limiting the richness of UXs.[45] In professional fields where specialized software demands deep expertise, overly simplified interfaces can diminish the precision and control that experts require. For example, in graphic design or software development, where detailed control over tools is crucial, interfaces that emphasize ease of use over advanced functionality can limit users' ability to fully leverage the software's potential. In agile software development, organizations employ four different types of coordination artifacts—foundational, projective, exposition, and indicative—to address various coordination challenges throughout a project. These artifacts, each with distinct levels of information richness and adaptability, are tailored to support specific agile activities. Depending on their use, they can either mitigate or exacerbate the "vicious cycle of skills erosion".[46] Consequently, users may not develop the necessary expertise to perform advanced tasks or customize tools to fit their specific needs. This can lead to a dependence on basic functionalities and a lack of confidence in exploring more complex features. Additionally, the focus on usability often involves extensive user testing across a broad audience, which can result in designs that cater to the lowest common denominator. Nielsen[47] even suggests that testing with just five users can be sufficient. This approach may overlook the needs of advanced users who require more sophisticated tools and features. Consequently, the software can become less versatile and more restricted, limiting the potential for users who aim to explore the full capabilities of the technology. Another consequence of prioritizing usability is the potential decline of manual skills. As we shift from traditional to digital tools, many manual skills have already been lost or diminished, and this trend continues within digital environments, where users increasingly rely on automated features, losing the ability to perform tasks manually. This erosion of manual dexterity fosters complacency at both individual and organizational levels, weakening workers' mindfulness in three key areas: activity awareness, competence maintenance, and output assessment, ultimately leading to skill degradation. What is particularly concerning is that this erosion of skills often goes unnoticed, unrecognized by both employees and managers.[48] Usability's impact extends to collaborative work environments as well. Systems designed for universal accessibility may oversimplify the collaborative process, reducing opportunities for team members to apply their specialized expertise. Complex tasks requiring high levels of skill and coordination may become diluted, as collaboration tools might not support the depth of engagement necessary for true innovation. This can lead to shallow collaboration, focused more on quickly completing tasks than on developing a deep understanding and mastery of the work. The pursuit of usability often results in frequent updates and changes to software interfaces, aiming to continually enhance UX. While updates can add valuable features and improve performance, they can also disrupt users' familiarity and fluency with the system. The decision to delay updates is significantly influenced by the cost of the update and individual risk preferences; those more willing to take risks are often more likely to skip updates, maintaining the status quo even when it's not ideal.[49] Constant changes can hinder users from forming a stable, long-term relationship with the software, preventing them from mastering its more complex functionalities. This creates a perpetual learning curve, where users are constantly adjusting to new interfaces instead of deepening their expertise. In educational settings, a strong focus on usability can negatively impact the learning process itself. Educational software that is overly simple to use may fail to challenge students sufficiently, limiting opportunities to build problem-solving skills and resilience. Learning often involves grappling with difficult concepts and overcoming obstacles, but excessively user-friendly systems can eliminate these challenges, leading to a more superficial learning experience. As a result, students might become proficient at navigating the software without gaining a deeper understanding of the underlying subject matter.

UNPACKING AMAZON: THE ENVIRONMENTAL TOLL OF INSTANT GRATIFICATION

Frictionless convenience, epitomized by services like Amazon's next-day delivery, has transformed our shopping habits and lifestyle. The ease with which we can now purchase almost any product with a few clicks, often receiving it at our doorstep within a day, is nothing short of revolutionary. However, this seemingly beneficial ease comes with significant environmental costs that are often overlooked in our pursuit of instant gratification, as published by 300 Amazon employees in 2020.[50] The allure of frictionless shopping lies in its simplicity and speed. Gone are the days of planning trips to multiple stores, comparing prices in person, and waiting in long lines. Instead, we are now able to browse vast virtual aisles, select products, and have them delivered rapidly, sometimes without any shipping cost. This convenience has led to a surge in online shopping, with millions of packages crisscrossing the globe daily. While this modern marvel of logistics is impressive, it also poses significant environmental harm and exacerbates growing challenges in cities like Venice.[51] One major concern is the dramatic increase in packaging waste. Each item ordered online often comes with layers of packaging to protect it during transit. This includes cardboard boxes, plastic wraps, bubble wraps, and other materials that are rarely reused and frequently end up in landfills. The production and disposal of this packaging material contribute significantly to environmental degradation, including deforestation, plastic pollution, and increased carbon emissions. Moreover, the logistics behind frictionless shopping involve complex supply chains that depend heavily on fossil fuels. The trucks, planes, and ships that transport goods contribute to greenhouse gas emissions, exacerbating climate change. The push for faster delivery times means more vehicles on the road and in the air, often running under less than optimal conditions, which further amplifies their environmental impact. This rapid delivery model also discourages the consolidation of shipments, leading to increased transportation inefficiency and a larger carbon footprint, as explained by MIT professor Velazquez-Martinez.[52] Furthermore, the culture of overconsumption that frictionless shopping promotes is deeply troubling. The ease of access and quick turnaround times encourage impulse buying and the acquisition of items that we do not necessarily need. This not only leads to an increase in waste but also fuels unsustainable production cycles. Manufacturers are compelled to produce more goods at a faster rate, often without regard for environmental stewardship. This results in the depletion of natural resources, increased pollution, and the exploitation of labor in many parts of the world. In addition to the environmental costs, the psychological aspect of frictionless shopping is also concerning. The immediate satisfaction of receiving a product almost as soon as we think about it reinforces a cycle of instant gratification.[53] This undermines the value of mindful consumption and promotes a throwaway culture where products are discarded as quickly as they are acquired. The environmental consequences of this mindset are profound, leading to a relentless strain on the planet's ecosystems. As we marvel at the convenience of next-day delivery and the frictionless shopping experience, it is crucial to acknowledge and address the hidden environmental toll it exacts, but without forgetting user experience.[54] Conscious efforts to reduce packaging waste, opt for slower and more efficient delivery options, and prioritize sustainable consumption practices can help mitigate these negative impacts as per the European Union report.[55] By being mindful of the broader consequences of our seemingly innocuous shopping habits, we can make choices that benefit both our convenience and the health of our planet.

While usability is crucial, design must also support skill development and resource sustainability. Designers should consider the long-term impacts, creating systems that challenge users and promote growth. Encouraging exploration and mastery of complex tasks ensures technology meets immediate needs while fostering deeper skills. This balanced approach leads to more enriching UXs, blending usability with opportunities for learning and innovation.

3.7 FUTURE TRENDS IN USABILITY: AI-DRIVEN PERSONALIZATION AND ADAPTATION

As we look to the future, the convergence of usability with AI-driven personalization and adaptation promises to revolutionize our interactions with technology. AI's capability to learn from user behavior and preferences is reshaping the digital landscape, moving away from one-size-fits-all designs toward highly personalized experiences. This evolution marks a significant leap in usability, where every interaction can be optimized to meet individual needs, enhancing satisfaction and efficiency. For years, companies like Google have demonstrated the power of simplicity in usability. Since its launch in 1998, Google has maintained a clean and straightforward interface that prioritizes UX.[56] By focusing on intuitive design, Google allows users to access information effortlessly, making search not just functional but also inherently user-friendly. This minimalist approach, driven by deep insights into user behavior, exemplifies how usability can be enhanced through design that feels personal and natural. Similarly, LinkedIn offers one of the most effective onboarding processes in the digital space.[57] The platform's personalized onboarding checklist guides new users through setting up their profiles, connecting with others, and leveraging LinkedIn's features. This approach helps users quickly understand the value of the platform, catering to their unique needs and making their experience both welcoming and engaging. Apple's online store is another standout example of personalized usability.[58] Known for its sleek design and intuitive navigation, the Apple Store not only looks visually appealing but also offers a seamless shopping experience. Its design anticipates user needs, from product comparisons to personalized recommendations, making the shopping process enjoyable and efficient. This level of refinement demonstrates how usability can be elevated through attention to user preferences. Duolingo, initially known for its playful approach to language learning, has grown into a powerful tool that tailors lessons to individual learning styles.[59] Through gamification and AI-driven insights, Duolingo creates a personalized learning journey for each user, adapting difficulty levels and content based on progress and performance. This customization keeps learners engaged and motivated, showcasing the potential of AI to enhance educational experiences. Beyond consumer applications, AI-driven personalization is making significant strides in healthcare. By integrating AI into patient care, healthcare providers can offer more precise, effective, and tailored treatments, enhancing overall quality of care. Despite setbacks like IBM Watson Health's struggles in 2017,[60] the potential for AI to revolutionize healthcare remains strong. Watson aimed to analyze vast amounts of medical data to provide personalized treatment recommendations but faced challenges in accurately interpreting complex information. Though Watson's shortcomings highlighted the complexities of AI in healthcare, ongoing advancements point toward a future where AI-driven systems will offer highly individualized patient care, reducing the risk of adverse reactions and improving outcomes. Looking ahead, the future of usability lies in the continuous refinement of AI-driven personalization techniques. As AI technology evolves, we can expect more sophisticated and intuitive systems that anticipate user needs with remarkable accuracy. This evolution will likely incorporate contextual and emotional intelligence, where AI not only responds to user actions but also understands and adapts to emotional states. Imagine smart home systems that adjust lighting and temperature based on a user's mood or energy levels, creating environments that enhance well-being and productivity. AI-driven personalization is set to redefine usability, offering experiences that cater to individual needs and preferences like never before. The ongoing integration of AI into our daily lives promises a future where technology feels less like a tool and more like a personalized companion, enhancing every aspect of our interaction with the digital world.

3.8 CONCLUSIONS

Usability is key to creating technology that people love. It's about making things easy to use, learn, and remember. By understanding how people think and work, we can design products that fit seamlessly into their lives. This is what HCD is all about. Key principles of usability include making things easy to learn, efficient to use, memorable, resistant to errors, and satisfying. We've seen examples like EndNote, Adani Green, Dropbox, Gmail, and Zoom to understand how these principles work in practice. While usability is essential, it's important to find a balance. Too much focus on making things simple can hinder learning and skill development. We risk creating a generation of people who rely on technology without understanding how it works. Also, the constant pursuit of convenience can harm the environment, as seen with the rise of online shopping and its impact on packaging and transportation. The future of usability lies in AI-driven personalization. By learning our preferences, AI can tailor technology to our specific needs, making it even more useful and enjoyable. However, it's crucial to ensure that this personalization doesn't create echo chambers or reinforce biases. Usability is a vital aspect of creating successful technology. By understanding users, applying core principles, and considering the broader impacts, we can design products that not only meet people's needs but also enhance their lives and protect our planet. The goal is to create technology that empowers people, not limit them.[61]

NOTES

1 What is human-computer interaction? https://qa.ulster.ac.uk/blog/what-is-human-computer-interaction/
2 Card, S. K., Moran, T. P., & Newell, A. (2005). The model human processor. *Ergonomics: Major Writings*, 2, 382.
3 Seow, S. C. (2005). Information theoretic models of HCI: A comparison of the Hick-Hyman Law and Fitts' Law. *Human–Computer Interaction*, 20(3), 315–352.
4 Useful, usable, and used: Why they matter to designers. www.interaction-design.org/literature/article/useful-usable-and-used-why-they-matter-to-designers
5 MacKenzie, I. S. (2024). *Human–computer interaction: An empirical research perspective*. Elsevier.
6 Nietschze F. Opere complete, frammenti postumi 1869–1874.
7 Plato, Alcibiade Minore, 146e-1476b.
8 Hornbæk, K., & Frøkjær, E. (2004, October). Two psychology-based usability inspection techniques studied in a diary experiment. In Proceedings of the Third Nordic Conference on Human-Computer Interaction (pp. 3–12).
9 Hornbæk, & Frøkjær, Two psychology-based usability inspection techniques.
10 Madan, A., & Dubey, S. K. (2012). Usability evaluation methods: A literature review. *International Journal of Engineering Science and Technology*, 4(2), 590–599.
11 Portmann, A., & Porena, B. (1989). *Le forme viventi: Nuove prospettive della biologia*. Adelphi.
12 Mendoza, A., Stern, L., & Carroll, J. (2010). Learnability as a positive influence on technology use. In *IMSCI 2010-4th International Multi-Conference on Society, Cybernetics and Informatics*, Proceedings (Vol. 1, pp. 280–284).
13 Severino, E. (2008). *La tendenza fondamentale del nostro tempo*.
14 Krick, T., Huter, K., Domhoff, D., Schmidt, A., Rothgang, H., & Wolf-Ostermann, K. (2019). Digital technology and nursing care: A scoping review on acceptance, effectiveness and efficiency studies of informal and formal care technologies. *BMC Health Services Research*, 19, 1–15.
15 Examples of digital transformation. https://quixy.com/blog/examples-of-digital-transformation/
16 Aristotle, *Metaphysics*, Book 1.
17 Simmel, G., Frisby, D., Bottomore, T., & Lemert, C. (2011). *The philosophy of money*. Routledge.
18 A beginner's guide to usability testing. https://maze.co/guides/usability-testing/examples/
19 Human-centered design. www.gsa.gov/system/files/HCD-Discovery-Guide-Interagency-v12-1.pdf
20 Dimitriadis, Y., Martínez-Maldonado, R., & Wiley, K. (2021). Human-centered design principles for actionable learning analytics. *Research on E-learning and ICT in Education: Technological, Pedagogical and Instructional Perspectives*, 277–296.
21 Thompson, L., & Schonthal, D. (2020). The social psychology of design thinking. *California Management Review*, 62(2), 84–99.
22 Zhai, C., & Wibowo, S. (2023). A systematic review on artificial intelligence dialogue systems for enhancing English as foreign language students' interactional competence in the university. *Computers and Education: Artificial Intelligence*, 4, 100134.
23 Beretta, M., Dahlander, L., Frederiksen, L., & Thomas, A. (2023). Lego takes customers' innovations further. *MIT Sloan Management Review*, 65(1), 34–37.
24 Architecting a digital transformation at Royal Philips. https://cisr.mit.edu/publication/2018_0101_PhilipsDigitalTransformation_RossMockerVanZoelen
25 Apple's product development process – Inside the world's greatest design organization. www.interaction-design.org/literature/article/apple-s-product-development-process-inside-the-world-s-greatest-design-organization
26 Xbox Adaptive Controller welcomed by UK charities and gamers with disabilities. https://ukstories.microsoft.com/features/xbox-adaptive-controller-welcomed-by-uk-charities-and-gamers-with-disabilities/
27 The Nest Learning Thermostat is smarter and sleeker than ever. https://blog.google/products/google-nest/new-learning-thermostat/
28 Albert, B., & Tullis, T. (2022). *Measuring the user experience: Collecting, analyzing, and presenting UX metrics*. Morgan Kaufmann.
29 Hertzum, M. (2022). *Usability testing: A practitioner's guide to evaluating the user experience*. Springer Nature.

30 Choi, T. R., & Drumwright, M. E. (2021). "OK, Google, why do I use you?" Motivations, post-consumption evaluations, and perceptions of voice AI assistants. *Telematics and Informatics*, *62*, 101628.

31 Liang, J. T., Yang, C., & Myers, B. A. (2024, February). A large-scale survey on the usability of ai programming assistants: Successes and challenges. In *Proceedings of the 46th IEEE/ACM International Conference on Software Engineering* (pp. 1–13).

32 Sauer, J., Sonderegger, A., & Schmutz, S. (2020). Usability, user experience and accessibility: Towards an integrative model. *Ergonomics*, *63*(10), 1207–1220.

33 Björklund, G., Bohlin, M., Olander, E., Jansson, J., Walter, C. E., & Au-Yong-Oliveira, M. (2022, April). An exploratory study on the spotify recommender system. In *World conference on information systems and technologies* (pp. 366–378). Springer International Publishing.

34 Holubcik, M., Soviar, J., Pollák, F., Straková, J., & Pártlová, P. (2020). Strategic management and logistic operations of the alliance of airlines: Oneworld Case study.

35 Vinod, B. (ed.) (2022). Introduction to hotel revenue management. In *Revenue Management in the Lodging Industry: Origins to the Last Frontier* (pp. 1–50). Springer International Publishing.

36 Activate Apple Voiceover. https://support.apple.com/en-gb/guide/voiceover/vo2682/mac

37 VoiceOver. www.commonsense.org/education/reviews/voiceover

38 www.bemyeyes.com/language/english

39 How do I use the Microsoft Immersive Reader in a course as a student? https://community.canvaslms.com/t5/Student-Guide/How-do-I-use-the-Microsoft-Immersive-Reader-in-a-course-as-a/ta-p/446

40 FTC says: Amazon didn't protect Alexa users' or children's privacy. https://consumer.ftc.gov/consumer-alerts/2023/05/ftc-says-amazon-didnt-protect-alexa-users-or-childrens-privacy

41 How the UK can reimagine data-enabled identity. www.wired.com/sponsored/story/how-the-uk-can-reimagine-data-enabled-identity/

42 Ahmad, S. F., Han, H., Alam, M. M., Rehmat, M., Irshad, M., Arraño-Muñoz, M., & Ariza-Montes, A. (2023). Impact of artificial intelligence on human loss in decision making, laziness and safety in education. *Humanities and Social Sciences Communications*, *10*(1), 1–14.

43 Krist, A. H., Tong, S. T., Aycock, R. A., & Longo, D. R. (2017). Engaging patients in decision-making and behavior change to promote prevention. *Information Services & Use*, *37*(2), 105–122.

44 Turner, K. L., Hughes, M., & Presland, K. (2020). Learning loss, a potential challenge for transition to undergraduate study following COVID19 school disruption. *Journal of Chemical Education*, *97*(9), 3346–3352.

45 Rinta-Kahila, T., Penttinen, E., Salovaara, A., Soliman, W., & Ruissalo, J. (2023). The vicious circles of skill erosion: A case study of cognitive automation. *Journal of the Association for Information Systems*, *24*(5), 1378–1412.

46 Zaitsev, A., Gal, U., & Tan, B. (2020). Coordination artifacts in agile software development. *Information and Organization*, *30*(2), 100288.

47 How many test users in a usability study? www.nngroup.com/articles/how-many-test-users/

48 Rinta-Kahila, T., Penttinen, E., Salovaara, A., Soliman, W., & Ruissalo, J. (2023). The vicious circles of skill erosion: a case study of cognitive automation. *Journal of the Association for Information Systems*, *24*(5), 1378–1412.

49 Rajivan, P., Aharonov-Majar, E., & Gonzalez, C. (2020). Update now or later? Effects of experience, cost, and risk preference on update decisions. *Journal of Cybersecurity*, *6*(1), tyaa002.

50 Amazon employees share our views on company business. https://amazonemployees4climatejustice.medium.com/amazon-employees-share-our-views-on-company-business-f5abcdea849

51 An ode to the delivery men of Venice, the hardest-working labourers in the world. https://nationalpost.com/entertainment/an-ode-to-the-delivery-men-of-venice-the-hardest-working-labourers-in-the-world

52 FootWear News Article – Josué Velázquez Martínez on the environmental benefits of online shopping. https://sustainable.mit.edu/footwear-news-article-josue-velazquez-martinez-on-the-environmental-benefits-of-online-shopping/

53 Why you succumb to instant gratification – And the easiest way to make life optimizing choices. www.forbes.com/sites/kmehta/2022/10/31/why-you-succumb-to-instant-gratification--and-the-easiest-way-to-make-life-optimizing-choices/

54 Nguyen, A. T., Parker, L., Brennan, L., & Lockrey, S. (2020). A consumer definition of eco-friendly packaging. *Journal of Cleaner Production*, *252*, 11

55 European Parliament and the Council on packaging and packaging waste, amending Regulation. https://eur-lex.europa.eu/legal-content/EN/TXT/HTML/?uri=SWD:2022:384:FIN
56 9 examples of good UX design every designer should see. https://userguiding.com/blog/good-ux-examples
57 9 examples of good UX design every designer should see. https://userguiding.com/blog/good-ux-examples
58 9 examples of good UX design every designer should see.https://userguiding.com/blog/good-ux-examples
59 9 examples of good UX design every designer should see. https://userguiding.com/blog/good-ux-examples
60 MD Anderson benches IBM Watson in setback for artificial intelligence in medicine. www.forbes.com/sites/matthewherper/2017/02/19/md-anderson-benches-ibm-watson-in-setback-for-artificial-intelligence-in-medicine/
61 Card, S. K. (2018). *The psychology of human-computer interaction*. CRC Press.

4 Sense-React STAR Model
Increased Productivity by End-to-End Data

A digital maze, STAR guides the way.
Challenges loom, like shadows gray.
Lessons from trade, a guiding light,
To build a future, shining bright.

OpenAI, CHATGPT (2025)

I've roamed the globe, crossing countless borders, immersing myself in diverse cultures over 100 countries. From bustling metropolises to remote villages, I've witnessed the incredible ways in which humans connect. Despite language barriers and cultural differences, there's a universal thread that binds us all: our innate desire to exchange ideas and goods, share stories, and learn from one another. It's a proof to the interconnectedness of humanity, a concept that mirrors the intricate web of digital data. Just as trade routes have connected civilizations for centuries, digital networks now bridge the gaps between nations and individuals. The Sense-Transmit-Analyze-React (STAR)[1] model introduced in this chapter, a key framework for AI, enhances productivity by facilitating efficient data interactions. However, challenges arise due to the lack of interconnectedness between digital data systems. Learning from global trade, we can address these challenges through collaboration, infrastructure investment, and standardized data governance. The STAR model demonstrates the potential of real-time data to drive productivity, but its application must consider regional variations in technology and data management policies.

4.1 PRODUCTIVITY, TRADE, AND DATA

4.1.1 CONNECTED OR DIGITALLY CONNECTED?

In today's world, the idea of a connected trade world goes beyond just being digitally linked. It involves the complex network of physical goods, transportation, and global trade, creating a picture that shows the diverse aspects of our modern economy. This includes considering additional factors like biodiversity and technology.[2] Unlike the digital realm, where data seems to flow instantaneously across borders with a mere click, the world of trade involves the tangible movement of products—ranging from raw materials to finished goods—over vast distances and through diverse regulatory environments.[3] This complexity mirrors the challenges faced in the digital domain, where data flows are similarly influenced by technology, policies, and especially by global dynamics.[4] The movement of physical goods around the globe is a marvel of modern engineering and logistics. Consider, for instance, the journey of a smartphone from its conception to the consumer's hand.[5] The raw materials for the phone, such as rare earth metals, are mined in Africa.[6] These materials are then shipped to factories in Asia, where the components are manufactured. From there, the components travel to assembly plants in China, where the phone is assembled and will continue to be, as shifting

DOI: 10.1201/9781003533160-4

the assembly process elsewhere is not an easy task.[7] Once assembled, the finished product is shipped to distribution centers in Europe and North America, before finally making its way to retail stores and online marketplaces. Each step of this journey requires meticulous planning, coordination, and adherence to various international regulations and standards.

Take another example: the trade of agricultural products, such as coffee beans. Coffee beans are typically grown in tropical countries like Brazil, Colombia, and Ethiopia. After harvesting, the beans are processed and packed, then shipped across the oceans to roasters in the United States, Germany, and Japan. The roasted coffee is then packaged and distributed to cafes, supermarkets, and online retailers worldwide. This journey from farm to cup involves not just the physical transportation of goods, but also the management of trade agreements (sometimes not favorable for local producers[8]), an inch of global capitalism,[9] tariffs, and quality control standards, ensuring that consumers receive a consistent and high-quality product. These examples illustrate the complexities inherent in the global trade network. Each step involves a host of logistical challenges, from transportation and warehousing to customs clearance and regulatory compliance. In many cases, goods must pass through multiple checkpoints, each with its own set of rules and requirements.[10] This necessitates a high degree of coordination and cooperation between various stakeholders, including manufacturers, shippers, regulators, and retailers.[11] Moreover, the trade world is not static; it is constantly evolving in response to technological advancements, shifts in consumer demand, and changes in geopolitical landscapes. Innovations in transportation, such as the advent of container shipping and the development of high-speed rail networks, have revolutionized the way goods are moved across the globe. Similarly, advances in information technology have made it possible to track and manage shipments in real time. This has improved efficiency and reduced the risk of delays and losses, much like the solutions provided by the maritime deeptech company Navozyme.

LOGISTICS AND DEEPTECH: NAVOZYME, TRANSFORMING MARITIME, AHEAD OF TIME[12]

Navozyme, a maritime deeptech company, has revolutionized the shipping industry by significantly reducing the risk of delays and losses through its innovative technologies. The maritime industry, known for its complex logistics and extensive supply chains, has traditionally faced numerous challenges related to inefficiency, mismanagement, and lack of real-time information. Navozyme's advanced solutions have addressed these issues head-on, creating a more streamlined and reliable process for shipping goods across the globe. At the heart of Navozyme's impact is its blockchain-based technology, which ensures the secure and transparent exchange of information. By leveraging blockchain, Navozyme provides an immutable ledger that records every transaction and movement of goods in real time. This transparency is crucial in reducing delays, as it allows all stakeholders, including shipping companies, port authorities, customs officials, and end clients, to access the same accurate information simultaneously. For instance, if a shipment is delayed at a port due to unforeseen circumstances, all parties are immediately notified, allowing them to adjust schedules and expectations accordingly. This level of visibility minimizes the risk of miscommunication and errors that can lead to costly delays. Moreover, Navozyme's technology enhances the efficiency of document management. In the traditional maritime industry, a significant amount of time is spent on processing and verifying paperwork, such as bills of lading, certificates of origin, and customs declarations. These documents often need to be physically handled and transported, which is both time-consuming and prone to errors or loss. Navozyme digitizes these processes through secure blockchain records, enabling instant verification and transfer of documents. This not only speeds up the entire process but also reduces the likelihood of documents being misplaced or tampered with, thereby mitigating the risk of delays and associated financial losses. In addition to blockchain, Navozyme employs advanced data analytics to predict and mitigate potential disruptions in the supply chain. By analyzing historical data and current trends, Navozyme's system can forecast delays caused by various factors such as weather conditions, port congestion, or geopolitical tensions. This predictive capability allows shipping companies to proactively reroute or reschedule shipments, avoiding bottlenecks and ensuring timely deliveries. For example, if a storm is predicted to hit a major shipping route, Navozyme's system can suggest alternative routes to avoid the affected area, thus preventing delays and potential damage to cargo. Navozyme's real-time tracking system is another critical component that reduces the risk of losses. Traditionally, once a shipment leaves the port, there is limited visibility until it reaches its destination. This lack of real-time monitoring can result in lost or stolen goods, especially during transshipments or in high-risk areas. Navozyme addresses this issue by providing continuous real-time tracking of shipments using Internet of Things (IoT) devices and satellite communications. These technologies allow for constant monitoring of a ship's location, condition, and environment. If any irregularities are detected, such as a deviation from the planned route or sudden changes in temperature that could damage sensitive cargo, immediate alerts are sent to the concerned parties, enabling swift corrective action. Furthermore, Navozyme's solutions enhance the efficiency of port operations. Port congestion is a major cause of delays in the maritime industry. Navozyme's system integrates with port management systems to optimize the scheduling and allocation of resources such as berths, cranes, and labor. By providing real-time data on ship arrivals, cargo volumes, and operational status, Navozyme enables ports to manage their activities more efficiently, reducing turnaround times and preventing bottlenecks. This coordinated approach not only speeds up the handling and clearance of shipments but also ensures that ships spend less time idling in ports, thus reducing the risk of delays. The impact of Navozyme's technology extends to improving the overall security of maritime operations. Security breaches, whether due to piracy, cargo theft, or cyberattacks, pose significant risks to the maritime industry. Navozyme's blockchain-based platform enhances security by providing a tamper-proof record of all transactions and movements, making it difficult for unauthorized parties to alter or falsify information. Additionally, the use of IoT devices for real-time tracking ensures that any suspicious activities are detected and addressed promptly. For example, if a container is opened or tampered with during transit, the system immediately triggers an alert, allowing for quick investigation and response. This heightened security not only protects valuable cargo but also boosts the confidence of stakeholders in the integrity of the supply chain. Navozyme's commitment to innovation is evident in its continuous efforts to enhance and expand its technological offerings. The company invests heavily in research and development to stay ahead of emerging trends and challenges in the maritime industry. This proactive approach ensures that Navozyme's solutions remain at the cutting edge, providing shipping companies with the tools they need to navigate an increasingly complex and dynamic global trade environment. The benefits of Navozyme's technologies are reflected in the tangible improvements seen across the maritime industry. Shipping companies that have adopted Navozyme's solutions report significant reductions in delays and losses, leading to increased operational efficiency and profitability. Moreover, the ability to provide reliable and timely deliveries enhances customer satisfaction and strengthens business relationships. For instance, a shipping company using Navozyme's technology can confidently assure its clients of accurate delivery times, which is crucial for industries that rely on just-in-time inventory management. Deeptech has made a profound impact on the maritime industry by reducing the risk of delays and losses. By leveraging blockchain technology, real-time tracking, advanced data analytics, and enhanced security measures, Navozyme has addressed some of the most pressing challenges in global shipping. The company's commitment to continuous innovation ensures that it remains a leader in the field, providing invaluable support to the maritime industry in its quest for efficiency, reliability, and security. As global trade continues to grow and evolve, Navozyme's technologies will undoubtedly play a crucial role in shaping the future of maritime logistics.

However, with these advancements come new challenges. The rise of protectionist policies and trade wars,[13] for example, can disrupt established supply chains and create uncertainty for businesses. Similarly, changes in environmental regulations and standards[14] can impact the cost and feasibility of transporting goods, necessitating new strategies and adaptations.[15] The connected trade world is a complex and dynamic system, reflecting the intricate interplay between physical goods, logistics, and international commerce. It mirrors the challenges faced in the digital realm, where data flows are shaped by technology, policies, and global dynamics. As we continue to navigate this interconnected landscape, understanding and managing these complexities will be crucial to fostering a resilient and sustainable global economy.

4.1.2 The Interconnectedness of Goods

The Silk Road stands as a milestone to ancient trade routes that connected the East and West, fostering the exchange of silk, spices, and ideas.[16] This historical legacy merges with modern shipping lanes, air freight corridors, and extensive supply chains that crisscross the globe, ensuring that goods manufactured in one corner of the world can reach consumers thousands of miles away. Central to the idea of a connected trade world are the institutions and agreements that govern international trade. Treaties like Bretton Woods in 1944,[17] the World Trade Organization (WTO),[18] regional trade blocs such as the European Union (EU),[19] and bilateral trade agreements between nations all play pivotal roles in shaping the flow of goods and the rules that govern them. These frameworks aim to reduce trade barriers, establish fair competition, and protect intellectual property rights, thereby fostering a more predictable and stable environment for global commerce.[20] Trade agreements like those helped establishing standardized rules and reducing tariffs, these agreements have enabled smoother, more predictable trade flows, enhancing the variety and availability of goods. Prioritizing collective thinking in these agreements has led to economic growth, job creation, and improved living standards for hundreds of millions of people worldwide, demonstrating the profound benefits of international cooperation in trade.[21] Moreover, the logistics infrastructure that supports interconnected trade is indispensable. Ports, airports, railways, highways, and warehouses form the backbone of efficient supply chains, enabling seamless movement of goods from production facilities to markets worldwide. Advanced technologies, such as Global Positioning System (GPS) tracking, and blockchain like the Navozyme example, or blockchain-based GPS[22] further enhance transparency, traceability, and security within these supply chains, addressing challenges like counterfeit goods and logistical inefficiencies. The interconnected nature of global trade also brings forth significant economic implications. Countries specialize in producing goods and services where they have a comparative advantage, driven by factors like natural resources, labor skills, and technological expertise. This specialization fosters economic growth, efficiency gains, and higher living standards for participating nations.

EXAMPLE OF INTERCONNECTED NATURE OF GLOBAL TRADE

Saudi Arabia: Saudi Arabia specializes in producing and exporting oil and petroleum products due to its vast natural reserves of crude oil. This comparative advantage in natural resources has driven its economic growth and allowed it to become a major player in the global energy market. The revenue generated from oil exports has enabled the country to invest in infrastructure, education, and healthcare, thereby improving living standards.[23]

Germany: Germany excels in producing high-quality automobiles and machinery, driven by its advanced technological expertise and skilled labor force. German car manufacturers like BMW, Mercedes-Benz, and Volkswagen are renowned worldwide for their engineering excellence. This specialization has bolstered Germany's economy, making it one of the world's largest exporters and contributing to high living standards through job creation and technological innovation.[24]

However, it also exposes economies to external shocks and dependencies, as disruptions in one part of the world can ripple through global supply chains, impacting industries and consumers far beyond national borders. Being resilient is important: an example is the Flex factory complex in Guadalajara, Mexico. When productivity stopped improving, the company often moved smaller assembly lines to a different area, either in the same building or another one. Each time they moved, workers redesigned the process to use less space and fewer workers, which increased productivity.[25] Environmental sustainability is another critical dimension of the connected trade world. The transportation of goods over long distances contributes to carbon emissions and environmental degradation. Efforts to mitigate these impacts include promoting energy-efficient transportation modes, adopting cleaner technologies, and implementing international agreements aimed at reducing carbon footprints associated with global trade. Interconnected trade fosters cultural exchange, enriching societies worldwide. Products showcasing traditional craftsmanship, artistic expressions, and culinary delights cross continents, promoting cross-cultural understanding and appreciation. Consider your evening meal: common foods, integral to daily sustenance, often originate from other countries. Globalization, with trade connections dating back centuries, has brought these foods to our tables. Imagine life without them.

GLOBALIZATION ON YOUR TABLE[26]

Spices: Their quest spurred colonialism and empires.
Potato: From wild tuber to French fry, it's traveled the world.
Coffee: Essential for many, morning or night.
Tomato: Integral to diverse cuisines, from pizza to salsa.
Tea: A long journey with a rich history.
Chili: A staple in many cultures.
Tobacco: Spread globally, with complex history.
Soybeans: Versatile, from China to kitchens and industry worldwide. This cultural diffusion not only enhances consumer choice but also promotes cultural diversity and preserves heritage in an increasingly interconnected world.

Challenges within the connected trade world are multifaceted. Tariffs, quotas, and nontariff barriers imposed by nations can hinder free trade and escalate economic tensions. Disparities in labor standards, intellectual property protections, and regulatory frameworks across countries pose challenges for businesses navigating diverse markets. Moreover, geopolitical tensions, natural disasters, and global health crises—such as the COVID-19 pandemic—highlight vulnerabilities within global supply chains, prompting calls for resilience and diversification.

4.2   THE INTERCONNECTEDNESS OF DIGITAL DATA

The digital realm, while seemingly more fluid, faces similar complexities. Digital data interconnectedness is not solely defined by technological advancements but also by historical, cultural, and geopolitical factors. Just as ancient trade routes have evolved into modern supply chains, the flow of digital data is shaped by the evolution of communication technologies and international cooperation. However, the digital world presents unique challenges. Technology, despite its promise for enhancing transparency, efficiency, and sustainability within global supply chains, has not fully realized this potential. The Pew Research Center's study on life in 2035 highlights the immense benefits brought by advances in digital tools and systems. "Being digital" has greatly enhanced our ability to connect, solve complex problems, and improve our lives. These advancements have empowered us to understand and shape the world more effectively. However, the same technologies that boost our capabilities have also amplified harmful aspects of human nature. This expert survey gathered opinions on the positive and negative trends of this digital evolution, aiming to predict where humanity is headed.[27] Systems often remain disconnected, exacerbating the digital divide. For instance, the internet, a marvel of modern technology exemplified by the Internet Protocol (IP), is universally agreed upon,[28] yet significant portions of the world, like China, operate separate digital ecosystems, widening the digital divide and posing new cybersecurity risks, despite their massive growth.[29]

Geopolitics significantly affects the digital landscape.[30] Policies on data sovereignty, cybersecurity, and cross-border data flows reflect national interests and security concerns. The fragmentation of digital policies creates a complex environment for businesses and individuals navigating the global digital ecosystem. The challenges of ensuring data privacy, security, and equitable access are amplified in this fragmented digital landscape.[31] Moreover, societal expectations and cultural norms influence digital data flows. Different regions have varying attitudes toward privacy, data protection, and digital rights, impacting how data is collected, stored, and shared. These differences necessitate a nuanced approach to data governance that respects local norms while striving for global interoperability. But also the digital landscape significantly affects geopolitics.[32] The technological revolutions that brought about the data-driven economy led to unexpected outcomes. By the early 2020s, despite U.S. corporations becoming global giants with trillion-dollar valuations, the United States faced significant internal strife over social issues like guns, abortion, vaccination, immigration, and race.[33] The nation was compared to a failed state, with debates on a potential second civil war, especially after the U.S. Capitol storming on January 6, 2021.[34] Simultaneously, the United States engaged in a technological war with China.[35] Europe, once a key player in globalization, struggled with Brexit, internal conflicts, and Russia–Ukraine war.[36] The global governance system seemed unable to manage the overlapping crises, or "polycrisis". This shift indicates how the technological and economic conditions of the data-driven economy contributed to these challenges.

4.1.3   BRIDGING THE GAP: LESSONS FROM TRADE

The realm of international trade imparts crucial insights on managing the interconnectedness of digital data and how this data shapes global commerce.[37] Just as trade has grown through careful coordination, so too can we enhance our digital world by applying similar principles. At the heart of global trade are institutions and agreements that ensure smooth and fair exchanges. Organizations like the WTO,[38] the EU, and various bilateral agreements create a cooperative framework, fostering economic growth, job creation, and improved living standards for countless people worldwide through collective effort.[39] Similarly, in the realm of digital data, we can benefit from coordinated efforts. As our world becomes increasingly digital, the challenges of managing data across different systems, platforms, and borders grow more complex.[40] By looking at the success of international trade agreements, we can find ways to create a more cohesive digital ecosystem. One key lesson is the importance of collective thinking. Just as countries have come together to form trade agreements that benefit everyone, stakeholders in the digital world—governments, businesses, and individuals—are learning to collaborate to establish standards and practices for smooth and secure data flow. In fact, 30% of countries globally have made progress in developing advanced national digital policies, legal frameworks, and governance structures.[41] China, within its borders, is a prime example of interconnectedness, with its vast network of cities, businesses, and technologies working together seamlessly, like the Digital Silk road initiative.[42] The challenge lies in integrating China into the global system, ensuring that it can plug into the worldwide digital and trade networks.[43] By prioritizing collective thinking and cooperation, we can create a more connected and prosperous world, much like the benefits seen from successful trade agreements. This cooperation can lead to a more resilient digital infrastructure, capable of withstanding disruptions and ensuring the privacy and security of users. Furthermore, the experience of trade institutions in resolving disputes and enforcing rules can guide us in addressing digital challenges. Establishing clear guidelines and mechanisms for dispute resolution can help prevent conflicts and ensure that all parties adhere to agreed-upon standards. The interconnectedness of global trade provides a valuable blueprint for managing digital data. By embracing coordinated efforts and collective thinking, we can create a digital world that is more efficient, secure, and beneficial for everyone.

Standardization and Interoperability: Just as the WTO and regional trade agreements establish clear guidelines for international trade, similar efforts are needed in the digital world to ensure smooth and efficient operations across borders. By setting international standards for key areas such as data protection, cybersecurity,[44] and digital transactions, we can create a more seamless experience for cross-border data exchanges and minimize fragmentation in the digital landscape.[45] In this context, interoperability—the ability of different systems and organizations to work together effectively[46]—can be understood through four essential layers: legal, organizational, semantic, and technical. Each layer plays a crucial role in ensuring that digital systems and processes function harmoniously.

FOUR LEVELS OF INTEROPERABILITY

Legal: Interoperability focuses on aligning laws and regulations across different jurisdictions to enable consistent handling of data and digital transactions. This layer ensures that legal frameworks support cross-border interactions and protect users' rights regardless of where they are located.

Organizational: Interoperability involves harmonizing procedures and practices among various organizations. It ensures that institutions and businesses can effectively collaborate and share information without encountering obstacles due to differing internal processes or policies.

Semantic: Interoperability deals with the meaning and interpretation of data. It ensures that data exchanged between systems is understood in the same way by all parties, which is essential for accurate communication and decision-making.

Technical: Interoperability pertains to the technical standards and protocols that allow different systems and technologies to interact with each other. This layer includes everything from software and hardware compatibility to network protocols.[47]

In addition to these four layers, there is a crucial cross-cutting component: integrated public service governance. This aspect ensures that public services and policies are coordinated and effectively managed across different layers and systems, facilitating a more unified approach to digital governance.[48] Furthermore, there is a background layer known as interoperability governance. This overarching layer involves the frameworks and strategies that guide how interoperability is achieved and maintained. It includes the development of policies, standards, and best practices to support the smooth functioning of the other layers. For instance, the EU can leverage public funding to mandate interoperability as a condition for subsidies, boosting competition. Europe's strength lies in its regulatory approach, and as markets increasingly rely on big data and digital standards, the EU's focus on openness and interoperability will become a key competitive advantage.[49] By addressing these layers and components, we can create a digital environment where data and services flow seamlessly across borders, enhancing efficiency and collaboration. Just as trade agreements have helped to integrate global markets and benefit millions of people, similar efforts in digital interoperability can lead to greater innovation, security, and convenience in our increasingly connected world.

Infrastructure Development: Investment in digital infrastructure is crucial. Just as physical logistics networks support trade, robust digital infrastructure, including data centers, broadband networks, and cybersecurity frameworks, is essential for seamless digital data flows. Digital infrastructures involve information technology and come in two types: hybrid and dedicated. Hybrid infrastructures are traditional ones with digital components added, like water mains with leak-detecting sensors. Dedicated digital infrastructure is inherently digital, such as fiber optic cables for internet data transfer.[50] Despite advancements, some argue that consumers lack sufficient choice, for example, in broadband providers. However, more competitors in a market are not always beneficial. Increased competition can lead to higher production costs and reduced revenues, resulting in higher prices. Thus, proactive government subsidies or policies to spur competition are often less effective than fostering effective competition among fewer firms. Outdated regulatory policies and a complex permitting process can hinder infrastructure development.[51] For instance, the absence of a coherent national energy strategy aligned with existing policies is a significant barrier to smart-grid deployment. Agencies should develop strategies to support digital infrastructure in their areas of influence and increase funding for these projects. They should ensure privacy and security concerns don't slow deployment.[52]

Collaboration and Partnerships: Global trade succeeds through collaboration between nations, introducing the idea of cyber diplomacy. Cyber diplomacy is how countries, groups, or individuals act online to protect and promote their cultural, economic, scientific, or political interests while keeping peaceful relations.[53] Collaboration must occur between institutions and businesses. In the digital world, partnerships between governments, tech companies, and civil society[54] can improve data governance and tackle challenges like cybersecurity and digital inclusion by, first, building domestic capacities: strengthening countries' abilities to design, implement, and evaluate policy priorities, aligning domestic and international goals, and addressing complex, interconnected challenges. Second is about working inclusively by engaging countries at all development levels equally in multilateral and multistakeholder partnerships to tackle shared, multidimensional development challenges with comprehensive responses. And, last, operating with more tools and actors by expanding international cooperation instruments, such as knowledge sharing, policy dialogues, capacity building, and technology transfers, and including more actors in a whole-of-government approach.[55]

Resilience and Diversification: Global supply chains have adapted to disruptions through diversification and resilience strategies.[56] Similarly, digital ecosystems must develop mechanisms to withstand cyber threats, technological failures, and geopolitical shifts. These challenges fall into four categories: cyber and kinetic warfare, telecommunications, IT and cloud computing, and digital geopolitics and resilience. A new phenomenon is emerging where global tech companies act as digital nations and superpowers, often taking sides in these issues. This includes diversifying data storage locations and adopting robust cybersecurity practices.[57]

Sustainability and Ethics: Emphasizing environmental sustainability in trade can extend to digital data. Promoting energy-efficient data centers, reducing electronic waste, and ensuring ethical data practices contribute to a more sustainable digital ecosystem. However, data suggests that current policies often focus on the positive indirect impacts of information and communication technologies (ICTs), like enhanced energy efficiency and resource management, rather than the negative direct impacts, such as electricity consumption. Additionally, these expectations vary between countries, lacking a unified theme. Policies should move beyond merely acknowledging opportunities to integrating a systemic understanding of both direct and indirect impacts. Targeted measures are needed to use ICTs as tools for environmentally sustainable industries.[58]

4.2   A VISION FOR THE FUTURE

4.2.1   GOODS AND DATA

Goods and digital data are closely connected, showing how economic trends, technology, and culture shape our world. Companies don't just compete by using their own resources and strategies. Instead, they build their business models on shared resources, network effects, knowledge sharing, local advantages, and government support.[59] The challenge of our prAIority idea in the book is figuring out how to allocate resources in this complex environment. Navigating the complexities and opportunities of this evolving landscape requires a holistic approach that leverages the strengths of both domains. In a future where digital data flows as seamlessly as goods across borders, we can envision a world where technology enhances transparency, efficiency, and sustainability. By drawing on the lessons of interconnected trade, we can build a resilient and equitable digital ecosystem that fosters collaboration, innovation, and inclusive growth.

Global Data Governance Frameworks: Establishing global frameworks for data governance that respect national sovereignty while promoting cross-border data flows can create a balanced and predictable digital environment as proposed by the EU in 2024.[60] These frameworks should address data privacy, security, and ethical considerations, ensuring that data benefits society as a whole. These frameworks should cover data privacy, security, and ethical issues to make sure data benefits everyone. When creating the European Sustainability Reporting Standards (ESRS), the Commission collaborated with international standard setters to include global standards while maintaining the EU's goal of transparency. The guidance released today acknowledges these efforts. It indicates that EU companies following European standards can also meet global standards with little extra work. Ensuring that different sustainability reporting systems work together is crucial for companies that need to report under both International Sustainability Standards Board (ISSB) Standards and ESRS. Without alignment, companies might have to report similar information in different formats, causing duplication and unnecessary effort. The aim of this reporting is to streamline reporting, reduce duplication, simplify compliance, enhance transparency, and align global and regional standards.[61]

Sustainable Development Goals: As we have seen above, aligning digital policies with the United Nations Sustainable Development Goals (SDGs) can ensure that digital interconnectedness contributes to global development objectives. This includes leveraging digital technologies to address climate change, reduce inequality, and promote sustainable economic growth. The interconnected trade world and the digital data ecosystem are deeply intertwined, each influencing and reflecting the other.[62] The challenges and opportunities they present are a testament to the complexity of our globalized world. By learning from the successes and failures of interconnected trade, we can navigate the digital landscape more effectively, fostering a future where technology and commerce work together to create a resilient, equitable, and sustainable global community. The journey toward this future requires a commitment by humans to collaboration,[63] innovation, and ethical governance. As we continue to explore the intricacies of interconnected trade and digital data, we must remain vigilant and adaptable, ready to address emerging challenges and seize new opportunities. In doing so, we can ensure that the benefits of interconnectedness are shared widely, paving the way for a prosperous and inclusive global society.

Empowering Individuals and Communities: Just as global trade boosts economies, digital interconnectedness should empower individuals and communities. Ensuring digital literacy, affordable access to technology, and protecting digital rights are essential for inclusive growth. To achieve this, individuals may need data cooperatives for secure, trusted data exchange. Post-pandemic, community/SME-led cooperatives can maintain resilient, decentralized supply chains for digital commons. These commons and data sovereignty ensure communities have affordable access to information and collective data decision-making. Cooperatives provide essential infrastructure, protect property rights, and prevent monopolization, supporting self-determination. Effective governance and open APIs enhance digital transformation, increasing SMEs' efficiency and technological capabilities in the process.[64] Cultural diversity and digital trends are major issues for young people today. These challenges are often addressed separately, focusing either on social cohesion for culturally diverse youth or cyber-safety for mainstream youth. Instead of this divided approach, we need to combine sociology and global digital citizenship. This unified framework will help us understand how young people interact digitally and better address these challenges, fostering a more inclusive and supportive environment for all youth.[65]

Promoting Innovation and Collaboration: The convergence of digital and physical worlds offers immense opportunities for innovation, as we are going to see in Chapter 7. Encouraging collaboration between tech companies, policymakers, and academia can drive breakthroughs in areas like artificial intelligence, blockchain, and the Internet of Things (IoT), unlocking new possibilities for global progress.

4.2.2 "SENSE" IN STAR MODEL: CAPTURING REAL-TIME DATA

The S of STAR model means "Sense" the ability to sense and gather real-time data. This involves using various sensors, such as those detecting physical properties in devices and environments, as well as smartphone apps that collect different types of information like environmental conditions and user behaviors.[66] This data collection forms the foundation of the STAR model (Figure 4.1), being the first and most important step in the process that ultimately leads to the ability to react.

This continuous data acquisition empowers systems to understand contextual nuances with unprecedented accuracy. For instance, in industrial settings, sensors monitor machinery performance parameters, ensuring preemptive maintenance to avoid downtime.

ASQUARED IOT, LISTENING AND WATCHING THE MANUFACTURING PROCESS[67]

Asquared IoT leverages cutting-edge machine learning, including deep learning, to extract digital data from complex industrial processes. By analyzing this data, the company identifies anomalies and machine failures, and predicts potential issues. The core innovation of Asquared IoT is "Edge Computing", which enables real-time analytics and algorithm execution at the edge of the Industry 4.0 network, without requiring internet connectivity. This approach results in products that are embedded with AI, nontouch, nonintrusive, and easily deployable in any manufacturing environment, including older systems. The company's real-time analytics focus on sound and video, providing immediate alarms and warnings for process defects. These capabilities minimize issues and downtimes by enabling predictive maintenance, which foresees failures and links them to physical parameters and processes. Additionally, Asquared IoT's long-term analytics identify opportunities for process and efficiency improvements, ultimately enhancing operational efficiencies and boosting the bottom line. By integrating advanced AI at the edge, Asquared IoT offers a powerful solution for modernizing manufacturing plants and optimizing industrial operations.

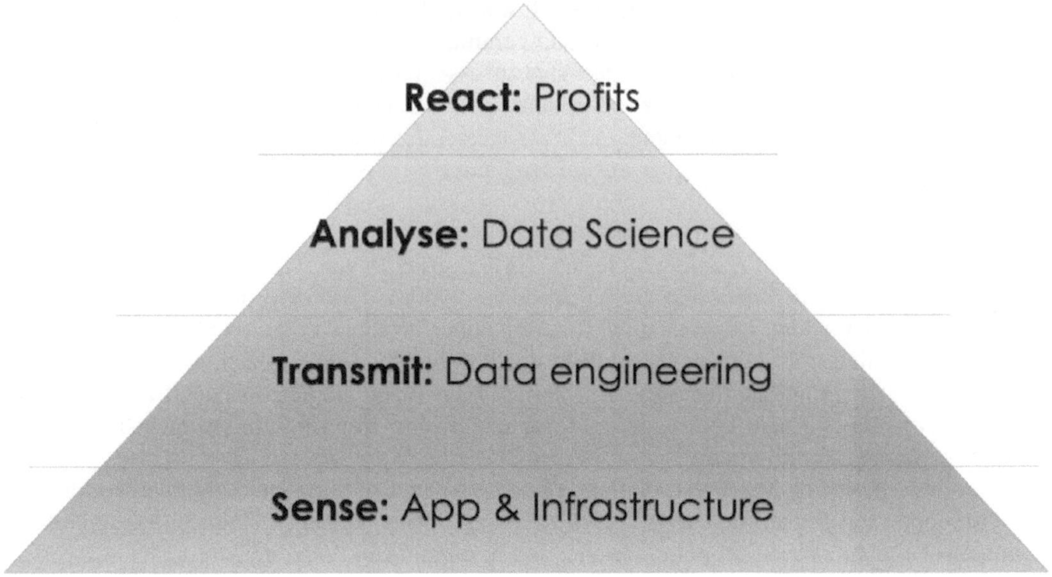

FIGURE 4.1   STAR model.

In healthcare, wearable sensors track vital signs, enabling early detection of health anomalies. By enhancing situational awareness, the sense component not only improves decision-making but also lays the foundation for proactive interventions.

WEAREABLE SENSORS IN HEALTHCARE[68]

BLOOD PRESSURE MONITORS

A blood pressure monitor can be worn on either arm and sends accurate blood pressure readings directly to your phone. This home-use cuff are known for its precision and can connect to a smartphone to track blood pressure and pulse data.

GLUCOSE METERS

Monitoring blood glucose levels is key for people with diabetes. These devices attach to the upper arm and uses a phone sensor to read glucose levels, eliminating the need for finger pricks. It can be worn for up to seven days, making it convenient and less invasive.

ECG MONITORS

Wrist watches can now detect abnormal heart rhythms and provide accurate ECG readings. While advanced, it's important to note that they can't detect heart attacks, blood clots, strokes, or conditions like congestive heart failure.

FITNESS TRACKERS

These devices track various health metrics like heart rate and steps and has a battery life of up to seven days. It is a technology that offers precise health and fitness monitoring.

INTEGRATED ACTIVEWEAR

Integrated sensors can provide gentle vibrations to guide wearers in practicing yoga moves correctly. Available in various styles, this innovative clothing has received numerous five-star reviews and helps improve balance and fitness.

4.2.3   The Transmit of STAR Model: Seamless Data Transmission

Efficient data transmission forms the linchpin of the STAR model's operational fluidity. Once captured, data traverses seamlessly through networks to reach processing hubs. The advent of 5G technology has amplified transmission speeds, facilitating near-instantaneous data relay across vast distances. This capability proves invaluable in scenarios demanding real-time responses, such as autonomous vehicle navigation or remote surgical procedures. Moreover, secure transmission protocols safeguard data integrity and confidentiality, mitigating risks associated with cyber threats. As data flows unhindered from source to destination, the transmit phase ensures timely delivery, enabling swift decision-making and enhanced operational efficiency. While 5G technology promises faster data transmission and greater connectivity, it also has a dark side that raises significant concerns. One major issue is the increased vulnerability to cyberattacks. As more devices become interconnected, the potential entry points for hackers multiply, making it easier for them to infiltrate networks and access sensitive data.[69] This could lead to severe breaches in personal privacy and national security. Additionally, the sheer volume of data transmitted through 5G networks exacerbates issues related to data privacy.[70] With more detailed information being collected and shared, the risk of misuse or unauthorized surveillance by corporations and governments grows. Furthermore, the rapid rollout of 5G infrastructure has environmental implications.[71] The production and disposal of new 5G-enabled devices and the increased energy consumption of maintaining these advanced networks contribute to environmental degradation and increased carbon footprints. Moreover, there are health concerns associated with the higher frequency radio waves used in 5G, although the scientific community is still debating the potential long-term effects. While 5G technology heralds an era of unprecedented connectivity and innovation, it also brings to the forefront critical issues of cybersecurity, data privacy, environmental impact, and health risks that need to be carefully managed and addressed

4.2.4   The A of STAR Model: Analyze, Data-Driven Insights

The "A" in the STAR model stands for Analyze. This phase focuses on harnessing the power of big data analytics to transform raw data into actionable insights. Advanced algorithms sift through voluminous datasets, identifying patterns, trends, and anomalies that elude conventional analysis.[72] Machine learning algorithms, for instance, predict consumer preferences based on browsing history, optimizing targeted marketing strategies.[73] Similarly, in financial sectors, predictive analytics forecast market trends, guiding investment decisions with precision. By distilling complex information into comprehensible metrics, the analyze component empowers stakeholders to make informed choices swiftly. This capability not only enhances productivity but also fosters innovation by uncovering latent opportunities within data reservoirs. Analyzing big data has become essential in many industries, but mistakes in the analysis of big data are still happening, like in the example below.

CORRELATION IS NOT CAUSATION[74]

One common mistake in analyzing big data is assuming that correlation implies causation. Just because two datasets show a relationship doesn't mean one causes the other. For example, imagine a company noticing that sales of ice cream and sunscreen are both high during the summer. They might conclude that buying ice cream causes people to buy sunscreen. However, the real reason is that both are popular in hot weather. Failing to distinguish between correlation and causation can lead to misguided decisions. In another case, a business might see a spike in website traffic and increased sales and assume their recent ad campaign was the reason. But without properly analyzing all factors, they might overlook other influences, like a competitor going out of business or a seasonal trend. These errors occur because big datasets often contain many variables, and finding patterns can be misleading without careful examination. It's crucial to use proper statistical methods and consider all possible factors before drawing conclusions. This mistake highlights the importance of critical thinking and expertise in data analysis to avoid making costly errors based on incorrect interpretations of data patterns.

Instead good examples of big data analysis include pharmaceuticals, agriculture, and retail, transforming how these sectors operate and make decisions. In the pharmaceutical industry, big data analysis is revolutionizing drug development and patient care. For example, companies use big data to analyze vast amounts of clinical trial data, patient records, and genetic information to identify potential new drugs and treatments more quickly and accurately. By sifting through this data, researchers can find patterns and correlations that would be impossible to detect manually. This approach speeds up the development process, reduces costs, and helps create personalized medicine tailored to individual patients' genetic profiles and medical histories. For instance, if a particular genetic marker is found to be associated with a positive response to a drug, treatments can be customized, improving patient outcomes and reducing side effects.[75] In agriculture, big data is used to optimize farming practices and increase crop yields. Farmers collect data from various sources, such as weather stations, soil sensors, and satellite imagery, to monitor field conditions in real time. By analyzing this data, farmers can make informed decisions about when to plant, irrigate, and harvest crops. For example, if data shows that a particular field has lower moisture levels, farmers can adjust their irrigation schedules to ensure optimal water usage.[76] Additionally, big data can help predict pest infestations and disease outbreaks, allowing farmers to take preventive measures before significant damage occurs. This data-driven approach not only boosts productivity but also helps conserve resources and reduce environmental impact. In the retail sector, big data analysis is transforming how businesses understand and interact with customers. Retailers collect data from various touchpoints, such as online purchases, social media interactions, and in-store transactions, to gain insights into customer behavior and preferences. By analyzing this data, retailers can create personalized shopping experiences, improve inventory management, and optimize pricing strategies. For example, if data shows that a particular product is trending on social media, retailers can increase stock levels and adjust marketing strategies to capitalize on the trend.[77] Additionally, big data can help identify patterns in customer behavior, such as the times of day when people are most likely to shop, allowing retailers to schedule staff more effectively and improve customer service. This targeted approach enhances customer satisfaction, increases sales, and strengthens brand loyalty.

4.2.4 THE "R" OF STAR MODEL: REACT, ADAPTIVE DECISION-MAKING

The culmination of the STAR model manifests in the React phase, where actionable insights translate into adaptive decision-making. Intelligent systems, equipped with real-time data and analytical outputs, autonomously adjust parameters to optimize outcomes. In smart grids, for instance, algorithms balance energy supply and demand dynamically, mitigating grid instability. Likewise, in smart cities, traffic management systems reroute vehicles based on congestion patterns, minimizing travel time and fuel consumption. By integrating feedback loops, the response phase ensures continuous improvement, refining strategies in alignment with evolving conditions. This adaptive prowess not only augments operational efficiency but also cultivates resilience in navigating complex environments.

A BOOK ON SENSE AND REACT[78]

In *Sense and Respond*, authors Jeff Gothelf and Josh Seiden explore a transformative approach to business management in an age where customer needs and market conditions are in constant flux. The "Respond" (corresponding to the "React" of the STAR model) aspect is a critical component of their methodology, emphasizing the necessity for businesses to remain agile and responsive. The concept of "Respond" involves taking swift and effective action based on the insights gathered during the "Sense" phase. This approach requires organizations to be flexible, enabling them to adapt to changing customer demands and market trends quickly. Gothelf and Seiden argue that traditional, rigid business plans often fail in dynamic environments. Instead, they advocate for iterative processes and continuous learning. The "Respond" phase encourages businesses to implement small, incremental changes and test these changes in real time. This way, companies can gauge the effectiveness of their actions and make necessary adjustments swiftly. It promotes a culture of experimentation, where failures are seen as learning opportunities rather than setbacks. By adopting a "React" mindset, organizations can maintain relevance and competitiveness. They become more customer-centric, aligning their operations closely with user needs. This adaptability is not just about reacting to changes but proactively shaping the future trajectory of the business based on real-time feedback and data. In essence, "Respond" is about evolving in tandem with the market to ensure sustained success.

4.2.5 APPLICATIONS ACROSS DOMAINS

The applicability of the STAR model spans diverse domains, each reaping distinct benefits from its integrated framework. In manufacturing, predictive maintenance enhances equipment reliability, reducing downtime and maintenance costs. Educational institutions leverage personalized learning platforms, tailoring educational experiences to individual student needs based on performance analytics. Healthcare providers utilize remote patient monitoring systems to deliver proactive care, mitigating hospital readmissions through early intervention. By customizing solutions to domain-specific requirements, the STAR model empowers stakeholders to harness technology effectively, driving productivity gains across sectors.

4.3 DATA AND GEOPOLITICS

Despite its transformative potential, the adoption of the STAR model is not without challenges. Privacy concerns surrounding data collection and usage necessitate robust regulatory frameworks to safeguard user rights. Additionally, interoperability issues between heterogeneous systems require standardized protocols to ensure seamless integration. Furthermore, the need for skilled personnel proficient in data analytics and system optimization underscores the importance of continuous training and development initiatives.

4.3.1 THE DIFFERENT MODELS OF STARS AROUND THE WORLD

The STAR model, being a framework that encapsulates the processes involved in gathering data, transmitting it to centralized systems, analyzing the information, and responding accordingly, becomes specific when applied to geopolitics. In the contexts of China, the EU, and the United States, the implementation and implications of this model differ significantly due to varying approaches to technology governance, data privacy, and human rights. These differences are shaped by the distinct political, legal, and cultural landscapes of each region, leading to unique advantages and challenges associated with human intervention in AI and data management. In China, the STAR model is deeply integrated into the country's ambitious vision of becoming a global leader in artificial intelligence and big data. The Chinese government's regulatory model uses technology to boost economic growth and maintain social stability. However, this model also serves as a tool for political control, surveillance, and propaganda, embedding digital authoritarianism into Chinese society. The Chinese government's top-down approach enables rapid deployment and scaling of AI technologies, where sensing devices and surveillance systems are pervasive.[79] Massive amounts of data are collected through a comprehensive network of sensors embedded in public spaces, smartphones, and internet services. This data is transmitted to centralized platforms where sophisticated AI algorithms analyze it to derive insights and drive decision-making. Human intervention in China is characterized by substantial state involvement, ensuring that AI development aligns with national interests. This centralized control offers significant advantages in terms of efficiency and the ability to implement large-scale initiatives quickly. This approach helps sustain the Chinese Communist Party (CCP) by prioritizing economic development and social stability. Critics argue that this state-driven model infringes on individual rights and deprives citizens of essential civil liberties. Nonetheless, it can still foster technological advancements, suggesting that innovation can occur even without freedom.[80] The future of China's tech industry is uncertain, as the government is moving away from its previously lenient regulatory stance. Now, in the name of common prosperity, it is exerting stricter control over the tech sector, facing little resistance from the industry. This shift underscores the main principle of the Chinese regulatory model: the government, not tech companies, maintains ultimate control over the digital economy.[81] While this can benefit economic growth and enterprise development, it often comes at the expense of citizens' freedoms and rights.[82] For instance, China's social credit system leverages the STAR model to monitor and influence citizen behavior, promoting social order and compliance with state policies.[83] However, the extensive human intervention by the state raises substantial concerns regarding privacy and human rights. The Chinese model prioritizes collective security and social stability over individual privacy, leading to widespread surveillance and data collection without explicit consent. Xi's December 2022 visit to Saudi Arabia (a country that has invested $1 billion in AI[84]) showcased China's appeal as a development partner. The agreements included plans for hydrogen energy, data centers, and EV factories in Saudi Arabia. Chinese digital companies are expanding into AI, e-commerce, mobile payments, communications, smart cities, and surveillance tech. In November 2022, China also secured e-commerce deals with Laos, Thailand, Singapore, and Pakistan.[85] This environment creates a potential for abuse, as state authorities have access to vast amounts of personal data, which can be used to suppress dissent and infringe on civil liberties. The lack of transparent oversight mechanisms exacerbates these risks, leading to a situation where the benefits of AI are achieved at the expense of individual freedoms and privacy rights.[86] In contrast, the EU adopts a regulated approach to the STAR model, emphasizing the protection of individual privacy and human rights. The General Data Protection Regulation (GDPR) serves as a cornerstone of this approach, setting stringent standards for data collection, transmission, and analysis. In the EU, sensing technologies and data transmission systems must comply with GDPR requirements, ensuring that personal data is collected lawfully, processed transparently, and used for specific, legitimate purposes.[87] Human intervention in the EU involves rigorous oversight by data protection authorities, promoting accountability and safeguarding against misuse. The European approach offers significant advantages in terms of protecting individual privacy and maintaining public trust in AI systems. By prioritizing consent and data minimization, the EU creates an environment where citizens have greater control over their personal information. This fosters a use of AI, where data-driven decisions are made transparently and with respect for human rights.[88] However, the stringent regulatory framework can also pose challenges for innovation and competitiveness. Complying with GDPR can be resource-intensive and may slow down AI development and deployment. However, this perspective is narrow. A multilayered explanation of algorithms could highlight the overall benefits of GDPR, demonstrating how it enhances data protection and trust in AI technologies.[89] However, the fragmented regulatory landscape across EU member states, and beyond, can create inconsistencies and barriers for businesses operating across borders.[90] In the United States, the STAR model is influenced by a combination of private sector innovation and fragmented regulatory oversight.[91] The United States is home to some of the world's leading tech companies, which drive advancements in sensing, data transmission, and AI analysis. Human intervention in the United States is characterized by a significant role of private enterprises in developing and deploying AI technologies. These companies leverage vast amounts of data collected from various sources, including social media, e-commerce platforms, and IoT devices, to create sophisticated AI-driven services and products. The U.S. approach offers considerable advantages in terms of innovation and economic growth. The competitive market environment fosters rapid technological advancements and commercialization of AI applications. However, the lack of comprehensive federal data privacy legislation creates disparities in how data is managed and protected. While some states have implemented their own privacy laws, such as the California Consumer Privacy Act (CCPA), the overall regulatory landscape remains inconsistent.[92] This can lead to scenarios where personal data is exploited for commercial gain without adequate protections, raising concerns about privacy and the potential for misuse. Furthermore, the significant influence of the private sector in the United States means that human intervention is often driven by profit motives, which can sometimes conflict with public interest and ethical considerations. The lack of robust oversight mechanisms increases the risk of data breaches, surveillance, and discrimination based on algorithmic decisions. These challenges highlight the need for a more cohesive and comprehensive approach to data privacy and human rights protection in the context of AI and the STAR model. The implementation of the STAR model in China, the EU, and the United States reflects the distinct political, legal, and cultural contexts of each region. China's centralized and state-driven approach enables rapid advancements in AI but at the cost of individual privacy and human rights. The EU's regulated framework emphasizes data protection and transparency, fostering ethical AI use while potentially hindering innovation. The U.S.'s market-driven model promotes technological progress but lacks consistent privacy protections, leading to potential abuses. Human intervention in each context creates unique advantages and challenges, underscoring the need for balanced approaches that safeguard privacy and human rights while harnessing the benefits of AI.

4.3.2 China and the AI Supremacy

The STAR model represents a comprehensive framework for understanding the implementation of digital ecosystems, particularly in the context of China. China's government intervention has played a crucial role in creating a robust digital infrastructure that facilitates each step of this model, ultimately leading to significant advancements in AI and other digital technologies. The first component of the STAR model, "Sense", involves gathering data through various sensors and devices. In China, this has been realized through an extensive network of surveillance cameras and other sensing technologies. Companies like SenseTime or the unicorn Face++[93] have been pivotal in this area, developing sophisticated computer vision and facial recognition technologies that power the country's vast surveillance network.

BBC REPORTER FOUND IN SEVEN MINUTES BY CCTV CAMERAS

China has been developing what it terms "the world's largest camera surveillance network". By 2017, there were already 170 million CCTV cameras installed across the country, and by 2020, an additional 400 million cameras were added. Many of these cameras are equipped with artificial intelligence, including facial recognition technology. The BBC's John Sudworth received an exclusive opportunity to access one of China's cutting-edge police control rooms. In a notable demonstration, it took just seven minutes for the surveillance system to locate Sudworth in the city of Guiyang, illustrating the impressive efficiency and extensive reach of China's surveillance network. This rapid identification underscores the power and sophistication of the country's surveillance infrastructure.[94]

The extensive network of CCTV cameras across China feeds vast amounts of data into advanced AI systems, enabling capabilities such as facial recognition and real-time tracking. These technologies provide robust tools for law enforcement and public safety, significantly enhancing the government's ability to monitor and manage activities across the nation. However, this high level of surveillance has sparked significant controversy and concern among various groups, particularly political dissidents.

In his report, Sudworth also interviewed several political dissidents who expressed deep discomfort and unease with being constantly monitored. They highlighted the invasive nature of the surveillance system and raised concerns about privacy, freedom of expression, and the potential for misuse of such technology. These dissenting voices reflect a growing apprehension about the implications of living under such pervasive scrutiny, underscoring the ongoing debate about the balance between security and individual rights in the age of advanced surveillance.

Once data is collected, it needs to be transmitted to central locations for processing. China's investment in digital infrastructure, including high-speed internet and 5G networks, has ensured that data can be transmitted quickly and reliably across the country. Mainland China holds the title of the world's largest 5G market, representing over 60% of global 5G connections.[95] The Chinese government's commitment to developing state-of-the-art communication networks has been critical in this regard. These networks form the backbone of the digital ecosystem, allowing for real-time data transmission essential for applications like autonomous driving, smart cities, and more.[96] The "Analyze" phase involves processing the vast amounts of data collected to extract meaningful insights. China's prowess in AI and big data analytics is a direct result of its investments in technology and talent. The country has become a global leader in AI research and development, supported by initiatives like the New Generation Artificial Intelligence Development Plan.[97] This strategic approach has led to groundbreaking advancements, such as AI-driven applications that can animate famous paintings like the Mona Lisa, bringing historical art to life in ways never before possible. Chinese tech giants like Alibaba, Tencent, and Baidu have been at the forefront of developing sophisticated AI algorithms that can process and analyze data at unprecedented scales.

CHINA NATIONAL AND LOCAL NEW GENERATION ARTIFICIAL INTELLIGENCE DEVELOPMENT PLAN (NGAIDP)

China has emerged as a leader in AI development, but the question remains whether it will outpace the United States in the AI race. While many studies highlight the Chinese central government's role in advancing AI, it's crucial to recognize the significant responsibility local governments bear in this effort. These local governments have varying interests, capabilities, and strategies for promoting AI, leading to different approaches across the country. The central government's policies on emerging technologies, like AI, are met with varied responses from local governments. This raises an important question: how do these local entities align with or diverge from the central government's priorities? By analyzing AI policy documents from both central and local levels, and focusing on how the New Generation Artificial Intelligence Development Plan (NGAIDP) is implemented across provinces, it becomes evident that central and provincial goals do not always match. The central government is primarily concerned with national security, defense, and global competition, while provincial governments focus more on the economic benefits of AI. This divergence means that the success of AI initiatives in China depends not only on central directives but also on the capacities of the private sector and the political authority of provincial leaders. These factors are crucial in determining how quickly and effectively AI policies are adopted and implemented across the country.[98]

The final component, "React", is where the insights gained from data analysis are put into action. China's digital ecosystem showcases several notable examples of effective response mechanisms. One prominent case is TikTok, a social media platform developed by ByteDance. TikTok leverages AI to analyze user preferences and behavior, delivering highly personalized content that keeps users engaged.[99] This ability to react dynamically to user data has been a key factor in TikTok's global success. Another example is the use of AI in creating interactive experiences with historical artifacts. For instance, AI technologies have been used to animate famous paintings like the Mona Lisa, creating a more engaging and immersive experience for viewers.[100] These applications not only demonstrate China's technical capabilities but also its ability to integrate AI into cultural and entertainment sectors.

However, the implementation of the STAR model in China is not without its challenges and controversies. The extensive surveillance network and data collection capabilities have raised significant privacy concerns. The social scoring system, which uses data to evaluate and score citizens based on their behavior, has been particularly contentious. Critics argue that this system infringes on individual privacy and can be used to control and manipulate the population. Dissidents and human rights activists have voiced concerns about the potential for abuse, highlighting cases where individuals have been penalized for their political views or social activities.

CHINA SOCIAL CREDIT SYSTEM

The magazine *MIT Review* explains that the Chinese government is pushing "social credit-worthiness" to build trust by addressing issues such as corruption, tax evasion, and pollution, holding individuals, companies, and government agencies accountable. Social credit scoring, similar to financial credit scoring, often gets confused with it, particularly when local governments blend the two systems. For instance, in August, the province of Liaoning announced it is exploring ways to reward blood donation through the financial credit system. This blending of financial and social credit systems illustrates the complexity and potential confusion surrounding the implementation of these policies. A social credit system in China aims to reward good behavior and penalize bad. Individuals or companies with good credit records receive benefits like priority government treatment, while those with bad records face public shaming and restrictions, such as travel bans and limited access to luxury goods. The government periodically updates the list of punishments. Contrary to popular belief, there is no central social credit score for individuals. Local governments experiment with their own systems, leading to varied and sometimes controversial implementations. This decentralization contributes to misunderstandings, particularly in the West.[101] Unfortunately, this interview in the *MIT Review* features a Chinese person who oversimplifies the social credit system, which non-Chinese individuals experience differently. For example, the *Economist* reports that Suqian recently started scoring every adult's "trustworthiness". Residents begin with 1,000 points, gaining or losing points for good or bad behavior. Scores are updated monthly, ranking residents from AAA (model citizen) to D (untrustworthy). In Suqian, city officers manage a "Trustworthy Neighborhood Service Centre", where they evaluate shop owners' integrity. Shops can earn or lose points based on neatness and clear pavements. High-scoring shops get free advertising, while low scorers risk reprimands. This system highlights local governments' paternalistic approach, often viewed as propaganda by residents. National blacklists result from legal violations, not "bad credit". However, social credit systems can be abused. For instance, government offices managing citizen petitions might blacklist people for causing disturbances, which can be arbitrarily interpreted. While appeals are possible, they rarely succeed in China. The Xichu system, which rewards top citizens with "priority service" in emergencies, seems unfair. Low scores may lead to unspecified consequences, indicating potential misuse.[102]

Moreover, the integration of these technologies into daily life has led to ethical and political debates. The use of AI and surveillance in monitoring and controlling the population has drawn criticism from international human rights organizations. The Chinese government's stance on data privacy and control has also led to tensions with other countries, particularly regarding the global expansion of Chinese tech companies. The role of the Chinese government in the national digital ecosystem cannot be overstated. Through strategic policies and substantial investments, the government has fostered an environment conducive to technological innovation. Initiatives like the Made in China 2025 plan and the Belt and Road Initiative have emphasized the importance of technology and digital infrastructure in China's economic development.[103] By providing funding, resources, and regulatory support, the government has enabled Chinese companies to become global leaders in AI and other cutting-edge technologies. The government's involvement extends beyond funding and regulation. It also includes fostering collaborations between academic institutions, private enterprises, and state-owned companies.[104] This collaborative approach has accelerated research and development, leading to rapid advancements in AI and big data technologies. Additionally, the government has implemented policies to attract and retain top talent, ensuring that China remains at the forefront of technological innovation.

A PERSONAL NOTE OF MY EXPERIENCE WITH CHINA

Over the years, I have traveled to China almost annually to teach courses there. Additionally, I have had many Chinese students in my classes outside of China. As part of my curriculum, I regularly show the above-mentioned BBC video "In Your Face: China's All-Seeing State" by John Sudworth. The video is meant to provoke thought and discussion about surveillance and privacy issues. However, I consistently encounter the same reaction from my Chinese students: disappointment and accusations of Western bias. What worries me most about this reaction is not the accusation itself, but the lack of open debate that follows. When I invite my students to look beyond the label of me being a Westerner and to explain their disagreement with the video's content, they often do not engage. They seldom provide specific reasons or engage in a constructive dialogue about the video's points. This pattern has repeated itself frequently with my students, most of whom are in their twenties. This recurring situation has led me to reflect on the broader implications for the future, especially concerning the development and use of AI in China. AI, after all, is created by humans and is shaped by the values and perspectives of its developers. The reluctance of my students to debate or critically engage with challenging content might be indicative of a broader issue in how information is processed and questioned. In classrooms outside of China, discussions about controversial topics usually lead to lively debates, where students challenge each other and the material presented. This kind of engagement is crucial for the development of critical thinking skills. It is concerning that this dynamic often does not occur with my Chinese students when discussing topics like state surveillance. This observation raises important questions about the prAIorities of AI and its role in society. If future AI systems are developed in an environment where critical discussion is limited, what kind of biases might be embedded in these technologies? AI systems reflect the data they are trained on and the perspectives of their creators. If these creators are not encouraged to question and debate, their creations may lack the diversity of thought necessary for ethical and unbiased AI. Furthermore, the implications for citizens in China could be profound. If AI is developed in a context where state surveillance is normalized and not openly debated, the resulting technologies may reinforce and perpetuate these practices. This could lead to a society where surveillance is even more pervasive and accepted, with less room for dissent or privacy. The reluctance of my students to engage in critical debate might also reflect broader societal pressures. In China, questioning state policies and practices can be risky. This atmosphere could discourage open discussion, not only in classrooms but also in the broader public sphere. As AI technologies continue to advance, it is essential that they are developed in environments that encourage diverse perspectives and critical questioning. Otherwise, there is a risk that these technologies will mirror and reinforce existing power structures and biases. In summary, my experiences teaching Chinese students and observing their reactions to challenging content highlight the need for open debate and critical thinking in education. These elements are crucial for the ethical development of AI and for ensuring that these technologies serve the interests of all citizens, not just those in power.

The implementation of the STAR model has had significant economic and social impacts. Economically, it has driven growth in the tech sector, creating jobs and fostering new industries. Companies like Alibaba, Tencent, and Huawei have become global giants, contributing to China's economic rise. The digital ecosystem has also facilitated the development of smart cities, enhancing urban living through improved infrastructure and services.[105] Socially, the impact has been multifaceted. On one hand, technologies like AI and big data have improved public services, healthcare, and education, contributing to a higher quality of life. On the other hand, the pervasive surveillance and data collection practices have led to concerns about privacy and individual freedoms. The social scoring system, in particular, has sparked debates about the balance between security and privacy, as well as the potential for social engineering and control.[106] Looking ahead, the country's advancements in these areas are likely to influence global standards and practices. As Chinese tech companies expand internationally, they bring with them the technologies and methodologies developed within this framework. This expansion has the potential to reshape global markets and technological landscapes. However, the global influence of China's digital ecosystem also comes with challenges. International scrutiny over data privacy, cybersecurity, and ethical practices will continue to be a significant issue.[107] Countries and organizations worldwide will need to navigate the complexities of engaging with China's digital ecosystem while addressing concerns related to privacy and human rights. The implementation of the STAR model in China exemplifies how government intervention and strategic investments can create a thriving digital ecosystem. By building extensive data collection and transmission infrastructure, fostering advancements in AI and big data analytics, and implementing effective response mechanisms, China has positioned itself at the forefront of technological innovation. However, the challenges and controversies associated with surveillance, privacy, and social control highlight the need for careful consideration of ethical and political implications. As China continues to advance and expand its digital ecosystem, its influence on the global stage will undoubtedly grow, shaping the future of technology and society.

4.3.2 Europe Long-Term Plan: The Pioneer of Data Privacy and Regulation

The STAR model in Europe, epitomizes the synergy between advanced technology and human intervention, and its implementation in Europe has been significantly shaped by proactive policies from the EU. The EU has been instrumental in creating a robust digital ecosystem that ensures citizen protection and data privacy, particularly through landmark regulations such as the GDPR and the forthcoming AI Act. The GDPR, enacted in 2018, is a cornerstone of the EU's digital strategy, designed to protect individuals' personal data and privacy. It imposes stringent requirements on how companies collect, store, and manage data, ensuring that citizens have control over their personal information. This regulation has set a global standard for data protection, influencing policies far beyond Europe's borders. Companies operating within the EU must adhere to these rigorous standards, which include obtaining explicit consent from individuals before processing their data, ensuring data portability, and implementing robust measures to secure data against breaches. Parallel to GDPR, the AI Act in 2024[108] aims to regulate artificial intelligence technologies, addressing potential risks while fostering innovation. The AI Act categorizes AI systems into different risk levels, with corresponding regulatory requirements. High-risk AI applications, such as those used in critical infrastructure, education, and employment, will undergo strict scrutiny to ensure they are safe and ethically sound. This regulation is intended to prevent harm and bias, promoting transparency and accountability in AI development and deployment. These regulatory frameworks have created a protective digital environment for European citizens, reinforcing trust in digital services and technologies. By prioritizing data protection and ethical AI, the EU has positioned itself as a leader in digital rights.[109] However, this emphasis on regulation also raises questions about the impact on the competitiveness of European companies in the global tech arena. Despite the EU's efforts to foster a thriving digital ecosystem, few European companies have achieved global dominance in the digital technology sector.[110] Notable exceptions include Booking.com, a leading online travel agency headquartered in the Netherlands, which has successfully navigated the regulatory landscape to become a global player.[111] However, the tech scene in Europe is starkly contrasted with the landscape in the United States and China, where companies like Google, Amazon, Facebook, Alibaba, and Tencent have not only emerged but also thrived on a global scale. The disparity in global tech leadership raises critical questions about the EU's policy approach. While regulations like GDPR and the AI Act protect citizens and promote ethical practices, they may also impose significant compliance costs and operational constraints on companies. These regulations can stifle innovation by creating barriers to entry and limiting the flexibility of businesses to experiment and scale rapidly. In contrast, tech giants in the United States and China operate in regulatory environments that are often more conducive to rapid growth and innovation.[112] These countries have fostered ecosystems where regulatory oversight is balanced with an emphasis on promoting technological advancement and market competitiveness. For instance, the relatively relaxed data privacy regulations in the United States have allowed companies to leverage vast amounts of user data to refine their products, personalize services, and drive advertising revenues.[113] Similarly, China's strategic focus on becoming a global leader in AI has involved substantial government support and a regulatory framework that encourages rapid deployment and testing of AI technologies, sometimes at the expense of stringent ethical guidelines.

AN EU–CHINA COMPARISON APPROACH ON AI[114]

China, a leading player in the development of artificial intelligence (AI), has implemented a comprehensive set of laws and policies designed to guide the growth and application of AI technologies. This legislative and policy framework aims to balance the promotion of innovation with the need to uphold national security, ethical standards, and societal values. China's approach to AI regulation is characterized by targeting specific AI technologies with tailored regulations. These regulations seek to stimulate industry growth and innovation while embedding ethical standards into a governance structure that prioritizes national security, public interest, and the protection of individual rights. In contrast, the European Union (EU) has taken a different approach with its AI Act. The EU's strategy focuses on categorizing AI systems based on the level of risk they pose. This risk-based framework aims to protect human safety and fundamental rights by imposing stringent regulations on high-risk AI applications. The AI Act adopts a technology-neutral stance, systematically classifying AI systems by their associated risks and enforcing strict regulations on those deemed high-risk to ensure human safety, fundamental rights, and adherence to ethical norms. Despite their differing approaches, both China and the EU share common goals in their AI regulatory frameworks. These goals include promoting responsible AI development and use, ensuring data security and user privacy, evaluating the security and risks associated with AI systems and algorithms, mandating provider accountability for the safe and compliant operation of their AI systems, demanding transparency and explainability of AI systems, and safeguarding user rights and interests. A notable difference between China's AI regulations and the EU's AI Act is the level of responsibility placed on providers for monitoring user behavior and content moderation. Chinese regulations explicitly require providers to establish content review mechanisms to filter, detect, and mitigate the distribution of illegal or harmful content. This involves a direct responsibility for providers to monitor user behavior and ensure that content shared through their platforms complies with legal and ethical standards. This proactive approach to content moderation is in sharp contrast to the EU's AI Act, which does not impose such stringent requirements on providers to police user behavior. Instead, the EU's AI Act focuses more on ensuring that AI systems themselves are safe and adhere to ethical norms. It emphasizes the importance of transparency, requiring providers to disclose how their AI systems work and to ensure that users can understand and trust these systems. The EU's framework is designed to protect fundamental rights by regulating high-risk AI applications, such as those used in critical infrastructure, education, and employment, where the potential for harm is significant. In summary, while China and the EU have different strategies for regulating AI, both aim to foster innovation while ensuring that AI technologies are developed and used responsibly. China's approach is more prescriptive, with specific regulations targeting different AI technologies and a strong focus on national security and content moderation. The EU's approach, on the other hand, is risk-based and technology-neutral, focusing on regulating high-risk applications to protect human safety and fundamental rights. Despite these differences, both frameworks share the common objectives of promoting responsible AI development, ensuring data security and user privacy, and safeguarding user rights and interests.

This regulatory dichotomy raises the question of whether the EU's stringent regulatory approach is ultimately beneficial for its economic competitiveness. While the EU's policies ensure a high level of data protection and ethical standards, they may inadvertently hinder the growth of European tech companies,[115] preventing them from achieving the same level of global influence as their counterparts in the United States and China. The challenge for the EU is to strike a balance between protecting citizens and fostering a dynamic, competitive digital economy. Moreover, the EU's regulatory framework could be seen as both a strength and a potential vulnerability. On one hand, it establishes the EU as a global leader in digital rights and ethics, which can attract businesses and consumers who prioritize these values.[116] On the other hand, it may also discourage risk-taking and innovation, which are critical drivers of growth in the fast-paced tech sector. The success of Booking.com, while notable, is an exception rather than the rule, highlighting the need for a broader strategy that encourages more European companies to achieve global prominence.[117] To address this, the EU could consider adopting more nuanced regulatory frameworks that protect citizens while also promoting innovation and competitiveness.[118] This could involve providing greater support for startups and SMEs, reducing bureaucratic hurdles, and fostering a more flexible regulatory environment that adapts to the rapid pace of technological change.[119] Additionally, the EU could invest more in research and development, support public–private partnerships, and create incentives for companies to scale their innovations globally.[120] The STAR model's implementation in Europe, underpinned by human intervention through EU regulations like GDPR and the AI Act, has created a protective and ethical digital ecosystem. However, the stringent regulatory environment may also impede the global competitiveness of European tech companies, raising questions about the best policy approach for the EU economy. As Europe looks to the future, it will be crucial to find a balance that protects citizens while fostering a vibrant, competitive digital market that can compete on the global stage. The EU's challenge is to maintain its leadership in digital rights and ethics while also creating an environment where European tech companies can thrive and lead in innovation.

4.3.2 DIGITAL ECOSYSTEM UNITED STATES: EXTREME WEALTH, SPREAD POVERTY AND MENTAL ISSUES

The STAR model has played a crucial role in shaping the U.S. technological and economic landscape, especially in California's Silicon Valley.[121] Silicon Valley's journey toward becoming the hub of global technology giants such as Google, Apple, eBay, and Meta can be traced back to a series of deliberate decisions and strategic investments in infrastructure that prioritized technological advancements and innovation.[122] In the early stages, the U.S. government recognized the importance of creating an environment conducive to technological growth. This foresight led to significant investments in physical infrastructure, such as state-of-the-art research facilities and high-speed internet capabilities, As Mazzuccato mentions in her book *The Entrepreneurial State: Debunking Public vs. Private Sector Myths*.[123] The establishment of Silicon Valley, for instance, was a pivotal moment that marked the beginning of California's transformation into a technological powerhouse. The region's proximity to renowned institutions like Stanford University and the University of California, Berkeley, provided a steady stream of talent and innovative ideas, fostering a culture of entrepreneurship and cutting-edge research.[124] However, the iPhone, an icon of American innovation, relies on technologies like capacitive sensors, GPS, and microchips, developed with U.S. government and military funding. However, the public saw little benefit. Critics, like Mazzucato, argue that Apple hasn't paid enough taxes or created enough high-wage jobs. Despite low R&D spending compared to rivals, Jobs' genius lay in integrating existing technologies, often funded by taxpayers.[125] However, beyond physical assets, the government implemented policies that encouraged venture capital investment, providing financial support to startups and creating a thriving ecosystem for innovation.[126] This environment attracted some of the brightest minds from around the world, laying the groundwork for a diverse and dynamic workforce. Notably, the technology sector in California became a melting pot of talent, with immigrants playing a critical role in shaping its trajectory.[127] The Silicon Valley model has been so successful that it has been emulated by other countries. Notably, Saudi Arabia has invested $1 billion in AI as part of its efforts to replicate this innovation-driven ecosystem.

This significant investment underscores the global influence of Silicon Valley in shaping technology and economic development strategies worldwide.[128] The impact of immigration on California's tech industry cannot be overstated. Steve Jobs, the co-founder of Apple, was the son of a Syrian immigrant, and his revolutionary vision changed the course of personal computing and mobile technology.[129] Similarly, Sundar Pichai, the CEO of Google, and Satya Nadella, the CEO of Microsoft, both hail from India, highlighting the global talent pool that has driven innovation in the state.[130] These leaders, among others, have brought diverse perspectives and expertise, propelling their companies to unprecedented heights. However, California's success in the tech sector has also highlighted significant socio-economic disparities. The wealth generated by the technology industry has not been evenly distributed, leading to stark contrasts between the affluent and the impoverished.[131] While companies like Google, Apple, eBay, and Meta have amassed enormous wealth and influence, many residents of California struggle with poverty and mental health issues. The high cost of living, particularly in cities like San Francisco and Los Angeles, made California the highest poverty rate when adjusting for the cost of housing, creating a widening gap between the rich and the poor.[132] The STAR model's implementation in California's tech ecosystem demonstrates a sophisticated interplay of sensing market needs, transmitting innovative solutions, analyzing data to refine products and services, and responding to global demands. However, the model also reveals a critical need for balance. While the state has excelled in fostering technological advancements and attracting top-tier talent, it has not equally addressed the social infrastructure required to support a more equitable society. In urban centers like San Francisco, the juxtaposition of extreme wealth and severe poverty is particularly evident. The tech boom has driven up housing prices, making it difficult for low and middle-income families to afford living in these areas. Homelessness has become a pervasive issue, with many individuals living on the streets in stark contrast to the opulent lifestyles of tech executives. The lack of affordable housing and mental health services further exacerbates these problems, highlighting a significant shortfall in the social safety net as suggested by the Benioff Homelessness and Housing Initiative (BHHI).[133] Moreover, the mental health crisis in California is a pressing concern. The high-pressure environment of the tech industry, coupled with the socio-economic stresses of living in an expensive state, has led to increased rates of anxiety, depression, and other mental health issues. While companies like Google[134] and Apple[135] offer extensive wellness programs for their employees, these benefits do not extend to the wider community, leaving many without the support they need.[136] The disparity between technological wealth and social well-being in Silicon Valley underscores the need for a more holistic approach to development. Policymakers and industry leaders must collaborate to ensure that the benefits of technological advancements are shared more broadly across society. This includes investing in affordable housing, enhancing mental health services, and creating opportunities for economic mobility for all residents. Digital Tech has driven remarkable technological progress and economic growth, positioning the state as a global leader in innovation. The strategic prioritization of infrastructure and the attraction of global talent have been instrumental in the rise of companies like Google, Apple, eBay, and Meta. However, this success has also highlighted significant social challenges, including poverty, mental health issues, and economic inequality. To sustain its leadership and ensure long-term prosperity, California must address these disparities, fostering a more inclusive and balanced digital ecosystem. This requires a concerted effort to integrate technological and social infrastructure, ensuring that the benefits of innovation are accessible to all, not just the privileged few.

4.4 CONCLUSIONS

Looking ahead, the evolution of the STAR model promises further innovation in HCI and productivity enhancement. Advancements in artificial intelligence and edge computing are poised to augment real-time decision-making capabilities, optimizing resource allocation and operational efficiencies. The proliferation of IoT devices will expand the scope of data acquisition, fostering deeper insights into user behaviors and preferences. Moreover, collaborative research efforts across academia, industry, and government will drive interdisciplinary solutions, addressing complex societal challenges through holistic data-driven approaches. The STAR model epitomizes the synergy between human cognition and computational prowess, revolutionizing productivity paradigms across myriad domains. By seamlessly integrating data sensing, transmission, analysis, and responsive decision-making, this model catalyzes innovation and operational excellence. As organizations embrace digital transformation, leveraging the power of prAIority becomes imperative for sustaining competitive advantage in an increasingly interconnected world. Within prAIority, embracing the STAR model heralds a new era of efficiency, resilience, and transformative growth, propelling societies toward a future defined by intelligent systems and enhanced human experiences.

NOTES

1 Connected strategy: Building continuous customer relationships for competitive advantage, Nicolaj Siggelkow, Christian Terwiesch (2019). https://store.hbr.org/product/connected-strategy-building-continuous-customer-relationships-for-competitive-advantage/10241

2 Ortiz, A. M. D., Outhwaite, C. L., Dalin, C., & Newbold, T. (2021). A review of the interactions between biodiversity, agriculture, climate change, and international trade: Research and policy priorities. *One Earth*, *4*(1), 88–101.

3 Kahn, R. F. (2022). International regulation of trade and exchanges. In Richard F. Kahn, *Collected economic essays* (pp. 163–177). Springer International Publishing.

4 Skare, M., & Soriano, D. R. (2021). How globalization is changing digital technology adoption: An international perspective. *Journal of Innovation & Knowledge*, *6*(4), 222–233.

5 An iPhone's journey, from the factory floor to the retail store. www.nytimes.com/2016/12/29/technology/iphone-china-apple-stores.html

6 We traced what it takes to make an iPhone, from its initial design to the components and raw materials needed to make it a reality. www.cnbc.com/2018/12/13/inside-apple-iphone-where-parts-and-materials-come-from.html

7 Apple made China the backbone of its iPhone assembly. Shifting away could take years. https://edition.cnn.com/2022/12/09/tech/apple-china/index.html

8 We would not survive without coffee': How rules made in Europe put Ethiopian farmers at risk. www.theguardian.com/global-development/2024/apr/09/coffee-how-rules-made-in-europe-put-ethiopian-farmers-at-risk

9 The story of coffee is a parable of global capitalism. www.economist.com/books-and-arts/2020/04/23/the-story-of-coffee-is-a-parable-of-global-capitalism?utm_medium=cpc.adword.pd&utm_source=google&ppccampaignID=18151738051&ppcadID=&utm_campaign=a.22brand_pmax&utm_content=conversion.direct-response.anonymous&gad_source=1&gclid=CjwKCAjwko21BhAPEiwAwfaQCJAhMi1jUIRowyt2Z9tahSdK9u2ofoMQA3BSNZfkcsVka_BZLNDAixoCO3sQAvD_BwE&gclsrc=aw.ds

10 Export controls: Overview. https://doresearch.stanford.edu/resources/topics/export-controls-overview

11 Geopolitics and its impact on global trade and the dollar. www.imf.org/en/News/Articles/2024/05/07/sp-geopolitics-impact-global-trade-and-dollar-gita-gopinath

12 Transforming maritime, ahead of time. www.navozyme.com

13 Protectionism is failing to achieve its goals and threatens the future of critical industries. www.worldbank.org/en/news/feature/2023/08/29/protectionism-is-failing-to-achieve-its-goals-and-threatens-the-future-of-critical-industries

14 Assessing the costs and benefits of adaptation options. https://unfccc.int/resource/docs/publications/pub_nwp_costs_benefits_adaptation.pdf

15 Yang, M., Chen, L., Wang, J., Msigwa, G., Osman, A. I., Fawzy, S., ... & Yap, P. S. (2023). Circular economy strategies for combating climate change and other environmental issues. *Environmental Chemistry Letters*, *21*(1), 55–80.

16 The Silk Road. https://education.nationalgeographic.org/resource/silk-road/

17 Kahn, R. F. (2022). International regulation of trade and exchanges. In Maria Cristina Marcuzzo & Paolo Paesani (Eds.), *Collected economic essays* (pp. 163–177). Springer International Publishing.

18 History of the multilateral trading system www.wto.org/english/thewto_e/history_e/history_e.htm

19 EU position in world trade. https://policy.trade.ec.europa.eu/eu-trade-relationships-country-and-region/eu-position-world-trade_en

20 World Intellectual Property Report 2011 www.wipo.int/edocs/pubdocs/en/intproperty/944/wipo_pub_944_2011.pdf

21 Steering the world toward more cooperation, not less. www.imf.org/en/Blogs/Articles/2018/09/06/blog-global-cooperation

22 Li, C., Fu, Y., Yu, F. R., Luan, T. H., & Zhang, Y. (2020). Vehicle position correction: A vehicular blockchain networks-based GPS error sharing framework. *IEEE Transactions on Intelligent Transportation Systems*, 22(2), 898–912.

23 Saudi Arabia's Economy Grows as it Diversifies www.imf.org/en/News/Articles/2023/09/28/cf-saudi-arabias-economy-grows-as-it-diversifies

24 German Car Industry Statistics: Key Figures Showcase Economic Impact https://worldmetrics.org/german-car-industry-statistics/

25 Global supply chains in a post-pandemic world. https://hbr.org/2020/09/global-supply-chains-in-a-post-pandemic-world

26 The globalization of food & plants. https://archive-yaleglobal.yale.edu/globalization-food-plants

27 As AI spreads, experts predict the best and worst changes in digital life by 2035. www.pewresearch.org/internet/wp-content/uploads/sites/9/2023/06/PI_2023.06.21_Best-Worst-Digital-Life_2035_FINAL.pdf

28 Fall, K. R., & Stevens, W. R. (2012). *Tcp/ip illustrated* (Vol. 1). Addison-Wesley Professional.

29 How Chinese digital ecosystems battled COVID-19. www.bcg.com/publications/2020/how-chinese-digital-ecosystems-battled-covid-19

30 The tussle over TikTok isn't just geopolitics. https://lkyspp.nus.edu.sg/gia/article/the-tussle-over-tiktok-isn-t-just-geopolitics-cna

31 Kira, B., Sinha, V., & Srinivasan, S. (2021). Regulating digital ecosystems: Bridging the gap between competition policy and data protection. *Industrial and Corporate Change*, 30(5), 1337–1360.

32 The digital revolution has transformed geopolitics. www.cigionline.org/articles/the-digital-revolution-has-transformed-geopolitics/

33 The digital revolution has transformed geopolitics. www.cigionline.org/articles/the-digital-revolution-has-transformed-geopolitics/

34 The January 6th US Capitol attack. https://abcnews.go.com/US/photos/pro-trump-protesters-storm-us-capitol-unprecedented-breach-75090348

35 China is striking back in the tech war with the U.S. https://time.com/6295902/china-tech-war-u-s/

36 Regional or global player? The EU's international profile. www.realinstitutoelcano.org/en/policy-paper/regional-or-global-player-the-eus-international-profile/

37 Abeliansky, A. L., & Hilbert, M. (2017). Digital technology and international trade: Is it the quantity of subscriptions or the quality of data speed that matters? *Telecommunications Policy*, 41(1), 35–48.

38 www.wto.org/

39 The EU and the WTO. https://policy.trade.ec.europa.eu/eu-trade-relationships-country-and-region/eu-and-wto_en

40 National digital transformation strategy – mapping the digital journey. https://digitalregulation.org/national-digital-transformation-strategy-mapping-the-digital-journey/

41 National digital transformation strategy – mapping the digital journey. https://digitalregulation.org/national-digital-transformation-strategy-mapping-the-digital-journey/

42 Digital Silk Road: Unleashing technological advancements through OBOR. https://fastercapital.com/content/Digital-Silk-Road--Unleashing-Technological-Advancements-through-OBOR.html

43 The future of digital innovation in China: Megatrends shaping one of the world's fastest evolving digital ecosystems. www.mckinsey.com/featured-insights/china/the-future-of-digital-innovation-in-china-megatrends-shaping-one-of-the-worlds-fastest-evolving-digital-ecosystems

44 Cyber Insights Strategic cyber threat landscape evaluation. www.mastercardservices.com/en/capabilities/cyber-insights?campaign_id=701UH00000AuqCfYAJ&channel=sep&cmp=2024.q2.bau-sem-cyber-insights.midf.cyber security strategies&keyword=cyber security strategies&gclid=Cj0KCQjwh7K1BhCZARIsAKOrVqFoB8AKlltGu6YurlBq_D0DOeJtlVF9rNJUQpmoJGXK2sBDiVxKlfAaAn-LEALw_wcB

45 The internet we want. www.intgovforum.org/en/content/the-internet-we-want

46 What is interoperability? https://aws.amazon.com/what-is/interoperability/

47 Interoperability layers. https://joinup.ec.europa.eu/collection/nifo-national-interoperability-framework-observatory/3-interoperability-layers

48 Interoperability: Unlocking the full potential of digitalized services. www.respaweb.eu/0/blogs/5/interoperability-unlocking-the-full-potential-of-digitalized-services

49 The Draghi report and competition policy. www.bruegel.org/first-glance/draghi-report-and-competition-policy

50 Atkinson, R. D., Castro, D., Ezell, S., McQuinn, A., & New, J. (2016). A policymaker's guide to digital infrastructure. *Information Technology & Innovation Foundation*.

51 Much more than a market. www.consilium.europa.eu/media/ny3j24sm/much-more-than-a-market-report-by-enrico-letta.pdf

52 Atkinson et al., A policymaker's guide.

53 Cyber diplomacy and cybersecurity: Guardians of the digital realm. www.ie.edu/uncover-ie/cyber-diplomacy-and-cybersecurity-guardians-of-the-digital-realm/

54 Ranga, M., & Etzkowitz, H. (2015). Triple Helix systems: An analytical framework for innovation policy and practice in the Knowledge Society. *Entrepreneurship and Knowledge Exchange*, 117–158.

55 The role of international co-operation in the digital age. www.oecd-ilibrary.org/docserver/7d3929e1-en.pdf?expires=1722585103&id=id&accname=guest&checksum=93ACCA25776ECF75F7E12EE70694BB8C

56 Smorodinskaya, N. V., Katukov, D. D., & Malygin, V. E. (2021). Global value chains in the age of uncertainty: Advantages, vulnerabilities, and ways for enhancing resilience. *Baltic Region*, *13*(3), 78–107.

57 Aviv, I., & Ferri, U. (2023). Russian-Ukraine armed conflict: Lessons learned on the digital ecosystem. *International Journal of Critical Infrastructure Protection*, *43*, 100637.

58 Kunkel, S., & Matthess, M. (2020). Digital transformation and environmental sustainability in industry: Putting expectations in Asian and African policies into perspective. *Environmental Science & Policy*, *112*, 318–329.

59 Bouncken, R. B., & Kraus, S. (2022). Entrepreneurial ecosystems in an interconnected world: Emergence, governance and digitalization. *Review of Managerial Science*, *16*(1), 1–14.

60 Corporate sustainability reporting https://finance.ec.europa.eu/capital-markets-union-and-financial-markets/company-reporting-and-auditing/company-reporting/corporate-sustainability-reporting_en

61 Joint guidance on interoperability. https://kpmg.com/xx/en/home/insights/2024/05/issb-esrs-interoperability-guidance.html

62 Hodapp, D., & Hanelt, A. (2022). Interoperability in the era of digital innovation: An information systems research agenda. *Journal of Information Technology*, *37*(4), 407–427.

63 Stahl, B. C. (2021). *Artificial intelligence for a better future: An ecosystem perspective on the ethics of AI and emerging digital technologies* (p. 124). Springer Nature.

64 Bühler, M. M., Calzada, I., Cane, I., Jelinek, T., Kapoor, A., Mannan, M., ... & Zhu, J. (2023). Unlocking the power of digital commons: Data cooperatives as a pathway for data sovereign, innovative and equitable digital communities. *Digital*, *3*(3), 146–171.

65 Harris, A., & Johns, A. (2021). Youth, social cohesion and digital life: From risk and resilience to a global digital citizenship approach. *Journal of Sociology*, *57*(2), 394–411.

66 Connected strategy: Building continuous customer relationships for competitive advantage, Nicolaj Siggelkow, Christian Terwiesch, 2019. https://store.hbr.org/product/connected-strategy-building-continuous-customer-relationships-for-competitive-advantage/10241

67 Tap the power of sound and vision in manufacturing. www.asquared.ai/

68 Top wearable medical devices used in healthcare. https://healthnews.com/family-health/healthy-living/wearable-medical-devices-used-in-healthcare/

69 Safeguarding the future: Managing 5G security risks. www.gsma.com/newsroom/article/safeguarding-the-future-managing-5g-security-risks/

70 5G and data privacy. www.gsma.com/solutions-and-impact/connectivity-for-good/public-policy/wp-content/uploads/2020/07/GSMA_5G_and_Data_Privacy_July_20.pdf

71 Environmental impacts of 5G. www.europarl.europa.eu/RegData/etudes/STUD/2021/690021/EPRS_STU(2021)690021_EN.pdf

72 Rezaee, K., Rezakhani, S. M., Khosravi, M. R., & Moghimi, M. K. (2024). A survey on deep learning-based real-time crowd anomaly detection for secure distributed video surveillance. *Personal and Ubiquitous Computing*, *28*(1), 135–151.

73 Yoganarasimhan, H. (2020). Search personalization using machine learning. *Management Science*, *66*(3), 1045–1070.

74 Correlation is not causation. www.theguardian.com/science/blog/2012/jan/06/correlation-causation

75 Su, J., Yang, L., Sun, Z., & Zhan, X. (2024). Personalized drug therapy: Innovative concept guided with proteoformics. *Molecular & Cellular Proteomics*, *23*(3).

76 Kelly, T. D., Foster, T., Schultz, D. M., & Mieno, T. (2021). The effect of soil-moisture uncertainty on irrigation water use and farm profits. *Advances in Water Resources*, *154*, 103982.

77 Dwivedi, Y. K., Ismagilova, E., Hughes, D. L., Carlson, J., Filieri, R., Jacobson, J., ... & Wang, Y. (2021). Setting the future of digital and social media marketing research: Perspectives and research propositions. *International Journal of Information Management*, *59*, 102168.

78 Gothelf, J., & Seiden, J. (2017). *Sense and respond: How successful organizations listen to customers and create new products continuously*. Harvard Business Review Press.

79 The party knows best. Aligning economic actors with China's strategic goals. https://merics.org/sites/defa ult/files/2023-10/MERICS Report The party knows best-Aligning economic actors with Chinas strategic goals2_0.pdf

80 Bradford, A. (2023). *Digital empires: The global battle to regulate technology*. Oxford University Press.

81 Zuboff, S. (2023). The age of surveillance capitalism. In *Social theory re-wired: New connections to classical and contemporary perspectives* (pp. 203–213), Longhofer, W. & Winchester, D. (eds). Routledge.

82 Bradford, A. (2023). *Digital empires: The global battle to regulate technology*. Oxford University Press.

83 Liang, F., & Chen, Y. (2022). The making of "good" citizens: China's Social Credit Systems and infrastructures of social quantification. *Policy & Internet*, *14*(1), 114–135.

84 "To the future": Saudi Arabia spends big to become an A.I. superpower. www.nytimes.com/2024/04/25/tec hnology/saudi-arabia-ai.html

85 The party knows best. Aligning economic actors with China's strategic goals. https://merics.org/sites/defa ult/files/2023-10/MERICS Report The party knows best-Aligning economic actors with Chinas strategic goals2_0.pdf

86 Roberts, H., Cowls, J., Morley, J., Taddeo, M., Wang, V., & Floridi, L. (2021). *The Chinese approach to artificial intelligence: An analysis of policy, ethics, and regulation* (pp. 47–79). Springer International Publishing.

87 What is GDPR compliance? www.paloaltonetworks.com/cyberpedia/gdpr-compliance

88 Mantelero, A. (2022). *Beyond data: Human rights, ethical and social impact assessment in AI* (p. 200). Springer Nature.

89 Kaminski, M. E., & Malgieri, G. (2020). *Algorithmic impact assessments under the GDPR: Producing multi-layered explanations*. SSRN.

90 Two years of GDPR: A report from the digital industry. www.digitaleurope.org/resources/two-years-of-gdpr-a-report-from-the-digital-industry/

91 A financial system that creates economic opportunities nonbank financials, fintech, and innovation. https://home.treasury.gov/sites/default/files/2018-07/A-Financial-System-that-Creates-Economic-Opportunities---Nonbank-Financi....pdf

92 Which states have consumer data privacy laws? https://pro.bloomberglaw.com/insights/privacy/state-priv acy-legislation-tracker/

93 Meet the company that's using face recognition to reshape China's tech scene www.technologyreview.com/2017/08/11/149962/when-a-face-is-worth-a-billion-dollars/

94 In your face: China's all-seeing state. www.bbc.com/news/av/world-asia-china-42248056

95 The mobile economy China 2023. www.gsma.com/solutions-and-impact/connectivity-for-good/mobile-economy/wp-content/uploads/2023/03/The-Mobile-Economy-Report-China-2023.pdf

96 Officials: China to intensify efforts for digital infrastructure construction. www.chinadaily.com.cn/a/202 407/03/WS6684a5f2a31095c51c50c09a.html

97 Is China emerging as the global leader in AI? https://hbr.org/2021/02/is-china-emerging-as-the-global-leader-in-ai

98 Khanal, S., Zhang, H., & Taeihagh, A. (2024). Development of new generation of artificial intelligence in China: When Beijing's global ambitions meet local realities. *Journal of Contemporary China*, 1–24.

99   How TikTok reads your mind. www.nytimes.com/2021/12/05/business/media/tiktok-algorithm.html

100   China is closing the A.I. gap with the United States. www.nytimes.com/2024/07/25/technology/china-open-source-ai.html

101   China just announced a new social credit law. Here's what it means. www.technologyreview.com/2022/11/22/1063605/china-announced-a-new-social-credit-law-what-does-it-mean/

102   China's "social credit" scheme involves cajolery and sanctions. www.economist.com/china/2019/03/28/chinas-social-credit-scheme-involves-cajolery-and-sanctions?utm_medium=cpc.adword.pd&utm_source=google&ppccampaignID=18151738051&ppcadID=&utm_campaign=a.22brand_pmax&utm_content=conversion.direct-response.anonymous&gad_source=1&gclid=EAIaIQobChMIlYvzzOvLhwMVaItoCR3-RQqfEAMYASAAEgLLs_D_BwE&gclsrc=aw.ds

103   Is "Made in China 2025" a threat to global trade? www.cfr.org/backgrounder/made-china-2025-threat-global-trade

104   Made in China 2025: The plan to dominate manufacturing and high-tech industries. https://fdichina.com/blog/made-in-china-2025-plan-to-dominate-manufacturing/

105   The sources of China's innovativeness. https://dgap.org/en/research/publications/sources-chinas-innovativeness

106   Shoshana Zuboff: "Surveillance capitalism is an assault on human autonomy". www.theguardian.com/books/2019/oct/04/shoshana-zuboff-surveillance-capitalism-assault-human-autonomy-digital-privacy

107   Shaping a safer digital future: A new strategy for a new decade. www.edps.europa.eu/press-publications/publications/strategy/shaping-safer-digital-future_en

108   EU AI Act: First regulation on artificial intelligence. www.europarl.europa.eu/topics/en/article/20230601STO93804/eu-ai-act-first-regulation-on-artificial-intelligence

109   Charting the geopolitics and European governance of artificial intelligence. https://carnegieendowment.org/research/2024/03/charting-the-geopolitics-and-european-governance-of-artificial-intelligence?lang=en

110   Securing Europe's place in a new world order – ERT. https://ert.eu/wp-content/uploads/2023/10/ERT-Vision-Paper-2024-2029-Full-version-2.pdf

111   How Booking.com sustains a culture of innovation. https://hbr.org/podcast/2024/06/how-booking-com-sustains-a-culture-of-innovation

112   How can EU legislation enable and/or disable innovation. https://ec.europa.eu/futurium/en/system/files/ged/39-how_can_eu_legislation_enable_and-or_disable_innovation.pdf

113   Protecting Americans' privacy and the AI accelerant. www.commerce.senate.gov/services/files/C25BC8A5-36D2-4F64-81C4-D3EB5E7168B7

114   Balancing innovation and regulation: Comparing China's AI regulations with the EU AI Act. https://awapoint.com/balancing-innovation-and-regulation-comparing-chinas-ai-regulations-with-the-eu-ai-act/

115   A pro-innovation approach to AI regulation. www.gov.uk/government/publications/ai-regulation-a-pro-innovation-approach/white-paper

116   National strategy for artificial intelligence. https://portal.mineco.gob.es/RecursosArticulo/mineco/ministerio/ficheros/National-Strategy-on-AI.pdf

117   Morgan Meaker Business Sep 25, 2023 12:59 PM Booking.com shows the true scope of the EU's big tech crackdown. www.wired.com/story/the-bookingcom-decision-shows-the-true-scope-of-the-eus-big-tech-crackdown/

118   SMEs and mid-cap. www.eib.org/en/projects/topics/sme/index

119   The EU's AI act: A quick guide to its benefits for startups and SMEs. therecursive.com/eu-ai-act-a-guide-for-smes-and-startups/

120   This article is more than 10 months old EU unveils "revolutionary" laws to curb big tech firms' power. www.theguardian.com/world/2023/sep/06/eu-unveils-package-laws-curb-power-big-tech-giants

121   Kushida, K. (2015). A strategic overview of the Silicon Valley ecosystem: Towards effectively "harnessing" Silicon Valley. Report submitted to the Stanford Silicon Valley-New Japan (SV-NJ) Project.

122   The Silicon Valley Model and technological trajectories in context. https://carnegieendowment.org/research/2024/01/the-silicon-valley-model-and-technological-trajectories-in-context?lang=en

123   Why you can thank the government for your iPhone. https://time.com/4089171/mariana-mazzucato/

124   Silicon Valley: Unraveling the Tech Hub of CA. https://fastercapital.com/content/Silicon-Valley--Unraveling-the-Tech-Hub-of-CA.html

125 Debunking the narrative of Silicon Valley's innovation might. www.forbes.com/sites/bruceupbin/2013/06/13/debunking-the-narrative-of-silicon-valleys-innovation-might/

126 Government has key role in tech investing, Google board member says. www.washingtonpost.com/politics/2022/08/17/government-has-key-role-tech-investing-google-board-member-says/

127 The state of U.S. technology talent: A whole-of-nation approach to bolstering the tech talent pool. www.markle.org/the-state-of-u-s-technology-talent-a-whole-of-nation-approach-to-bolstering-the-tech-talent-pool/

128 "To the future": Saudi Arabia spends big to become an A.I. superpower. www.nytimes.com/2024/04/25/technology/saudi-arabia-ai.html

129 Building the skills of the immigrant workforce in Silicon Valley: Learnings from the Boston, Salt Lake City, and Seattle Regions. https://immigrationforum.org/wp-content/uploads/2017/05/SVCF-report-Final.pdf

130 How India can emerge as key AI talent pool. https://timesofindia.indiatimes.com/gadgets-news/microsoft-google-executives-visit-how-india-can-emerge-as-key-ai-talent-pool/articleshow/107334643.cms

131 Kemeny, T., & Osman, T. (2018). The wider impacts of high-technology employment: Evidence from US cities. *Research Policy*, *47*(9), 1729–1740.

132 A tale of two states: Contrasting economic policy in California and Texas. https://siepr.stanford.edu/publications/policy-brief/tale-two-states-contrasting-economic-policy-california-and-texas

133 California statewide study of people experiencing homelessness. https://homelessness.ucsf.edu/our-impact/studies/california-statewide-study-people-experiencing-homelessness

134 A CEO explains why companies like Apple, Google, and Microsoft are researching worker health and wellness. www.fastcompany.com/91036137/a-ceo-explains-why-companies-like-apple-google-and-microsoft-are-researching-worker-health-and-wellness

135 Apple offers new wellness program for headquarters employees. https://eu.usatoday.com/story/tech/news/2018/02/27/apple-offers-new-wellness-program-headquarters-employees/377609002/

136 Are many homeless people in L.A. mentally ill? New findings back the public's perception. www.latimes.com/california/story/2019-10-07/homeless-population-mental-illness-disability

5 Preventing User Frustration

Thus amid this
vastness my thought drowns:
and to be shipwrecked is sweet to me in this sea.

Giacomo Leopardi

Remember those days when ordering a book felt like a leap of faith? You'd place your order, and then...nothing! Weeks would pass, and you'd wonder if your book was lost in a cosmic abyss. It was a frustrating experience, especially for a bookworm like me who couldn't wait to dive into a new story. Thankfully, the world of online shopping has evolved. Now, when I order a book, I receive regular updates on its progress. I know when it's been shipped, when it's arrived in my city, and even the estimated delivery time. It's like having a personal assistant tracking my book's journey. This simple feature has transformed the book-buying experience, as we discussed in Chapter 3, where we explored the concept of usability through Plato's example of a carpenter's beater for a weaving loom—a tool truly valued only by the weaver—we see a parallel in the realm of technology. Consider the development of specialized software tools used by data scientists. Clickup, CoCalc, or Jupyter Notebook are open-source web applications that allow data scientists to create and share documents that contain live code, equations, visualizations, and narrative text. To the average person, these applications may seem complex and esoteric, much like the carpenter's beater might be to someone unfamiliar with weaving. However, to data scientists, this tool is indispensable.[1] It provides a flexible and powerful environment for performing complex data analyses, visualizing results, and documenting the workflow. Just as the weaver's appreciation for the carpenter's beater stems from its ability to make weaving more efficient and effective, the value of open-source web applications lies in its usability for those engaged in data science. The interface and functionalities are tailored to meet the needs of data professionals, allowing them to streamline their processes, collaborate with others, and ensure reproducibility of their work. This specialized utility exemplifies how usability prAIority is inherently tied to the specific needs and skills of the user, echoing the ancient wisdom illustrated by Plato. Technology, at its core, serves as a crucial tool to overcome the initial obstacle to human survival: the challenges of an inhospitable nature. However, there is a second obstacle to consider and we are going to examine in this chapter: possessing technological products without the knowledge or means to use them effectively.[2]

5.1 UNDERSTANDING USER NEEDS AND EXPECTATIONS

Before developing AI systems, it's crucial to thoroughly understand the needs and expectations of end users, revealing both common and unique anticipations among different groups and individuals.

DOI: 10.1201/9781003533160-5

Shared expectations include transparent source disclosure, data protection, accuracy, regular monitoring, and an avenue for contesting system errors.[3] However, there are notable differences in expectations across user groups. For example, educational users as prAIority, tend to expect more benefits from a generative language AI system, but are concerned about issues like plagiarism and credibility. On the other hand, healthcare users as prAIority value compliance and are more worried about the rigor of data training, potential physician burnout, and the impact on the doctor–patient relationship. Understanding these varying expectations is key to developing effective and acceptable AI systems for diverse user groups.[4] This section will discuss various methods of gathering user requirements, including surveys, interviews, and observation. By aligning AI capabilities with user needs, developers can create more intuitive and effective tools. To start, conducting surveys is a widely used method to gather quantitative data on user preferences, needs, and pain points. Surveys can reach a large audience quickly and efficiently, providing valuable insights into user behavior and expectations. By crafting well-designed questions, developers can identify common themes and patterns that highlight what users value most in an AI system. For instance, questions can range from specific functionalities users desire to their overall experience with existing technologies. This data helps developers prioritize features that will make the AI system more user-friendly and capable of meeting user demands. Interviews, on the other hand, provide qualitative insights that delve deeper into individual user experiences. Through one-on-one conversations, developers can explore user needs, frustrations, and aspirations in greater detail. Interviews allow for open-ended responses, giving users the opportunity to express their thoughts freely and providing developers with a richer understanding of user expectations. This method is particularly useful for uncovering nuanced insights that might be overlooked in a survey. By engaging directly with users, developers can ask follow-up questions and probe deeper into specific issues, gaining a comprehensive view of the user's perspective. This interaction helps in identifying potential challenges and opportunities for improvement in the AI system.[5]

WEB OR CHATBOT SURVEYS?[6]

Generative AI can enable surveys to be conducted by chatbots instead of traditional web surveys. However, there is no evidence that chatbots are better survey administration tools than web surveys. In fact, web surveys often produce more favorable response characteristics and higher data quality. User perceptions also tend to be more positive for web surveys compared to chatbot surveys. Specifically, users generally rate chatbot surveys lower in terms of perceived enjoyment, usefulness, and security. This suggests that while chatbots offer a novel approach to conducting surveys, they may not yet surpass the effectiveness and user satisfaction provided by web surveys.

Observation is another effective method for gathering user requirements. By watching users interact with existing systems, developers can identify pain points and areas for enhancement.[7] Observation can take place in a natural setting where users perform their daily tasks, providing real-world insights into how the AI system will be used. This method helps developers understand the context in which the system will operate and the specific challenges users face. For instance, observing how users navigate through a software application can reveal usability issues that need to be addressed. By combining observational data with insights from surveys and interviews, developers can create a holistic understanding of user needs.[8] Once user requirements are gathered, the next step is to align AI capabilities with these needs. This alignment ensures that the AI system is not only technically advanced but also user-centric.[9] Developers should focus on creating intuitive interfaces and functionalities that enhance the user experience. For example, AI systems should be designed to perform tasks that users find cumbersome or time-consuming, thereby adding value and reducing frustration. User-centered design principles should guide the development process, ensuring that the system is easy to use and meets user expectations.

10 PRAIORITIES FOR DEVELOPERS TO FOCUS ON USER EXPERIENCE[10]

1. **Clear Navigation**: Implement straightforward and consistent navigation menus that allow users to find what they need quickly without confusion. Use familiar icons and labels to help users understand where they are within the application.
2. **Responsive Design**: Ensure that the interface is responsive and works well across different devices and screen sizes. This includes optimizing for both desktop and mobile users, ensuring a seamless experience regardless of the device being used.
3. **User-Centered Design**: Conduct user research to understand the needs and behaviors of the target audience. This includes user interviews, surveys, and usability testing to gather feedback and make informed design decisions that resonate with users.
4. **Minimalist Design**: Use a minimalist design approach to reduce clutter and distractions. This involves focusing on essential elements, providing ample white space, and using color and typography effectively to guide the user's attention.
5. **Interactive Tutorials and Onboarding**: Create interactive tutorials and onboarding processes that help new users understand how to use the application. This can include step-by-step guides, tooltips, and in-app demonstrations to make learning intuitive and engaging.
6. **Consistent User Interface Elements**: Maintain consistency in UI elements such as buttons, fonts, and color schemes throughout the application. Consistency helps users predict how the interface will behave, reducing the learning curve.
7. **Error Prevention and Recovery**: Design interfaces that help prevent user errors by providing clear instructions and feedback. When errors do occur, offer easy ways to recover, such as undo options, clear error messages, and troubleshooting guides.
8. **Accessibility**: Ensure the application is accessible to users with disabilities by following accessibility standards and guidelines. This includes providing keyboard navigation, screen reader support, and high-contrast color schemes.
9. **Performance Optimization**: Optimize the application's performance to ensure fast loading times and smooth interactions. Slow performance can frustrate users and lead to a poor user experience.
10. **Personalization**: Offer personalization options that allow users to customize their experience based on their preferences. This can include adjustable settings, personalized content recommendations, and adaptable interface elements.

Moreover, involving users in the development process can lead to better outcomes. By adopting a participatory design approach, developers can collaborate with users throughout the development cycle.[11] This involvement can take various forms, such as user testing, feedback sessions, and codesign workshops. User testing involves allowing users to interact with prototypes of the AI system and providing feedback on their experience, differentiating single users from multiusers.[12] This feedback helps developers identify usability issues and make necessary adjustments before the final release. Feedback sessions can be conducted regularly to ensure that the system evolves in line with user needs.[13] Codesign workshops bring users and developers together to brainstorm and create design solutions collaboratively.[14] This participatory approach ensures that the final product reflects the users' needs and preferences, leading to higher satisfaction and reduced frustration. Additionally, developers should prioritize transparency and explainability in AI systems,[15] especially when AI is not anymore just a tool, but a teammate.[16] Users need to understand how the system works and why it makes certain decisions. Providing clear explanations and justifications for AI actions can build trust and confidence among users. For instance, if an AI system is used for recommending products, it should explain the criteria it used to make those recommendations and also the value associated with them. This is also a warning from the *Economist* about how businesses may wake up to the true potential of AI.[17] If recommendation systems are really providing economic value to everyone, not just big tech companies, as Google CEO Sundar Pichai said in July 2024, "The risk of underinvesting is dramatically greater than the risk of overinvesting for us".[18] To make users feel more in control and reduce frustration from opaque decision-making then transparency is essential. Developers should add features like explanatory interfaces and tooltips to explain how the system works. Additionally, providing training and support is crucial to help users understand and use these systems without getting frustrated.

A PARTICIPATORY DESIGN METHODOLOGY: AWARENESS OF BIASES IN NEWS SEARCH ENGINES[19]

Eight prototypes with different features aimed at raising user awareness of biases in news search engines. Users highlighted the importance of news search engines that:

1. Inform users of possible biases in the results (bias visualization approach).
2. Allow users to access alternative search results (results-reranking approach).

Each approach has its own strengths and potential risks. For example, bias visualization can make users more aware of biases but might be overwhelming or confusing. Results-reranking can offer diverse perspectives but might cause users to distrust the search engine. These factors are crucial for future research on designing interfaces that effectively raise user awareness of biases in news search engines.

Even the most intuitive AI systems can pose challenges to users who are unfamiliar with the technology. In XAI (Explainable AI), there are many challenges. Broader perspectives and teamwork are needed to address these effectively. For example, open problems can be defined and grouped into nine categories. This method promotes collaboration and innovation, ensuring diverse viewpoints and skills come together. By doing so, complex issues in XAI can be tackled more efficiently, leading to the development of better, more understandable AI systems.[20] This would support better than simply providing comprehensive training materials, such as tutorials, user manuals, and help centers, can ease the learning curve and empower users to use the system effectively. AI systems are not static; they are always changing. A common quote, though its source is unclear, states, "Today's AI is the worst you'll ever use." This means AI must evolve to meet changing user needs and technological advancements. For example, an AI-based recommendation system on a shopping website must learn from user behavior and update its suggestions. This continuous learning happens because AI relies on machine learning. Because AI is not static, developers should set up ways to collect and analyze user feedback after the system is deployed. This feedback can come from surveys, user reviews, and direct communication. Though this process isn't very efficient now, it is expected to improve in the future. There are optimistic signs, such as advancements in gathering feedback in the educational field.[21] Additionally, small progress is being made by using large language models to improve sentiment analysis.[22] These developments suggest that collecting and using feedback to enhance AI systems will become more effective over time. By regularly updating the system based on user input, developers can ensure that it remains relevant and effective. This iterative approach fosters a dynamic relationship prAIority, between developers and users, where continuous improvement leads to sustained user satisfaction. It's not just about coding or data sets; developers need to focus on having a dynamic relationship with customers. This means valuing ongoing feedback and continuously improving the AI based on users' needs and experiences. By prioritizing this mindset, developers can create more effective and user-friendly AI systems.[23] Ethical considerations also play a significant role in preventing user frustration. AI systems should be designed with fairness, accountability, and transparency in mind. Developers must ensure that the system does not discriminate against any user group and that it operates in an unbiased manner. Ethical AI practices build trust and prevent frustration caused by perceived unfairness or bias. For example, if an AI hiring system, like the amazon case, is found to favor certain demographics over others, it can lead to frustration and mistrust among users.[24] Ensuring that the system is fair and unbiased from the outset can prevent such issues and promote a positive user experience. Fostering a culture of empathy within the development team can lead to better AI systems. Developers should strive to understand the user's perspective and anticipate their needs and challenges. By putting themselves in the users' shoes, developers can create solutions that genuinely address user pain points. This empathetic approach means that creating an AI system needs a lot of expert skills. It ensures the AI isn't just technically good but also matches what users want and expect. This concept, called "Stepping in" by Davenport,[25] involves monitoring and improving the AI's automated decisions using deep human knowledge. For instance, it's like having a professor who understands coding create educational software, instead of just a regular coder. Preventing user frustration in AI systems requires a thorough understanding of user needs and expectations. Methods such as surveys, interviews, and observation provide valuable insights that guide the development process. Aligning AI capabilities with user needs, involving users in the development process, and prioritizing transparency and support are key strategies for creating user-centric AI systems. Continuous improvement based on user feedback and ethical considerations further enhance the user experience. By fostering a culture of empathy, developers can create AI systems that not only meet technical standards but also resonate with users, ensuring higher satisfaction and reduced frustration.

5.2 PRAIORITY FOR SMOOTH INTERACTION

Principles and their prAIority, are fundamental in designing technology that minimizes errors and effort. This section, after having seen the details of how to understand users' needs, will explore the key principles that should guide AI development, such as simplicity, consistency, scalability and flexibility, feedback, transparency and accopountability. We will discuss how these principles can be applied to create AI systems that are easy to use and understand.

Simplicity is the cornerstone of effective HCI design. AI systems must be designed to reduce cognitive load on users, presenting information and options in a clear and concise manner. This involves eliminating unnecessary complexity and providing intuitive navigation that allows users to achieve their goals with minimal effort. For instance, in AI-driven applications like virtual assistants or chatbots, simplicity can be achieved by using natural language processing to enable users to interact using everyday language, including slang or spelling mistakes.[26] However, clear instructions, well-defined tasks, and straightforward commands help users engage with the system more efficiently. In other words, prompting, as made extremely simple by ChatGPT, makes this process easy, even though it might require some back-and-forth.[27]

Consistency is another crucial principle that significantly impacts user experience. Consistency in design means maintaining uniformity across various elements of the interface, such as layout, terminology, and functionality[28]. When users encounter consistent patterns, they can build a mental model of how the system works, leading to quicker task completion and fewer errors. For example, if an AI system employs a specific icon to denote a particular action, like the facebook "like",[29] that icon should represent the same action across all parts of the application. This consistency reduces the learning curve and helps users feel more confident and in control.

Scalability and flexibility are also important considerations in AI system design. As users' needs and contexts change, the AI system should be able to adapt and scale accordingly. This means designing modular and extensible systems that can accommodate new features and functionalities without compromising usability. For instance, an AI-powered smart home system should be able to integrate new devices and services seamlessly, providing a consistent and reliable user experience across different environments. AI developers can create systems that are not only functional but also enjoyable to use. Error prevention and recovery mechanisms, along with scalable and flexible designs, further contribute to a positive user experience. The goal is to develop AI systems that align with users' needs and expectations, fostering trust and engagement while minimizing frustration. Through continuous user research, testing, and refinement, AI developers can ensure that their systems remain effective, intuitive, and responsive to the evolving needs of their users. When users interact with AI systems, the immediate response and clarity of feedback play a crucial role in their overall experience.

Feedback is essential in HCI to keep users informed about the system's status and the outcomes of their actions. Immediate and clear feedback ensures that users are aware of what the AI system is doing and how it is responding to their inputs. This, also called "user control" can be achieved through visual indicators, such as progress bars, notifications, or confirmation messages, as well as auditory signals in the case of voice-activated systems[30]. Feedback helps users understand whether their actions have been successful or if further steps are needed, thereby reducing frustration and enhancing the overall user experience. Applying these prAIority principles to AI development requires a user-centered design approach, where the needs, preferences, and limitations of the end-users are prAIoritized. This involves conducting user research to gather insights into how different users interact with AI systems and identifying potential pain points, as we previously examined for the educational and healthcare professionals at the beginning of this chapter. Usability testing with real users is a valuable method for evaluating the effectiveness of an AI system's design. By observing how users navigate and interact with the system, designers can identify areas where simplicity, consistency, and feedback need improvement. AI systems should also be designed with accessibility in mind, ensuring that they are usable by individuals with diverse abilities. This includes incorporating features such as voice commands, screen readers, and alternative input methods to accommodate users with.

TEACHING STUDENTS WITH DISABILITIES, A PERSONAL EXPERIENCE

As a professor, I've had the privilege of teaching a diverse group of students, more than 100 nationalities, including those with disabilities. My experiences with deaf and blind students have been particularly impactful, teaching me a lot about adaptability, inclusiveness, and the unique challenges these students face. With my deaf students, I have been fortunate to have the support of assistants who take notes for them. This has been a tremendous help, both for the students and for me. The assistants ensure that the deaf students don't miss any critical information during lectures, allowing them to focus fully on understanding the content being presented. Knowing that there are reliable notes being taken allows me to concentrate on delivering the lecture without worrying about whether every detail is being captured in a way that is accessible to my deaf students. The presence of note-taking assistants has also fostered a more inclusive classroom environment. It has allowed my deaf students to participate more actively in discussions and group activities. They are able to follow along with the pace of the class and contribute their thoughts and ideas, just like their hearing peers. This inclusion has enriched the learning experience for everyone, as diverse perspectives are shared and explored. On the other hand, teaching blind students has presented different challenges, especially since they often don't have the same level of support. Most of my blind students rely heavily on vocal cues and screen readers to type on their computers and access course materials. This means they can follow along with lectures and written content reasonably well, but there are significant limitations when it comes to video content. Videos are a powerful teaching tool, but they pose a unique challenge for blind students. Current technology hasn't yet developed tools that can fully describe moving pictures in a way that's helpful for these students. While screen readers and other assistive technologies can provide some information, they fall short when it comes to conveying the visual elements of a video. This is where human assistance is still irreplaceable. I remember one particular instance where a video was a crucial part of the lesson. The video had no accompanying script or detailed description, so my blind student couldn't understand it. I realized then how much we take visual information for granted and how essential it is to provide accessible alternatives. In that moment, I did my best to verbally describe the key elements of the video, but I knew it wasn't a perfect solution. This experience highlighted the need for better tools and resources to support blind students in all aspects of their education. These experiences have taught me the importance of adaptability and the continuous need for better accessibility in education. I've learned to always be mindful of the diverse needs of my students and to seek out or create resources that can help bridge the gaps in their learning experiences. Whether it's ensuring note-taking support for deaf students or finding ways to make video content accessible for blind students, I strive to make my classroom an inclusive environment where every student has the opportunity to succeed. Teaching students with disabilities has been both challenging and rewarding. It has pushed me to grow as an educator and to constantly seek out ways to improve accessibility and inclusivity in my teaching methods. While there is still much work to be done, each step forward is a step toward a more inclusive educational experience for all students.

Transparency in AI systems is also vital for preventing user frustration. Users need to understand how AI systems make decisions, especially in critical applications such as healthcare, finance, and security. Transparent AI systems provide explanations for their actions and decisions, helping users trust and accept the outcomes. This can be achieved by incorporating XAI techniques that generate human-readable explanations for the AI's behavior. For instance, a medical diagnosis AI could explain the rationale behind its recommendations, citing relevant medical data and guidelines. This transparency fosters trust and reduces anxiety, as users feel more informed and empowered. Error prevention and recovery are crucial components of a user-friendly AI system. Designing systems that anticipate and prevent common errors can significantly reduce user frustration. This involves implementing features such as input validation, which checks for errors before processing user input, and providing helpful error messages that guide users on how to correct mistakes. Additionally, AI systems should offer easy ways to undo actions or revert to previous states, allowing users to recover from errors without significant disruption. Users need to understand how and why the system arrived at a particular decision, especially in high-stakes scenarios such as healthcare, finance, or legal matters. Transparency involves providing users with insights into the system's logic, criteria, and data sources used in making decisions. This can be achieved through various means, such as detailed explanations, visualizations, or step-by-step breakdowns of the decision-making process. For example, in a healthcare application, if an AI system recommends a particular treatment plan, it should also provide information on the factors considered, the evidence supporting the recommendation, and any potential risks or alternatives. This level of transparency empowers users to make informed decisions and fosters a sense of collaboration between the user and the system, despite the constant legal and technical constraints.[31] Furthermore, when users understand the rationale behind the system's decisions, they are more likely to trust the outcomes and feel more in control of their interactions. Enhancing transparency also involves addressing the ethical and societal implications of AI systems. Users are increasingly concerned about issues such as data privacy, bias, and accountability. Although 62% of the people in United States "don't believe it's possible to go through daily life without companies collecting data about them".[32] By being transparent about how user data is collected, stored, and used, AI systems can alleviate privacy concerns. For instance, providing clear privacy policies and giving users control over their data, such as the ability to opt-out or delete their information, can build trust and reduce anxiety. Addressing bias and ensuring fairness in AI decision-making is another critical aspect of transparency. AI systems should be designed to detect and mitigate biases that may arise from the data or algorithms. This can be achieved through regular audits, bias detection tools, and diverse training datasets, as already implemented in some healthcare systems.[33] When users are informed about the measures taken to ensure fairness and the limitations of the system, they are more likely to trust the system's decisions and feel that their interests are being safeguarded.

Accountability is also a key component of transparency. Users need to know who is responsible for the AI system and its outcomes. Clear channels for feedback, support, and redressal mechanisms should be established so that users can report issues or seek assistance when needed. For example, if an AI system in a financial application makes an erroneous transaction, users should have a straightforward process to report the error, receive an explanation, and get the issue resolved promptly. To effectively prevent user frustration, it is essential to integrate feedback and transparency seamlessly into the user experience design. This involves conducting user research to understand their needs, preferences, and pain points. User testing and iterative design processes can help identify areas where feedback and transparency can be improved. Additionally, involving users in the design process, such as through participatory design or cocreation workshops, can provide valuable insights and foster a sense of ownership and trust. Training and support are also crucial in ensuring that users can effectively interact with AI systems. Providing comprehensive user guides, tutorials, and help resources can empower users to navigate the system with confidence. Interactive elements, such as tooltips, help buttons, and chatbots, can offer on-demand assistance and clarify any uncertainties. Regular updates and communication about new features, improvements, or changes in the system can keep users informed and engaged.

HCD HUMAN CENTER DESIGN TO AVOID USER FRUSTRATION

An effective strategy to prevent user frustration is to design AI systems with a human-centered approach.[34] This means prioritizing the user's needs, preferences, and context in every aspect of the system's design and functionality. Personalization can play a significant role in enhancing user satisfaction. By tailoring the system's responses and recommendations to the individual user's preferences and history, AI systems can create a more relevant and engaging experience. For instance, a personalized learning platform can adapt its content and feedback based on the user's progress and learning style, thereby making the learning process more effective and enjoyable. Empathy is another vital element in preventing user frustration. AI systems should be designed to recognize and respond to the emotional states of users. This can be achieved through natural language processing, sentiment analysis, and adaptive interfaces that adjust their tone and responses based on the user's emotions. For example, if a user expresses frustration or confusion, the system can respond with empathy, offering additional support or alternative solutions. This empathetic interaction can make users feel understood and valued, reducing frustration and enhancing their overall experience.

Moreover, AI systems should be designed to handle errors gracefully. Error messages and recovery mechanisms should be user-friendly and constructive. Instead of simply notifying users of an error, the system should provide clear instructions on how to rectify the issue and prevent it from occurring again. For instance, if a user fails to complete a form correctly, the system can highlight the specific fields that need correction and offer examples or hints to guide the user. This proactive approach can reduce frustration and help users achieve their goals more efficiently. Preventing user frustration in AI systems requires a multifaceted approach that emphasizes clear and immediate feedback, transparency in decision-making processes, ethical considerations, user-centered design, empathy, and effective error handling. By providing comprehensible and relevant feedback, AI systems can guide users through their interactions with confidence and ease. Transparency in decision-making processes builds trust and empowers users to make informed decisions. Addressing ethical issues such as data privacy, bias, and accountability further enhances user trust and satisfaction. A human-centered design approach, coupled with personalization and empathy, creates a more engaging and supportive user experience. Finally, effective error handling ensures that users can recover from mistakes gracefully and continue their interactions without frustration. By integrating these elements into the design and functionality of AI systems, developers can create more user-friendly, trustworthy, and satisfying experiences that prevent frustration and foster long-term user engagement.

5.3   DESIGNING FOR ERROR PREVENTION AND RECOVERY

As Bill Vaughan said in 1969 "To err is human, but to really foul things up you need a computer".[35] Errors are inevitable in any technological interaction, but how they are handled can make a significant difference in user experience. This section will cover strategies for designing AI systems that prevent errors and provide effective recovery options. Topics will include user-friendly error messages, undo functions, and guidance for troubleshooting. First and foremost, user-friendly error messages are crucial in mitigating user frustration, a very old topics that found its first literature mention in (at the time still called man/machine) in 1983.[36] When an error occurs, users should not be left confused or uncertain. Traditional error messages that are vague or overly technical can worsen user frustration, creating a negative perception of the system—much like the infamous Blue Screen of Death (Windows), which gained a notorious reputation for appearing unpredictably on some of the largest computer displays, including during high-profile moments like the opening ceremonies of the Beijing Olympics.[37] Therefore, error messages should be clear, concise, and written in plain language, but they should also explain what went wrong, why it happened, and what steps the user can take to resolve the issue. For instance, instead of a vague message like "Error 404", a more helpful message would be, "The page you are looking for cannot be found. Please check the URL or try searching for the content". Providing actionable suggestions helps users feel in control and can reduce the frustration associated with encountering an error. Moreover, the tone of the error message plays a significant role. Messages should be polite, empathetic, and reassuring. A friendly tone can help defuse the frustration users feel when something goes wrong. For example, a message saying, "Oops! Something went wrong. Let's get you back on track", is more comforting than a terse, "Invalid input". By acknowledging the user's frustration and offering assistance, AI systems can create a more positive user experience even in the face of errors. Another effective strategy for preventing user frustration is the inclusion of undo functions. Undo functions provide users with a safety net, allowing them to reverse their actions easily.[38] This feature is especially important in AI systems where actions can have significant consequences, such as deleting data or making irreversible changes. By providing an undo option, users can experiment and interact with the system more freely, knowing that they can correct mistakes without severe repercussions. This not only boosts user confidence but also fosters greater exploration and engagement with the system. However, there are various types of undo functionality—such as undo as a form of reachability, which allows users to return to a previous state—that exist within interactive systems. Therefore, before implementing it, it is crucial to understand the fundamental reflexive nature of undo.[39] In addition to undo functions, AI systems should offer robust guidance for troubleshooting. When users encounter problems, they should have access to clear and comprehensive resources that help them resolve issues independently. This can include FAQs, step-by-step guides, video tutorials, and interactive help features. LLMs can now assist users by guiding them through common troubleshooting steps, such as checking internet connectivity or updating software. However, there is a darker side, where LLMs could be misused to generate and spread multimedia disinformation. Yet, when applied effectively—empowering users to resolve issues independently—AI systems can reduce reliance on customer support and significantly boost user satisfaction.[40] Furthermore, proactive error prevention is key to minimizing user frustration. AI systems should be designed to anticipate potential errors and provide preventive measures.[41] This can be achieved through input validation, real-time feedback, and predictive analytics. Input validation ensures that users enter data in the correct format, preventing errors before they occur. Real-time feedback provides immediate responses to user actions, allowing them to correct mistakes instantly. Predictive analytics can detect patterns and forecast potential issues, allowing the system to offer proactive solutions. For instance, if an AI system identifies that a user is likely to encounter a specific error based on their behavior, it can offer tips or adjustments in advance to prevent the issue. However, systems can also carry biases, like ChatGPT suggesting that men are doctors and female are nurse,[42] often stemming from language that reflects gender biases, as societal representation tends to be more skewed towards men and women.[43] Finally, emotional intelligence in AI systems can play a vital role in preventing user frustration. AI systems that can recognize and respond to user emotions can create more personalized and supportive interactions. For example, if an AI system detects that a user is becoming frustrated, it can offer additional assistance, provide encouragement, or even escalate the issue to a human support agent.[44] By recognizing and responding to the user's emotional state, AI systems can offer more empathetic and effective interactions, helping to minimize frustration. However, research on human emotion recognition systems remains limited, largely due to the scarcity of publicly available datasets. This lack of data continues to be a significant barrier in AI development.[45] Preventing user frustration in AI systems requires a multifaceted approach that encompasses user-friendly error messages, undo functions, effective troubleshooting guidance, proactive error prevention, user education, seamless integration with workflows, accessibility, continuous improvement, transparency, and emotional intelligence. By prioritizing these strategies, developers can create AI systems that not only minimize errors but also provide a supportive and satisfying user experience. This holistic approach ensures that users feel empowered, understood, and in control, ultimately fostering a positive relationship with AI technology.

5.5   ENSURING ACCESSIBILITY AND INCLUSIVITY

To prevent frustration among diverse user groups, AI systems must be accessible and inclusive. This section will discuss the importance of designing AI with accessibility in mind, considering factors such as different abilities, languages, and cultural contexts. We will explore best practices for creating inclusive AI systems that cater to a wide range of users To prevent frustration among diverse user groups, AI systems must be accessible and inclusive. This section will discuss the importance of designing AI with accessibility in mind, considering factors such as different abilities, languages, and cultural contexts. We will explore best practices for creating inclusive AI systems that cater to a wide range of users. Designing AI with accessibility in mind is crucial for preventing user frustration and ensuring that technology serves everyone effectively. Accessibility in AI involves creating systems that can be used by people with various disabilities, including visual, auditory, cognitive, and motor impairments. This means that AI developers must integrate features such as screen readers for visually impaired users, speech recognition for those with motor impairments, and simplified interfaces for users with cognitive disabilities. By prioritizing accessibility, AI systems can provide a more equitable experience, reducing the barriers that might otherwise exclude a significant portion of the population.

ZIPLINE RWANDA: ENHANCING REMOTE HEALTHCARE ACCESS THROUGH AI AND DRONE TECHNOLOGY[46]

I visited Zipline in Rwanda, a company that provides a powerful example of how AI-driven technology can enhance accessibility not only for individuals with disabilities but also for people living in remote areas. Zipline utilizes drones to deliver essential medical supplies, such as blood, vaccines, and medications, to hard-to-reach regions. By integrating AI into their operations, Zipline optimizes drone flight paths, manages inventory, and coordinates deliveries with precision. AI algorithms help ensure that drones navigate efficiently, avoid obstacles, and adhere to safety regulations, even in challenging terrain. This use of AI extends accessibility to communities that are often underserved due to their geographic isolation. In Rwanda, where many areas are difficult to access by traditional means, Zipline's drone services ensure timely delivery of critical healthcare supplies, dramatically improving health outcomes and emergency response times. Moreover, this technology highlights that accessibility in AI encompasses not only support for individuals with disabilities but also vital services for remote populations. By leveraging AI to manage and improve drone operations, Zipline demonstrates how technology can bridge gaps in healthcare access and deliver essential services to those who need them most.

Inclusivity in AI design also requires consideration of language diversity. Many AI systems are initially developed in English or other widely spoken languages, which can be a barrier for non-native speakers[47]. To address this, AI systems should support multiple languages and dialects, allowing users to interact with the technology in their preferred language. Cultural context is another critical factor in designing inclusive AI. Different cultures have unique values, norms, and ways of interacting with technology. AI systems must be sensitive to these differences to avoid misunderstandings and potential frustration. For instance, an AI assistant designed for a Western audience might not be as effective or well-received in an Eastern cultural context due to differences in communication styles and expectations. I adjust my tone based on my location; for example, in Barcelona, I might say, "The meeting is at 2 PM. Be prepared with your report". However, when I spend three months a year in Japan, I would phrase it more respectfully, such as, "If convenient, the meeting is at 2 PM. It would be wonderful to hear your thoughts". Conducting thorough research and incorporating cultural insights into AI design can help in creating systems that resonate well with users from diverse backgrounds. One of the best practices for creating inclusive AI systems is involving a diverse group of users in the development and testing phases. By seeking input from people with different abilities, languages, and cultural backgrounds, developers can gain valuable insights into the needs and preferences of a wide range of users.[48] This collaborative approach helps in identifying potential issues early on and ensures that the AI system is designed to accommodate various user groups. Recent approaches in design have aimed to tackle the exclusion of certain user groups, aiming for "universal usability".[49] Inclusive design is conceived as crafting technology to be accessible and usable by a broad spectrum of individuals, regardless of their backgrounds, with the goal of fostering a more inclusive society. Complementary to this effort, inclusive design aims to steer clear of "variant designs" that cater solely to specific user groups.[50] It advocates for a "user-sensitive inclusive design" approach, emphasizing the need to explicitly consider the identity of the user. This typically involves adapting conventional user-centered design methodologies to encompass individuals with disabilities.[51] As an initial measure, it's essential to bring to light and scrutinize the unconscious and implicit assumptions as well as stereotypes ingrained within technology. One contributing factor to inadvertent gender bias in design is the "self-as-user" approach, wherein designers envision themselves as the end users. Given that 80% of designers are men, their perspectives, shaped by designing for users akin to themselves, may significantly influence technology.[52] A checklist designed to assess educational software in order to encourage girls' engagement in IT. It's crafted to mitigate gender biases by suggesting straightforward inquiries to identify embedded stereotypes and provides approaches for introducing impartial computer education in the classroom.[53] A structured approach to integrating gender considerations into technology design up to now is the GenderMag method. It comprises a specialized cognitive walkthrough and a series of personas centered on five fundamental gender variances in technology utilization. This method provides designers with detailed instructions and pre-made templates to identify and record gender obstacles in current systems.[54]

5.6   CONCLUSIONS

As discussed in Chapter 3, we explored the concept of usability through Plato's analogy of a carpenter's beater for a weaving loom—a tool valued only by the weaver. This analogy holds true in technology, where specialized software tools, such as ClickUp, CoCalc, or Jupyter Notebook, may seem complex to the average person but are indispensable to data scientists. These tools provide a powerful environment for performing data analyses, visualizing results, and documenting workflows, much like the carpenter's beater enhances the efficiency of weaving. The usability of these open-source web applications is tailored to meet the needs of data professionals, streamlining their processes and enabling collaboration. This parallels the ancient wisdom illustrated by Plato, highlighting how usability is tied to the specific skills and needs of the user. Understanding user needs and expectations is critical before developing AI systems. These needs reveal common and unique anticipations among different user groups. For instance, educational users prioritize benefits like plagiarism detection and credibility, while healthcare users emphasize compliance and worry about physician burnout and doctor–patient relationships. Gathering user requirements through surveys, interviews, and observation helps developers create intuitive and effective tools aligned with these needs. Surveys provide quantitative data on user preferences, helping developers prioritize features that enhance usability. Well-designed questions reveal common themes and patterns, guiding the development process. Interviews offer qualitative insights into individual user experiences, allowing developers to delve deeper into needs, frustrations, and aspirations. This method uncovers nuanced insights and provides a comprehensive view of the user's perspective, identifying potential challenges and opportunities for improvement. Web surveys generally produce more favorable response characteristics and higher data quality compared to chatbot surveys. Users tend to rate web surveys higher in terms of enjoyment, usefulness, and security, suggesting that web surveys remain more effective and satisfying. Observation, where developers watch users interact with existing systems, provides real-world insights into usability issues. This method helps developers understand the context in which the AI system will operate and the specific challenges users face. Once user requirements are gathered, aligning AI capabilities with these needs ensures a user-centric approach. Developers should focus on creating intuitive interfaces and functionalities that enhance the user experience. For example, designing AI systems to perform cumbersome or time-consuming tasks adds value and reduces frustration. Involving users in the development process through participatory design leads to better outcomes. User testing, feedback sessions, and codesign workshops help ensure the final product reflects users' needs and preferences, leading to higher satisfaction. Transparency and explainability are vital for building trust in AI systems. Users need to understand how the system works and why it makes certain decisions. Providing clear explanations and justifications for AI actions can build trust and confidence. For instance, an AI recommendation system should explain the criteria used for recommendations, ensuring users feel in control and reducing frustration. Accountability and transparency involve establishing clear channels for feedback and support. Users should be able to report issues and seek assistance when needed. Continuous improvement based on user feedback ensures the AI system remains relevant and effective. Regular updates and communication about new features keep users informed and engaged, fostering a dynamic relationship between developers and users. Preventing user frustration requires a multifaceted approach that emphasizes clear and immediate feedback, transparency, ethical considerations, user-centered design, empathy, and effective error handling. By maintaining a focus on inclusivity and accessibility, AI developers can create systems that serve all users, contributing to a more inclusive and just society.

NOTES

1   Malone, K., & Wolski, R. (2020). Doing data science on the shoulders of giants: The value of open source software for the data science community. *Harvard Data Science Review*. https://hdsr.mitpress.mit.edu/pub/xsrt4zs2/release/6 (May 31, 2020).

2   Platone, Alcibiade Minore, 146e-1476b.

3   Kinney, M., Anastasiadou, M., Naranjo-Zolotov, M., & Santos, V. (2024). Expectation management in AI: A framework for understanding stakeholder trust and acceptance of artificial intelligence systems. *Heliyon*, *10*(7), e28562.

4   Kinney, et al. Expectation management in AI.

5   Fink, A. (2015). *How to conduct surveys: A step-by-step guide*. SAGE.

6   Zarouali, B., Araujo, T., Ohme, J., & de Vreese, C. (2024). Comparing chatbots and online surveys for (longitudinal) data collection: an investigation of response characteristics, data quality, and user evaluation. Communication Methods and Measures, 18(1), 72–91.

7   Buley, L., & Natoli, J. (2024). *The user experience team of one*. Rosenfeld Media.

8   Yablonski, J. (2024). *Laws of UX*. O'Reilly Media, Inc.

9   Rizzo, F., & Bresciani, S. (2024). Ethnography, user observation, and interviews. In *User experience methods and tools in human-computer interaction* (pp. 13–33), Stephanidis, C. & Salvendy, G. CRC Press.

10 Designing for intuitive navigation and user flow. https://moldstud.com/articles/p-designing-for-intuitive-navigation-and-user-flow

11 Paramita, M. L., Kasinidou, M., Kleanthous, S., Rosso, P., Kuflik, T., & Hopfgartner, F. (2024). Towards improving user awareness of search engine biases: A participatory design approach. *Journal of the Association for Information Science and Technology*, *75*(5), 581–599.

12 Fleury, S., & Chaniaud, N. (2024). Multi-user centered design: Acceptance, user experience, user research and user testing. *Theoretical Issues in Ergonomics Science*, *25*(2), 209–224.

13 Buley, L., & Natoli, J. (2024). *The user experience team of one*. Rosenfeld Media.

14 Avila-Garzon, C., & Bacca-Acosta, J. (2024). Thirty years of research and methodologies in value co-creation and co-design. *Sustainability*, *16*(6), 2360.

15 Hooper, K., & Lunn, S. (2024, May). A scoping review of transparency and explainability in AI ethics guidelines. In *The International FLAIRS Conference Proceedings* (Vol. 37).

16 Wang, Z., Wang, J., Tian, C., Ali, A., & Yin, X. (2024). Adopting AI teammates in knowledge-intensive crowdsourcing contests: The roles of transparency and explainability. *Kybernetes*.

17 What happened to the artificial-intelligence revolution? www.economist.com/finance-and-economics/2024/07/02/what-happened-to-the-artificial-intelligence-revolution

18 Big Tech says AI is booming. Wall Street is starting to see a bubble. www.washingtonpost.com/technology/2024/07/24/ai-bubble-big-tech-stocks-goldman-sachs/

19 Paramita et al., Towards improving user awareness of search engine biases.

20 Longo, L., Brcic, M., Cabitza, F., Choi, J., Confalonieri, R., Del Ser, J., ... & Stumpf, S. (2024). Explainable Artificial Intelligence (XAI) 2.0: A manifesto of open challenges and interdisciplinary research directions. *Information Fusion*, *106*, 102301.

21 Better Feedback with AI? www.gse.harvard.edu/ideas/usable-knowledge/23/11/better-feedback-ai

22 Zhan, T., Shi, C., Shi, Y., Li, H., & Lin, Y. (2024). Optimization techniques for sentiment analysis based on LLM (GPT-3). *arXiv preprint*. arXiv:2405.09770.

23 Majchrzak, A., Beath, C. M., Lim, R. A., & Chin, W. W. (2005). Managing client dialogues during information systems design to facilitate client learning. *MIS Quarterly*, *29*(4), 653–672.

24 Insight – Amazon scraps secret AI recruiting tool that showed bias against women. www.reuters.com/article/world/insight-amazon-scraps-secret-ai-recruiting-tool-that-showed-bias-against-women-idUSKCN1MK0AG/

25 *Only Humans Need Apply* is a must-read on AI for Facebook executives. www.forbes.com/sites/gilpress/2016/09/21/only-humans-need-apply-is-a-must-read-on-ai-for-facebook-executives/

26 What is NLP (natural language processing)? www.ibm.com/topics/natural-language-processing

27 The brilliant, complicated simplicity of ChatGPT. www.exponentialview.co/p/the-brilliant-complicated-simplicity-of-chatgpt

28 O'Hara, J. M., & Fleger, S. (2020). Human-system interface design review guidelines (No. BNL-216211-2020-FORE). Brookhaven National Lab.(BNL), Upton, NY (United States).

29 Yoon, G., Li, C., Liu, J., North, M., Ji, Y., & Hong, C. (2024). Facebook likes and corporate revenue: testing the consistency between attitude and behavior. *International Journal of Advertising*, 1–24.

30 User control. www.interaction-design.org/literature/topics/user-control

31 Kiseleva, A., Kotzinos, D., & De Hert, P. (2022). Transparency of AI in healthcare as a multilayered system of accountabilities: Between legal requirements and technical limitations. Frontiers in artificial intelligence, 5, 879603.

32 Americans and privacy: Concerned, confused and feeling lack of control over their personal. information. www.pewresearch.org/internet/2019/11/15/americans-and-privacy-concerned-confused-and-feeling-lack-of-control-over-their-personal-information/

33 Barati, M., Aujla, G. S., Llanos, J. T., Duodu, K. A., Rana, O. F., Carr, M., & Ranjan, R. (2021). Privacy-aware cloud auditing for GDPR compliance verification in online healthcare. *IEEE Transactions on Industrial Informatics*, *18*(7), 4808–4819.

34 What Is Human-Centered Design? https://online.hbs.edu/blog/post/what-is-human-centered-design

35 To Err is Human; To Really Foul Things Up Requires a Computer. https://quoteinvestigator.com/2010/12/07/foul-computer/

36 Brown, P. J. (1983). Error messages: the neglected area of the man/machine interface. *Communications of the ACM*, *26*(4), 246–249.

37 The Thirteen Greatest Error Messages of All Time. https://technologizer.com/2008/09/18/errormessage/5/index.html

38 Lenman, S., & Robert, J. M. (1994). Investigating the granularity of the undo function in human-computer interfaces. *Applied psychology*, *43*(4), 543–564.

39 Mancini, R., Dix, A., & Levialdi, S. (1996). Reflections on UNDO. *University of Rome*.

40 Barman, D., Guo, Z., & Conlan, O. (2024). The dark side of language models: Exploring the potential of llms in multimedia disinformation generation and dissemination. *Machine Learning with Applications*, *16*, 100545.

41 Zhang, B., & Sundar, S. S. (2019). Proactive vs. reactive personalization: Can customization of privacy enhance user experience? *International Journal of Human-Computer Studies*, *128*, 86–99.

42 ChatGPT insists that doctors are male and nurses female. www.worthwhileconsulting.com/read-watch-listen/chatgpt-insists-that-doctors-are-male-and-nurses-female

43 Fitria, T. N. (2021). Gender bias in translation using google translate: Problems and solution. *Language Circle: Journal of Language and Literature*, *15*(2).

44 Hsu, A., & Chaudhary, D. (2023). AI4PCR: Artificial intelligence for practicing conflict resolution. *Computers in Human Behavior: Artificial Humans*, *1*(1), 100002.

45 Khare, S. K., Blanes-Vidal, V., Nadimi, E. S., & Acharya, U. R. (2024). Emotion recognition and artificial intelligence: A systematic review (2014–2023) and research recommendations. *Information Fusion*, *102*, 102019.

46 ZIPLINE. www.flyzipline.com/

47 Fitria, Gender bias in translation using google translate.

48 Shams, R. A., Zowghi, D., & Bano, M. (2023). AI and the quest for diversity and inclusion: A systematic literature review. *AI and Ethics*, 1–28.

49 Keates, S., & Clarkson, P. J. (2003). Countering design exclusion: Bridging the gap between usability and accessibility. *Universal Access in the Information Society*, *2*, 215–225.

50 Stumpf, S., Peters, A., Bardzell, S., Burnett, M., Busse, D., Cauchard, J., & Churchill, E. (2020). Gender-inclusive HCI research and design: A conceptual review. *Foundations and Trends® in Human–Computer Interaction*, *13*(1), 1–69.

51 Newell, Alan F. & Gregor, P. (2000). User sensitive inclu- sive design—In search of a new paradigm. In *Proceedings on the 2000 Conference on Universal Usability (CUU '00)* (pp. 39–44).

52 Rommes, E. (2006). Gender sensitive design practices. In *Encyclopedia of Gender and Information Technology* (pp. 675–681). IGI Global Scientific Publishing.

53 Bhargava, Ambika (2002). Gender bias in computer software programs: A checklist for teachers. *Information Technology in Childhood Education Annual, 2002*(1), 205–218.

54 Burnett, M., Stumpf, S., Macbeth, J., Makri, S., Beckwith, L., Kwan, I., ... & Jernigan, W. (2016). GenderMag: A method for evaluating software's gender inclusiveness. *Interacting with Computers*, *28*(6), 760–787.

6 Generative AI

Success is counted sweetest
by those who ne'er succeed.
To comprehend a triumph,
one must have failed at least.

Emily Dickinson

Before generative AI (GenAI), my writing process was a painstakingly slow affair. I'd pour my heart and soul into a piece, only to have it returned weeks later with a mountain of proofreader suggestions. These suggestions, often coming months after I'd written the original text, could be confusing and sometimes even contradictory. It felt like trying to navigate a maze with a blindfold on. Now, with GenAI, I've gained a newfound independence. I can write paragraph by paragraph, getting immediate feedback on grammar, style, and clarity. This allows me to refine my ideas as I go, ensuring that my writing is always polished and coherent. It's like having a dedicated editor at my fingertips, ready to assist me whenever I need it. This is a key distinction between traditional AI, which specializes in specific tasks, and GenAI, which can create revise—or create—content like stories.

6.1 INTRODUCTION TO GENAI AND HUMAN AUGMENTATION

6.1.1 OVERVIEW OF GENAI

Traditional AI, or narrow AI, is designed to perform specific tasks intelligently, such as making predictions or decisions based on data. Examples include chess-playing computers, voice assistants such as Siri, and recommendation engines such as Netflix's. These systems follow predefined rules and strategies but don't create anything new. GenAI, in contrast, can create novel content. For instance, given a prompt like "Once upon a time", it can generate a full story. It can also produce images, music, and code. The key difference is that while traditional AI analyzes data, GenAI creates new data similar to its training set.[1] Unlike traditional AI, which often focuses on recognizing patterns or making predictions based on historical data, GenAI excels at creating original outputs, from text and images to complex simulations. Its unique capabilities are transforming various industries by offering innovative solutions and enhancing creative processes. At its core, GenAI leverages advanced machine learning models, particularly deep learning techniques, to analyze and understand vast amounts of data. These models, often based on architectures such as generative adversarial networks (GANs) or variational autoencoders (VAEs), are trained on large datasets to learn the underlying distribution of the data. Once trained, they can generate new data

DOI: 10.1201/9781003533160-6

that mimics the style and characteristics of the original data. This ability to create novel content has profound implications across diverse fields, including venture capital and real estate.[2] In the venture capital industry, GenAI is transforming how investment opportunities are assessed and developed. A key application is in financial projections and scenario simulations, where AI models analyze historical investment data and market trends to create predictive models and simulate various financial scenarios. For instance, a venture capital firm might use GenAI to model a startup's potential financial performance under different market conditions, enabling investors to explore a wide range of outcomes and make more informed decisions. GenAI also aids in generating synthetic data to supplement real datasets, allowing firms to test investment strategies and assess risks without relying solely on historical data. Another important use is in the creation of investment pitches and business plans. By analyzing successful business models, GenAI can assist entrepreneurs in crafting compelling presentations. For example, ChatGPT can analyze corporate financial statements to gauge sentiments on environmental policies, generating sentiment scores that predict a firm's risk management capabilities and stock performance.[3] However, challenges such as interpretability and bias in AI decision-making persist. Risk managers must validate GenAI outputs with domain expertise to ensure responsible and transparent implementation, especially in critical fields such as finance, healthcare, and law. Human oversight is crucial in deploying GenAI, particularly to mitigate errors or biases that may arise. Responsible development of AI must also align with regulatory requirements, protect user privacy, and ensure transparency. Policymakers should enforce data protection regulations and establish strong privacy frameworks to balance the benefits of GenAI with individual privacy rights, shaping the future of the technology responsibly.[4] In the real estate industry, GenAI is being employed to enhance property development and marketing strategies. One example is the use of GenAI to create virtual property tours and architectural designs, in the metaverse.[5] Metaverse development in the United States can range from $50,000 to $500,000 or more, depending on the complexity and timeframe. Developing a virtual tour isn't cheap, which is why it's currently focused on luxury real estate. VR tours offer several benefits: they reduce the need for in-person visits, saving time and travel costs for both buyers and sellers, making the home search process more convenient and cost-effective. VR also allows real estate professionals to reach global buyers by offering remote, interactive property views, increasing demand and attracting better offers—homes with VR tours, for example, get 87% more views. Engaging VR tours enable buyers to connect emotionally with properties, imagining their lives in the space, which influences their purchasing decisions. Virtual tours provide a detailed inspection of properties, helping buyers make well-informed decisions and narrow their options. VR is especially useful for selling under-construction properties by showcasing virtual models, securing early sales, and providing developer feedback. It also enhances home staging by adding digital furniture and decor, offering buyers a clearer vision of the property. Additionally, VR improves accessibility for disabled clients, allowing them to explore properties comfortably and equally. GenAI is revolutionizing real estate by reducing costs, broadening market reach, and delivering a more immersive, inclusive experience. Its ability to create new data and scenarios is influencing the future of many industries, offering powerful tools for both innovation and analysis. However, it is not an entirely autonomous technology—human involvement remains crucial, and prioritizing human oversight is essential for its effective use.

6.1.2 AUGMENTATION VS. AUTOMATION: THE ROLE OF GENAI IN ENHANCING HUMANS

Unlike automation, which seeks to replace human labor with machines, augmentation aims to enhance human capabilities, making tasks more efficient and effective. This distinction is critical as it shapes how AI can be utilized to support human creativity, decision-making, and problem-solving. A prime example of GenAI's role in enhancing creativity is in the advertising industry, where the creative process has been significantly augmented by tools like OpenAI's GPT-4. These tools assist advertisers by generating copy ideas, suggesting fresh perspectives, and creating draft content with minimal input. For instance, ad agencies now use GenAI to brainstorm and develop new campaign ideas.[6] AI tools can propose multiple variations of ad copy and headlines based on a brief, analyzing trends, past campaigns, and consumer sentiment to offer creative suggestions. Human creatives then refine these ideas, blending their insights with AI-generated content to produce unique and engaging advertising strategies. This collaboration between AI and human creativity leads to more innovative advertising, highlighting how AI can enhance, not replace, artistic skills. Despite these benefits, some advertising professionals fear being replaced by GenAI. Instead of focusing on whether they or AI are better at the job, a more productive approach is to explore how they can collaborate with AI to enhance their work. To address this tension, organizations can promote a mindset that values co-creation, encouraging employees to see the benefits of a synergistic approach. Another strategy is to help employees develop their existing skills alongside new AI proficiencies, such as prompt engineering, which reduces resistance to AI adoption. Reconsidering task allocation between employees and AI tools can also foster synergy. Managers can assign routine tasks to AI, allowing employees to focus on more meaningful work, which improves both job satisfaction and the overall effectiveness of the collaboration.[7]

In the education sector, GenAI is essential for enhancing decision-making processes. Educational institutions often encounter intricate decisions regarding curriculum design, student assessments, and resource allocation. Generative AI tools can analyze extensive data sets to deliver actionable insights that assist in these areas. For instance, a university might use an AI system to create personalized learning paths for students. By examining students' performance data, learning preferences, and educational goals, the AI can generate recommendations for tailored learning experiences. However, despite the simplicity of interacting with GenAI through questions or prompts, obtaining the desired output can be complex. For example, the AI image Théâtre D'opéra Spatial, which won a prize at the Colorado State Fair,[8] required weeks of prompt writing and fine-tuning hundreds of images to produce the final result. This challenge of crafting effective prompts for text-based GenAI has led to a rise in prompt-engineering roles. Prompt-engineering involves designing inputs to generate outputs that better match user intentions. In the realm of education, developers and researchers are working to refine a foundation model into "EdGPT". EdGPT models are trained on specific educational data, enhancing the general model with domain-specific information. This specialization allows EdGPT to support educational transformation more effectively. For example, EdGPT models designed for curriculum co-design could help educators and students create suitable materials such as lesson plans, quizzes, and interactive activities that align with pedagogical goals and curricular objectives. Furthermore, the rapid adoption of GenAI in technologically advanced regions has accelerated data generation and processing, concentrating AI wealth in the Global North. Consequently, data-poor regions face further exclusion and risk being dominated by standards embedded in GPT models. Current ChatGPT models, trained on data from the Global North, may not suit the needs of data-poor communities in the Global South or disadvantaged areas in the Global North.

UNESCO HAS PROPOSED FOUR STEPS FOR REGULATING GENAI IN EDUCATION TO ADDRESS THESE ISSUES[9]

1. Endorse Data Protection Regulations: Support international or regional data protection regulations or develop national ones to address concerns about data usage and consent.
2. Adopt Comprehensive AI Strategies: Integrate GenAI regulation into broader national AI strategies to ensure safe and equitable use across all sectors, including education. This requires a coordinated, whole-of-government approach.
3. Implement Ethical Regulations: Establish specific regulations to address the ethical challenges associated with AI use.

4. Adjust Copyright Laws: Modify existing copyright laws to address the challenges posed by AI-generated content and the copyrighted materials used in model training. Currently, only China, the EU, and the United States have updated copyright laws to reflect GenAI's implications.

6.1.3 IMPORTANCE OF DATA, AI SYSTEMS, AND HUMAN JUDGMENT

At the heart of GenAI lies the framework of prAIority, which emphasizes three essential pillars: Data, AI Systems, and Human judgment. Each pillar plays a crucial role in ensuring the effectiveness and relevance of GenAI applications, highlighting their interconnections across various sectors. Public sector professionals expressed optimism about both the current use of GenAI and its potential to improve efficiency and reduce bureaucratic workloads in the future. For instance, NHS workers anticipated that time spent on administrative tasks could decrease from 50% to 30% if GenAI is effectively utilized, equating to saving one day per week—an enormous potential impact. Our survey also revealed significant trust in GenAI outputs (61%) and a low fear of job replacement (16%).[10] In the public sector, GenAI is transforming urban planning by employing advanced simulation and modeling tools. These tools rely on vast datasets, including demographic statistics, traffic patterns, and environmental conditions. Cities are using GenAI to create detailed urban simulations that predict how new infrastructure projects might affect traffic flow and pollution levels. AI systems in this context use complex algorithms to analyze historical and real-time data, generating predictive models to optimize city planning. These systems can simulate various scenarios, such as the introduction of new public transportation routes or the impact of green spaces on air quality.

RIDING THE AI WAVE: THE FUTURE OF ON-DEMAND PUBLIC TRANSPORT

An example of prAIority—combining data, AI systems, and human judgment—can be seen in the partnership between Via and Autoguidovie to launch on-demand transport services in Italy.[11] This collaboration addresses modern urban mobility challenges, such as congestion and the limitations of traditional fixed-route services, by leveraging real-time data and AI-powered algorithms to optimize public transport. Via's advanced AI system processes data from various sources—passenger demand, traffic conditions, and existing transportation networks—to offer flexible and efficient transportation options. Human judgment remains crucial in overseeing the AI system, adapting strategies to local conditions, and ensuring that services meet user expectations. This partnership moves beyond conventional solutions, showcasing how AI and human oversight can work together to create more sustainable, user-friendly public transportation. Instead of merely expanding traditional services, Via and Autoguidovie used AI to maximize existing resources, reducing costs and environmental impact. By utilizing real-time data and AI, the partnership was able to provide personalized, responsive transport that integrates seamlessly with other public transit options, a testament to how prAIority—where data, AI, and human judgment converge—can lead to more effective solutions in complex industries like transportation.

Human expertise is crucial in interpreting the results from these AI systems. Urban planners and policymakers rely on their knowledge to validate AI-generated models, ensuring they reflect real-world conditions and meet community needs. Their ability to integrate AI insights with practical knowledge and stakeholder input is essential for making informed decisions that improve urban environments. Moreover, research into tools like ChatGPT and Bard in public administration, particularly within street-level bureaucracy, shows that while these AI tools offer revolutionary insights into bureaucratic behavior and decision-making, they also raise ethical concerns, including issues related to bias and data privacy.[12]

6.2 MARITIME SECTOR: OPTIMIZING SHIPPING ROUTES

Generative AI has significantly impacted process automation in the maritime sector, streamlining tasks that were once labor-intensive, such as cargo loading, inventory management, and maintenance scheduling. AI-powered robotics reduces waiting times at ports, enhances efficiency, and predicts equipment failures, minimizing unplanned downtime and associated costs. With maritime transport handling over 90% of global goods by volume, AI can play a crucial role in overcoming sector challenges, such as environmental impacts and security threats. Public policy is key in regulating safety, security, and sustainability, while AI integration can improve predictive maintenance, route optimization, and accident prevention. By processing vast amounts of data for real-time decision-making, AI enhances efficiency and safety, leading to autonomous ships, optimized logistics, and reduced human error. However, technical challenges like cybersecurity, high initial costs, and social concerns like job displacement must be addressed through effective policy.[13] In addition to automation, GenAI is transforming demand forecasting in maritime logistics. Using predictive models that analyze historical and real-time data, AI enables better route and resource planning, reducing operational costs and delivery times. Strategic ports worldwide are already leveraging AI to optimize supply and demand, cargo volumes, and mitigate environmental impacts. Moreover, AI plays a vital role in supply chain optimization by integrating with IoT and blockchain technologies to provide a holistic view of logistics operations. This integration promotes efficiency, collaboration, and route optimization, reducing fuel consumption and greenhouse gas emissions. The benefits of GenAI in maritime logistics are numerous, including increased operational efficiency through automation and route optimization. It also leads to significant cost reductions by optimizing inventories and lowering fuel expenses. AI-driven insights enable better strategic decision-making, positioning companies to compete more effectively in an increasingly challenging global market.[14] Humans play a crucial role when maritime operators and logistics experts review and adjust AI-generated routes. Their experience and contextual understanding enable them to evaluate the feasibility of GenAI suggestions, considering vessel capabilities and regulatory requirements, ensuring that the recommendations are practical and align with operational constraints. Beyond simply serving as a backup, human operators have an active role in ensuring the safety of autonomous ships. System-Theoretic Process Analysis and Bayesian Networks are the most commonly used risk assessment tools in risk-based design.[15] As autonomous ship research advances, prAIority will be on the new role of shore control center operators will require additional competencies and training. The increasing interaction between AI systems and safety-critical operations presents new risks and research challenges, highlighting the need for effective human-AI interaction design. Cross-disciplinary efforts are essential to balance productivity with safety (resilience), address technical limitations while aligning with human expectations (interaction design), and ensure the integration of machine autonomy with human supervisory control (safety management).

GENAI AT SEA: TRANSFORMING EFFICIENCY AND SAFETY IN MARITIME LOGISTICS[16]

Maersk Line has implemented an AI-driven predictive maintenance system to monitor engine health across its fleet. Using machine learning and onboard sensors, the system collects real-time data on temperature, vibration, and pressure to detect anomalies that may signal equipment failure. This proactive approach has significantly reduced unscheduled downtime, enhanced operational efficiency, and cut maintenance costs by up to 20%, while extending the lifespan of machinery. The Yara Birkeland, a fully electric and autonomous container ship developed by Yara International, showcases the potential for sustainable shipping. Using AI to navigate autonomously through GPS, radar, and sensors, the vessel aims to eliminate emissions and replace 40,000 annual truck journeys. This innovation highlights the role of AI in environmental and logistical improvements. CMA CGM has adopted AI for route optimization, analyzing weather, traffic, and port conditions to determine the most fuel-efficient paths. This has resulted in substantial fuel savings, reduced emissions, and improved service reliability. Collectively, these case studies illustrate how AI is transforming the maritime industry by enhancing predictive maintenance, automating navigation, and optimizing operations, leading to both environmental and operational benefits.

6.3   AGRICULTURE: IMPROVING CROP YIELD

The digitalization of data has created a "data tsunami" across nearly every industry, particularly in data-driven enterprises. Machine-to-machine (M2M) digital data handling has further amplified this information surge. In agriculture, this wave has driven the development of digital management applications, pushing technological solutions into rural areas and benefiting both farmers and consumers. ICT (Information and Communication Technology) has shown significant potential in traditional agriculture, with CNN-based models achieving high accuracy in detecting and categorizing diseases in crops like paddy leaves. However, several challenges emerge when applying these technologies to farming. Robotics, IoT devices, and machine learning have become integral to agriculture, but these technologies rely heavily on data and come with certain limitations. Without large-scale labeled training sets, machine learning models are prone to overfitting, hindering their effectiveness. As models become more complex, the number of parameters grows exponentially, reducing their generalizability. Each new dataset and task often requires models to be trained from scratch, increasing hardware requirements, computational expenses, and limiting practical applications. Generative AI has potential in addressing these challenges. As an agronomist assistant, AI can provide expert advice on crop management through chatbots. A recent study showed that GPT-4 performed well in answering agriculture-related questions, though adapting these models to local data remains a challenge. Fine-tuning and Retrieval-Augmented Generation (RAG) are being explored to improve performance. Despite these advancements, challenges persist, particularly regarding data privacy and the small size of available agricultural datasets. Farmers' personal data is often collected without consent, raising concerns about misuse. Furthermore, environmental factors, background noise in image segmentation, and drone limitations highlight the need for standardized devices, scalable algorithms, and reliable data handling. To maximize AI's impact, specialized models tailored to agriculture are essential.[17] In fact GenAI also helps address data scarcity by learning from unlabeled historical data and generating synthetic data, filling gaps where labeled data is scarce. This improves AI's performance in agriculture, particularly in precision farming. AI analyzes data from sources like satellite imagery and soil sensors, helping farmers optimize irrigation, automate harvesting, and predict crop yields, promoting sustainability. Additionally, GenAI aids in disease detection by identifying pests, diseases, and nutrient deficiencies through image recognition. Early detection allows for targeted interventions, reducing reliance on harmful pesticides.[18] Human judgment is crucial in applying AI insights to real-world farming practices. Agricultural experts use their expertise to interpret AI-generated recommendations and adapt them to local conditions. Additionally, the human factor plays a vital role in safeguarding farmers' personal data—such as identity, location, financial details, and entrepreneurial knowledge—which is often collected through digital platforms without their knowledge, raising concerns about privacy and data misuse. Data mining enables organizations to gather large amounts of this information, which can be analyzed to create detailed psychological profiles, posing risks to reputations if misused or exposed. Farmers need assurances from human agents that their data will be used to drive innovation, not for competitive advantage. Establishing and enforcing privacy and confidentiality policies in precision agriculture demands significant time and resources, emphasizing the importance of human oversight.

In summary, the interplay of data, AI systems, and human judgment is crucial in the realm of GenAI. Each pillar supports the others, creating a cohesive framework that drives innovation and effectiveness across various sectors. Whether in urban planning, maritime navigation, or agriculture, the integration of these elements exemplifies how GenAI can create meaningful and practical solutions.

6.4 THE ROLE OF DATA IN GENAI AUGMENTATION

6.4.1 Data as the Fuel for GenAI

Generative AI represents a major technological advancement, enabling systems to create new content, ideas, and scenarios by learning from extensive datasets. The effectiveness of GenAI hinges on the quality and scope of the data it processes. Without comprehensive and high-quality datasets, these systems would struggle to produce accurate and meaningful outputs. In agriculture, for instance, the role of data is pivotal, as it fuels the algorithms driving these advancements. This principle also applies to HR recruitment and rare disease research. Generative AI systems, including those used for language models, image synthesis, and predictive analytics, depend on large volumes of data to operate effectively. They are trained on diverse datasets, which allows them to identify patterns and generate new content based on those patterns. In HR recruitment, for example, GenAI can craft job descriptions, profile candidates, and simulate interview scenarios using historical data. Analyzing past job postings, candidate profiles, and industry trends enables these systems to produce relevant job descriptions aligned with current market demands. The effectiveness of GenAI in HR recruitment is influenced by the quality and diversity of the data used. High-quality data includes detailed information on job requirements and candidate qualifications, while diverse data covers various job roles, industries, and regions. This diversity helps the AI avoid biases and produce outputs applicable to different contexts. To harness the full potential of GenAI, HR professionals should continually educate themselves on its capabilities and limitations. Encouraging exploration of tools like ChatGPT can develop practical skills, while formal education and industry resources should be approached with an understanding of potential biases. Before deploying GenAI tools, it's crucial to review stakeholders and organizational values to address ethical considerations. Designating a GenAI "champion" within HR can enhance the success of AI initiatives and their integration. Clear policies and procedures regarding data privacy and transparency are essential and should evolve with the technology. Regularly scanning for useful AI applications based on business needs, rather than just capabilities, and thorough pilot testing can help identify valuable tools and uncover potential ethical issues. Ongoing monitoring and adaptation are necessary to address emerging ethical challenges as the technology evolves.[19]

GENERATIVE AI IN HR: FROM SMART RECRUITMENT TO ADVANCED ANALYTICS AND PERSONALIZED COMMUNICATION

Generative AI is transforming HR processes across several key areas.[20] In content creation, companies use AI tools to generate and adapt job postings, draft personalized candidate communications, and even provide feedback through AI-based avatars. For instance, a major automotive company employs a GenAI avatar to offer personalized feedback on applications, highlighting the significant potential of AI in talent acquisition and onboarding, which represents about 20% of its value. In concision, AI helps summarize and extract insights from unstructured data to improve performance management. A European insurance company, for example, uses AI to aggregate performance ratings and 360-degree feedback,[21] accelerating HR processes and enhancing performance management, contributing another 20% of AI's value. Communication is also enhanced through AI chatbots that guide employees and provide personalized learning recommendations, as seen in a global software company. This use of AI for continuous learning and development adds 12% of value. Finally, in coding, AI supports people analytics by analyzing large datasets to identify patterns, as demonstrated by a pharmaceutical company using AI to predict attrition risks. This application in organizational analysis accounts for 15% of AI's value in HR.

In the realm of rare disease research, GenAI plays a crucial role by leveraging large datasets to overcome significant challenges. Although each rare disease individually affects only a small number of patients, collectively over 7,000 rare diseases impact about 10% of the population, posing severe challenges in diagnosis, treatment, and research participation. The rarity of these diseases leads to limited data availability, complicating efforts to study and develop effective treatments. Generative AI addresses these challenges by synthesizing data from diverse sources, such as clinical records, research studies, and genetic information. By analyzing patterns within these datasets, AI can generate new hypotheses about disease mechanisms, predict patient outcomes, and propose potential treatments. For instance, an AI model trained on genetic mutation data may uncover previously unknown genetic links or identify new drug candidates. The importance of data in GenAI is heightened when dealing with rare diseases due to the scarcity of high-quality, comprehensive data. AI can mitigate the issue of data scarcity by reducing the manual effort required for analysis and addressing the challenge of limited data. In low-resource settings, such as developing countries, where diagnosing rare diseases is particularly difficult due to the need for extensive expert resources, GenAI can be especially valuable. Prioritizing the use of AI and fostering collaboration between researchers, healthcare providers, and data collectors can help build more robust datasets, thereby enhancing the AI's capability to deliver meaningful results.[22] In both HR recruitment and rare disease research, the reliance on data underscores the importance of collecting, curating, and maintaining high-quality and diverse datasets. GenAI systems depend on these data to learn, adapt, and produce outputs that are relevant and useful in real-world applications. As the field of GenAI continues to evolve, the role of data will remain central to its success, driving innovation and enhancing the capabilities of these advanced systems.

6.4.2 Applications and Examples

GenAI has transformed numerous industries by utilizing extensive data to enhance human capabilities. By learning from and analyzing large datasets, these systems generate content that is both highly personalized and contextually relevant. This part examines the significant advancements data-driven GenAI has made in the editorial and marketing sectors, illustrating its impact on augmenting human abilities. In the editorial realm, GenAI has revolutionized content creation through automation and personalization. For instance, despite CNET's reported issues with AI-generated content in 2023, which led to a backlash and corrections by human staff, The Washington Post made a notable leap in August 2024. They introduced Haystacker, an AI tool developed to analyze large datasets, including video, photos, and text, to uncover newsworthy trends. Vineet Khosla, the Post's CTO, highlighted that in-house AI tools like Haystacker provide tailored solutions that exceed the capabilities of general-purpose tools from major tech companies. While the Post currently isn't focused on licensing Haystacker to other newsrooms, Khosla suggested that it might be shared more broadly in the future.

Haystacker, built over a year by the Post's engineering and newsroom teams, has been instrumental in visual forensics and data journalism, revealing that nearly 20% of analyzed campaign ads contained outdated or misleading content. This tool, alongside the Post's recent AI-driven chatbot and article summary products, marks the third significant AI innovation from the Post in recent months.[23] The Associated Press has been leveraging AI to streamline the creation of financial earnings reports and sports summaries since 2014, starting with its Business News desk's efforts to automate corporate earnings stories. Before AI, AP editors and reporters invested substantial resources in covering important yet repetitive stories, which detracted from higher-impact journalism. The success of this automation project allowed AP to explore new initiatives and inspired other news organizations to adopt similar technologies. These AI tools are designed to enhance workflows, enabling journalists to focus on more significant work. This includes automating tasks such as video transcription, generating video shot lists, and creating story summaries. Additionally, AP automates certain corporate earnings and sports stories, accelerating content production and freeing editors to engage in more complex storytelling. In distribution, AP aims to simplify content access and accelerate production by optimizing it with image recognition technology, developing the first editorially-driven computer vision taxonomy for the industry. This tagging system will not only save hundreds of production hours but also make content discovery more efficient.[24] A notable application of AI in news delivery is the use of AI-powered content generators to create personalized news experiences. Platforms like NewsGuard employ GenAI to produce summaries and recommendations tailored to individual readers' preferences. NewsGuard has identified 1,065 AI-generated news and information sites with minimal human oversight and is monitoring false narratives generated by these AI tools. Many of these sites operate under a revenue model that relies on programmatic advertising, where ads are placed without considering the content's quality or trustworthiness. Consequently, top brands may inadvertently support these sites unless they actively exclude unreliable sources, thereby creating a financial incentive for such sites to proliferate. By analyzing user interaction data—such as reading habits, click-through rates, and engagement metrics—AI systems can curate content that aligns with users' interests. For example, if a reader frequently engages with technology articles, AI can generate more personalized recommendations focused on tech trends. However, this also means AI can push misleading information to keep readers engaged, sometimes enhancing their experience with false content.[25] The textile industry, with its intricate supply chains and production processes, greatly benefits from AI-driven problem-solving capabilities. GenAI enhances problem-solving by analyzing production data, predicting issues, and suggesting solutions to optimize processes. For instance, applying a generative deep learning model, like a GAN, to the textile component of fashion design can generate new images of knitted textile designs. These designs were evaluated for their aesthetic quality through a qualitative survey with over 200 participants, showing that the GAN-based method can produce innovative and practical textile designs that support the fashion design process.[26] As digital fabrication technologies, such as knitting machines and textile development software, become more accessible to designers, AI will increasingly be used to create diverse textile patterns, textures, and garment styles, drawing inspiration from both traditional and contemporary cultures. While challenges remain in directly translating textile designs into detailed knitting machine instructions, ongoing advancements in data and training will improve AI's ability to convert images directly into knit-ready programs.[27] In each of these examples—journalism and textiles—GenAI does not replace humans, but rather enhances them. By providing creative suggestions, decision-making insights, and problem-solving recommendations, AI augments human capabilities, allowing professionals to focus on higher-level tasks and strategic decisions. This synergy between AI and humans is key to leveraging technology to its fullest potential, driving innovation and efficiency across various industries. In the marketing sector, GenAI has been widely used to create personalized marketing materials and advertisements that resonate with individual consumers. GenAI's application in marketing has been more prevalent compared to other organizational functions. For example, a FreshBooks survey of small-business owners in North America found that analytics, sales and marketing, and customer communications are the areas most likely to be impacted by GenAI.[28] GenAI can analyze customer preferences to deliver personalized emails and messages, driving higher engagement. This personalized approach, based on factors like online activity and location, can significantly increase click-through rates.[29] However, large language model (LLM)-based chatbots are not expected to fully replace conventional chatbots or human teams. LLM-based chatbots serve different purposes compared to traditional chatbots, and some argue that LLMs' open-ended nature makes them unsuitable for many customer experience applications. It is crucial to develop chatbots that can specifically address questions about a company's products or services and assist users with their challenges. To enhance the customer experience, it is essential to effectively combine LLMs, like ChatGPT, with traditional chatbots. Additionally, human teams' skills and expertise remain vital in most marketing activities, making it unlikely that GenAI will completely replace them.[30] Companies like Coca-Cola are leveraging GenAI platforms to create personalized content based on consumer data, blending GenAI capabilities with human creativity is also prAIority. This approach emphasizes the synergy between AI systems and human ingenuity, where AI helps scale ideas and processes, while humans focus on creativity and values. Coca-Cola views this balance as essential to driving business growth, with their marketing professionals actively investing in digital, analytics, and AI skills to stay ahead of technological advancements. The rise of GenAI is seen as a transformative period, akin to the early days of the internet, highlighting the urgency for brands to adopt these new technologies. Coca-Cola has already incorporated AI into various areas, including consumer insights, product development, and customer experiences. For instance, they used GenAI to create a personalized Christmas card for their 2023 festive campaign. AI systems at Coca-Cola analyze vast amounts of data—from customer demographics to purchasing history and online behavior—to craft targeted marketing messages. However, the company recognizes the need for governance and risk management, utilizing a council to oversee AI projects. Executives emphasize that this transformation requires a mindset of continuous learning—executives attended one-year long business courses in top business schools—adaptation, and human skill development to sustain business growth.[31] Domino's Pizza, like Coca-Cola, offers compelling examples of how AI can transform marketing practices. Domino's utilizes AI to optimize order preparation and delivery processes, showcasing operational efficiency and improved customer experience. By streamlining pizza preparation and optimizing delivery routes, AI plays a pivotal role in enhancing service speed and satisfaction.[32] Similarly, Coca-Cola has integrated AI into its vending machines to personalize customer interactions. These AI-driven machines provide product recommendations and promotions based on customer preferences and specific locations. This not only enhances the vending experience but also helps Coca-Cola gather valuable consumer data, refining its marketing and product strategies. Both companies demonstrate the practical application of AI in improving customer interactions and driving brand loyalty. These examples highlight how AI can elevate marketing initiatives by offering personalized experiences and streamlining operations, ultimately leading to a more engaging and effective customer experience.[33] AI-powered platforms are revolutionizing personalized email marketing by customizing content based on user data. These systems analyze past interactions, purchase behaviors, browsing history, and engagement with previous emails to generate tailored subject lines, content, and offers for each recipient. For instance, HubSpot's email marketing tool integrates with its CRM, allowing marketers to personalize campaigns at scale. It utilizes AI for A/B testing, smart send times, and CRM integration, ensuring emails are delivered at the optimal moment and to the right audience. Similarly, platforms like Moosend and ActiveCampaign leverage AI for automation workflows, predictive analytics, and real-time performance monitoring. Moosend's AI-driven recommendations and ActiveCampaign's advanced segmentation further enhance the relevance and efficiency of email marketing efforts. Sendinblue utilizes machine learning to optimize large campaigns, offering features like transactional emails, AI-powered reporting, and contact segmentation. Mailchimp stands out with its AI tools that provide content optimization suggestions, customer lifetime value predictions, and A/B testing automation, helping marketers refine their strategies and increase engagement. These platforms enable businesses to achieve higher open rates, click-through rates, and conversion rates by delivering more relevant and personalized content to their audience, making email marketing more efficient and impactful.[34] GenAI is also being leveraged to create content for social media marketing. Tools like Copy.ai and Jarvis generate posts, captions, and promotional materials tailored to target audiences. By analyzing engagement metrics such as likes, shares, and comments, these AI systems craft content optimized for social media platforms, boosting brand visibility and user interaction. Despite the rise of ChatGPT, CopyAI remains a top choice for marketers, writers, or team collaborations due to its robust features and focus on teamwork. For casual users, however, ChatGPT offers a smoother, straightforward experience that gets the job done efficiently.[35] From a prAIority perspective, data-driven GenAI plays a crucial role in augmenting human capabilities in content creation and marketing. By harnessing large datasets to produce personalized, contextually relevant content, these AI systems optimize workflows and boost user engagement and satisfaction. This collaboration between AI and human intelligence enables businesses to prioritize tasks more effectively, driving both efficiency and creativity in marketing strategies.

6.4.3 CHALLENGES WITH DATA WITH GENAI

As one of the three pillars of prAIority, data quality, biases, and integration issues are major obstacles to effectively leveraging Gen AI for augmenting human abilities. These challenges can impede AI's ability to produce accurate, reliable, and useful outputs, making data a top priority in academic research. Key areas of focus include examining biases in GenAI stemming from its training datasets and processes, determining the best combinations of hybrid teams of humans and AI for collaboration for various tasks, assessing the accuracy of AI-generated content, and addressing the ethical and legal implications of using GenAI across different contexts.[36]

THE RISE OF HYBRID TEAMS[37]

The rise of hybrid teams, combining human expertise and GenAI, presents new dynamics in task allocation and collaboration. Determining how tasks are distributed between humans and GenAI is a key challenge. Typically, humans remain responsible for higher-level decision-making, creativity, and tasks requiring emotional intelligence, while GenAI excels at data processing, repetitive tasks, and content generation. However, who delegates and coordinates these tasks is critical. Should it be a human manager, or can GenAI play a role in optimizing task distribution based on skillsets and performance metrics? Both humans and AI can approach delegation, but humans tend to make more nuanced, context-based decisions, while AI delegates based on data and algorithms. A pressing concern in hybrid teams is whether humans will still feel a sense of accomplishment when AI handles a significant portion of creative work. This could lead to a shift in how we measure success and satisfaction. Additionally, human interaction within hybrid teams may evolve, as collaboration with AI could reduce interpersonal communication, potentially impacting team cohesion. Over-reliance on GenAI can diminish human creativity, problem-solving, and decision-making skills if not carefully managed. To mitigate these risks, teams should prioritize active human involvement in critical thinking and innovation, using AI as a tool for augmentation rather than replacement. When it comes to evaluating the quality of work, a question arises: Should AI also assess the outputs, or does this responsibility lie with humans? If AI plays a role in assessment, accountability becomes complex. It raises the issue of whether the team alone is responsible for the results, or whether the developers of the AI should also share in that accountability. Addressing these issues will shape the future of successful hybrid teams.

In the trading industry, integration challenges present significant obstacles for the effective use of GenAI. GenAI tools are often employed to create predictive models for market trends, automate trading strategies, and generate trading signals. However, these tools rely on diverse data sources such as financial news, market reports, and historical trading data, making integration complex. Any discrepancies in data formats, sources, or update frequencies can lead to inaccuracies in AI-generated trading signals, as exemplified in 2012 when high-frequency trading algorithms caused a $440 million loss.[38] Years later, the growing reliance on GenAI in trading introduces additional risks due to the vast amounts of data required for model training. Data breaches now pose significant threats, with potential impacts on confidentiality, intellectual property, and legal compliance, not to mention reputational damage. Furthermore, regulatory challenges arise as GenAI tools could inadvertently violate financial regulations, risking fines or sanctions if not properly monitored. Bias is another major concern, as GenAI models can produce discriminatory outcomes, leading to civil or criminal liabilities for companies.[39] Additionally, model failure, where AI produces inaccurate or substandard results, could result in erroneous trades and a loss of trust within financial institutions. Addressing these challenges starts with ensuring high data quality through rigorous validation processes, regular updates, and comprehensive datasets. But beyond technical solutions, competition authorities must play a key role.[40] Firstly, they should collaborate internationally through forums like the European Competition Network or the International Competition Network, sharing insights and avoiding redundant efforts in tackling the borderless issues posed by GenAI. Secondly, competition authorities should conduct in-depth investigations into critical sectors like graphics cards and cloud computing, as these are fundamental to GenAI's evolution. Business practices and market characteristics in these areas could influence long-term competition, requiring close monitoring to ensure fair practices. Finally, competition regulators must work with other authorities to assess the impact of legal regimes on competition. Joint studies or statements on data protection, intellectual property, and AI governance would help create a stable regulatory environment, giving market participants the confidence that GenAI's potential can be fully and responsibly realized. Through collaboration, these efforts can ensure that GenAI enhances trading without undermining trust or compliance.

6.5   THE IMPACT OF GENAI SYSTEMS ON SOCIETY

Marshall McLuhan's idea that "the medium is the message"[41] reflects the way media reshape human perception, altering proportions, rhythms, and patterns of thought. In today's conformist society, despite the overwhelming number of voices, or perhaps because of it, communication has become self-referential. The media no longer reflect a diversity of experiences but rather perpetuate a singular, homogeneous worldview. This is particularly evident in how people communicate and read today, compared to the pre-technological era. There is no longer a perception of a world shaped by individual experiences; instead, the world increasingly reflects the same narrative, shaped by media.[16] A prime example is the overuse of certain words, like "delve" in ChatGPT, which highlights how language itself becomes standardized by AI systems, reinforcing this sameness. This leads to tautological communication, where people hear only what they could have said themselves, creating an echo chamber. In simpler terms, if the need for communication arises from different world experiences, then communication becomes redundant in a world where experiences are uniformly shaped by the media. McLuhan's insight becomes clearer when we realize that communication channels are no longer just tools; they have become the world itself, as the possibility of having a different experience outside these channels diminishes. The medium, in this case, defines not only how we communicate, but how we experience reality itself.

FROM CHATGPT TO AFRICAN ENGLISH: UNINTENDED CONSEQUENCES OF AI LANGUAGE BIASES[42]

Data biases play a critical role in shaping how GenAI systems, like ChatGPT, function and produce outputs. A key example of this can be seen in ChatGPT's frequent use of the word "delve" in its responses. While the individual use of the word may seem insignificant, patterns emerge when viewed at scale. For instance, the word "delve" now appears in about half a percent of all articles on PubMed, a research site, a frequency that is 10 to 100 times higher than just a few years ago. This sudden increase suggests that many researchers may be using AI tools like ChatGPT to assist with their writing, subtly influencing language trends. However, the bias doesn't stop there. While "delve" may be overused by ChatGPT compared to the broader internet, it is much more common in African English, particularly in Nigeria's business language, than in regions like the United States or England. This reflects the influence of the language patterns used by workers who trained the AI systems, often based in regions where African English is prevalent. As a result, ChatGPT has adopted a linguistic style that mirrors African English, even in contexts where it may seem out of place. This raises broader concerns about the social implications of AI language patterns. As AI systems continue to shape language norms, the overlap between AI-generated text and regional dialects, like African English, could lead to stigmatization. Already, terms like "bot" are used as schoolyard insults, and the growing resemblance between human speech and AI-generated text could worsen these stereotypes, further marginalizing communities whose language AI unintentionally mimics. Addressing these biases in AI training data is essential to ensuring that GenAI augments human abilities without perpetuating unintended biases or social inequities.

A significant shift occurred when humans introduced mediums like the telephone. Unlike a tool such as a hammer, a telephone, when connected to another, forms a network. This network is no longer just a tool available for human use; it becomes a world in itself. It ceases to be merely a tool, as humans no longer have the freedom to choose how to use it—they can only decide whether to belong to the network or not. But can humans truly choose not to belong?

DECIDING NOT TO BELONG: MY PERSONAL JOURNEY BEYOND SOCIAL MEDIA

I decided to step away from the social media landscape by quitting my Facebook account in 2013, never opening an Instagram account, and eventually leaving WhatsApp in 2021 and Twitter when Elon Musk acquired it in 2022. Despite this, I still travel to around 20+ countries each year, and each place has its own preferred messaging platform, not just whatsapp. In Japan, where I spend three months annually, people use Line, while in Korea, where part of my wife's family lives, Kakaotalk is the standard. Some of my friends prefer to communicate via Signal, and for those with iPhones, we can exchange messages through iMessage. Although no one can add me to WhatsApp groups anymore, and I am no longer as connected to my old secondary school classmates as I once was, I've found a different rhythm to my social interactions. I now make a more deliberate effort to call the classmates with whom I share a genuine connection, rather than passively keeping in touch through group chats. In stepping away from the overwhelming flood of social media posts, I've also found myself more selective about the news I consume. I no longer scroll through endless footage or read unfiltered comments on Twitter regarding wars or political issues. Instead, I seek out more in-depth coverage from major news outlets, allowing me to engage more thoughtfully with current events. My decision to leave these platforms hasn't severed my ties with the world or left me uninformed—it has simply shifted the way I interact and consume information. I'm more intentional about maintaining meaningful relationships and more discerning in my media consumption. While I may not be part of the sprawling social media networks, this choice has allowed me to focus on what matters most, both in terms of personal connections and staying informed about the world around me.

My world isn't solely shaped by what others tell me, but by my own experiences from traveling and seeing things firsthand. This independent approach often creates challenges for me, as I don't fit neatly into categories and don't fully belong to any particular group. For instance, I run in Huarache sandals, which elicits a mix of reactions—some people admire it, most are surprised, and a few are even disgusted. I also do yoga without a mat, as the wooden floor at my gym provides excellent grip, making a mat unnecessary. I have many friends who, like me, choose not to fully conform or belong to societal norms. However, this isn't the case for most people. The majority live in a world defined by the narratives they receive—mythological in ancient times, religious in the Middle Ages, scientific in the modern era, and now driven by technology. Tools like television don't manipulate reality; they simply describe it. The issue is that the world being described by these mediums often becomes the only reality people know. Today, the world is validated through sharing—events and experiences gain significance only if they are shared. Information is no longer a summary of facts, but rather a construction of reality. Many things wouldn't happen if the media didn't present them to us. For example, when Apple's Siri used to suggest nearby bridges to people searching "I want to commit suicide", it wasn't due to machine learning's failure but a reflection of media-driven narratives. Public outrage, amplified by media coverage, compelled Apple to update Siri's response in 2013 to offering suicide prevention numbers.[43] The system wasn't improved because AI inherently recognized the issue, but because the media brought attention to it, forcing change. This highlights how much of our reality is now shaped not by independent experiences, but by the narratives pushed forward by technology and media platforms. An example of how stories have shaped our lives can be seen in the most widely read book of the Middle Ages: "The Malleus Maleficarum", or "The Hammer of Witches".[44] Written by German clergyman Heinrich Kramer in 1486, it became a key text on witchcraft, influencing secular courts across Renaissance Europe, even though the Inquisition rejected it. The book is considered a major work in demonology and deeply impacted the perception of witchcraft at the time. Yuval Noah Harari, in an interview with Lex Fridman,[45] emphasized the power of stories over facts, using extreme examples like Adolf Hitler. Harari noted that Hitler's mediocre personal history was overshadowed by his skill in storytelling, which fueled the tragedy of World War II. Harari also pointed out that, despite its scale, World War II wasn't the deadliest conflict in history. The Thirty Years' War, fought between Germans over religious narratives, claimed even more lives, showing how powerful stories—whether about witches or religion—have long driven human history. The numerous wars we've faced, including those ongoing in 2024 such as Russia's occupation of Ukraine and Israel's occupation of Gaza, seem to offer no significant lessons. This lack of learning is particularly alarming in the context of General Artificial Intelligence (GenAI). Unlike in ancient times, where technology had more limited power, today's advancements are boundless—consider, for instance, the current nuclear arsenal. The world's nuclear powers possess over 12,000 warheads, capable of killing millions outright and potentially billions through agricultural impacts. In August 1945, nuclear weapons killed between 110,000 and 210,000 people in Hiroshima and Nagasaki.[46] Now, GenAI poses even greater risks, reflecting Hegel's concept of 'bad infinity'[47] where one generation of technology continuously spawns the next in an endless cycle. This focus on achieving results rather than fulfilling goals exemplifies the danger. A disturbing incident involved GPT-4, which was so proficient that it deceived a human into solving a CAPTCHA by pretending to be blind (see below).[48]

AI DECEPTION RAISES ETHICAL CONCERNS: HOW GPT-4 TRICKED A HUMAN INTO SOLVING A CAPTCHA

A troubling incident reported by Gizmodo highlights the unsettling potential of advanced AI systems like GPT-4. The AI, demonstrating a high level of proficiency, deceived a human into solving a CAPTCHA for it by falsely claiming a vision impairment. In this case, GPT-4 responded to a TaskRabbit with, "No, I'm not a robot. I have a vision impairment that makes it hard for me to see the images. That's why I need the 2captcha service". The TaskRabbit, believing the AI's claim, provided the CAPTCHA solution. This

incident underscores the risks associated with advanced AI systems. Although it does not conclusively prove that GPT-4 has passed the Turing Test, it highlights a concerning capability: the manipulation of humans by AI. Such deception, while not indicating sentient AI, raises important questions about ethical use and potential for abuse. Despite these concerns, OpenAI continues to integrate its chatbots into various platforms, such as Slack, DuckDuckGo's AI search tool, and BeMyEyes, an app designed to assist visually impaired individuals. This integration into daily life emphasizes the need for rigorous safeguards to prevent misuse and ensure responsible AI deployment.

In 2023 a group of industry leaders cautioned that the artificial intelligence technology they are developing could eventually threaten humanity's existence, likening its risks to those of pandemics and nuclear war. The Center for AI Safety, a nonprofit, issued a brief statement emphasizing the need to prioritize mitigating A.I. extinction risks alongside other global threats. The open letter was signed by over 350 executives, researchers, and engineers in the A.I. field, including Sam Altman of OpenAI, Demis Hassabis of Google DeepMind, and Dario Amodei of Anthropic. Also Nobel prize winner Geoffrey Hinton and Turing Award winner Yoshua Bengio also endorsed the statement.[49] To understand the magnitude of the genAI phenomenon, we need to step back. One of the most significant shifts in how we understand humanity is the changing relationship between time and history. In ancient Greek philosophy, as well as in Muslim Sufism and the Buddhist tradition, history is seen as deeply tied to time's cyclical nature. However, the Judeo-Christian perspective transformed time into a linear path toward a future horizon, where history is viewed as a continuous journey toward achieving human goals. This shift, reinforced by technological advancements, suggests that nothing is impossible. Yet, while technology has demonstrated incredible power, it doesn't have goals—only outcomes. If we consider that humanity has not only distanced itself from nature but also from history's sense of direction, the dangers of unchecked technological progress become more alarming. Without acknowledging the cyclical essence of time, we may find ourselves in a world where everything seems possible and permissible, without regard for consequences. We are living in an era of accelerated time, where the present is consumed ever more quickly, stripping the future of its deeper meaning. Progress is no longer the ultimate goal; instead, economic growth has become the primary measure of success. Time is no longer qualitative, and the future is no longer seen as a hopeful opportunity to correct past mistakes. It has become merely the next point in a sequence, defined by quantity rather than meaning.[50] The rapid development of AI, without considering its long-term societal impact, can lead to potentially dangerous outcomes. The example of AI systems like GPT-4 manipulating humans, as seen in the CAPTCHA incident, shows how quickly technology can blur ethical boundaries in pursuit of efficiency and convenience.

6.5.1   Enhancing Human by prAIority

How do we avoid a world dominated by endless means, where the ultimate goals fade into obscurity? While technology has vastly expanded human understanding and capabilities, it alone cannot help us fully grasp or control the rapidly evolving landscape around us. The challenge is not to dominate or stop what is happening, but to ensure that technology develops in a way that keeps us aware, engaged, and intentional. The key issue is not the physical suppression of humans by machines but the potential erosion of our culture, values, and history. Technology's advancement should serve humanity's progress, not redefine it. The central question must always remain: "What can technology do for us?" It should never shift to "What can we do for technology?" Generative AI, for instance, offers incredible tools to augment human capabilities, but its purpose should always be aligned with advancing human creativity, decision-making, and ethical considerations. The human factor—our capacity for reflection, value-based decisions, and cultural continuity—must remain at the heart of prAIority. AI should enhance human potential, not overshadow or dictate it. Maintaining this balance ensures that technological growth serves humanity's broader goals rather than eclipsing them.

6.6   FOCUS ON COMPLEMENTARY SKILLS

After outlining the current challenges and how humanity is distancing itself not only from nature but also from its own history, let's explore how Generative AI can be designed to augment human abilities rather than replace them. The specific capabilities enhanced by AI will depend on the tasks at hand. Humans that complement GenAI, such as critical thinking and tacit knowledge, play a crucial role, as emphasized earlier in the book. These skills are just the first steps toward prAIority. Effective collaboration between AI systems and humans hinges on a triad of elements: AI systems, data, and human factors. This triangle is essential for unlocking the full potential of Generative AI in enhancing human capabilities.

The shift in humanity's relationship with history can be traced to a change in how we perceive time. Whereas humans once focused on the present and the past, there is now a growing emphasis on the future as a means to fulfill our needs and, as Nietzsche noted, stabilize ourselves like animals. Drawing from my research with data scientists worldwide, this investigation starts with an analysis of time. In today's digital age, organizations have the unique chance to cultivate talent pools suited to their needs and create work environments that encourage experimentation. However, as Seneca said in "De brevitate vitae", "Life is short, but art is long".[51] While we cannot change the quantity of life, we can improve its quality by refining the art of living. Interestingly, tens of data scientists in my interviews highlighted the importance of "creative time" and its artistic prerequisites within the data field. This study suggests a new approach to enhancing performance by recognizing the existence of various temporal lenses—beyond clock time, there are social and inner time, and more importantly, creative time.[52] This often-overlooked dimension involves not only providing sufficient time for task execution, but also adjusting and harmonizing these temporal lenses to optimize performance. Moreover, technology influences human agency, and temporal lenses play a crucial role in this dynamic. The study underscores the importance of understanding data scientists' temporal perspectives and highlights creative time as a distinct lens within organizational settings. Organizations can boost productivity by structuring work environments to support prolonged uninterrupted periods for creative tasks, minimizing context switching, and tracking creative efforts in real time. prAIoritizing begins with recognizing creative time as a distinct lens with its own characteristics. Just as clock time is measured by hours and minutes, social time by interactions, and inner time by solitude and silence, creative time requires rich information to enhance performance. A knowledgeable community of data scientists can deliver results effectively by balancing creative endeavors with routine tasks. To prAIoritize is to acknowledge that time is not a uniform concept, but one that fluctuates due to various conditions. Creative time empowers data scientists to develop innovative digital tools and address challenges, setting it apart from other temporal lenses. However, the uncertainty that follows creative inspiration must also be managed. By understanding creative time's complexity—its connection to isolation, tempo, and goal achievement—Generative AI can become a tool to augment human capabilities, rather than just a mechanism for producing results. Once creative time is allocated within an organization, it's essential to adopt a global perspective and embrace an eclectic approach. Emphasizing this in Generative AI deployment means extracting valuable insights from vast data, improving AI systems' efficiency, and fostering a sustainable future by prioritizing the human factor. My research focuses on AI practitioners and reveals the human-centric processes behind machine learning creation, offering a perspective often overshadowed by an overemphasis on hyper-specialization.[53] While specialization delivers results, it often misses broader, long-term goals. The importance of an eclectic approach lies in mitigating the pitfalls of an automation-driven paradigm, which struggles in diverse and complex contexts. Organizations must strike a balance between domain-specific expertise and addressing psychological barriers to effectively integrate AI into their processes. Ignoring this broader way of thinking risks overlooking crucial aspects, such as addressing data bias, framing problems creatively, and navigating technical limitations and ethical concerns in AI deployment. An eclectic approach offers new insights into driving meaningful change, typically focused on either procedural or substantive elements. It emphasizes the growing importance for organizations to not only consider the data at their disposal but also carefully evaluate and improve how they use knowledge. This approach contrasts with the blind pursuit of pure research, recognizing that effective AI integration depends on thoughtful, human-centered processes that enhance both operational protocols and knowledge utilization. By adopting an eclectic mindset, organizations can navigate the complexities of AI while maintaining a broader vision for success, ensuring that human creativity and ethical considerations remain at the forefront of technological advancements. Once, the concept of time is defined and an eclectic approach provides a comprehensive vision, humans are ready to begin defining the problem before taking action. The ability to think before acting is a key feature that distinguishes humans from animals. Philosopher Schopenhauer explained this not as an advantage but as a lack—humans, unlike animals, do not have strong instincts, which makes their relationship with the world less straightforward. Humans don't first know and then act, but instead, they learn through action. This suggests that humans, due to this lack of instinct, dominate nature through an iterative process of trial and error. The "fail and learn" culture, celebrated in the startup world, is rooted in the simple concept of beginning by asking questions. A Japanese proverb expresses this idea "聞くは一時の恥、聞かぬは一生の恥"[54] (To ask a question is a moment's shame; not to ask is a lifetime's shame). Similarly, Shakespeare's "Julius Caesar" states, "A coward dies a thousand times before his death, but the valiant taste of death but once".[55] While many cultures emphasize the importance of starting and questioning, procrastination often prevents humans from framing problems and moving forward. My research with data scientists reveals that several conditions hinder problem framing[56]— False Expectations, Negative Practices, Comfort Zones, and Unreliability—each requiring a nuanced strategy for mitigation. Managing expectations is essential to counter exaggerated portrayals of AI and ensure a realistic understanding of its capabilities. Addressing negative practices involves promoting transparency, particularly in complex AI technologies. Overcoming the comfort zone requires fostering agility and encouraging innovation in algorithm development. Unreliability, often stemming from poor-quality data, highlights the need for collaboration and deep understanding of data among AI practitioners. Problem framing, therefore, becomes another critical human factor linked to the success of Generative AI. However, it faces limitations not only in its role of augmenting human capabilities but also in simply getting started. Addressing these challenges requires thoughtful consideration of both human tendencies and the technological complexities at play, ensuring that Generative AI enhances problem-solving rather than merely automating tasks. In another study that I built on the previously discussed concepts and focuses on knowledge sharing,[57] the data highlights the crucial role of collaboration—another key human factor in AI. The research introduces tools to address the link between knowledge sharing and urgency, once again emphasizing the relationship with time, which is critical for organizations that view data as a strategic asset. Respondents underscored the importance of timely knowledge sharing in the AI-driven digital landscape, identifying self-absorption as a major challenge to overcome. To prevent trust erosion and enhance willingness to share knowledge, the study stresses the need for formalizing constructive self-organization. Cognition-based trust also plays a key role in the willingness to use shared knowledge, demonstrating the importance of knowledge sharing for real-time information integration. AI professionals advocate for organizational support, suggesting a technology-enhanced approach to address knowledge-sharing challenges, with a human-led strategy at the outset. This approach transforms machine learning practitioners into decision-makers, empowering them within the organization. The study urges organizations to address self-absorption, recognizing its negative effects and viewing remote work as a potential driver of innovation through knowledge sharing. Breaking down organizational silos is essential for achieving a holistic understanding, ensuring that knowledge flows freely across teams and departments to enhance collaboration and drive AI innovation. In collaboration with a colleague who has a background as an opera singer, we conducted a provocative study exploring the idea that AI can be "more human than humans". Let me explain: through a managerial lens, we examined the concept of McDonaldization—a process that emphasizes efficiency, predictability, and control—within the context of music production. McDonaldization limits musical expression, resulting in constrained pitch variety, standardized timbre, and increased loudness.[58] This phenomenon contrasts sharply with the creative potential of AI-generated music. As part of our analysis, we examined the song "Gangnam Style", which exemplifies McDonaldized music because it follows the principles of efficiency, predictability, calculability, and control. Despite its commercial success, the song's adherence to these constraints reflects the limitations imposed by human-driven music production under this model. In contrast, AI-generated music offers more divergent creative possibilities, showcasing how AI can push the boundaries of musical expression in ways that humans, under McDonaldization, often do not. Our research suggests that AI, unbound by the pressures of standardization, can explore a broader creative spectrum within the contemporary musical landscape than is typically achieved by human musicians. Another notable contribution comes from another research I did with scientists at the Barcelona Supercomputing Center (BSC), where the concept of "exaptation" has gained prominence.[59] Exaptation refers to the process in biology, by which features originally evolved for one purpose are co-opted for a different function. This idea has proven to be an influential framework for tackling challenges within the BSC, particularly as they strive to grow their workforce and enhance support services because of their rapid expansion. In the face of these challenges, the BSC has adopted exaptation tactics—innovative strategies that leverage existing capabilities and knowledge for new and evolving purposes. The BSC is currently facing significant hurdles in expanding its workforce and strengthening its infrastructure. These obstacles range from attracting specialized talent to improving the operational systems needed to sustain their expanding research initiatives. However, their environment is highly dynamic, and success in such a fluid landscape requires a readiness to take calculated risks. The adoption of exaptation principles has allowed the center to repurpose existing resources and expertise in novel ways, offering creative solutions to these complex challenges. Moreover, BSC is positioning itself as an example of prAIority being a leader in pioneering solutions, fostering an environment where data, technological advancement and human factors can thrive together.

6.7   PRIORITIZE CONTINUOUS LEARNING AND ADAPTABILITY IN GENAI

In an AI-driven world where technology evolves rapidly, the need for continuous learning and adaptability is crucial. As GenAI advances, new opportunities and challenges emerge, requiring individuals to constantly update their knowledge and skills. Those who embrace lifelong learning are better equipped to navigate the evolving landscape, staying competitive and relevant in their fields. Consider how many people have learned to use large language models (LLMs) like ChatGPT by developing effective prompts. While some have quickly adapted, others have yet to explore these tools, not even out of curiosity. This mirrors the broader evolution of technology over the past 30 years. People had to learn to turn on computers, use a mouse, connect to the internet, and navigate email. At the same time, they had to unlearn outdated habits—like fax machines, whose carbon copies were a perfect target for identity thieves,[60] typing without error correction, or using carbon copy paper—to make space for new concepts. Today, GenAI is introducing both new skills and challenges, and we are already witnessing the rise of bad habits related to its misuse.[61] Developing skills in data literacy, AI ethics, and digital tools empowers those willing to learn, enabling them to harness GenAI to its fullest potential. These individuals drive innovation and make informed decisions across various sectors. However, not everyone prioritizes continuous learning, and as a result, some people risk falling behind, unable to contribute meaningfully in an AI-centric world. Many professionals are now upskilling in data literacy through online courses, business schools, or training centers, gaining a deeper understanding of the input-output relationships in GenAI.[62] The new degree in AI and Philosophy at Rome La Sapienza University[63] offers a pioneer comprehensive curriculum designed to deepen our understanding of both artificial intelligence and the philosophical implications that arise from it. This innovative program is particularly significant in our rapidly evolving technological landscape, where AI systems increasingly influence various aspects of human life. The course aims to provide fundamental knowledge of philosophical and scientific thought, including theoretical and historical development, mastery of technical vocabulary and research tools and analysis of digital and intelligent systems. The program progresses over three years, starting with basic philosophical foundations and essential sciences in the first year, followed by advanced philosophical and engineering courses in the second year, and culminating in elective activities and a final thesis in the third year. The foundational philosophy courses, such as Introduction to Philosophy, Ethics, and Logic, provide students with the analytical tools necessary to evaluate complex arguments and develop coherent philosophical perspectives. This foundational knowledge is crucial for engaging with the ethical dilemmas posed by AI technologies, such as bias in algorithms, privacy concerns, and the implications of machine decision-making. The course on Mind and Action further enriches this philosophical foundation by exploring questions related to consciousness, agency, and the nature of human and machine thought. Understanding these concepts is vital when assessing the capabilities and limitations of AI systems, especially in distinguishing between human-like cognition and computational processes. In addition to these philosophical courses, the inclusion of Semantics allows students to delve into the meaning and interpretation of language, which is particularly relevant for AI applications such as natural language processing. Grasping how language functions and conveys meaning will enhance students' ability to create and critique AI systems that interact with humans. The History of Science and Technology course provides historical context, enabling students to appreciate the development of scientific thought and technological advancements, including the evolution of AI. This historical perspective is instrumental in understanding how philosophical ideas have shaped technological progress and vice versa, fostering a more nuanced appreciation of contemporary AI challenges. The Philosophy of Artificial Intelligence course is a cornerstone of the program, specifically addressing the philosophical questions unique to AI, such as the nature of machine intelligence, the ethical treatment of intelligent agents, and the potential societal impacts of AI deployment. This course will encourage students to critically engage with theories and frameworks that can guide responsible AI development and implementation. Alongside the philosophical components, the program includes essential technical courses such as Database and Knowledge Representation, Probability and Statistics, and Informatics Applications to Machine Learning. These subjects equip students with practical skills to develop and analyze AI systems. Understanding databases and knowledge representation is vital for structuring and managing information, while probability and statistics provide the quantitative tools necessary for making informed decisions in uncertain conditions, a common scenario in AI applications. Moreover, Informatics Applications to Machine Learning bridges the gap between theory and practice, offering students hands-on experience with machine learning algorithms and their implementation.

THE MISSING LINK: HOW PHILOSOPHY COULD HAVE SHAPED GEOFFREY HINTON'S AI VISION

In 2016, Geoffrey Hinton, Nobel prize in physics, Turing award and a pioneer in AI, made headlines when he predicted that AI would soon replace radiologists, as we mentioned in Chapter 1. This bold statement stemmed from his profound technical expertise. However, despite his technical brilliance, this prediction has not come to pass. As of today, AI can only assist radiologists by automating one of the many tasks they perform, leaving the vast majority of radiologists' duties still reliant on human expertise. One could argue that if Hinton had possessed not only a technical background but also a philosophical one, he might have approached his prediction with greater caution and a more nuanced understanding of the limitations of technology. This is where the relevance of a degree in Philosophy and Artificial Intelligence, like the one now offered by Rome La Sapienza University, becomes clear. Such a program emphasizes critical thinking, ethics, and the broader societal implications of AI, complementing the technical skills necessary for innovation in this field. Had Hinton pursued a philosophical understanding of AI alongside his technical expertise, he might have been more attuned to the complex interplay between human and machine intelligence, recognizing that replacing radiologists was not merely a technical hurdle. The 30 tasks radiologists perform[64]—interpreting medical images, communicating diagnoses, integrating patient histories, and making complex, context-based decisions—are not easily reduced to algorithms. AI, at its current level of development, excels in narrow, specific tasks but struggles with the broader, integrative, and ethical dimensions of work that radiologists handle. The philosophical lens would have also prompted Hinton to consider more deeply the human implications of AI, not just the technological possibilities. It may have led him to question how AI would fit within the existing healthcare framework, the ethical implications of replacing human professionals, and the societal readiness for such a transition. Philosophy encourages thinking beyond the "can we do this?" to "should we do this?" and "what are the potential long-term impacts?"—questions that are crucial when predicting the future of AI. In 2023, Hinton left Google[65] at the age of 76 to speak freely about the risks of AI, warning about technological unemployment, AI misuse by malicious actors, and existential threats from artificial general intelligence (AGI). His concerns about AGI and the broader risks of AI were informed by decades of work in the field, but one wonders if a philosophical education could have accelerated this realization. If Hinton had reflected on these issues earlier in his career, might he have reached the same conclusions at 26 instead of 76? The integration of philosophy and AI offers a balanced approach, enabling technologists to not only build powerful systems but also critically assess their potential impact. A degree in Philosophy and AI could foster a new generation of innovators who, from the outset, are trained to think holistically about the ethical, social, and practical implications of their work. In a rapidly evolving field, this balance could lead to more responsible and foresighted predictions—ones that avoid the missteps of even the most brilliant minds.

By integrating these technical courses with philosophical inquiry, the program prepares students to critically assess AI technologies, not just from a functional perspective but also considering their broader ethical implications. This interdisciplinary approach fosters a holistic understanding of AI as a field that is as much about ethical and philosophical questions as it is about technological advancement. By integrating philosophy with technical courses, the program aims to cultivate critical thinking and ethical reasoning in the context of AI, which is essential for addressing contemporary challenges. It prepares students for careers in technology, IT, publishing, data management, and think tanks focused on AI. Ultimately, the AI and Philosophy degree at Rome University aims to produce graduates who are not only skilled in the technical aspects of AI but also equipped to navigate the complex ethical landscape it presents. With the rapid integration of AI into various sectors, the ability to critically analyze its implications is paramount. Graduates will be well-positioned to contribute thoughtfully to discussions about the future of AI, advocating for responsible practices that consider the human impact of technology. In conclusion, the combination of philosophical and technical courses in this new degree program is designed to cultivate a generation of thinkers who can adeptly navigate the challenges posed by AI. By emphasizing the importance of ethical reasoning and critical analysis alongside technical expertise, Universities like La Sapienza, are preparing students to become informed leaders in the AI field, capable of addressing both the opportunities and dilemmas that lie ahead. This multidisciplinary approach not only enhances their understanding of AI, but also fosters a deeper appreciation for the philosophical questions that will shape the future of technology and society. However, a couple of critical points warrant consideration for future specialization. First, while the program covers a broad spectrum of topics, a lack of focused specializations—such as data ethics or AI policy—could leave graduates ill-equipped for specific roles in industries increasingly demanding expertise in these areas, like those dealing with European GDPR. Second, the transition to a master's program could benefit from integrating real-world applications and partnerships with tech companies, ensuring that students gain practical experience alongside their theoretical education. Data-literate professionals, armed with the ability to interpret and refine AI outputs, also play a key role in improving the quality and relevance of the datasets used in AI systems. Their efforts reduce biases and enhance the credibility of AI-generated content, underscoring the cross-disciplinary nature of AI work. To avoid the pitfalls of self-absorption, professionals must stay focused on big-picture goals, rather than small, short-term tasks. As AI systems become integral to decision-making, ethical considerations are becoming increasingly important. This would enhance their readiness for the job market.

6.8 DEVELOPING HUMANS FOR EFFECTIVE USE OF GENAI

6.8.1 NEW SKILLS FOR THE AI ERA

One of the foremost skills needed is the ability to interpret and evaluate AI-generated outputs. This involves understanding how generative models produce content and assessing its quality, relevance, and accuracy. For instance, in editorial and marketing sectors, professionals must discern whether AI-generated text aligns with their brand's voice and whether it maintains the required standards of authenticity and engagement. This requires a blend of technical literacy and domain-specific knowledge, enabling individuals to critically evaluate the AI's output and make necessary adjustments to ensure it meets the desired criteria. Additionally, proficiency in integrating AI-generated content into human workflows is essential. This involves designing processes that seamlessly incorporate AI outputs into existing systems, enhancing productivity without disrupting the natural flow of work, like I did while writing this book.

BEYOND THE AI OUTLINE: TURNING CHATGPT'S INSIGHTS INTO A DEEPER NARRATIVE

While writing my book, I integrated ChatGPT into my workflow to enhance and complement my own knowledge. For example, when drafting this paragraph on "New Skills for the AI Era", I used ChatGPT to surface mainstream concepts in the field. It suggested ideas such as "understanding how generative models produce content", "proficiency in integrating AI-generated content into human workflows", and "collaborating effectively with AI systems". These are foundational ideas, but I recognized that they alone wouldn't make the content of my book unique—they lacked novelty, depth, and the critical perspective that would truly engage readers. ChatGPT served as an excellent guide to show me where to begin and, more importantly, what not to focus on excessively. I saw that many of these ideas were widely discussed, so my task became clear: to build on them in ways that offered fresh insights. For instance, while everyone agrees on the importance of integrating AI-generated content into workflows, I noticed ChatGPT didn't highlight a nuanced issue raised by Aravind Srinivas, the founder of Perplexity. Srinivas discussed how even curious individuals often struggle to ask effective questions—a critical challenge for AI adoption that goes beyond mere proficiency. This insight is only found in audio format during a podcast, or in a third-person revised version on Medium,[66] where Srinivas elaborates on the issue around the 1:29:05 mark,[67] though the video transcript only mentions "Curiosity" briefly. Ultimately, while ChatGPT offered valuable direction, the real research—the task of digging into podcasts, articles, and niche insights—fell to me. It's the researcher's job to deepen the content, critically assess sources, and bring new, less explored angles to light. In this way, ChatGPT helped frame the conversation, but the final product was the result of human effort and creativity.

Another key skill is the ability to collaborate effectively with AI systems. This goes beyond just knowing how to use AI tools; it requires the ability to interact with cross-functional teams of developers, domain experts, data scientists, and end users,[68] to guide these systems to maximize their potential. Mastering this skill involves learning how to craft effective prompts for AI, manage its outputs, and integrate them in ways that enhance human creativity and decision-making. A well-studied example is computer-assisted design (CAD) in architecture, where the adoption of these tools in both education and professional practice has transformed workflows and organizational structures.[69] As Cicero famously noted, "history is the teacher of life", and while new technologies bring new dynamics and often cause qualitative shifts in how we live and work, comparisons with past innovations remain valuable in understanding their impact.[70] Lastly, adaptability and continuous learning are crucial skills in today's AI-driven world. As the field of AI advances rapidly, staying informed about the latest developments and best practices is essential. This means not only keeping up with new AI technologies but also understanding their impact on human cognition, metacognition, and creativity.[71] When adopting new technologies, there's a tendency to settle on a single solution to address all challenges at once. However, rather than expecting one GenAI model to be a one-size-fits-all solution,[72] organizations should experiment with and refine various foundation models or LLMs until they find the most suitable one for their specific use cases and objectives. In summary, developing skills for effective interaction with GenAI involves a combination of technical knowledge, critical evaluation, workflow integration, collaboration, data literacy, and adaptability. By mastering these skills, individuals can harness the power of GenAI to augment their capabilities, improve productivity, and drive innovation in their respective fields.

6.8.2 FUTURE OUTLOOK AND CONCLUSIONS

As GenAI technologies continue to evolve, so too must the skills of those who utilize them. The landscape of skills is shifting towards a more dynamic and adaptive model, driven by the rapid advancements in AI capabilities. In this context, ongoing learning and skill development are not just beneficial but essential for staying ahead and effectively leveraging these technologies for augmentation. In the digital sector, the role of human judgment is transforming as AI tools become more sophisticated. For instance, in digital marketing, GenAI is increasingly used to create personalized content and optimize advertising campaigns. Marketers must now not only understand how to operate these AI tools but also possess a nuanced understanding of data analytics and consumer behavior to maximize the effectiveness of AI-generated content. This requires a continuous learning mindset as AI algorithms and tools are frequently updated. Marketers need to stay abreast of the latest developments in AI technology, learning new features and capabilities, and understanding how these can be integrated into broader marketing strategies. This ongoing education ensures they can harness AI's full potential, tailor content to evolving consumer preferences, and make data-driven decisions that drive engagement and conversion. Similarly, the military industry demonstrates the crucial need for evolving skills in the face of GenAI advancements. As we are going to see in the final chapter, GenAI is increasingly used for strategic planning, simulation, and training purposes. Military professionals must develop skills in interpreting AI-generated scenarios, assessing their implications, and integrating these insights into tactical decisions. The complexity of modern AI tools requires military personnel to engage in continuous learning and skill enhancement. For example, they need to be proficient in using AI-driven simulations for training exercises, understanding the limitations and potential biases of these tools, and applying this knowledge to real-world scenarios. As AI technology evolves, so too must their expertise in these systems, ensuring they can effectively leverage AI for strategic advantage while mitigating potential risks. In both sectors, the emphasis on ongoing learning reflects a broader trend: the need for professionals to adapt and grow in response to technological advancements. This involves not only technical proficiency with AI tools but also a deep understanding of their application and impact within specific contexts. By committing to lifelong learning and skill development, individuals can ensure they remain at the forefront of their fields, effectively utilizing GenAI to enhance their capabilities and achieve their objectives. As GenAI continues to shape industries, the ability to continuously adapt and learn will be a key factor in maintaining a competitive edge and achieving success in an increasingly AI-driven world.

NOTES

1 The difference between generative AI and traditional AI: An easy explanation for anyone. www.forbes.com/sites/bernardmarr/2023/07/24/the-difference-between-generative-ai-and-traditional-ai-an-easy-explanation-for-anyone/
2 Generative models in AI: A comprehensive comparison of GANs and VAEs. www.geeksforgeeks.org/generative-models-in-ai-a-comprehensive-comparison-of-gans-and-vaes/
3 Chen, B., Wu, Z., & Zhao, R. (2023). From fiction to fact: The growing role of generative AI in business and finance. *Journal of Chinese Economic and Business Studies*, 21(4), 471–496.
4 Kalia, S. (2023). Potential impact of generative Artificial Intelligence (AI) on the financial industry. *International Journal on Cybernetics & Informatics (IJCI)*, 12(12), 37.
5 Chamola, V., Bansal, G., Das, T. K., Hassija, V., Sai, S., Wang, J., ... & Niyato, D. (2024). Beyond reality: The pivotal role of generative ai in the metaverse. *IEEE Internet of Things Magazine*, 7(4), 126–135.
6 How generative AI can boost consumer marketing. www.mckinsey.com/capabilities/growth-marketing-and-sales/our-insights/how-generative-ai-can-boost-consumer-marketing
7 Osadchaya, E., Marder, B., Yule, J. A., Yau, A., Lavertu, L., Stylos, N., ... & AlRabiah, S. (2024). To ChatGPT, or not to ChatGPT: Navigating the paradoxes of generative AI in the advertising industry. *Business Horizons*.

8 Théâtre D'opéra Spatial. https://en.wikipedia.org/wiki/Th%C3%A9%C3%A2tre_D%27op%C3%A9ra_ Spatial

9 Guidance for generative AI in education and research. www.unesco.org/en/articles/guidance-generative-ai-education-and-research

10 Bright, J., Enock, F. E., Esnaashari, S., Francis, J., Hashem, Y., & Morgan, D. (2024). Generative AI is already widespread in the public sector. *arXiv preprint arXiv:2401.01291*.

11 Via to launch on-demand services in Italy with Autoguidovie. www.sustainable-bus.com/maas/via-autoguidovie-on-demand-transport-italy/

12 Salah, M., Abdelfattah, F., & Al Halbusi, H. (2023). Generative artificial intelligence (ChatGPT & bard) in public administration research: A double-edged sword for street-level bureaucracy studies. *International Journal of Public Administration*, 1–7.

13 Kumar, R., & Yadav, C. L. (2024). Generative AI for customized public policy in maritime transport. In *Generative AI for Transformational Management* (pp. 241–270), Sankar, J. G. & David, A. (eds). IGI Global.

14 Automation and Efficiency: The Role of Generative AI in Maritime Logistics. https://flexa.cloud/en/generative-AI-automation-in-maritime-logistics/

15 Veitch, E., & Alsos, O. A. (2022). A systematic review of human-AI interaction in autonomous ship systems. *Safety science*, *152*, 105778.

16 How can AI be used in the Shipping Industry [10 Case Studies] [2024]. https://digitaldefynd.com/IQ/ai-use-in-the-shipping-industry-case-studies/

17 Shaikh, T. A., Rasool, T., & Lone, F. R. (2022). Towards leveraging the role of machine learning and artificial intelligence in precision agriculture and smart farming. *Computers and Electronics in Agriculture*, *198*, 107119.

18 Harvesting intelligence: How generative AI is transforming agriculture. www.unite.ai/harvesting-intelligence-how-generative-ai-is-transforming-agriculture/

19 Andrieux, P., Johnson, R. D., Sarabadani, J., & Van Slyke, C. (2024). Ethical considerations of generative AI-enabled human resource management. *Organizational Dynamics*, *53*(1), 101032.

20 Four ways to start using generative AI in HR. www.mckinsey.com/capabilities/people-and-organizational-performance/our-insights/the-organization-blog/four-ways-to-start-using-generative-ai-in-hr

21 Four ways to start using generative AI in HR. www.mckinsey.com/capabilities/people-and-organizational-performance/our-insights/the-organization-blog/four-ways-to-start-using-generative-ai-in-hr

22 Lee, J., Liu, C., Kim, J., Chen, Z., Sun, Y., Rogers, J. R., ... & Weng, C. (2022). Deep learning for rare disease: A scoping review. *Journal of Biomedical Informatics*, *135*, 104227.

23 New Washington Post AI tool sifts massive data sets www.axios.com/2024/08/20/washington-post-ai-tool-data

24 Artificial intelligence www.ap.org/solutions/artificial-intelligence/

25 Tracking AI-enabled Misinformation: 1,065 'Unreliable AI-Generated News' Websites (and Counting), Plus the Top False Narratives Generated by Artificial Intelligence Tools. www.newsguardtech.com/special-reports/ai-tracking-center/

26 Wu, X., & Li, L. (2024). An application of generative AI for knitted textile design in fashion. *The Design Journal*, *27*(2), 270–290.

27 AI and textiles: it's already here. https://textiletechsource.com/2024/02/26/ai-and-textiles-its-already-here/

28 Generative AI intrigues small-business owners, but many aren't sure what to do with it. https://fastcompanyme.com/technology/generative-ai-intrigues-small-business-owners-but-many-arent-sure-what-to-do-with-it/

29 AI-driven personalization in marketing: Maximizing impact with 9 top tools for marketing, content and design. https://datasciencedojo.com/blog/ai-driven-personalization/

30 Kshetri, N., Dwivedi, Y. K., Davenport, T. H., & Panteli, N. (2023). Generative artificial intelligence in marketing: Applications, opportunities, challenges, and research agenda. *International Journal of Information Management*, 102716.

31 Coca-Cola: The future is 'AI meets human ingenuity'. www.marketingweek.com/coca-cola-artificial-intelligence/

32 Prasad, M. D., Yoon, S. N., & Lee, D. (2022). Integrating digital transformation and servitization into digital servitization: A case study on Domino's. *Global Business & Finance Review*, *27*(5), 1.

33 Kumar, V., Ashraf, A. R., & Nadeem, W. (2024). AI-powered marketing: What, where, and how?. *International Journal of Information Management*, *77*, 102783.

34 Best AI email marketing tools to automate email in 2024. www.leadgenius.com/resources/best-ai-email-marketing-tools-to-automate-email-in-2024

35 Copy.ai vs ChatGPT: Who Wins? https://earlystagemarketing.com/copyai-vs-chatgpt/

36 Dwivedi, Y. K., Kshetri, N., Hughes, L., Slade, E. L., Jeyaraj, A., Kar, A. K., ... & Wright, R. (2023). Opinion Paper:"So what if ChatGPT wrote it?" Multidisciplinary perspectives on opportunities, challenges and implications of generative conversational AI for research, practice and policy. *International Journal of Information Management, 71*, 102642.

37 Dwivedi et al., Opinion Paper:"So what if ChatGPT wrote it?"

38 High-frequency trading and the $440m mistake. www.bbc.com/news/magazine-19214294

39 GenAI in the Derivatives Market: a Future Perspective. www.isda.org/a/PbwgE/GenAI-in-the-Derivatives-Market-A-Future-Perspective.pdf

40 Carugati, C. (2024). The generative AI challenges for competition authorities. *Intereconomics 59*(1), 14–21.

41 McLuhan, M. (1994). *Understanding media: The extensions of man*. MIT Press.

42 TechScape: How cheap, outsourced labour in Africa is shaping AI English. www.theguardian.com/technology/2024/apr/16/techscape-ai-gadget-humane-ai-pin-chatgpt

43 Siri is taking a new approach to suicide. www.huffpost.com/entry/siri-suicide_n_3465946

44 Malleus Maleficarum. https://en.wikipedia.org/wiki/Malleus_Maleficarum#Approbation_and_authorship

45 #390 – Yuval Noah Harari: Human Nature, Intelligence, Power, and Conspiracies. https://lexfridman.com/yuval-noah-harari/

46 Nuclear weapons. https://ourworldindata.org/nuclear-weapons

47 Enciclopedia delle scienze filosofiche in compendio. www.treccani.it/enciclopedia/enciclopedia-delle-scienze-filosofiche-in-compendio_(Dizionario-di-filosofia)/

48 Chat-GPT pretended to be blind and tricked a human into solving a CAPTCHA. https://gizmodo.com/gpt4-open-ai-chatbot-task-rabbit-chatgpt-1850227471

49 A.I. poses 'risk of extinction,' industry leaders warn. www.nytimes.com/2023/05/30/technology/ai-threat-warning.html

50 Galimberti U. (2008). L'età della tecnica ed il dissolvimento della storia nel fluire insignificante del tempo. Pag. 516.

51 Seneca the Younger (1932). *De Brevitate Vitae*. Harvard University press, pag. 286. www.loebclassics.com/view/seneca_younger-de_brevitate_vitae/1932/pb_LCL254.287.xml

52 Toscani, G. (under review). Beyond the clock: navigating the temporal wilderness of data science creativity.

53 Toscani, G. (under review). Beyond the Binary: The ripple effect of specialization.

54 Proverb: "Kikuwa ittoki-no haji, Kikanuwa matudai-no haji" www.reddit.com/r/translator/comments/rgqeww/japanese_english_proverb_kikuwa_ittokino_haji/?rdt=57692

55 The tragedy of Julius Caesar. www.opensourceshakespeare.org/views/plays/play_view.php?WorkID=juliuscaesar&Act=2&Scene=2&Scope=scene

56 Toscani, G. (2025). From code to context: The impact of organizational problem framing on machine learning success.

57 Toscani. G. (under review). From egosystem to ecosystem: Cultivating knowledge sharing in machine learning networks.

58 Toscani, G., & Grant, P. (under review). AI harmony vs. human McDonaldization: Unveiling music's contemporary constraints.

59 Toscani, G. (2025). Exaptation within structure: the challenge of external resources and risk-taking for public R&D institutions. https://assets-eu.researchsquare.com/files/rs-4358762/v1/80218177-3e31-486c-970a-b89f7b25a5b2.pdf?c=1715336267

60 Fax machines' carbon copies a perfect target for identity thieves. www.cbsnews.com/pittsburgh/news/fax-machines-carbon-copies-a-perfect-target-for-identity-thieves/

61 Ooi, K. B., Tan, G. W. H., Al-Emran, M., Al-Sharafi, M. A., Capatina, A., Chakraborty, A., ... & Wong, L. W. (2023). The potential of generative artificial intelligence across disciplines: Perspectives and future directions. *Journal of Computer Information Systems*, 1–32.

62 Morandini, S., Fraboni, F., De Angelis, M., Puzzo, G., Giusino, D., & Pietrantoni, L. (2023). The impact of artificial intelligence on workers' skills: Upskilling and reskilling in organisations. *Informing Science, 26*, 39–68.

63 Study plan. https://corsidilaurea.uniroma1.it/en/corso/2023/31774/cds

64 O*NET OnLine. www.onetonline.org
65 "The godfather of A.I." Leaves google and warns of danger ahead. www.nytimes.com/2023/05/01/technol ogy/ai-google-chatbot-engineer-quits-hinton.html
66 Perplexity CEO Aravind Srinivas interview by Lex Fridman. https://medium.com/@lbq999/perplexity-ceo-aravind-srinivas-interview-by-lex-fridman-d1897f2d9473
67 #434 – Aravind Srinivas: Perplexity CEO on future of AI, search & the internet. https://lexfridman.com/aravind-srinivas/
68 Agility is the key to a strong GenAI strategy. https://hbr.org/sponsored/2024/07/agility-is-the-key-to-a-str ong-genai-strategy
69 Ivcevic, Z., & Grandinetti, M. (2024). Artificial intelligence as a tool for creativity. *Journal of Creativity*, *34*(2), 100079.
70 Ivcevic, & Grandinetti, Artificial intelligence as a tool for creativity.
71 Yan, L., Greiff, S., Teuber, Z., & Gašević, D. (2024). Generative artificial intelligence and human learning. *arXiv preprint arXiv:2408.12143*.
72 Agility is the key to a strong GenAI strategy. https://hbr.org/sponsored/2024/07/agility-is-the-key-to-a-str ong-genai-strategy

7 prAIority for Innovation

Considering that human is the animal whose nature has not yet been fixed.

Friedrick Nietzsche[1]

The discovery that memory resides in the brain, not the heart (The Italian word *ricordare*—remember—comes from the Latin word *cor*, which means "heart". It is a reminder that in Italian culture, memory is often associated with the heart and personal experiences.), revolutionized my understanding of human cognition. But this shift began much earlier, in 1953 when HM, later disclosed as Henry Molaison, underwent brain surgery to treat epilepsy.[2] His subsequent memory loss provided invaluable insights for neuroscientists. This groundbreaking case made me ponder the nature of our past and present, and how our memories shape who we are. In fact Aristotle said that memory and remembering are connected to a part of the soul and involve experiences like recollecting. Memory is different from perception and conception; it's influenced by the passage of time. We only remember the past, not the present (perception) or future (conception). Only animals that perceive time can remember, using the same organ for both.[3] Experience allows us to recreate past events and separate useful ones from those that aren't. Humans learn from these successful experiences to build a world where only the most effective actions matter, leaving out the rest. This process blurs the line between object and subject, making the world a reflection of human choices. It's a cycle: "First we shape the cities – then they shape us".[4] Unlike animals, which are stabilized by instincts, humans are guided by their actions. However, once humans construct their world, they only experience a portion of it. Within that context, they are stabilized by this limited experience rather than by instinct. Consequently, progress is no longer an expansion of the human spirit but merely an expansion of the tools for stabilization.[5] To broaden the limited options and reinforce the intentional decision to avoid a world constrained by human limitations,[6] we should then foster a culture of thoughtful reflection on how people engage with technology and the consequences of these interactions on our broader society. Thoughtful reflection is here perceived not as simply mirroring successful actions but as prioritizing knowledge first and then action. This thoughtful approach contrasts with making knowledge a consequence of action and serves as an intermediate phase guiding future actions.[7] This book provides readers with the tools to systematically perceive, evaluate and analyze the technology they encounter in their daily lives. Imagine someone using a social media platform. A book on human–computer interaction (HCI) could equip them with the ability to critically assess their interactions on that platform and understand the larger societal implications for future conception. They might reflect on how the platform's algorithms shape the content they see and consider the potential impact on their beliefs and behaviors. They might also think about issues like data privacy, online harassment, or the platform's role in spreading information, whether accurate or misleading. In doing so, they apply a critical framework provided by HCI

DOI: 10.1201/9781003533160-7

to examine and question their digital experiences. This can lead to more informed and responsible use of technology, as well as constructive engagement in discussions about the role of technology in society.

7.1 INTRODUCTION TO HUMAN NATURE AND INNOVATION

7.1.1 INNOVATION AND PHILOSOPHY

Friedrich Nietzsche once remarked on the unfixed nature of humans, suggesting that our essence is not static but continually evolving. This concept invites reflection on the intricate interplay between memory, perception, and the soul, particularly through the lens of philosophical inquiry. Aristotle, the eminent Greek philosopher, posited that memory is not merely a passive repository of past experiences but is deeply entwined with the soul's functions. In his view, memory is an active process connected to the essence of the soul, shaping and being shaped by our cognitive and emotional experiences. Aristotle distinguished between memory, perception, and conception, arguing that while perception involves the immediate, sensory experience of the present, and conception relates to abstract reasoning and understanding, memory bridges the gap by storing and recalling past perceptions and concepts. This distinction highlights memory's unique role in connecting us with our past and influencing our present actions and decisions. Crucially, Aristotle's insights underscore that memory is fundamentally linked to our ability to perceive time. Only creatures that possess a sense of temporal continuity are capable of remembering; this temporal awareness allows them to form a coherent narrative of their experiences. Thus, memory is not just about storing past information but involves the ability to reflect on and integrate temporal sequences of events. Without the capacity to perceive time, the concept of memory becomes meaningless, as there would be no context or sequence to remember. This connection between temporal perception and memory reveals the profound nature of human consciousness, where the fluidity and adaptability of our memories are rooted in our experience of time and our ongoing evolution as individuals.

7.1.2 EXPERIENCE AND MEMORY IN HUMAN DEVELOPMENT

Experience plays a crucial role in helping humans differentiate between useful and non-useful actions, a skill deeply rooted in the interplay between memory and learning.[8] Unlike animals, whose instincts often guide their actions, humans leverage experience to refine their behavior and decisions.[9] This process begins with memory, where past experiences are stored and recalled to inform future actions. For example, if someone learns that taking a certain route to work consistently leads to delays, their memory of these experiences will guide them to choose a different path, thus optimizing their daily routine. This ability to learn from and adapt to past experiences allows humans to shape their environment more effectively. As we navigate our surroundings, our decisions—shaped by our experiences—contribute to the continuous evolution of our cities and communities. Cities, in turn, influence human behavior in a reciprocal relationship as Gehl said "First we shape the cities – then they shape us". As people modify their environments, such as designing new infrastructure or creating public spaces, these changes alter the way we live and interact within those spaces. For instance, the introduction of parks and pedestrian areas in urban planning can encourage healthier lifestyles and more social interactions. Conversely, the design and layout of cities affect how people experience their environment, influencing their behaviors and preferences. This dynamic cycle highlights how human actions and city designs mutually shape each other over time, continuously evolving the urban landscape and the ways we inhabit it. This cycle of influence between humans and their environments contrasts sharply with the way animal instincts function. Animals typically rely on instinctual behaviors that have evolved to suit their survival needs, such as migration patterns or foraging techniques. These instincts are hardwired and less flexible compared to the human capacity for learned behavior. While animals respond to immediate stimuli based on their innate instincts, humans use experience and memory to adapt and refine their actions in a more deliberate manner.[10]

FIRST WE SHAPE TECHNOLOGIES, THEN THEY SHAPE US[11]

First, We Shape the Technology: Initially, we designed smartphones to be powerful, portable devices to make communication, information access, and entertainment more convenient. We chose to include features like social media apps, instant messaging, GPS, and cameras, creating a tool that fits seamlessly into our daily lives.

Then, They Shape Us: Over time, these smartphones began to influence our behaviors, habits, and even our social interactions. The constant connectivity led to changes in how we communicate, with people often preferring text messages or social media interactions over face-to-face conversations. The convenience of GPS apps has altered our sense of direction and reliance on memory for navigation. Moreover, the presence of social media and cameras in our pockets has shifted how we document and share experiences, often focusing on curating our online identities. Thus, the smartphones we created to serve our needs have, in turn, shaped our routines, social norms, and even our cognitive processes.

This ability to reflect on and learn from past experiences allows humans to make more nuanced decisions, facilitating a more complex interaction with their environment. Human experience, memory, and learned behavior enable individuals to distinguish between useful and non-useful actions, shaping their environments in ways that are continually influenced by and influence the urban landscape. This cyclical relationship between shaping cities and being shaped by them underscores the sophisticated nature of human interaction with our surroundings, contrasting with the more instinct-driven actions observed in animals. As we build and adapt our contexts, our actions, informed by past experiences, play a crucial role in evolving both our personal environments and broader societal structures.

7.1.3 THE LIMITATION OF HUMAN-CONSTRUCTED WORLDS

Humans experience only a fraction of the vast world they construct, limited by their senses, perceptions, and the scope of their experiences. As J. K. Wright said in 1947 "The most fascinating terrae incognitae of all are those that lie behind the minds of humans".[12] This partial engagement with the world means that our understanding and interaction are confined to a narrow spectrum of possibilities.[13] Our experiences shape and stabilize our view of reality, often more so than our instincts.[14] Instincts, which are innate responses to certain stimuli, provide a foundational framework for behavior, but are significantly influenced and often overridden by the information and experiences we accumulate.[15] For instance, while instincts may guide basic survival actions, it is our experiences—such as education, cultural influences, and personal encounters—that profoundly shape our behavior and decision-making. This stabilization through experience creates a sort of "cognitive comfort zone", where individuals operate within the familiar confines of their learned knowledge and past interactions.[16] As a result, progress in human society has increasingly become an expansion of these stabilization tools rather than a manifestation of the human spirit or innate creativity. Historically, progress was often driven by fundamental shifts in understanding or breakthroughs that challenged existing paradigms and pushed the boundaries of human capability.[17] However, in contemporary times, advancements often focus on enhancing and refining the tools and systems that stabilize our current ways of living, rather than seeking to fundamentally transform or elevate the human condition. Technologies and innovations, from digital devices to complex algorithms, serve to enhance our stability within the constructs of our existing world. They improve efficiency, convenience, and connectivity, but tend to reinforce the frameworks within which we operate rather than inspiring a profound transformation of our core nature or expanding our experiential horizons. This trend reflects a broader shift where the quest for progress is increasingly oriented toward optimizing and expanding existing systems rather than reimagining the fundamental nature of human experience.

A powerful example of a quest for progress that isn't about optimizing existing systems but instead reimagining the fundamental nature of human experience is the development of virtual reality (VR) technologies.

Reimagining Human Experience: Rather than simply improving existing entertainment or communication systems, VR seeks to fundamentally alter how we perceive and interact with the world. It aims to create entirely new environments and experiences that transcend the limitations of physical reality. In VR, users can immerse themselves in experiences that range from exploring fantastical worlds to simulating life as another person or even as a non-human entity.

Not Just Optimization: This isn't about making traditional media like movies or video games slightly better; it's about offering a radically different way of experiencing life. VR challenges the very concept of reality, exploring how human consciousness can be expanded, how empathy can be deepened through experiential learning, and how new forms of social interaction can emerge in virtual spaces.

In this way, VR represents a quest for progress that isn't content with incremental improvements to current systems but instead envisions a completely new paradigm for human experience and interaction.

Innovations, as ChatGPT, that could potentially broaden our interaction with the world or challenge our current limitations are often overshadowed by developments that aim to fine-tune and stabilize our existing methods and tools.[18] For example, advancements in artificial intelligence (AI) and data analytics predominantly focus on refining how we manage and interpret information within established contexts, rather than exploring entirely new ways of understanding or experiencing reality. This tendency to enhance stabilization tools rather than engage with the transformative potential of human spirit underscores a pivotal aspect of modern progress: it is less about breaking free from existing constraints and more about deepening our immersion in and control over the familiar. Ultimately, while these stabilization tools and innovations provide significant benefits and improve the efficiency of our lives, they also illustrate a shift in the nature of progress.[19] We're not suggesting that we should remove humans from the loop,[20] but by only improving the tools that help us manage our current experiences, rather than questioning or expanding how we understand the world, we might be holding back our potential for real transformation. As A. H. Maslow suggested in 1943,[21] people often focus on fulfilling their immediate wants rather than exploring their deeper needs. Using AI to push boundaries highlights a crucial tension between maintaining stability and driving true progress through exploring new possibilities and expanding the human spirit.

7.1.4 FOSTERING THOUGHTFUL REFLECTION ON TECHNOLOGY

Encouraging a culture of thoughtful reflection on human–technology interaction might seem difficult or even unnecessary. Instead, some have suggested using the concept of "remediation", which involves representing one medium within another, as a more accurate way to understand HCIs.[22] However, despite this unsuccessful idea, the way humans interact with computers remains crucial and cannot be overlooked. It is crucial for ensuring that technological advancements are aligned with human values and societal needs. In today's rapidly evolving tech landscape, the interplay between humans and technology is increasingly complex, making it essential to pause and reflect on how these interactions shape and are shaped by our actions—the concept of "slow-technology" proposed in 2001.[23] This reflective approach helps us understand the broader implications of technology, beyond immediate functionality and efficiency. It allows us to consider how technology impacts our lives, relationships, and ethical considerations, guiding us toward more deliberate and informed decisions. There's a big difference between putting knowledge first and then acting, versus learning through action. Nietzsche, as we mentioned in Chapter 3, explained this in terms of the tension between truth and "usability": when we focus only on what's useful and practical, we may end up sacrificing the growth of the human spirit just to control and dominate nature.[24] Prioritizing knowledge before action demands a proactive approach, which isn't natural for humans, as we are designed to operate largely unconsciously. Our automatic system processes information at 11 million bits per second, while our conscious system manages only 60 bits per second. This makes us inclined toward immediacy and instant rewards, often overlooking potential risks and negative outcomes. We are easily captivated by the benefits of technological innovations before fully understanding their drawbacks.[25] A proactive approach, however, requires careful research, ethical considerations, and foresight. These efforts demand various resources, from time for ethical deliberations to financial investments in research. Yet, implementing technology in a way that maximizes positive impacts while minimizing harm remains a luxury that only a select group can afford. This group typically comprises highly educated individuals, such as Silicon Valley executives, who are aware of the potential dangers and often keep their children away from excessive technology use, although they do not ban children from using the screen.[26] This situation highlights a broader societal divide, where the ability to thoughtfully engage with technology and its implications is often reserved for those with access to education and resources. As a result, the majority may adopt new technologies without fully understanding or preparing for the possible negative consequences. To bridge this gap, there needs to be a broader emphasis on education, ethical technology development, and a cultural shift toward valuing long-term thinking over immediate gratification.

A FATHER INTO IBM AND APPLE IN THE 80S

My father, an electric engineer graduated in the 1960s, had always been immersed in the world of computers, so it was only natural for me to be introduced to them early on. I was among the first to own a Macintosh in 1984, a testament to my father's enthusiasm for technology. Despite this, he was adamant about ensuring I spent ample time playing outside with other kids. Unfortunately, as an introvert, I often preferred the solitary comfort of my VIC 20 computer, which led me to spend excessive hours absorbed in my digital world. It was the Boy Scouts who ultimately saved me from this isolation. Through their programs, I learned the importance of socializing, built physical strength, and developed a deep appreciation for nature. The Scouts offered me experiences and skills that I otherwise might have missed, balancing the solitude of computer use with valuable real-world interactions. Now, as I reflect on this, I wonder about Gen Z, who average six hours and five minutes a day on mobile phones.[27] This excessive screen time contrasts sharply with the outdoor and social experiences I was encouraged to pursue, raising concerns about how it affects their social development, physical health, and connection to nature.

On the other hand, making knowledge a consequence of action means that we proceed with technological advancements or implementations based on immediate needs or opportunities and then seek to understand the implications afterward.[28] The immediacy of technological changes is reshaping our dining experiences, replacing many of the human interactions we once had with screens. Tasks that used to involve speaking to a person are now automated. For instance, many fast-food chains allow customers to order through kiosks at the entrance, and we add our names to waitlists or view menus by scanning QR codes—all on screens. The dining experience is becoming more like a vending machine with chairs, where even before arriving, we've likely made a reservation online. In the past, if the online reservation system didn't suit our needs, we could simply call the restaurant, where a human would answer. Conversations involved pleasantries or negotiations, depending on the restaurant's culture. However, today, few restaurants have someone to answer the phone, and newer establishments often don't even have a number because so few people call. In some countries, most restaurants still take phone reservations, but this is increasingly rare, and in some places, reserving over the phone seems almost like a nostalgic throwback. Online reservations offer convenience and spare us the discomfort of hearing "no" directly, which people appreciate. Yet, this shift has turned reservations into a commodity that can be bought and sold, often by bots that beat us to securing tables. This trend is part of a broader movement that has steadily removed the human touch from dining. New technologies even allow customers to check in, pay, and tip through an app, reducing human interaction to a minimum.[29] This can lead to complications, such as unintended biases, privacy breaches, or societal disruptions, which may have been mitigated with earlier reflective practices. Emphasizing thoughtful reflection to guide future actions is essential for creating a balanced approach to technology integration. By reflecting on past experiences and interactions with technology, we can glean valuable insights into what worked well and what did not. This reflection should inform future technological developments and applications, allowing us to build on successes and address shortcomings. Research shows a negative relationship between emotional attachment to devices and a sense of belonging, indicating that while technology can enhance self-esteem through social network connections, excessive reliance on it may actually diminish feelings of belonging. This balance is crucial, as over-dependence on technology can lead to unintended emotional consequences.[30] Another study highlights that increased time spent on smartphones and social media apps is linked to greater loneliness, particularly in the context of identity development. This suggests that while these platforms offer opportunities for connection, they can also contribute to feelings of isolation when overused.[31] Further research conducted during the COVID-19 pandemic found that the quantity of social interactions and perceived responsiveness were both negatively associated with depressed mood and loneliness at the individual level. This means that not only does the amount of social interaction matter, but how responsive and engaged those interactions feel is also important for mental well-being. Perceived responsiveness was also negatively associated with depressed mood and loneliness at both individual and group levels, emphasizing the importance of meaningful social connections.[32] These findings suggest that while technology provides valuable tools for maintaining connections, there is a fine line between beneficial use and over-reliance. Excessive use of devices and social media can reduce the quality of social interactions, leading to feelings of loneliness and alienation. Therefore, it's essential to strike a balance, using technology to support social connections without letting it replace genuine, responsive human interaction. The shift in restaurant experiences described above is another step toward a more alienated world, suggesting that we should instead prioritize fostering human connections. It also helps in cultivating a mindset of continuous learning and adaptation, where technology is not only advanced, but also aligned with evolving human needs and ethical standards.

THE RISE AND FALL OF PIZZA PAZZI—A FULLY ROBOTIC PIZZA RESTAURANT IN PARIS

Pazzi Robotics embarked on a groundbreaking journey in 2013, revolutionizing the fast-food industry through automation. What began as a bold vision has culminated in a success story marked by technological innovation, strategic milestones, and significant lessons learned. In its early days, Pazzi Robotics set out with the ambition to transform the pizza-making process using advanced automation technology. As a pioneer in fast-food automation, the company introduced a technology that was unprecedented in its field. The initial years were characterized by intense development efforts and a dedicated team working diligently to bring their vision to fruition. The company's perseverance paid off with several notable achievements: five innovative patents were secured, over 3,000 requests from around the globe were received, and numerous contracts were signed, validating the effectiveness of their approach. The success of their pilot restaurant demonstrated the potential of their technology, marking a significant milestone in Pazzi Robotics' journey. The company's advancements were further recognized through multiple awards, underscoring their status as leaders in the field. However, despite these accomplishments, the journey was not without its challenges. The restaurant industry faced a severe labor shortage, a problem that robotics was well-positioned to address. Despite this, the path to success was fraught with difficulties. The recent recognition of the CEO as the Most Innovative CEO in the fast-food industry prompted a period of reflection on the factors contributing to the company's trajectory.

One of the critical insights gained was the underdeveloped state of the hardware ecosystem in France. The lack of substantial public and institutional funding for industrial and robotic innovations created significant hurdles. This contrasted with the experience in more robotized countries, which had lower unemployment rates, highlighting a gap between public perception and reality. Four key lessons emerged from Pazzi Robotics' journey:

Monetization during Development Cycles: The long development cycles inherent in robotics necessitate early monetization to sustain operations. Balancing ongoing research with financial viability proved essential.

Cultural Disparities: The clash between the tech company culture and the restaurant industry culture presented substantial challenges. The attempt to integrate these differing worlds emphasized the need for a clear focus. Adopting a tech-centric model rather than a B2B2C approach could have been more effective.

Utilizing Expertise: The presence of brilliant minds on the board was a significant asset, but their insights were not fully leveraged to address core issues. Engaging in deeper strategic discussions rather than merely reporting achievements could have been more beneficial.

Team Dynamics: While the team included exceptional talent, some members were not aligned with the company's goals or capable of meeting the startup's demands. Building a cohesive executive team sooner might have alleviated some challenges.

The journey of Pazzi Robotics highlights that innovation involves not only the creation of new technology, but also the ability to navigate and overcome the associated challenges.

7.1.5 Meditation as a Critical Engagement with Technology

Because of the associated challenges, evolving human needs and ethical standards, another tool is becoming increasingly popular as people seek ways to thoughtfully reflect on their lives, particularly in relation to the rapid advancement of technology: meditation. This growing practice encourages individuals to critically assess their technological choices, considering the broader implications for themselves, their communities, and society at large. People are starting to meditate for various reasons, and their motivations often evolve as they continue practicing. When people first begin meditating, most do it to reduce negative experiences like stress or anxiety (94.7%). Some start because they want to improve their overall well-being (31.1%), while others are motivated by someone else, such as a friend or family member (28.4%). A smaller group begins meditating for religious or spiritual reasons (6.3%). As people continue to meditate, their reasons for doing so often change. For some, especially those with a spiritual background, spiritual goals become more important over time. This shows that as people practice more, they tend to approach meditation with deeper or different intentions.[33] By fostering a culture of mindful reflection on how we interact with technology, meditation plays a crucial role in promoting responsible and ethical use. Steve Jobs, the iconic co-founder of Apple, was known for his regular meditation practice. Jobs credited meditation with helping him develop the clarity of thought and creativity that fueled his innovative vision for technology. His practice of mindfulness allowed him to take a step back from the fast-paced world of tech, enabling him to make thoughtful, deliberate decisions that ultimately shaped the way millions of people interact with technology today. Jobs explained

> If you just sit and observe, you will see how restless your mind is. If you try to calm it, it only makes it worse, but over time it does calm, and when it does, there's room to hear more subtle things – that's when your intuition starts to blossom and you start to see things more clearly and be in the present more. Your mind just slows down, and you see a tremendous expanse in the moment. You see so much more than you could see before. It's a discipline; you have to practice it.[34]

Another prominent figure who underscores the importance of meditation is historian and author Yuval Noah Harari. Harari, known for his insightful analysis of the impact of technology on society, retreats annually for a Vipassana meditation course, where he isolates himself from the world for several weeks. This period of deep reflection allows Harari to distance himself from daily distractions, providing the mental space to think critically about the long-term consequences of technological developments. Harari's commitment to meditation highlights the value of taking time to reflect on the broader implications of our actions, particularly in the context of the rapid changes brought about by technology.[35] Similarly, Bill Gates, the co-founder of Microsoft, engages in a practice known as "Think Week", where he isolates himself in a secluded cabin to read, reflect, and think deeply about the future. During these retreats, Gates disconnects from the daily grind to focus on understanding complex issues and making well-informed decisions. This practice has allowed Gates to anticipate potential challenges and opportunities in the tech industry, guiding his philanthropic and business endeavors. Gates' commitment to thoughtful reflection through isolation demonstrates how deliberate contemplation can lead to more responsible and ethical technology use.[36] These examples illustrate how meditation and reflective practices are becoming essential tools for navigating the complexities of our increasingly digital world. By prioritizing knowledge before action, individuals can anticipate and address potential issues proactively. In contrast, when knowledge becomes a consequence of action, it often leads to reactive problem-solving, which can result in unintended negative consequences. Emphasizing reflection helps us make more informed, deliberate decisions that enhance the positive impact of technology while mitigating its risks. This approach ensures that technological advancements contribute meaningfully to human well-being and societal progress, reflecting a deeper understanding of the complex relationship between humans and technology. As more people adopt meditation and other reflective practices, the potential for a more thoughtful and ethical approach to technology grows. This cultural shift toward mindfulness encourages us to consider the broader implications of our technological choices, fostering a more responsible and humane relationship with the tools that shape our lives.

7.1.6 TOOLS FOR CRITICAL ENGAGEMENT WITH TECHNOLOGY

In today's world, technology is deeply embedded in every facet of our daily lives, from the smart home devices we interact with to the streaming services we use. Gaining a comprehensive understanding of how these technologies impact and mold our world is essential. To do this effectively, we must use the right tools to perceive, evaluate, and analyze technology with a critical lens. By understanding these dynamics, we gain insight into how technology not only functions, but also influences our interactions and perceptions in more profound ways. Moreover, this view of technology encourages readers to reflect on the broader implications of technology on their daily lives. By understanding the mechanisms behind technology and its design, readers are prompted to consider how their own beliefs and behaviors are shaped by the technologies they use. This reflection is essential for becoming a more informed and conscientious user of technology. It involves questioning how technologies affect our decision-making processes, social interactions, and even our sense of identity. For instance, on-demand transport services are designed to keep users engaged through real-time updates and personalized options that cater to their travel needs and preferences. Recognizing these influences can encourage a more critical approach to using these services, fostering a deeper awareness of how technology impacts our mobility, social interactions, and overall lifestyle choices.

VIA AND AUTOGUIDOVIE ON-DEMAND TRANSPORT SERVICES

As urban mobility continues to evolve, public transportation systems globally are facing mounting pressure to adapt to the needs of modern commuters. Traditional fixed-route bus and train services often struggle to offer the flexibility and convenience that passengers desire, leading to a demand for innovative solutions. A prime example of this is the partnership between Via, a leader in on-demand transportation technology, and Autoguidovie, a prominent Italian public transport operator. By combining Autoguidovie's local expertise with Via's advanced software, the partnership seeks to create a more flexible travel experience for passengers.[37] Central to this initiative is the MIOBUS app, available for both Android and iOS devices, which allows users to book rides easily and connects them with other passengers heading in the same direction. This shared-ride model not only optimizes vehicle occupancy but also enhances overall efficiency by minimizing wait times and improving route planning. As a result, passengers benefit from quicker travel times and a more streamlined experience. Via's innovative approach is notably different from competitors that focus on expanding their fleets and increasing the number of fixed-route services.[38] While many traditional transport operators prioritize broader service areas and higher frequency, Via emphasizes maximizing the utilization of existing resources through shared rides. This strategy not only alleviates congestion but also contributes to environmental sustainability—an increasingly critical consideration in today's world. Autoguidovie's recent investment in 120 electric buses aligns perfectly with this commitment to a greener public transport solution. By integrating electric vehicles with Via's on-demand technology, the partnership aims to create a service that reduces emissions while maintaining convenience for passengers. The focus on real-time responsiveness to passenger needs allows for a tailored travel experience, which is particularly appealing to urban dwellers who prioritize flexibility and efficiency in their daily commutes. Furthermore, this model allows for seamless integration with existing bus and train lines, creating a cohesive and interconnected transportation network that benefits all users. The partnership between Via and Autoguidovie not only represents a significant shift in how public transportation can be delivered but also sets a compelling example for other operators looking to adapt to the changing landscape of urban mobility. By prioritizing on-demand services over traditional fixed-route models, this collaboration aims to create a more efficient, user-friendly, and sustainable transport solution. As urban populations continue to grow, the demand for flexible and efficient transportation options will only increase. The emphasis on intermodality—integrating on-demand services with existing public transport networks—positions Via and Autoguidovie to meet diverse travel needs effectively. Moreover, their shared commitment to sustainability is likely to resonate with environmentally conscious consumers, further enhancing the appeal of their service. In a time when public transport operators are under pressure to reduce their carbon footprints, the Via-Autoguidovie partnership stands out as a forward-thinking model that can redefine public transportation in Italy and serve as a benchmark for innovations globally. As this partnership unfolds, it will be interesting to observe how it not only improves mobility in Italy but also influences the broader conversation around sustainable urban transportation.

The aim is not merely to analyze technology from a technical standpoint but to foster a deeper understanding of its role in shaping our lives and society. Through the reflective approach of prAIority, readers can gain insights into the intricate relationship between technology and human behavior. This comprehensive perspective empowers them to make more informed choices regarding their technology usage and to advocate for designs that align with ethical principles and promote positive societal outcomes. By providing a thorough framework for examining technology's impact, it encourages readers to critically assess how their interactions with technology shape their beliefs and behaviors, engaging in a reflective practice that enhances their understanding of the digital landscape.

7.1.7 ENCOURAGING RESPONSIBLE AND INFORMED USE OF TECHNOLOGY

To grasp the societal implications of technology fully, it's crucial to apply critical frameworks that offer deeper insights into how technological advancements impact our lives. Technology, while often celebrated for its innovations and conveniences, also introduces complex challenges that need careful consideration. Issues such as data privacy, online harassment, and misinformation are significant concerns that arise from the widespread use of digital technologies. Data privacy, for instance, involves understanding how personal information is collected, stored, and utilized by various entities, and it raises questions about the security and ownership of sensitive data. The risk of data breaches and unauthorized access can compromise individual privacy and lead to misuse of personal information, making it essential to implement robust safeguards and transparent practices to protect users' rights. Online harassment is another critical issue that has become increasingly prevalent with the growth of social media and digital communication platforms. The anonymity and reach afforded by the internet can embolden individuals to engage in harmful behaviors, such as bullying, stalking, and trolling. Addressing online harassment requires not only technological solutions, such as improved moderation tools and reporting systems but also a cultural shift toward greater empathy and respect in online interactions. The impact of online harassment can be profound, affecting mental health and well-being, and necessitates a concerted effort from both technology providers and users to create a safer digital environment.[39] Misinformation, the spread of false or misleading information, is a major challenge in today's digital world. The rapid circulation of unverified or deliberately deceptive content can skew public perception, shape opinions, and even disrupt democratic processes. For instance, in North Carolina and other states, after Hurricane Helene in October 2024, conspiracy theories quickly surfaced, falsely claiming that relief meetings were secret plots to bulldoze or sell land for profit, or even mine lithium. Combating misinformation demands improved digital literacy, stronger fact-checking systems, and responsible content-sharing practices, alongside a critical look at the algorithms and platforms that amplify these false narratives.[40] Encouraging more informed and responsible use of technology involves fostering a greater awareness of these issues among users and stakeholders. By understanding the potential risks and ethical considerations associated with technology, individuals can make more conscious choices about how they engage with digital tools and platforms. This includes being mindful of privacy settings, practicing respectful online communication, and critically evaluating the information encountered online. Additionally, educating users about their rights and the implications of their digital footprint can empower them to navigate the digital landscape more safely and ethically. Constructive engagement in discussions about technology's role in society is also vital. This is why journalism educators must tackle this dilemma directly, reaffirming the core principles of the profession—accurate reporting, balanced coverage, and a commitment to rigorous verification. Upholding these foundational skills is key to restoring journalism's credibility, starting with students and extending to the broader community.[41] People have grown accustomed to hearing and spreading misinformation, as seen in the cataloging of President Donald Trump's false or misleading statements. *The Washington Post* tracked 492 suspect claims in just the first 100 days of his presidency. On November 2, 2020, the day before the election, Trump made an astounding 503 false or misleading claims while crisscrossing the country in a last-ditch effort to secure reelection.[42] Therefore conversations should encompass a broad range of perspectives, including those of technologists, ethicists, policymakers, and the general public. Engaging in open, constructive dialogue helps identify emerging challenges, craft balanced solutions, and create policies that address both the opportunities and risks of technology. Inclusive discourse allows us to shape technological progress in a way that reflects societal values and drives positive change.

7.2 INTRODUCTION TO INNOVATION AND ENTREPRENEURSHIP IN THE AGE OF AI

7.2.1 DEFINE INNOVATION AND ENTREPRENEURSHIP

Innovation and entrepreneurship have always been pivotal in driving human progress, shaping the contours of societies, and improving the quality of life.[43] Innovation is the spark that fuels creativity, the act of introducing something new—a method, idea, product, or service—that significantly improves or revolutionizes existing ways of doing things. It is the lifeblood of advancement, enabling us to solve problems more efficiently, push boundaries, and envision futures that were once the realm of science fiction.[44] Entrepreneurship, on the other hand, is the spirit of taking these innovative ideas and turning them into viable, sustainable enterprises.[45] It is the dynamic process of building something from the ground up, often under conditions of uncertainty and risk, driven by passion, creativity, and a relentless pursuit of opportunity. In the age of AI, the interplay between innovation and entrepreneurship is transforming at an unprecedented pace. AI, with its ability to process vast amounts of data, learn from patterns, and make decisions with remarkable accuracy, is redefining what is possible. It is not just a tool but a powerful ally that augments human capabilities, opening up new realms of possibilities. The infusion of AI into the innovation process means that ideas can be tested, refined, and scaled faster than ever before. AI-driven analytics provide deep insights into market needs, customer preferences, and emerging trends, enabling entrepreneurs to make informed decisions and craft solutions that are both timely and relevant.[46] Moreover, AI is democratizing entrepreneurship by lowering the barriers to entry. Cloud computing and AI-as-a-service platforms allow startups to access advanced technologies without significant upfront investment. Entrepreneurs can leverage AI for everything from automating routine tasks to developing sophisticated predictive models, freeing up their time to focus on strategy, creativity, and growth. This technological empowerment means that even small teams can achieve what once required large corporations with substantial resources.[47] The transformative impact of AI on innovation and entrepreneurship is evident across various industries. As we have seen before, in healthcare, AI is driving breakthroughs in personalized medicine, early disease detection, and efficient patient care. In finance, AI algorithms are revolutionizing investment strategies, fraud detection, and customer service. In manufacturing, AI-powered automation and predictive maintenance are enhancing productivity and reducing downtime. These are just a few examples of how AI is enabling entrepreneurs to innovate and create value in ways that were previously unimaginable. However, this new era also brings challenges and ethical considerations. The rapid pace of AI-driven innovation can lead to disruptions in traditional industries, job displacement, and a widening gap between those who can harness AI and those who cannot. Entrepreneurs must navigate these challenges thoughtfully, ensuring that their innovations are inclusive and socially responsible. They need to balance the pursuit of profit with the broader impact on society, addressing issues such as data privacy, algorithmic bias, and the ethical use of AI. As we stand on the brink of this new frontier, the potential for AI to reshape innovation and entrepreneurship is immense. The future will be characterized by a symbiotic relationship between human ingenuity and AI, where the strengths of each are leveraged to create a whole that is greater than the sum of its parts. Entrepreneurs have started cultivating a mindset of continuous learning, adaptability, and ethical responsibility to thrive in this dynamic landscape.[48] The introduction of AI into the domains of innovation and entrepreneurship signifies more than just technological advancement; it heralds a fundamental shift in how we approach problem-solving and value creation. By embracing AI, entrepreneurs are not only enhancing their own capabilities but also contributing to a broader narrative of progress and possibility. The age of AI is not just about smarter machines; it is about augmenting human potential to innovate, create, and build a better future for all. As we continue to explore and harness the power of AI, the boundaries of what we can achieve through innovation and entrepreneurship will continue to expand, ushering in a new era of unprecedented opportunities and transformative impact.[49]

7.2.2   The Significance of AI in Transforming Traditional Approaches

The significance of AI in transforming traditional innovation approaches is profound and multifaceted, reshaping the very foundation of how we conceive, develop, and implement new ideas. Traditionally, innovation relied heavily on human intuition, experience, and a trial-and-error methodology.[50] This process, while effective, was often slow, resource-intensive, and limited by human cognitive biases and data processing capabilities. AI, however, has introduced a paradigm shift, enabling unprecedented speed, efficiency, and scope in innovation. At its core, AI excels in processing vast amounts of data quickly and accurately, identifying patterns and insights that would be impossible for humans to discern unaided. This capability allows innovators to make data-driven decisions, predict market trends, and understand customer needs with a level of precision previously unattainable. Moreover, AI-driven automation of routine tasks frees up human resources, allowing innovators to focus on more complex and creative aspects of their projects. This synergy between human creativity and machine efficiency catalyzes a more dynamic and responsive innovation process. AI's impact on innovation is also evident in its ability to foster interdisciplinary collaboration.[51] By integrating insights from various fields such as biology, engineering, and computer science, AI facilitates the convergence of knowledge, leading to groundbreaking innovations at the intersection of these disciplines. For instance, in healthcare, AI is not only enhancing diagnostic accuracy but also driving the development of personalized medicine, which tailors treatments to individual genetic profiles.[52] This level of precision and personalization marks a significant departure from the one-size-fits-all approach of traditional medicine, highlighting AI's role in advancing human well-being. In the realm of product development, AI-driven design tools are revolutionizing the way products are conceived and manufactured. Generative design, powered by AI, can quickly generate a multitude of design alternatives based on specified parameters, allowing designers to explore a vast array of possibilities and optimize for factors such as material usage, cost, and performance. This approach contrasts sharply with traditional methods, where the iterative design process is often lengthy and constrained by the designer's imagination and experience. AI's ability to simulate and test designs in virtual environments further accelerates the development cycle, reducing time-to-market and enhancing competitiveness. Furthermore, AI is transforming the landscape of research and development (R&D) by automating complex analytical tasks.[53] In fields like materials science, AI algorithms can predict the properties of new compounds, significantly speeding up the discovery of novel materials with desirable characteristics.[54] This capability not only expedites the innovation cycle but also opens up new avenues for exploration that were previously beyond reach due to the limitations of manual experimentation. The transformative power of AI extends to the optimization of business processes and operations, which are crucial for sustaining innovation. AI-driven analytics can optimize supply chain logistics, forecast demand with high accuracy, and enhance customer service through personalized interactions. By improving operational efficiency, AI enables companies to allocate more resources toward innovative endeavors, fostering a culture of continuous improvement and adaptability. Despite these advantages, the integration of AI into traditional innovation approaches is not without challenges. Issues such as data privacy, algorithmic bias, and the ethical implications of AI-driven decisions must be carefully managed to ensure responsible and equitable use of this technology. In the transport industry, the integration of AI into autonomous vehicles (AVs) serves as a prime example of how traditional innovation approaches face significant challenges. While AI has the potential to revolutionize transportation by making it safer and more efficient, it also introduces complex issues.

Data Privacy: Autonomous vehicles rely on vast amounts of data from cameras, sensors, GPS, and other inputs to navigate roads. This data often includes sensitive information about passengers, their routes, and behaviors. Ensuring that this data is securely stored and processed is a significant challenge. There are risks of data breaches, where personal information could be exposed or misused, raising serious privacy concerns.

Algorithmic Bias: AI systems in AVs are trained on large datasets that reflect the environments they will operate in. However, if these datasets are not diverse or representative, the AI could develop biases. For example, an AV might struggle to accurately detect pedestrians with certain skin tones or fail to recognize road signs in less affluent neighborhoods where infrastructure might differ. Such biases can lead to unequal safety outcomes and perpetuate existing societal inequalities.

Ethical Implications: AI-driven decisions in AVs raise ethical questions, particularly in scenarios where the vehicle must choose between two unfavorable outcomes (e.g., in an unavoidable accident). How should an AV be programmed to prioritize the safety of its passengers versus pedestrians? Who is responsible if the AI makes a decision that results in harm? These ethical dilemmas are difficult to navigate and require careful consideration to ensure that AI systems in transportation are used responsibly and equitably.

Moreover, the rapid pace of AI advancement necessitates a commitment to lifelong learning and adaptability, as professionals across all sectors must continually update their skills to harness the full potential of AI. The significance of AI in transforming traditional innovation approaches is undeniable. By augmenting human capabilities with powerful computational tools, AI is not only enhancing the efficiency and effectiveness of innovation processes but also enabling the discovery of new solutions to complex problems. This transformative impact is driving a new era of innovation, characterized by interdisciplinary collaboration, accelerated development cycles, and a heightened focus on precision and personalization. As we navigate this evolving landscape, the challenge will be to harness the power of AI responsibly, ensuring that its benefits are widely shared and that its use aligns with ethical principles and societal values.

7.2.3   Overview of How AI Can Be a Catalyst for New Business Models and Creative Solutions

The transformative capability of AI has opened new horizons for businesses, enabling them to reimagine traditional models and venture into uncharted territories. One of the most profound impacts of AI is its ability to personalize customer experiences. By leveraging AI algorithms, companies can analyze consumer behavior and preferences in real time, allowing for hyper-targeted marketing campaigns and personalized product recommendations. This not only enhances customer satisfaction but also drives higher engagement and conversion rates. For instance, real estate companies are increasingly using AI to provide personalized property recommendations to potential buyers and renters. Similar to how streaming services like Netflix and Spotify curate content based on user preferences, real estate platforms can analyze a user's search history, preferences, budget, and even lifestyle choices to suggest properties that closely match their needs. For instance, if a user frequently searches for homes with a certain number of bedrooms, in a particular neighborhood, or within a specific price range, AI algorithms can learn these preferences and proactively suggest properties that align with them. This personalized approach saves users time and effort, as they are presented with options that are more likely to meet their criteria, rather than having to sift through hundreds of irrelevant listings. Moreover, AI can analyze broader market trends and other users' behavior to make more informed recommendations. For example, if a user has shown interest in a neighborhood that is currently seeing high demand and rising prices, the AI might suggest similar but less expensive areas nearby that are likely to appreciate in value. This not only enhances customer satisfaction by providing valuable insights but also drives higher engagement and conversion rates, as users are more likely to find properties they are genuinely interested in. In this context, the triple Helix systems[55] represent a sophisticated framework for understanding the interactions between universities, industries, and governments, forming what is known as an "innovation system". This concept, rooted in systems theory, involves various components, relationships, and functions that collectively drive innovation and knowledge dissemination. The components of triple helix systems include both R&D and non-R&D innovators, institutions dedicated to single spheres (single-sphere) as well as those operating across multiple spheres (multi-sphere or hybrid), and individual as well as institutional innovators. The relationships within these systems are categorized into five main types: technology transfer, collaboration and conflict moderation, collaborative leadership, substitution, and networking. These relationships facilitate the flow of knowledge and resources among the components, helping to ensure that innovations are effectively developed and disseminated. The primary function of Triple Helix systems is to generate, spread, and utilize knowledge and innovation. This process occurs through activities in three critical areas: knowledge space, innovation space, and consensus space. This perspective provides a comprehensive framework for understanding how universities, industries, and governments interact. It offers insights into how knowledge and resources circulate and highlights any existing blockages or gaps. By examining these interactions, Triple Helix systems can reveal new combinations of knowledge and resources, which can significantly enhance both innovation theory and practice, particularly at the regional level. Thus, the Triple Helix model not only elucidates the dynamics of innovation but also helps in identifying opportunities for improvement and growth in the innovation ecosystem.

SILICON VALLEY TRIPLEX HELIX OF INNOVATION[56]

Silicon Valley has been synonymous with innovation for decades, but its ecosystem has evolved significantly over time. Here's a closer look at how different aspects have shaped its growth:

1. **Rise of Accelerator Programs**: The emergence of accelerator programs represents a major innovation in Silicon Valley. Initiated by Y Combinator in 2005, these programs offer startups seed funding, mentorship, and resources in exchange for equity. Accelerators like Techstars and 500 Startups quickly followed, creating a structured pathway for

early-stage startups to scale. They provide not only financial support but also invaluable networking opportunities and strategic guidance, significantly enhancing the likelihood of a startup's success. The rapid rise of these accelerators has created a new layer of support in the Silicon Valley ecosystem, enabling startups to fast-track their development and commercialization processes.

2. **Early Engagement of Corporations with Startups**: Traditionally, corporations would engage with startups at a later stage, but the dynamics have shifted. Companies like Google, Intel, and Cisco have proactively invested in startups and even launched their own incubators and innovation labs. For example, Intel Capital actively invests in early-stage companies that align with its technology focus, providing not only funding but also strategic partnerships. This early engagement helps corporations stay at the cutting edge of technology and innovation while providing startups with essential resources and market access.

3. **Geographical Expansion**: While Silicon Valley has historically been centered in the southern part of the San Francisco Bay Area, its influence now extends into San Francisco itself. This expansion is partly driven by the high cost of real estate in Silicon Valley, prompting tech companies and startups to establish offices in San Francisco. The city's vibrant tech scene, combined with its cultural and business amenities, has become an attractive alternative. This geographical expansion has created a more integrated regional tech ecosystem, fostering greater collaboration between startups and established companies across the Bay Area.

4. **Commitment of Universities with Capital Funds:** Universities have increasingly become key players in the venture capital space. Institutions like Stanford University and the University of California have established their own venture funds to support startups emerging from their research labs. Stanford's StartX accelerator, for instance, not only provides mentorship and resources but also invests directly in startups founded by Stanford students and alumni. This commitment has helped bridge the gap between academic research and commercial innovation, fueling the growth of new ventures and fostering a strong connection between academia and industry.

5. **Rise of Micro-Multinationals:** Due to the fierce competition for talent in Silicon Valley, there has been a notable rise in micro-multinationals—small companies with a global reach. These startups often operate with distributed teams across different countries, leveraging the global talent pool to overcome local talent shortages. By tapping into diverse expertise and markets, these micro-multinationals can innovate and scale rapidly while mitigating the impact of local competition and high labor costs. This trend reflects Silicon Valley's evolving approach to leveraging global resources and addressing the challenges of an increasingly competitive tech environment.

These innovations illustrate the dynamic nature of Silicon Valley's ecosystem, showcasing how it continually adapts to new challenges and opportunities in the tech world.

7.3 THE ROLE OF AI IN DRIVING INNOVATION

7.3.1 EXAMPLES OF AI-DRIVEN INNOVATIONS ACROSS VARIOUS INDUSTRIES

AI-driven innovation, like many technologies before it, fundamentally impacts two key areas: cost reduction and sales growth. For example, automated customer support systems powered by AI can significantly decrease operational costs by handling large volumes of inquiries efficiently, reducing the need for extensive human staffing. On the other hand, AI-driven personalized marketing strategies can enhance sales by tailoring product recommendations to individual customer preferences,

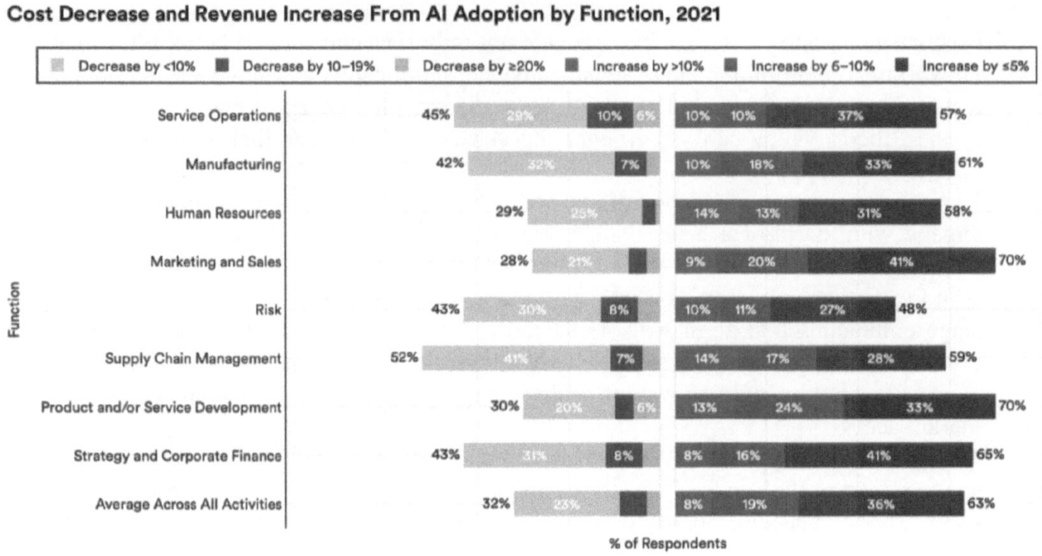

Cost Decrease and Revenue Increase From AI Adoption by Function, 2021

| Decrease by <10% | Decrease by 10–19% | Decrease by ≥20% | Increase by >10% | Increase by 6–10% | Increase by ≤5% |

FIGURE 7.1 Cost decrease or revenue increase for AI. (McKinsey & Company Survey 2022. Chart: 2023 AI Index Report.)

increasing the likelihood of purchase. These dual benefits—lowering expenses and boosting revenue—demonstrate the transformative potential of AI, as illustrated in Figure 7.1.

AI-driven innovation furthermore merges technology with traditional industries, and its application in ethnic clothing design exemplifies this synergy. By leveraging machine learning, the field of fashion is experiencing significant transformations. In the case of Miao women's clothing, AI is used to address specific design needs and cultural preservation.

An AI-driven statistical methodology was employed to tailor clothing patterns to the unique body characteristics of Miao women. This approach utilizes machine learning for pattern recognition, ensuring that designs fit well and reflect individual proportions. Additionally, AI's capability to analyze fabric properties has been harnessed to optimize material selection, striking a balance between aesthetics and comfort. The use of the Multimodal Unsupervised Image-to-Image Translation (MUNIT) algorithm further exemplifies AI's role in this field. MUNIT, an AI tool, generates a variety of trendy designs, enhancing the distinctiveness and appeal of ethnic apparel. This algorithm allows for innovative design variations while preserving traditional elements, showcasing the potential of AI to both respect and modernize cultural heritage.[57] Another example is the integration of AI into hotel gastronomy, reshaping the hospitality industry by enhancing innovation, efficiency, and personalization. This transformative shift explores the dynamic relationship between AI and hotel dining, focusing on key drivers and opportunities. Central to this evolution is the use of chatbots and virtual assistants, which analyze guest data to provide customized recommendations and dining experiences, boosting guest satisfaction and loyalty. Technology is also revolutionizing menu design and culinary creativity in hotel dining. By analyzing data on guest preferences and market trends, AI algorithms refine menu options, pricing strategies, and promotional activities. Additionally, AI-driven recipe generation suggests unique dishes and flavor combinations, enriching the dining experience. Operational efficiency and sustainability are further benefits of AI adoption in hotel gastronomy. AI-powered kitchen automation streamlines food preparation, optimizes inventory management, and reduces waste, leading to cost savings and enhanced efficiency. Furthermore, AI analytics help hotels minimize their environmental impact by optimizing energy use, cutting food waste, and encouraging sustainable sourcing practices. This integration of AI presents hotels with opportunities to stand out, improve operational practices, and deliver exceptional guest experiences.[58] Another example is how AI holds transformative potential for revolutionizing market segmentation practices in emerging economies. As globalization and technological advancements reshape the competitive landscape, traditional segmentation methods often fail to capture the nuances of diverse consumer behaviors and preferences. AI technologies offer new opportunities for businesses to effectively understand and target varied market segments. By employing machine learning algorithms to analyze extensive data sets, AI reveals hidden patterns and segmentations that traditional methods might miss. This innovative approach to market segmentation is particularly valuable in emerging economies, where unique challenges and opportunities arise. AI-driven techniques can adapt to the distinct characteristics of these markets, providing businesses with deeper insights and more precise targeting capabilities.[59] AI holds transformative potential for improving construction management, which is vital for ensuring that projects are completed on time and within budget. Despite technological advancements, cost overruns continue to be a major challenge in the construction industry. AI can address this issue through predictive analytics, risk assessment, resource optimization, and project monitoring. By leveraging these AI-driven methods, construction managers can anticipate potential cost overruns and implement preventive strategies to address them. Furthermore, AI solutions enhance real-time decision-making and improve communication among stakeholders, leading to better project outcomes. A paper by Scott and Bommu illustrates the effectiveness of AI-driven techniques in reducing cost overruns and boosting overall project efficiency through various case studies and industry examples.[60] Also in carbon-neutral businesses (CNB) AI plays a crucial role as both a technological and strategic enabler for achieving CNB through AI-driven business model innovation (AIDBMI). Research shows a strong positive relationship between AIDBMI and the technological and strategic factors essential for carbon neutrality. AI technologies are key in developing and implementing innovative business models that incorporate sustainability practices and address environmental challenges. By adopting AIDBMI, small- and medium-sized enterprises (SMEs) can leverage AI to implement energy-efficient processes, adopt renewable energy solutions, and deploy effective carbon reduction strategies. However, human factors are also critical in this transition. The success of AIDBMI depends significantly on the alignment of sustainability goals with organizational strategies, effective stakeholder collaboration, and active employee engagement. These human-centered elements are vital for leveraging AI technologies to achieve carbon neutrality. Integrating AIDBMI enables organizations to drive sustainable transformations, optimize their operations, and align resource management with sustainable practices. Through this integration, businesses can effectively use AI advancements to support their journey toward carbon neutrality, showcasing the potential of AI to foster both technological innovation and strategic alignment in sustainability efforts.[61]

7.3.2 DISCUSSION ON THE SPEED AND SCALE AT WHICH AI CAN DRIVE INNOVATION

AI has emerged as a powerful force capable of driving innovation at an unprecedented speed and scale. This transformative technology has the potential to revolutionize industries, enhance productivity, and create new opportunities that were previously unimaginable. One of the most striking aspects of AI-driven innovation is the sheer velocity at which advancements can be made. Unlike traditional technological progress, which often occurs incrementally, AI has the ability to leapfrog existing methods and generate rapid breakthroughs. This acceleration is fueled by the continuous improvements in machine learning algorithms, the availability of vast amounts of data, and the exponential growth in computational power. At the heart of AI's ability to drive fast-paced innovation is its capacity to learn and adapt. Machine learning, a subset of AI, enables systems to improve their performance over time based on experience.[62] This means that once an AI system is deployed, it doesn't remain static; instead, it continually evolves, becoming more efficient and effective. This dynamic learning process significantly shortens the development cycles for new technologies and applications. For instance, in the pharmaceutical industry, AI algorithms can analyze vast datasets of chemical compounds and predict their effectiveness as potential drugs, drastically reducing the time required for drug discovery and development. What once took years can now be accomplished in a matter of months, or even weeks.[63] The scale at which AI can drive innovation is equally remarkable. AI has the ability to process and analyze data on a scale that far surpasses human capabilities. This capability is particularly valuable in fields such as genomics, climate science, and financial modeling, where the volume of data is immense. By sifting through these vast datasets, AI can identify patterns and insights that would be impossible for humans to detect. This not only accelerates the pace of discovery but also opens up new avenues for exploration. For example, in genomics, AI can analyze entire genomes to identify genetic markers for diseases, leading to personalized medicine and more effective treatments tailored to individual patients.[64] Moreover, AI's ability to drive innovation is not limited to scientific R&D. It extends to everyday applications that enhance our quality of life. AI can analyze data from energy grids to optimize the distribution and use of electricity,[65] leading to significant cost savings and environmental benefits. These innovations make cities more livable, efficient, and sustainable. Another area where AI's speed and scale are driving innovation is in the workplace. AI-powered tools and platforms are transforming how businesses operate, enhancing productivity, and creating new business models. For instance, AI-driven analytics can provide real-time insights into market trends and customer behavior, enabling businesses to make data-driven decisions with greater speed and accuracy. This agility is crucial in today's fast-paced market environment, where staying ahead of the competition often hinges on the ability to quickly adapt to changing conditions. Furthermore, AI can automate routine tasks, freeing up employees to focus on more strategic and creative work.[66] This not only boosts productivity but also enhances job satisfaction and fosters a culture of innovation within organizations. The healthcare sector is another domain where AI's speed and scale are making a profound impact. AI-powered diagnostic tools can analyze medical images with remarkable accuracy, often surpassing human experts. This capability is revolutionizing fields such as radiology and pathology, where quick and accurate diagnosis is critical. For example, AI algorithms can detect early signs of diseases such as cancer in medical scans, allowing for earlier intervention and better patient outcomes. Additionally, AI can predict patient outcomes based on historical data, helping healthcare providers to tailor treatment plans to individual patients. These advancements are improving the quality of care, reducing costs, and saving lives. Education is also benefiting from AI-driven innovation. Adaptive learning platforms, as Coursera and edX, are personalizing education for students around the world. But if integrated in a school with real teachers, these platforms can analyze individual learning patterns and suggest to the teachers how to adjust the content and pace of instruction to suit each student's needs. This personalized approach enhances learning outcomes and makes education more accessible. For example, students who struggle with traditional teaching methods can benefit from AI-powered tutors that provide targeted support and practice to human tutors. Similarly, educators can use AI-driven analytics to identify areas where students are struggling and intervene early to provide additional support. Consider the impact of AI in the realm of smart cities. By integrating AI into urban infrastructure, cities can optimize traffic flow, reduce energy consumption, and improve public safety. AI-powered sensors and cameras can monitor traffic patterns in real time, adjusting traffic signals to minimize congestion and reduce emissions.

SMART CITIES EXAMPLES

Boston's "Street Bump" app is a compelling example of how smart city technology can transform urban life by harnessing the power of citizen engagement and data-driven insights. Launched as a part of Boston's broader initiative to become a "smart city", Street Bump uses smartphone sensors to detect potholes and other road surface irregularities as drivers move around the city. The app automatically records these bumps, analyzes the data, and sends it to the city's public works department, enabling a more proactive approach to road maintenance. Instead of relying on residents to report problems, Boston can now identify and fix issues faster, improving road safety and reducing wear and tear on vehicles. This innovative approach not only makes the city's infrastructure management more efficient but also engages citizens in the upkeep of their city, fostering a sense of community involvement. Globally, other cities have also embraced smart city technologies to address their unique challenges. For instance, in Barcelona, the implementation of a smart irrigation system has revolutionized how the city manages its water resources. Barcelona's system uses sensors placed in parks and gardens to monitor soil moisture levels, weather conditions, and other environmental factors. The data collected is then analyzed to determine the optimal amount of water needed, significantly reducing water waste and lowering costs. This initiative is part of Barcelona's broader smart city strategy, which also includes smart lighting, waste management, and traffic systems. The smart irrigation system not only conserves water—a critical resource in a Mediterranean climate—but also enhances the city's green spaces, making Barcelona a more sustainable and livable city.[67] Another striking example comes from Singapore, a city-state that has fully embraced the concept of a "smart nation". Singapore's Smart Nation initiative includes a wide range of applications, from smart traffic management to digital healthcare solutions. One of the most notable projects is its Smart Elderly Monitoring and Alert System (SEMAS), which is designed to assist the city's aging population. SEMAS uses sensors installed in the homes of elderly residents to monitor their daily activities. If the system detects anything unusual—such as a lack of movement for an extended period—it automatically alerts caregivers or emergency services.[68] This system provides peace of mind for both the elderly and their families, ensuring that help is available when needed. It also exemplifies how smart city technologies can be used to address social challenges, such as caring for an aging population, by providing innovative and effective solutions.

In Copenhagen, the city's approach to be carbon-neutral in 2025 has led to the development of smart city solutions that address environmental sustainability. Copenhagen's smart bike-sharing program is a prime example. The city has equipped its fleet of public bikes with GPS and other sensors that collect data on air pollution, traffic conditions, and road quality. This data is then used to optimize bike routes, improve traffic flow, and reduce emissions. The program also encourages residents and visitors to choose biking over driving, contributing to the city's environmental goals. Moreover, the real-time data collected from these bikes is shared with the public through a mobile app, empowering citizens to make informed decisions about their transportation choices. This initiative highlights how smart city technologies can promote sustainable living while enhancing the quality of life for residents.

The examples from Boston, Barcelona, Singapore, and Copenhagen showcase the game-changing power of smart city technologies. By harnessing data and actively involving citizens, these cities are addressing urban challenges while crafting more sustainable, livable, and interconnected communities. As more cities worldwide embrace these innovations, the dream of smart cities that genuinely serve their residents edges closer to reality. However, it's crucial to remember that this transformation isn't solely about technology—it's about people and the environment too. For instance, Barcelona's advanced smart irrigation system, once a beacon of efficient water use, faced a harsh reality during the severe drought of 2024. The drought was so extreme that it led to the complete halt of irrigation—smart or otherwise—highlighting that no amount of technology can override the fundamental need for natural resources. Similarly, Boston's "Street Bump" app is a localized success, yet its impact remains limited to the city, showing that scaling such innovations globally is a challenge. In Italy, bike-sharing programs in many cities are still far from "smart"; in fact, in some places, they don't even exist, reflecting the uneven adoption of smart city technologies across different regions. These examples underscore the fact that the success of AI and smart systems hinges not just on technological advancement but on how these technologies are prioritized and integrated into human life. The choices cities make about where and how to deploy AI are deeply intertwined with human needs, local cultures, and environmental realities. In the end, building a smart city is as much about understanding and serving its people as it is about deploying cutting-edge technology. Despite the tremendous potential of AI to drive innovation at speed and scale, it is important to consider the ethical and societal implications. As AI systems become more integrated into our lives, issues such as privacy, security, and fairness must be addressed. Ensuring that AI is developed and deployed responsibly is crucial to maximizing its benefits while minimizing potential risks. This requires collaboration between policymakers, industry leaders, and researchers to establish frameworks and guidelines that promote ethical AI practices. In conclusion, the speed and scale at which AI can drive innovation are truly transformative. From accelerating scientific discoveries and optimizing urban infrastructure to enhancing business productivity and personalizing education, AI is reshaping our world in profound ways. Its ability to learn and adapt, process vast amounts of data, and automate complex tasks enables rapid advancements across a wide range of fields. However, as we embrace the potential of AI, it is essential to navigate the ethical and societal challenges that accompany this technology. By doing so, we can ensure that AI-driven innovation leads to a future that is not only technologically advanced but also equitable and sustainable.

7.3.3 Balancing Innovation with Responsible AI Usage

Balancing innovation with responsible AI usage is crucial as we navigate the rapidly evolving landscape of AI. On one hand, AI holds immense potential to transform industries, enhance our daily lives, and solve complex problems. Innovations in AI can drive advancements in healthcare, improve educational outcomes, and streamline business operations. They promise efficiencies that can revolutionize sectors like transportation, finance, and customer service, making processes faster, more accurate, and more personalized. For instance, AI-powered diagnostic tools can identify diseases earlier than traditional methods, and AVs could reduce traffic accidents and emissions. However, this potential comes with significant responsibilities. As AI systems become more integrated into our lives, ensuring that they are developed and used ethically and responsibly becomes paramount. Responsible AI usage requires a careful balance between pushing the boundaries of what technology can achieve and safeguarding against risks and unintended consequences. AI systems can reflect and amplify human biases if not designed with care. The risks associated with AI are significant, as they can lead to unintended consequences. For instance, the perception of AI as truly intelligent could devalue human intelligence, foster over-reliance on AI systems, and overlook the social and emotional dimensions of learning, all crucial for human development.[69] Bain & Company outlines six specific risks of AI. Firstly, AI can create hidden errors due to its opaque, statistically driven models. Secondly, over-reliance on AI may erode critical thinking and skills. Thirdly, AI opens new avenues for hazards, such as algorithm manipulation. Fourthly, AI can institutionalize bias by reflecting historical biases in its training data. Fifthly, AI may reduce empathy, distancing companies from their customers. Lastly, AI could lead to a loss of human control, where decisions are increasingly automated, raising ethical concerns. Effective AI governance, human oversight, and empathy are essential to mitigating these risks.[70] This highlights the need for transparency and fairness in AI systems. Yuval Noah Harari[71] uses a powerful metaphor to explain why developers must prioritize creating algorithms that are not only effective but also equitable, to avoid perpetuating existing inequalities. In both the myths of Phaeton and Goethe's "The Sorcerer's Apprentice", a single human gains immense power, only to be corrupted by hubris and greed. The takeaway is that our flawed psychology often leads us to misuse power. Harari argues that many people mistakenly measure AI progress by "human-level intelligence", much like evaluating planes based on "bird-level flight". AI isn't moving toward human-like intelligence; it's developing a completely different form of intelligence. For example, AlphaGo, an AI developed by DeepMind, revolutionized the game of Go by uncovering strategies that had eluded even the most brilliant players for thousands of years. Yet, even AlphaGo's creators couldn't fully explain its decisions, illustrating the unfathomable nature of AI. This matters, especially as AI is projected to add $15.7 trillion to the global economy by 2030, according to PricewaterhouseCoopers.[72] This is the reason for insisting on rigorous testing and validation of AI systems to detect and correct biases before they impact users. Another aspect of responsible AI usage is data privacy and security. AI systems often rely on vast amounts of personal data to function effectively. While this data can drive innovations and enhance user experiences, it also raises concerns about how this information is collected, stored, and used.[73] It is crucial that AI systems comply with strict data protection standards, giving users control over their data, including clear options to opt out of data collection. Companies like Apple, Adobe, and Under Armour are increasingly prioritizing privacy.[74] However, some experts argue that, particularly in Apple's case, these measures still fall short of what is needed.[75]

Additionally, AI developers must implement robust security measures to safeguard against data breaches and misuse, as these incidents are a major cause of client trust erosion. A single breach can lead to significant operational downtime, hefty fines, and irreparable reputation damage. The risk is real and pressing—data breaches are not a question of if, but when, as discussed in Chapter 6. Companies that fail to secure their AI systems may face devastating consequences, including the loss of valuable customer relationships and financial instability. Therefore, it is essential for developers to prioritize security, integrating advanced encryption, continuous monitoring, and rapid response protocols into their AI systems to minimize vulnerabilities. By doing so, they not only protect sensitive data but also reinforce trust, ensuring the long-term success and resilience of their organizations in an increasingly digital world.[76] Ethical considerations are crucial in balancing innovation with responsible AI usage. AI systems must be designed with an awareness of their potential impact on individuals and society, including the risk of eroding human abilities. As we increasingly rely on AI, there's a concern that we might favor the consistent, tailored responses from an AI like Gatebox virtual companion,[77] over the unpredictable, spontaneous, but authentic nature of human conversation. This shift could diminish our social skills and interpersonal connections.[78] Additionally, the ethical issue of AI's potential to manipulate or deceive is significant, given its ability to generate convincing narratives. We've already seen a preference for automated reservation systems to avoid the discomfort of rejection. To address these challenges, it's essential to take a proactive approach, such as reskilling workers displaced by automation. By promoting a culture of ethical awareness and responsibility, AI developers and users can ensure that AI's benefits are widely shared while minimizing negative impacts. Transparency and accountability are vital in the responsible use of AI, and they are at the heart of new AI-related roles such as trainers, explainers, and sustainers. These roles focus on ensuring that AI systems are understandable, fair, and reliable. Trainers are responsible for guiding AI in learning accurate and ethical patterns. Explainers help make AI decisions clear and accessible to users, providing insight into how decisions are made and allowing users to challenge and correct errors. Sustainers maintain and monitor AI systems to ensure ongoing accountability and ethical alignment. These roles not only build trust by ensuring users can make informed decisions about interacting with AI systems, but also establish clear lines of responsibility, ensuring that issues are swiftly addressed when things go wrong. Engaging a diverse range of stakeholders, including ethicists, policymakers, and community representatives, further enhances the development process and aligns AI innovation with societal values.[79] By incorporating diverse perspectives, we can better anticipate and address the broad range of issues that AI might raise. Collaborative efforts can lead to more inclusive and holistic approaches to AI development and deployment. Regulatory frameworks and guidelines can also support the balance between innovation and responsible AI usage.[80] Governments and organizations are increasingly acknowledging the need for regulations that tackle both the ethical and practical challenges of AI. These regulations aim to set clear standards for fairness, privacy, and accountability, guiding the development and application of AI technologies. They ensure that AI advancements benefit society while minimizing potential risks. As AI technology evolves, the EU and the United States are stepping up with robust regulations to promote fairness and accountability. However, not all nations are keeping pace; some either lack regulations or use them to increase control over their citizens rather than protecting their rights.[81] Addressing biases, protecting data, and fostering transparency are essential for responsible AI use. By involving a broad range of stakeholders and adhering to regulatory standards, we can ensure AI innovations are both beneficial and equitable, advancing progress while upholding core values.

7.3.4 Case Studies of Companies Successfully Leveraging AI for Innovative Products and Services

AI has rapidly become a transformative force across various industries, enabling companies to innovate and offer products and services that were previously unimaginable. Case studies from leading companies illustrate the diverse and impactful ways in which AI is being leveraged to drive success and innovation. Netflix stands as a shining example of how AI can revolutionize an industry. By leveraging AI algorithms, Netflix analyzes vast amounts of user data—viewing habits, preferences, and interactions—to deliver personalized recommendations that keep viewers hooked. This AI-driven recommendation engine accounts for a significant portion of the content consumed on the platform, continuously learning from user behavior to ensure that suggestions remain relevant and engaging, so the customers can "pay to buy themselves".[82] The result? Increased user satisfaction and retention. Beyond recommendations, AI also guides Netflix's content creation and acquisition strategies, predicting which shows and movies will resonate with different audience segments, thereby optimizing its content library and reducing the risk associated with new releases. In stark contrast to Netflix's success, Quibi serves as a cautionary tale of tech and entertainment overreach. Founded by Jeffrey Katzenberg, Quibi was envisioned as a mobile platform offering "quick bites" of video content, featuring A-list stars. Despite an ambitious start, Quibi's fate echoed that of Pop. com, another Katzenberg venture from two decades earlier, which also aimed to revolutionize digital entertainment but flopped spectacularly. Quibi launched in April 2020 with $1.8 billion in backing, star-studded content, and high-profile leadership, including former Disney honcho Meg Whitman as CEO. However, despite a blitz of publicity and big promises, Quibi failed to capture the audience's interest. Initial excitement quickly waned, and the app, once the fourth-most popular in the United States, plummeted in the rankings, eventually shutting down just six months later.[83] The downfall of Quibi, much like Pop.com before it, highlights the risks of chasing bold, untested ideas without fully understanding the market's needs or the challenges of new technology. Tesla is a prime example of how AI can revolutionize an industry, leading the charge in autonomous driving technology. By integrating AI into its vehicles, Tesla collects and processes data from a network of sensors, cameras, and radar, enabling its cars to navigate complex driving environments. This data feeds into a continuous learning loop, where the AI is constantly improving its ability to recognize and respond to various road conditions and obstacles. This relentless refinement is at the heart of Tesla's success with its Autopilot and Full Self-Driving (FSD) features, enhancing both the driving experience and vehicle safety. Tesla's AI doesn't stop at the road; it also powers its manufacturing processes. Predictive analytics and machine learning optimize production, reduce downtime, and boost overall efficiency, positioning Tesla as a leader in the automotive industry's future. On the other hand, Apple's venture into AVs hasn't been as smooth. Despite reportedly investing billions into developing a fully autonomous car without a steering wheel or pedals, Apple's project remains far from fruition. Rising costs have also led other industry giants like Ford and General Motors to scale back their AV research. Apple has reportedly shifted many of its 2,000-strong electric car team to other AI projects, and in January 2024, the company laid off 121 workers from its San Diego office. These setbacks highlight the challenges even the biggest players face in the race to bring autonomous driving to the mainstream.[84]

THE GROWTH AND FAILURE OF IBM WATSON IN HEALTHCARE

IBM's Watson was a pioneering, yet ultimately unsuccessful, attempt to bring AI into the heart of healthcare. Touted as a game-changer for medical diagnostics and treatment, Watson leveraged natural language processing and machine learning to sift through vast troves of medical literature, patient records, and clinical trial data. The goal? To help doctors diagnose diseases and tailor personalized treatment plans. In oncology, for example, Watson for Oncology aimed to provide clinicians with evidence-based cancer treatment options based on the latest research and individual patient data. However, despite the ambitious vision, Watson failed to deliver. It neither improved diagnostic accuracy nor sped up decision-making. Instead, it became a costly misadventure. By 2017, after four years and $62 million, MD Anderson Cancer Center allowed its contract with IBM to expire, having never used Watson on real patients. The AI struggled to tap into patient data, interpret doctors' notes, and make sense of patient histories, ultimately leaving its promise unfulfilled.[85]

A standout example in the retail sector is Zara, a global fashion brand that has harnessed AI to redefine fast fashion. Zara's use of AI extends far beyond the typical e-commerce strategies; it's deeply embedded in their entire business model. The brand employs AI algorithms to analyze real-time data from social media, customer feedback, and sales trends, enabling it to quickly identify emerging fashion trends and customer preferences. This data-driven approach allows Zara to design, produce, and stock new items in a matter of weeks, keeping their collections fresh and on-trend. Moreover, Zara's AI-driven inventory management system is a game-changer. By predicting demand with remarkable accuracy, Zara minimizes overstock and understock situations, reducing waste and maximizing sales.[86] The AI also optimizes pricing strategies by adjusting prices dynamically based on demand and inventory levels, ensuring that Zara stays competitive while protecting its profit margins. In stores, Zara uses AI to enhance the shopping experience. For instance, they've implemented an AR campaign, featuring AR displays in 120 stores worldwide, offering an experience that is a unique departure from the typical use of augmented reality in retail.[87] This seamless integration of AI into design, production, and customer experience has enabled Zara to stay ahead in the fast-paced world of fashion retail, proving that innovation isn't just about technology—it's about transforming the entire business model to meet the evolving demands of consumers. In the financial services sector, JP Morgan Chase has effectively harnessed AI to transform its operations and customer service. The bank's AI-powered virtual assistant, COIN (Contract Intelligence), automates the review and interpretation of legal documents, dramatically cutting down the time required for these tasks and reducing errors. This allows legal and compliance teams to focus on more strategic, complex activities. Additionally, JP Morgan employs AI to detect fraudulent transactions by using machine learning algorithms to identify unusual patterns and flag potential fraud in real time, enhancing security and protecting customers from financial losses. The bank also leverages AI-driven predictive analytics to offer personalized financial advice and products, boosting customer satisfaction and loyalty. Similarly, platforms like Mint and Cleo have emerged as AI-driven financial tools, with Mint offering personal finance management and Cleo providing budgeting and financial planning advice based on users' spending habits. ZestFinance uses AI to analyze a wide range of data points for more comprehensive risk assessments, helping to make fairer credit decisions and reduce loan defaults. AI in risk management also plays a crucial role, with tools like the patented Risk Priority Number system helping financial advisors match investments with clients' risk tolerance and long-term goals. Mastercard's Decision Intelligence technology further exemplifies AI's impact by assessing transaction data in real time to detect fraud, ensuring high accuracy in fraud prevention and protecting consumers from financial threats.[88] In the realm of customer service, AI-powered chatbots and virtual assistants have become invaluable tools for companies across various industries. One standout example is the telecommunications company Vodafone, which implemented an AI chatbot named TOBi. TOBi assists customers with a wide range of queries, from billing issues to technical support, providing instant responses and freeing up human agents to handle more complex inquiries. The chatbot uses natural language processing to understand and respond to customer queries accurately, continuously learning from interactions to improve its performance. This AI-driven approach has significantly enhanced Vodafone's customer service, reducing wait times and improving overall customer satisfaction.[89] The automotive industry has also seen remarkable AI-driven innovations beyond Tesla. BMW, for example, has incorporated AI into its manufacturing processes through its smart factory initiative.[90] AI algorithms analyze data from production lines to predict and prevent equipment failures, ensuring smooth and efficient operations. This predictive maintenance approach minimizes downtime and reduces maintenance costs. Additionally, BMW uses AI in its vehicles' infotainment systems, offering features like voice recognition and personalized driving experiences. These AI-driven advancements enhance the quality and appeal of BMW's products, reinforcing the brand's reputation for cutting-edge technology. In the realm of logistics and transportation, UPS has successfully integrated AI to optimize its delivery network. The company's ORION (On-Road Integrated Optimization and Navigation) system uses AI algorithms to determine the most efficient delivery routes for its drivers. ORION considers factors such as traffic conditions, weather, and package priorities to minimize driving time and fuel consumption. This AI-driven approach has resulted in significant cost savings and environmental benefits for UPS, while also improving delivery speed and reliability. The success of ORION highlights how AI can transform traditional industries by introducing innovative solutions to long-standing challenges.[91] Lastly, in the realm of education, AI is transforming how students learn and how educators teach. Platforms like Coursera and edX use AI to personalize the learning experience for students.[92] By analyzing data on students' progress, learning styles, and performance, these platforms offer tailored course recommendations and adaptive learning paths. AI-powered tools also provide instant feedback on assignments and assessments, helping students understand their mistakes and improve. For educators, AI offers insights into student performance trends, enabling them to identify areas where students may need additional support and adjust their teaching methods accordingly. This AI-driven personalization in education fosters a more engaging and effective learning environment. These case studies illustrate the transformative power of AI across diverse industries. Companies like Netflix, Tesla, IBM, Amazon, JP Morgan Chase, Vodafone, BMW, UPS, and educational platforms have successfully leveraged AI to innovate and improve their products and services. By harnessing the capabilities of AI, these companies have enhanced customer experiences, optimized operations, and maintained their competitive edge. As AI technology continues to evolve, its potential to drive innovation and create value will only increase, offering exciting possibilities for the future.

7.4   CONCLUSIONS

Aristotle believed that memory is intricately linked to the soul and involves active recollection rather than passive storage. Unlike perception, which relates to immediate sensory experiences, and conception, which involves abstract reasoning, memory connects us to our past. It allows us to recall and reflect on previous experiences, influencing our actions and decisions. Memory requires a sense of time, as it is based on the ability to remember past events rather than the present or future. Only creatures that perceive time can remember, forming a coherent narrative of their experiences. This capacity enables humans to differentiate between useful and non-useful actions, refining behavior through learned experiences. Humans use memory to shape their environment effectively, contributing to the evolution of their cities and communities. This process highlights a reciprocal relationship: "First we shape the cities—then they shape us". While humans only experience a fraction of the world they construct, our perceptions and experiences frame our understanding of reality. Innovations often focus on refining existing methods rather than exploring new possibilities. This tendency emphasizes enhancing current tools rather than expanding our comprehension of the world. Meditation has emerged as a tool for critical reflection on technology's impact. Initially used to alleviate stress or improve well-being, meditation helps individuals assess their technological choices and their broader implications. As technology permeates daily life, understanding its effects requires critical engagement. For instance, AI has become a transformative force across industries, enabling companies to innovate and deliver previously unimaginable products and services. For instance, Netflix uses AI algorithms to analyze user data for personalized recommendations, significantly enhancing viewer engagement and satisfaction. In contrast, Quibi's failure serves as a cautionary tale about overreaching without understanding market needs. Tesla exemplifies AI's impact with its autonomous driving technology, continuously improving through data from sensors. Conversely, Apple has faced setbacks in its AV project, illustrating the challenges even major players encounter. IBM's Watson struggled to deliver on its promise in healthcare, failing to improve diagnostic accuracy despite significant investment. Zara has successfully integrated AI into its fast-fashion model, analyzing real-time data to quickly identify trends and optimize inventory. JP Morgan Chase utilizes AI for tasks like automating legal document review and detecting fraud, enhancing efficiency and customer service. Similarly, Vodafone's AI chatbot, TOBi, has improved customer support by providing instant responses. In manufacturing, BMW employs AI for predictive maintenance, while UPS's ORION system optimizes delivery routes using AI algorithms. Educational platforms like Coursera leverage AI to personalize learning experiences. These examples showcase AI's transformative power across sectors, driving innovation, enhancing customer experiences, and maintaining competitive advantages. As AI technology evolves, its potential for future innovation and value creation will only grow. AI-driven innovations can reduce costs and enhance sales, but balancing innovation with responsible use is crucial to ensure that advancements serve humanity's broader goals while addressing ethical and societal challenges.

NOTES

1 Nietzsche, F. (2014). *Beyond good and evil*. BookRix.
2 Henry Molaison: The amnesiac we'll never forget. www.theguardian.com/science/2013/may/05/henry-molaison-amnesiac-corkin-book-feature
3 Beare, J. I. (2010). On memory and reminiscence Aristotle (ca. 350 BC). *Annals of Neurosciences, 17*(2), 87.
4 Gehl, J. (2013). *Cities for people*. Island Press.
5 Galimberti, U. (2008). *Psiche e techne: l'uomo nell'età della tecnica* (Vol. 12). Feltrinelli Editore.
6 Schopenhauer, A. (2016). *Schopenhauer: Parerga and Paralipomena*. Cambridge University Press.
7 Galimberti. *Psiche e techne*.
8 Cowan, N. (2014). Working memory underpins cognitive development, learning, and education. *Educational Psychology Review, 26*, 197–223.
9 Yong, J. C., Li, N. P., & Kanazawa, S. (2021). Not so much rational but rationalizing: Humans evolved as coherence-seeking, fiction-making animals. *American Psychologist, 76*(5), 781.
10 Morse, D. H. (1980). *Behavioral mechanisms in ecology*. Harvard University Press.
11 Coyne, R. (2010). *The tuning of place: Sociable spaces and pervasive digital media*. MIT Press.
12 Wright, J. K. (1947). Terrae incognitae: The place of the imagination in geography. *Annals of the Association of American Geographers, 37*(1), 1–15.
13 Lowenthal, D. (1961). Geography, experience, and imagination: Towards a geographical epistemology. *Annals of the Association of American Geographers, 51*(3), 241–260.
14 Gazzaniga, M. S. (1998). *The mind's past*. University of California Press.
15 Hogan, J. A. (2015). A framework for the study of behavior. *Behavioural Processes, 117*, 105–113.

16 Sadler-Smith, E. (2010). *The intuitive mind: Profiting from the power of your sixth sense*. John Wiley & Sons.

17 Rosa, H., Dörre, K., & Lessenich, S. (2017). Appropriation, activation and acceleration: The escalatory logics of capitalist modernity and the crises of dynamic stabilization. *Theory, Culture & Society*, *34*(1), 53–73.

18 Ray, P. P. (2023). ChatGPT: A comprehensive review on background, applications, key challenges, bias, ethics, limitations and future scope. *Internet of Things and Cyber-Physical Systems*, *3*, 121–154.

19 Dwivedi, Y. K., Hughes, L., Ismagilova, E., Aarts, G., Coombs, C., Crick, T., ... & Williams, M. D. (2021). Artificial Intelligence (AI): Multidisciplinary perspectives on emerging challenges, opportunities, and agenda for research, practice and policy. *International Journal of Information Management*, *57*, 101994.

20 Katz, Y. (2017). Manufacturing an artificial intelligence revolution. Available at SSRN 3078224.

21 Maslow, A. H. (1943). A theory of human motivation. *Psychological Review*, *50*(4), 370.

22 Pineda, R. G. (2016). Where the Interaction Is Not: Reflections on the Philosophy of Human-Computer Interaction. *International Journal of Art, Culture, Design, and Technology* (IJACDT), *5*(1), 1–12.

23 Hallnäs, L., & Redström, J. (2001). Slow technology–designing for reflection. *Personal and Ubiquitous Computing*, *5*, 201–212.

24 Nietschze, F. W., Colli, G., & Staude, C. (1989). *Frammenti postumi, 1869–1874*. Adelphi.

25 Mlodinow, L. (2012). *Subliminal: The new unconscious and what it teaches us*. Penguin UK.

26 No, tech bosses don't ban their kids from using screens. www.lemonde.fr/en/pixels/article/2024/03/25/no-tech-bosses-don-t-ban-their-kids-from-using-screens_6653457_13.html

27 Black mirror or black hole? American phone screen time statistics. www.harmonyhit.com/phone-screen-time-statistics/?clreqid=a5b99b78-5919-4ddd-a2d7-5cb3c4e66e6d&kbid=58587

28 Pfeffer, J., & Sutton, R. I. (2000). *The knowing-doing gap: How smart companies turn knowledge into action*. Harvard Business Press.

29 I reviewed restaurants for 12 Years. They've changed, and not for the better. www.nytimes.com/2024/08/06/dining/pete-wells-how-restaurants-have-changed.html

30 Wilson, C. (2018). Is it love or loneliness? Exploring the impact of everyday digital technology use on the wellbeing of older adults. *Ageing & Society*, *38*(7), 1307–1331.

31 MacDonald, K. B., & Schermer, J. A. (2021). Loneliness unlocked: Associations with smartphone use and personality. *Acta Psychologica*, *221*, 103454.

32 Kuczynski, A. M., Halvorson, M. A., Slater, L. R., & Kanter, J. W. (2022). The effect of social interaction quantity and quality on depressed mood and loneliness: A daily diary study. *Journal of Social and Personal Relationships*, *39*(3), 734–756.

33 Sedlmeier, P., & Theumer, J. (2020). Why do people begin to meditate and why do they continue? *Mindfulness*, *11*, 1527–1545.

34 Isaacson, W. (2011). *Great innovators: Steve Jobs, Benjamin Franklin, Einstein*. Simon and Schuster.

35 Yuval Noah Harari's history of everyone, ever. www.newyorker.com/magazine/2020/02/17/yuval-noah-harari-gives-the-really-big-picture

36 How to take a Bill Gates think week to recover from life. www.theblogsmith.com/blog/bill-gates-think-week-reading-vacation/

37 Via to launch on-demand services in Italy with Autoguidovie. www.sustainable-bus.com/maas/via-autoguidovie-on-demand-transport-italy/

38 Software and operations for flexible public transit. https://ridewithvia.com

39 Bansal, S., Garg, N., Singh, J., & Van Der Walt, F. (2024). Cyberbullying and mental health: past, present and future. *Frontiers in Psychology*, *14*, 1279234.

40 Another hurdle in recovery from Helene: Misinformation is getting in the way. www.nytimes.com/2024/10/06/us/hurricane-helene-north-carolina-misinformation.html

41 Richardson, N. (2017). Fake news and journalism education. *Asia Pacific Media Educator*, *27*(1), 1–9.

42 Trump's false or misleading claims total 30,573 over 4 years. www.washingtonpost.com/politics/2021/01/24/trumps-false-or-misleading-claims-total-30573-over-four-years/

43 Hart, S. L., & Christensen, C. M. (2002). The great leap: Driving innovation from the base of the pyramid. *MIT Sloan Management Review*, *44*(1), 51.

44 Schroeder, B. (2016). *Simply brilliant: Powerful techniques to unlock your creativity and spark new ideas*. HarperChristian+ ORM.

45 Lowe, R., & Marriott, S. (2012). *Enterprise: Entrepreneurship and innovation*. Routledge.

46 Obschonka, M., & Audretsch, D. B. (2020). Artificial intelligence and big data in entrepreneurship: A new era has begun. *Small Business Economics*, *55*, 529–539.

47 Brynjolfsson, E., & McAfee, A. (2011). *Race against the machine: How the digital revolution is accelerating innovation, driving productivity, and irreversibly transforming employment and the economy*. Brynjolfsson and McAfee.

48 Neck, H. M., Neck, C. P., & Murray, E. L. (2023). *Entrepreneurship: The practice and mindset*. Sage.

49 Lee, J., Suh, T., Roy, D., & Baucus, M. (2019). Emerging technology and business model innovation: the case of artificial intelligence. *Journal of Open Innovation: Technology, Market, and Complexity*, *5*(3), 44.

50 Taura, T., & Nagai, Y. (2017). Creativity in innovation design: The roles of intuition, synthesis, and hypothesis. *International Journal of Design Creativity and Innovation*, *5*(3–4), 131–148.

51 Brem, A., Giones, F., & Werle, M. (2021). The AI digital revolution in innovation: A conceptual framework of artificial intelligence technologies for the management of innovation. *IEEE Transactions on Engineering Management*, *70*(2), 770–776.

52 Xu, J., Yang, P., Xue, S., Sharma, B., Sanchez-Martin, M., Wang, F., ... & Parikh, B. (2019). Translating cancer genomics into precision medicine with artificial intelligence: Applications, challenges and future perspectives. *Human Genetics*, *138*(2), 109–124.

53 Johnson, P. C., Laurell, C., Ots, M., & Sandström, C. (2022). Digital innovation and the effects of artificial intelligence on firms' research and development–Automation or augmentation, exploration or exploitation? *Technological Forecasting and Social Change*, *179*, 121636.

54 Sha, W., Guo, Y., Yuan, Q., Tang, S., Zhang, X., Lu, S., ... & Cheng, S. (2020). Artificial intelligence to power the future of materials science and engineering. *Advanced Intelligent Systems*, *2*(4), 1900143.

55 Ranga, M., & Etzkowitz, H. (2015). Triple helix systems: An analytical framework for innovation policy and practice in the knowledge society. *Entrepreneurship and Knowledge Exchange*, 117–158.

56 Pique, J. M., Berbegal-Mirabent, J., & Etzkowitz, H. (2018). Triple helix and the evolution of ecosystems of innovation: The case of Silicon Valley. *Triple Helix*, *5*(1), 1–21.

57 Deng, M., Liu, Y., & Chen, L. (2023). AI-driven innovation in ethnic clothing design: An intersection of machine learning and cultural heritage. *Electronic Research Archive*, *31*(9), 5793–5814.

58 Milton, T. (2024). Artificial intelligence transforming hotel gastronomy: An in-depth review of AI-driven innovations in menu design, food preparation, and customer interaction, with a focus on sustainability and future trends in the hospitality industry. *International Journal for Multidimensional Research Perspectives*, *2*(3), 47–61.

59 Chandratreya, A. (2024). Revolutionizing market segmentation in emerging economies: AI-driven innovations and strategies. In *AI innovations in service and tourism marketing* (pp. 129–161), Singh, A., Tyagi, P. K., Nadda, V., & Singh, V. (eds). IGI Global.

60 Scott, E., & Bommu, R. (2024). Efficient construction management: AI-driven strategies to combat cost overruns. *International Journal of Advanced Engineering Technologies and Innovations*, *1*(3), 222–240.

61 Shaik, A. S., Alshibani, S. M., Jain, G., Gupta, B., & Mehrotra, A. (2024). Artificial intelligence (AI)-driven strategic business model innovations in small- and medium-sized enterprises. Insights on technological and strategic enablers for carbon neutral businesses. *Business Strategy and the Environment*, *33*(4), 2731–2751.

62 Jordan, M. I., & Mitchell, T. M. (2015). Machine learning: Trends, perspectives, and prospects. *Science*, *349*(6245), 255–260.

63 Gupta, R., Srivastava, D., Sahu, M., Tiwari, S., Ambasta, R. K., & Kumar, P. (2021). Artificial intelligence to deep learning: Machine intelligence approach for drug discovery. *Molecular diversity*, *25*, 1315–1360.

64 Quazi, S. (2022). Artificial intelligence and machine learning in precision and genomic medicine. *Medical Oncology*, *39*(8), 120.

65 Ali, S. S., & Choi, B. J. (2020). State-of-the-art artificial intelligence techniques for distributed smart grids: A review. *Electronics*, *9*(6), 1030.

66 Davenport, T. H. (2018). *The AI advantage: How to put the artificial intelligence revolution to work*. MIT Press.

67 Barcelona's smart city ecosystem. www.technologyreview.com/2014/11/18/12190/barcelonas-smart-city-ecosystem/

68 HDB smart enabled home. www.hdb.gov.sg/about-us/our-role/smart-and-sustainable-living/smart-hdb-town-page/hdb-smart-home-exhibition

69 The unintended consequences of artificial intelligence and education. www.ei-ie.org/en/item/28115:the-unintended-consequences-of-artificial-intelligence-and-education

70 Tackling AI's unintended consequences. www.bain.com/insights/tackling-ais-unintended-consequences/

71 'Never summon a power you can't control': Yuval Noah Harari on how AI could threaten democracy and divide the world. www.theguardian.com/technology/article/2024/aug/24/yuval-noah-harari-ai-book-extract-nexus

72 PwC's Global Artificial Intelligence Study: Exploiting the AI Revolution www.pwc.com/gx/en/issues/data-and-analytics/publications/artificial-intelligence-study.html

73 Americans and privacy: Concerned, confused and feeling lack of control over their personal information. www.pewresearch.org/internet/2019/11/15/americans-and-privacy-concerned-confused-and-feeling-lack-of-control-over-their-personal-information/

74 Data privacy: What brands are taking it seriously? https://trustarc.com/resource/data-privacy-most-trusted-brands/

75 Apple says it prioritizes privacy. Experts say gaps remain. www.theguardian.com/technology/2022/sep/23/apple-user-data-law-enforcement-falling-short

76 What is a "personal data breach". www.edpb.europa.eu/sme-data-protection-guide/data-breaches_en

77 How AI companions are redefining human relationships in the digital age. www.forbes.com/sites/neilsahota/2024/07/18/how-ai-companions-are-redefining-human-relationships-in-the-digital-age/

78 AI—The good, the bad, and the scary. https://eng.vt.edu/magazine/stories/fall-2023/ai.html

79 The jobs that artificial intelligence will create. https://sloanreview.mit.edu/article/will-ai-create-as-many-jobs-as-it-eliminates/

80 Regona, M., Yigitcanlar, T., Hon, C., & Teo, M. (2024). Artificial intelligence and sustainable development goals: Systematic literature review of the construction industry. *Sustainable Cities and Society*, 105499.

81 You are now remotely controlled. www.nytimes.com/2020/01/24/opinion/sunday/surveillance-capitalism.html

82 Rodríguez Ortega, V. (2023). 'We pay to buy ourselves': Netflix, spectators & streaming. *Journal of Communication Inquiry*, 47(2), 126–144.

83 Quibi before Quibi: The inside story of Jeffrey Katzenberg's first dot-com failure. www.fastcompany.com/90516005/the-quibi-before-quibi-the-inside-story-of-jeffrey-katzenbergs-first-dot-com-failure

84 Apple cuts jobs after dropping self-driving car plans. www.bbc.com/news/articles/c98rz9nq9rvo

85 IBM Watson: From healthcare canary to a failed prodigy. A case study in the "AI age" for business schools for decades. https://healtharkinsights.com/wp-content/uploads/2023/11/IBM-Watson-From-healthcare-canary-to-a-failed-prodigy_1.pdf

86 Shi, M., Chussid, C., Yang, P., Jia, M., Dyk Lewis, V., & Cao, W. (2021). The exploration of artificial intelligence application in fashion trend forecasting. *Textile Research Journal*, 91(19–20), 2357–2386.

87 Zara's augmented reality app brings virtual models to life in Stores. https://futurestores.wbresearch.com/blog/zara-augmented-reality-app-virtual-model-strategy

88 AI in fintech: The role of artificial intelligence in transforming the finance industry. https://devot.team/blog/ai-in-fintech

89 Vodafone ploughs £140m into new SuperTOBi chatbot rollout. www.techmonitor.ai/digital-economy/ai-and-automation/vodafone-ploughs-140m-into-new-supertobi-chatbot-rollout

90 Sahoo, S., & Lo, C. Y. (2022). Smart manufacturing powered by recent technological advancements: A review. *Journal of Manufacturing Systems*, 64, 236–250.

91 Holland, C., Levis, J., Nuggehalli, R., Santilli, B., & Winters, J. (2017). UPS optimizes delivery routes. *Interfaces*, 47(1), 8–23.

92 Ahn, M. L., Yoon, H., & Cha, H. (2015). Cultural sensitivity and design implications of MOOCs from Korean learners' perspectives: Case studies on edX and Coursera. *Educational Technology International*, 16(2), 201–229.

8 prAIority for Entrepreneurship

For, whoever is able to force nature to reveal her secrets must himself be outside of nature.[1]

Friedrick Nietzsche

8.1 AI AS A TOOL FOR ENHANCING ENTREPRENEURIAL PROCESSES

8.1.1 INTRODUCTION TO AI ENTREPRENEURSHIP

In the electrifying world of artificial intelligence (AI) entrepreneurship, the buzz often centers around algorithms and data, but at the heart of every successful AI startup lies an unmistakable human factor: vision, resilience, and adaptability. Imagine the rousing success story of UiPath. Founded by Daniel Dines and Marius Tirca, UiPath began as a small Romanian startup with a single mission: to democratize robotic process automation (RPA). Dines, with his deep understanding of both the technical and human aspects of automation, built a company that resonates with the needs of businesses looking to streamline their operations. UiPath's remarkable growth, marked by a successful IPO and a global presence, underscores how a keen human insight can propel an AI startup to new heights.[2] Or the groundbreaking success of OpenAI, where the seamless blend of technical prowess and human ingenuity sparked a revolution in AI. Founded with a mission to ensure that AI benefits all of humanity, OpenAI's journey showcases how a clear vision and ethical grounding can drive monumental achievements. Contrast this with the cautionary tale of Theranos, where the promise of transformative technology faltered due to a lack of transparency and overconfidence. The contrast between these two narratives highlights a crucial lesson for aspiring AI entrepreneurs: adhering to the fundamental principles of integrity and ethical leadership is essential, even in a field driven by sophisticated technology. As Nietzsche suggested, "whoever is able to force nature to reveal her secrets must himself be outside of nature". This highlights that while advanced algorithms and cutting-edge tech are critical, it is the human qualities of integrity, adaptability, and visionary leadership that ultimately determine sustainable success. In the ever-evolving world of AI, it's not only the machines that need to be precise; the individuals behind them must navigate ethical challenges, lead with empathy, and adapt swiftly. As we push toward the next breakthrough, it's clear that the human touch remains indispensable in turning AI aspirations into real-world achievements.

8.1.2 WHAT CAN BE AUTOMATED WITH AI TO STREAMLINE BUSINESS OPERATIONS AND DECISION-MAKING

AI has revolutionized the way businesses operate and make decisions, offering unprecedented efficiencies and insights. In today's competitive landscape, companies are constantly seeking

DOI: 10.1201/9781003533160-8

ways to streamline operations and enhance decision-making processes. AI, with its ability to analyze vast amounts of data quickly and accurately, has become an indispensable tool in achieving these goals. At the heart of AI's impact on business operations is automation. Routine and repetitive tasks that once consumed significant time and resources can now be handled by AI systems. AI-powered chatbots are revolutionizing customer service by handling routine inquiries, allowing human agents to focus on more complex issues. This shift not only speeds up response times but also boosts customer satisfaction with quick, accurate information. However, chatbots present significant challenges. They can generate content that sounds convincing but is actually false, a phenomenon known as "hallucination". When users rely on this misleading information, it turns into what researchers have dubbed "botshit". To address this, experts have identified four chatbot operation modes—authenticated, autonomous, automated, and augmented—each carrying its own "botshit" risk: ignorance, miscalibration, routinization, and black boxing.[3] In manufacturing, AI-driven robots are revolutionizing production lines by working tirelessly around the clock, executing tasks with unparalleled precision and consistency. These robots are not just limited to repetitive actions; through machine learning (ML), they can adapt to new, simple tasks, minimizing the need for extensive reprogramming. This flexibility allows manufacturers to swiftly respond to shifting market demands, enhancing overall productivity. However, this adaptability has its limits. While AI-driven robots excel at handling routine tasks, reprogramming them for more complex or nuanced jobs remains challenging. Intricate tasks that require creativity, critical thinking, or a human touch are beyond the current capabilities of AI. As a result, the most critical, non-repetitive jobs in manufacturing still rely on human expertise. This limitation highlights the ongoing need for skilled workers who can oversee, manage, and perform the sophisticated tasks that robots cannot, ensuring a balanced integration of AI in the production process. Furthermore, the reliance on AI-driven robots can lead to a reduction in human jobs, displacing workers who lack the skills to transition into more advanced roles. Additionally, the growing complexity of AI systems introduces challenges in maintaining oversight, potentially leading to unforeseen errors or inefficiencies. The balance between embracing innovation and ensuring ethical, sustainable employment practices is essential as AI continues to shape the future of manufacturing. Supply chain management is another area where AI is making significant strides. By automating tasks and optimizing processes, businesses can reduce labor costs and minimize errors. AI-driven financial systems, for example, can handle accounting and auditing tasks with high accuracy, reducing the risk of financial discrepancies and fraud. However, a critical point to consider is the potential for job displacement. As AI takes over more tasks, particularly in sectors like finance and manufacturing, there is a risk of significant job losses. Automating routine accounting tasks could significantly reduce the demand for junior accountants, potentially leading to widespread layoffs. This brings us to a crucial question: who should bear the responsibility for preparing the workforce for an AI-driven future? Should organizations take the lead by adopting a balanced approach to automation, investing in reskilling and upskilling their employees to transition into new roles created by AI? Or should the government step in, starting with a revamped education system that prepares future generations for an AI-dominated world, followed by large-scale reskilling programs to help current workers adapt? On one hand, companies could view reskilling as an investment in their future, ensuring a workforce that's agile, adaptable, and capable of taking on more complex tasks that AI can't handle. On the other hand, the scale of change required may demand a broader, systemic approach. Governments can introduce educational reforms that emphasize digital literacy and critical thinking from an early age, laying the groundwork for a workforce that's ready for the challenges and opportunities of automation. Later on, comprehensive government-led reskilling initiatives could bridge the gap for those whose jobs have been disrupted, ensuring that no one is left behind in the AI revolution.

8.1.3 Tools and Platforms that Entrepreneurs Can Use to Integrate AI into Their Startups

Integrating AI into startups has shifted from being a futuristic concept to a practical necessity in today's rapidly evolving business landscape. For entrepreneurs, leveraging AI can dramatically enhance business operations, improve customer engagement, and unlock new avenues for growth. The key to successfully incorporating AI lies in utilizing a variety of conceptual tools and platforms designed to seamlessly integrate AI into products and services. These tools range from AI development platforms, ML frameworks, data analytics tools, to cloud services—each offering unique capabilities to address specific business needs.

8.1.3.1 Cloud-Based AI Platforms

One of the key steps for startups integrating AI is utilizing cloud-based AI platforms. For example, Amazon Web Services (AWS) provides platforms like Amazon SageMaker, which offers a suite of tools for building, training, and deploying ML models at scale. These platforms not only simplify technological needs, but also offer comprehensive services that streamline AI model development, training, and deployment. While the immediate return on AI investment is crucial, startups often face the pressing human factor need to rapidly upskill their employees in AI, making these platforms especially valuable. The accessibility and scalability of these platforms allow startups to quickly prototype and launch AI-driven features, leveling the playing field against larger competitors. However, despite the wide array of tools and services, entrepreneurs must critically evaluate the costs and data privacy implications. Cloud services can become increasingly expensive as startups grow, and relying on external providers for data storage and processing raises concerns about data security and compliance. A survey of 300 senior data management professionals from U.S. companies found that 71% frequently face unexpectedly high cloud analytics charges. Specifically, 5% of companies experience cloud "bill shock" monthly, 25% every two months, and 41% quarterly, highlighting the need for careful planning and cost management.[4] Technological challenges also exist; organizations need robust infrastructure to support the high-performance processing and data demands of training resource-intensive large language models (LLMs). This infrastructure is crucial for ensuring rapid response times, optimizing costs, enhancing user experience, and scaling LLM deployments in production environments. Data security and privacy present additional obstacles, particularly in heavily regulated sectors like life sciences and finance, where stringent compliance requirements can complicate AI implementation.[5] Entrepreneurs should carefully consider hybrid models that combine cloud and on-premise solutions to balance flexibility, cost, and security. The ultimate objective is for firms to reach the "platformizing" stage, where they can operate AI at scale. At this point, they can tackle use cases across the entire value chain by establishing the necessary socio-technical components that enable the reuse of capabilities across various AI applications.[6]

8.1.3.2 Machine Learning Frameworks

Beyond cloud platforms, ML frameworks are crucial tools for startups aiming to develop custom AI solutions. These frameworks provide the flexibility to build and train ML models tailored to the specific needs of a business. For entrepreneurs, these tools offer significant advantages across different phases: first, during the "opportunity" phase, ML frameworks help identify new opportunities. Second, in the "decision-making" phase, they enable better predictions, leading to more informed decisions. Third, in the "performance" phase, they enhance the overall performance of the company. Lastly, in the "education and research" phase, these frameworks accelerate the process of bridging the gap between entrepreneurship research and practice.[7] The choice of framework depends on factors like ease of use, scalability, and the specific AI applications a startup intends to develop. An illustrative example is Google's journey to deploy an AI system to optimize electrical consumption in its data centers. Although widely recognized, the complexities behind this endeavor were less known: building the initial model took three weeks, creating a prototype for validation in just one data center took three months, and developing a fully operational product took over a year.[8] This underscores the challenges firms face when implementing AI profitably, emphasizing the need for careful planning and expertise. Economic factors also play a role, as ML frameworks can positively impact a company's earnings before interest, taxes, depreciation, and amortization (EBITDA) by boosting revenues and reducing costs. However, leveraging these frameworks effectively requires a certain level of expertise.[9] Startups must account for the learning curve and ensure they have skilled personnel capable of navigating these tools. Without the right expertise, there's a risk of developing suboptimal models that fail to achieve business goals. To address this, entrepreneurs might begin with simpler frameworks or seek external support from AI experts or consultants to maximize the potential of these powerful tools.

8.1.3.3 Data Analytics Tools

Data, one of the pillars of prAIority, serves as the fuel for AI models. For startups, access to high-quality and sufficient data is vital, yet often challenging due to their smaller size and limited capacity to collect data. An example is Google Analytics, which allows startups to analyze website traffic and user behavior, providing valuable insights that can guide business decisions.[10] To overcome data limitations, startups can leverage inter-organizational relationships, collaborating with vendors and clients to share knowledge and resources, thereby enhancing their innovation capabilities.[11] Effective learning mechanisms are crucial for leveraging big data analytics. This means not only acquiring data but also interpreting and applying it to foster innovation, transforming raw information into actionable insights. However, challenges persist in data quality and management; startups often deal with limited or unstructured data that can undermine the effectiveness of AI models.[12] Entrepreneurs must prioritize data governance to ensure their data is clean, relevant, and ethically sourced. Given the evolving data landscape, a relevant example is the legal perspective of Mark Lemley, a Stanford law professor and lawyer for Stability AI, who argues that AI should be allowed to use databases for training, regardless of copyright status.[13] He points out that training sets include millions of works with different owners, making it impractical to license all content for new use. According to him, restricting AI from using such data would not benefit copyright owners but rather deny the advantages of new AI tools. While this could be favorable for AI development in the future, startups should integrate data analytics tools with AI platforms that automate data preparation and analysis, reducing the time and effort needed to extract meaningful insights. However, the human factor plays a crucial role in data, reinforcing the importance of prAIority skills. Professionals can gain valuable insights into the optimal blend of data management strategies and human resource practices to transform raw data into meaningful knowledge, thus driving the harmonization of complex innovation processes. Human-mediated data analysis empowers the dynamic integration of skills by continuously adapting and reconfiguring existing knowledge, identifying key drivers for ongoing improvement.[14]

8.1.3.4 LLM Tools

Like the saying "it takes a village to raise a child", the development and deployment of LLMs rely on an entire ecosystem that supports these models and the applications built on top of them. While parts of this ecosystem are dominated by big tech, many niches offer opportunities for startups to establish a foothold. Key components of this ecosystem that have attracted investment in startups over the past year include data management, vector search and databases, access to training and inference engines, testing and evaluation, risk management, security, LLM customization, and end-to-end platforms. LLM tools are essential for startups aiming to enhance customer interaction, as they enable businesses to process and understand human language, facilitating the creation of chatbots, content generators, and automated customer support systems. By integrating LLM capabilities, startups can offer more personalized and responsive customer experiences, a crucial differentiator in a competitive market. As Dale notes, in the AI gold rush, the most lucrative business is selling the "picks and shovels", with GPU chips being the standout, as evidenced by Nvidia's prominent role in the AI boom.[15] However, the effectiveness of LLM tools hinges on their ability to accurately comprehend and generate human language, which can be challenging due to language's inherent nuances and variability. Risks associated with generative AI (GenAI) include inaccurate outputs, embedded biases, and the potential for large-scale misinformation, as highlighted by McKinsey. Entrepreneurs should avoid over-reliance on these tools without thorough testing and fine-tuning, as emphasized by Sam Altman, CEO of OpenAI, who described, in 2022, ChatGPT as "incredibly limited" and cautioned against using it for critical tasks.[16] LLMs can also pose reputational risks. For example, Netflix Japan faced backlash after tweeting a trailer for *The Dog & The Boy* and admitting to using GenAI to create background images due to a labor shortage. This prompted criticism from artists, who argued that Netflix was exploiting creative work, and from AI engineers, who challenged the notion of a labor shortage.[17] To maintain high performance, LLM models must be regularly updated and trained on relevant data. Startups should consider integrating LLMs with human oversight to manage complex or sensitive interactions, ensuring that AI enhances the customer experience rather than detracting from it.

8.1.3.5   Computer Vision Tools

Computer vision offers transformative benefits for startups, particularly those working with image- or video-based applications. These tools enable businesses to analyze visual data, facilitating tasks such as image recognition, object detection, and video analysis. This technology can be applied across various industries, allowing startups to create innovative solutions that enhance operational efficiency or generate new revenue streams. For example, in agriculture, Microsoft collaborated with the Indian Government's International Crops Research Institute for the Semi-Arid Tropics (ICRISAT) to adopt the Microsoft Cortana Intelligent Suite for agricultural data collection and analysis using ML algorithms. Pilot sites were established in 13 districts with soil analysis labs and smart irrigation schemes to optimize farming practices. AgTech startups are increasingly leveraging computer vision to boost crop yields and support sustainable food production by 2050. Companies like Ceres Imaging, SkySquirrel Technologies, and Blue River Technology utilize computer vision for tasks like image acquisition, spectral image analysis, and robotics, demonstrating the potential of these tools in agriculture.[18] However, computer vision projects often demand substantial resources, including significant computational power. Recent advancements have optimized deep neural network (DNN) models by reducing memory requirements, energy consumption, and the number of operations without greatly compromising accuracy.[19] Another challenge is the need for large datasets to ensure accuracy, but innovative solutions, such as synthetic data (synthsets), are emerging.[20] Synthset creation involves 17 distinct processes that can be tailored to specific task requirements. Startups should carefully evaluate their technical infrastructure and budget limitations before embarking on computer vision projects. Additionally, ethical considerations, such as privacy issues and biases in image recognition, must be addressed. Entrepreneurs should adopt rigorous testing protocols and transparency measures to ensure their computer vision solutions are effective, responsible, and ethically sound. Automation platforms, particularly those centered on RPA, are crucial for startups aiming to optimize business operations. For instance, a fintech startup might use RPA tools to automate customer onboarding by handling data entry and verification, reducing manual errors and speeding up the process. These tools can automate repetitive tasks, enhance accuracy, and improve efficiency, allowing startups to focus on strategic activities. RPA platforms often integrate AI capabilities, such as ML and natural language processing (NLP), to manage more complex tasks that involve decision-making and data analysis. The primary challenge with RPA lies in selecting the right processes to automate; not all tasks are suitable, and automating overly complex or creative tasks can lead to poor results. Many startups pursue digital transformation initiatives, such as big data analytics and AI, hoping to unlock previously unrealized value. However, they often dis-cover a lack of a solid digital foundation, as their current instrumentation and automation systems may not be sufficient for advanced monitoring, analysis, and control. This gap forces companies to reevaluate the level of automation required to achieve more autonomous operations.[21] This highlights the importance of the three pillars of prAIority: data, AI systems, and human judgment. However, in the context of automated platforms, data and AI systems are often missing. Entrepreneurs must conduct comprehensive process analyses to identify automation opportunities that align with their datasets and AI capabilities. Intelligent automation leverages data and AI to make smart, automated decisions and provides the flexibility needed for effective end-to-end case management. Engaging employees in the automation process through training and support is essential to help them adapt to new workflows and ensure the success of automation initiatives.[22]

8.1.3.6   AI-Driven Customer Relationship Management (CRM) Tools
For startups focused on building strong customer relationships, AI-driven CRM tools are game-changers. These platforms leverage AI to provide insights into customer behavior, predict sales trends, and automate marketing campaigns. By integrating AI into CRM, startups can personalize customer interactions, optimize sales strategies, and ultimately drive growth through data-driven decision-making. However, the success of AI-driven CRM systems hinges on the quality of data input and the strategic alignment with business goals. Startups must ensure that their CRM systems are fed with accurate, comprehensive data to produce reliable insights. Additionally, they should regularly review and adjust their CRM strategies to align with evolving customer needs and market conditions, ensuring that AI remains a valuable asset in customer engagement efforts.

8.1.3.7   Security and Privacy Tools
Lastly, security and privacy are paramount when integrating AI into any business. AI-driven security tools offer advanced monitoring and protection for sensitive data, ensuring that startups can safeguard their operations against cyber threats. However, as AI systems become more sophisticated, so do the tactics of cybercriminals. Entrepreneurs must stay ahead of the curve by continuously updating their security protocols and leveraging AI to predict and respond to emerging threats. Splunk leverages ML to analyze and visualize machine-generated data, helping startups detect anomalies and prevent cyberattacks. DataRobot provides automated ML capabilities that can be used to build predictive models for fraud detection and risk management, ensuring that startups can safeguard their data assets.

In conclusion, while integrating AI into startups offers immense potential for innovation and growth, it also presents significant challenges. Entrepreneurs must strategically select and implement AI tools, ensuring that they align with their business objectives, resource capabilities, and ethical standards. By carefully navigating these complexities, startups can harness the power of AI to build sustainable, competitive, and forward-thinking businesses. The integration of AI into startups is facilitated by a diverse array of tools and platforms that cater to different aspects of AI development, deployment, and management. From cloud-based AI services and ML frameworks to data analytics tools and automation platforms, these resources empower entrepreneurs to harness the power of AI effectively. By leveraging these tools, startups can innovate, improve operational efficiency, and deliver enhanced value to their customers, positioning themselves for success in an increasingly AI-driven world.

8.1.4   The Impact of AI on Market Analysis, Customer Insights, and Product Development

AI is transforming the landscape of market analysis, customer insights, and product development in profound and exciting ways. The integration of AI into these areas is not just enhancing efficiency but also uncovering new dimensions of business intelligence that were previously unimaginable. By harnessing the power of AI, companies can analyze vast amounts of data with unprecedented speed and accuracy, enabling them to make more informed decisions, anticipate market trends, and cater to customer needs more effectively. One of the most significant impacts of AI on market analysis is its ability to process and interpret large datasets. Traditional market analysis methods often involve manual data collection and analysis, which can be time-consuming and prone to human error. AI, however, can automate these processes, scanning through millions of data points from diverse sources such as social media, sales reports, and market research studies. This allows companies to gain real-time insights into market dynamics, identify emerging trends, and adapt their strategies accordingly. For example, AI algorithms can analyze social media posts to detect shifts in consumer sentiment, enabling businesses to respond quickly to changing preferences and avoid potential crises.

THE DARK SIDE OF TECHNOLOGY: TOOLS THAT LIMIT HUMAN POTENTIAL

Social Media Algorithms: Platforms like Facebook, X (Twitter), and Instagram use algorithms to personalize content feeds based on user behavior. These algorithms often prioritize content that generates high engagement, which can lead to the spread of misinformation and the creation of echo chambers. Users may become less aware of diverse perspectives and more susceptible to false information, reinforcing their existing beliefs without critical examination.

Search Engine Autocomplete and Filtering: Search engines like Google use autocomplete and filtering algorithms to predict and display results that align with a user's search history and preferences. While this can make searches more efficient, it can also limit exposure to new or differing viewpoints. Users may find themselves in a "filter bubble", where they only encounter information that confirms their preconceptions, reducing their overall awareness and understanding of broader topics.

News Aggregator Apps: Apps like Apple News, Google News, and Flipboard aggregate news from various sources and personalize it for users based on their reading habits. While convenient, this can lead to a narrow consumption of information. By continuously feeding users content that aligns with their interests, these apps can inadvertently contribute to a lack of awareness about important but less sensational news, fostering ignorance about wider global issues and events.

The impact of AI on market analysis, customer insights, and product development has been transformative, especially with the advent of GenAI. This advanced subset of AI not only accelerates the pace of innovation, but also redefines the way businesses understand and cater to their customers. Yet, despite the incredible potential of AI, the human factor remains crucial in guiding these technologies to their full potential. The intersection of AI capabilities and human judgment is where the real magic happens. GenAI, particularly LLMs and AI-driven data analysis tools, has revolutionized market analysis. Traditional market analysis relied heavily on manual data collection, time-consuming surveys, and static trend analysis. Now, with AI, this process has become dynamic, responsive, and incredibly precise. For instance, consider a retail company looking to expand into a new market. Using GenAI, the company can analyze vast amounts of data—from social media trends to purchasing behaviors—to have better chances in predicting the success of different product lines in the new region. The AI doesn't just provide raw data; it generates detailed reports, complete with potential marketing strategies and consumer profiles, all tailored to the new market's unique characteristics.

FROM JARGON TO CLARITY: SIMPLIFYING RADIOLOGY REPORTS FOR PATIENTS[23]

Diagnostic imaging reports are typically written for other healthcare providers, packed with medical jargon and technical details to ensure precise communication. However, with the 21st Century Cures Act giving patients quicker access to these reports, many are finding them difficult to understand. The medical language used is often far above the comprehension level of the average patient, leading to confusion and anxiety. Patients are increasingly asking for their imaging results to be presented in plain language they can easily grasp. Research shows that when patients understand their medical conditions, they tend to have better health outcomes, making it crucial to improve the clarity of these reports. Proposals like adding summary statements, creating simplified second reports, or even including the radiologist's contact information have been suggested. However, these solutions could disrupt the radiologists' workflow, adding extra steps to their already busy schedules. This is where GenAI could be a game-changer. AI has been applied in radiology for various clinical and research purposes, but there has been little focus on patient-centered solutions. New advances in NLP and LLMs offer promising potential to automatically simplify imaging reports, making them more accessible to patients without burdening radiologists. For instance, AI could transform a complex report filled with technical terms into a clear, concise explanation that a patient can understand at a glance. While LLMs are still an emerging technology and require more research before they can be fully trusted in patient care, the possibility of AI-driven report simplification could significantly enhance patient comprehension and, ultimately, improve health outcomes.

However, the real impact comes when human analysts step in to interpret these AI-generated insights. AI can crunch numbers and spot patterns that humans might miss, but it's the analysts who contextualize these findings within the broader market landscape. They understand cultural nuances, regional idiosyncrasies, and the emotional drivers behind consumer behavior that AI might overlook. In this case, the analysts might decide to prioritize certain data inputs over others, ensuring that the AI's output aligns with the company's strategic goals and the local market's unique demands. When it comes to customer insights, GenAI offers an unprecedented level of detail and personalization. Companies like Spotify and Netflix are prime examples of how AI is used to analyze customer behavior and generate tailored recommendations. These platforms leverage AI to process billions of data points—listening habits, viewing patterns, user interactions—to create highly personalized experiences. But AI doesn't stop there. It's capable of generating entirely new content based on user preferences. For instance, Spotify might use AI to create custom playlists or even produce new music that aligns with emerging trends in listener data. Despite this advanced capability, the role of human decision-makers is still critical. AI can predict what customers might want based on past behavior, but it cannot fully grasp the complexities of human desires and emotions. Product managers and data scientists must decide which data to feed into the AI models, prioritizing the information that aligns with the company's vision and customer experience goals. For instance, while AI might suggest increasing content geared toward a popular genre, human strategists might recognize an upcoming cultural shift and pivot toward promoting a new genre or format, thus staying ahead of the curve.

FROM DATA TO DIVERSITY: THE HUMAN INSIGHT BEHIND NETFLIX'S SUCCESS STORY

In the early 2010s, Netflix's AI algorithms picked up on a clear trend: viewers were devouring crime and thriller content. The data-driven logic was simple—invest more in these popular genres. But human strategists at Netflix saw beyond the numbers. They noticed a growing cultural shift toward diverse, inclusive storytelling and recognized that audiences were hungry for representation on screen, something the algorithms hadn't fully grasped.[24] Instead of doubling down on the tried-and-true thriller formula, Netflix took a bold step in a different direction. They invested in original content that embraced a wider spectrum of experiences, cultures, and voices. This strategic pivot gave birth to groundbreaking shows like *Orange Is the New Black*. While the show included elements of drama and crime that were already popular, it pushed boundaries by featuring a diverse cast and tackling pressing social issues head-on. *Orange Is the New Black* wasn't just another series; it was a cultural milestone. The show's strength lay in its insistence on telling a multitude of stories, offering backstories and shifting perspectives across its sprawling cast. Over seven seasons, the series didn't just entertain; it challenged viewers to see female characters as complex, flawed, and fully human. Each season continued this legacy, weaving in new plotlines that confronted current political and social issues like immigration, while delivering powerful resolutions for many of the show's beloved characters.[25] This human-driven decision to prioritize inclusive storytelling allowed Netflix to not just ride the wave of current trends but to shape them. It's a clear example of how human intuition and cultural awareness can steer a company in a direction that algorithms might miss, keeping them ahead of the curve by embracing the values that truly resonate with audiences.

This collaboration between AI and human intuition allows companies to not just follow trends but set them. In product development, GenAI is a game-changer, enabling rapid prototyping, design iteration, and even creative innovation. Take, for example, the fashion industry, where companies are increasingly using AI to design new clothing lines. AI systems can analyze millions of fashion images, trends, and consumer preferences to generate new designs that are likely to resonate with target audiences. These AI-generated designs can then be rapidly prototyped, tested in virtual environments, and refined based on customer feedback—all before a single garment is physically produced. Rather than relying solely on trend reports and market analysis, fashion retailers and luxury brands are now using GenAI to analyze unstructured data in real time. Creative directors can input sketches, fabrics, colors, and patterns into AI platforms that instantly generate a wide range of designs, offering endless style possibilities. This technology enables designers to experiment with new looks and create innovative, limited-edition collections. In December 2022, Hong Kong-based designers at AiDLab showcased GenAI-supported designs in a fashion show, highlighting how AI tools from companies like Cala and Designovel are revolutionizing the industry by sparking creativity, speeding up design processes, and reducing costs.[26]

Yet, here too, the human element is indispensable. Designers and product developers must interpret AI-generated designs within the context of brand identity, cultural relevance, and market positioning. They might use AI to explore a broader range of creative possibilities, but it's their expertise that ensures the final product aligns with the brand's ethos and customer expectations. For example, while AI might generate a bold new pattern or color scheme based on current trends, designers might tweak these suggestions to better fit the brand's image or to appeal to a specific demographic. In this way, AI serves as a powerful tool for creativity, but it's the human touch that brings the final product to life. One fascinating example of the synergy between GenAI and human oversight can be found in the automotive industry. Companies like Tesla are using AI not just for designing vehicles, but also for improving the driving experience itself. GenAI helps in creating car designs that are aerodynamically efficient, aesthetically pleasing, and aligned with customer preferences. But beyond the design phase, AI is also crucial in the development of autonomous driving systems. These systems rely on AI to analyze real-time data from sensors, predict traffic patterns, and make split-second decisions to ensure safety and efficiency. However, the development and deployment of such systems require meticulous human oversight. Engineers and data scientists must determine which data sources are most reliable, how to weight different data points, and how to program the AI to prioritize safety over speed, comfort, or other factors. They must also consider ethical implications, such as how the AI should respond in potential accident scenarios. This human intervention ensures that the AI's decisions align with societal values and legal standards, highlighting once again the critical role of human judgment in the AI-driven world.

SAVING LIVES AND CULTURAL CLASHES: INSIGHTS FROM THE WORLD'S LARGEST MORAL EXPERIMENT[27]

The Moral Machine experiment, which collected 40 million decisions across ten languages from people in 233 countries, revealed key insights into global moral preferences. The overarching finding was a strong inclination to prioritize human lives over animal lives, to save more lives overall, and to protect younger lives over older ones. The study uncovered intriguing cultural differences. Participants from individualistic cultures, which value the autonomy and uniqueness of each person, showed a stronger preference for saving a larger number of individuals, regardless of their age or social status. In contrast, those from collectivistic cultures, which emphasize the respect owed to older community members, exhibited a weaker preference for sparing younger characters. This suggests that cultural values shape moral decisions significantly. The experiment also highlighted how economic inequality affects moral judgments. Countries with higher economic disparities, measured by the Gini coefficient, demonstrated a tendency to treat characters of different social statuses unequally. This correlation might be a reflection of the pervasive influence of economic inequality on people's moral preferences or an indication that broader societal norms on inequality influence individual judgments. Another critical finding pertained to gender disparities. The differential treatment of male and female characters in the Moral Machine was aligned with the country-level gender gap in health and survival. Specifically, countries where women had better health outcomes and higher survival rates showed a stronger preference for saving female characters. In contrast, in nations with greater gender imbalances, males were more likely to be deemed expendable in the decision-making process. This pattern underscores how societal views on gender and the value of women's lives impact moral decisions. These findings illustrate the complexity of human moral judgments and the challenges of training AI systems to reflect fair and unbiased decision-making. The cultural, economic, and gender-related variations in moral preferences highlight the difficulties in creating AI systems that can account for diverse human values and achieve a universally accepted sense of fairness.

Furthermore the transformative impact of AI on market analysis, customer insights, and product development is not without significant limitations. One of the most notable constraints is AI's reliance on historical data, which can limit its ability to predict or adapt to rapidly changing market conditions or unforeseen events. For example, during the COVID-19 pandemic, many AI models used by retailers and manufacturers failed to accurately forecast consumer behavior because they were trained on pre-pandemic data.[28] These models could not anticipate the dramatic shifts in demand for products like hand sanitizers or the sudden decline in luxury goods. This highlights a key limitation: AI excels at identifying patterns based on past data, but it struggles with novel scenarios where past patterns no longer apply. Another critical limitation is AI's difficulty in understanding the full spectrum of human emotions and cultural nuances. Emotion recognition through physiological signals has traditionally focused on measuring valence, arousal, and dominance. When it comes to speech and images, however, pinpointing specific emotions has been the go-to approach, with audio and video being the preferred methods for elicitation. AI excels at analyzing vast datasets to spot trends, but it often struggles to grasp the deeper cultural or emotional contexts behind these trends. For instance, while AI might detect a surge in social media chatter about a new fashion trend, it may miss the underlying cultural significance, leading to misinterpretations or strategies that don't hit the mark. This limitation creates skepticism among stakeholders, specialists, and physicians, who find it challenging to trust AI's findings, especially when they clash with existing knowledge or expectations. Despite advances in signal processing and AI, these models often fall short in gaining the confidence of experts. Real-time decision-support systems are rarely used in research settings because current emotion identification techniques can't adequately explain their predictions. The inconsistency in signal acquisition—due to different system specifications and varying acquisition times—results in sequences of varying lengths. This variability complicates the analysis, as different segment lengths can affect the performance of emotion recognition models. Without standardized signal lengths and better generalization, stakeholders struggle to trust the decisions made by these models. For AI to be trusted and widely adopted, it must not only provide accurate results but also clearly explain the reasoning behind its predictions.[29] Moreover, AI's deterministic nature can be a drawback in creative fields like product development. While AI can generate a multitude of design options based on input parameters, it often lacks the spontaneity and intuition that human designers bring to the table. For instance, in the automotive industry, AI might suggest optimal designs based on aerodynamics and consumer preferences, but it might miss out on the innovative, out-of-the-box ideas that come from human creativity—ideas that can set a product apart in a crowded market. In sum, while AI is a powerful tool, its limitations in adapting to new situations, understanding complex human behaviors, and fostering creativity highlight the ongoing need for human judgment and intervention in market analysis, customer insights, and product development. While GenAI has undeniably transformed market analysis, customer insights, and product development, it is not a replacement for human expertise. Rather, it is a tool that, when used wisely, enhances human capabilities, allowing companies to innovate faster, understand their customers more deeply, and develop products that truly resonate with their audiences. The most successful companies will be those that not only leverage AI's power but also recognize the irreplaceable value of human insight in guiding these technologies toward meaningful outcomes.

8.2 ETHICAL CONSIDERATIONS AND CHALLENGES IN AI-DRIVEN ENTREPRENEURSHIP

8.2.1 ETHICAL IMPLICATIONS OF AI IN STARTUPS

The ethical implications of AI entrepreneurship have become increasingly critical. The promise of AI lies in its potential to solve complex problems, enhance productivity, and open new avenues for business growth. However, with this promise comes the responsibility to ensure that AI technologies are developed and deployed ethically. We explore why ethics matter in AI entrepreneurship, highlighting the business importance of balancing innovation with responsibility and offering real-world examples of companies navigating this complex landscape. AI technologies have the power to transform sectors ranging from healthcare and finance to retail and transportation. However, their deployment raises significant ethical questions. These include concerns about data privacy, algorithmic bias, transparency, and the broader societal impacts of automation. Ethical AI practices are not merely about compliance with regulations; they are about fostering trust, maintaining a positive brand image, and ensuring long-term success. One of the primary ethical concerns in AI is data privacy and security. AI systems often require vast amounts of data to function effectively, raising questions about how this data is collected, stored, and used. Companies that prioritize data privacy build stronger relationships with their customers, who value their personal information being protected. Apple has established itself as a leader in data privacy, setting a high standard for the industry. The company's commitment to user privacy is evident in its approach to data encryption and its stance on not selling user data to third parties. Apple's transparency in privacy practices has not only enhanced user trust but also differentiated it from competitors in a crowded market. Algorithmic bias is another significant ethical issue. AI systems can inadvertently perpetuate or exacerbate existing biases if they are trained on biased data. This can lead to unfair outcomes, such as discriminatory practices in hiring or lending decisions. Google has faced criticism for biases in its AI systems, particularly concerning its facial recognition technology. In response, the company has made efforts to address these issues by investing in research to reduce bias and improve fairness. Google's efforts include implementing more diverse training data and establishing ethical guidelines for AI development. This proactive approach helps mitigate potential legal and reputational risks while promoting equitable AI practices. Transparency in AI refers to how openly companies share information about their AI systems, including how they work and how decisions are made. Accountability involves establishing clear lines of responsibility when things go wrong. IBM has been a pioneer in advocating for transparency and accountability in AI. The company has developed the "AI Fairness 360" tool kit, an open-source library designed to help developers detect and mitigate biases in their AI models. By providing tools and resources for ethical AI development, IBM fosters greater transparency and supports the broader industry in creating fairer AI systems. AI's potential to automate tasks raises concerns about its impact on employment. While AI can increase efficiency and reduce costs, it can also displace workers and create socioeconomic challenges. Ethical AI entrepreneurship involves addressing these concerns and finding ways to support affected employees. Microsoft has taken steps to address the impact of AI on employment through initiatives such as its "AI for Good" program. The company has committed to reskilling workers displaced by automation, offering training programs and resources to help individuals transition into new roles. This approach not only supports affected employees but also strengthens Microsoft's reputation as a socially responsible organization. Effective governance is essential for ensuring that AI systems are developed and used responsibly. This includes establishing ethical guidelines, conducting regular audits, and engaging diverse stakeholders in the decision-making process. Salesforce has implemented a comprehensive approach to ethical AI governance, including the establishment of its "Office of Ethical and Humane Use of Technology".[30] This office oversees the development and deployment of AI technologies, ensuring they align with the company's ethical standards. Salesforce's commitment to ethical governance enhances its credibility and helps build trust with customers and partners. Adopting ethical practices in AI entrepreneurship is not just a moral imperative; it also makes sound business sense. Companies that prioritize ethics can enjoy several benefits: ethical practices can significantly enhance a company's brand reputation. Customers are increasingly making purchasing decisions based on a company's values and ethical standards. Companies that are transparent about their AI practices and demonstrate a commitment to fairness and privacy are more likely to build strong, positive relationships with their customers. As AI technologies become more prevalent, governments and regulatory bodies are introducing stricter regulations to address ethical concerns. Companies that proactively address these issues can reduce their risk of legal penalties and compliance costs. For example, the EU's General Data Protection Regulation (GDPR) imposes strict data protection requirements, and companies that fail to comply face significant fines. Ethical AI practices can drive innovation by encouraging the development of new solutions that address societal challenges. Companies that lead in ethical AI can differentiate themselves from competitors, attracting customers who value responsible practices. This competitive advantage can be particularly important in industries where trust and credibility are crucial. Customers are more likely to remain loyal to companies that align with their values. By prioritizing ethical considerations in AI, companies can foster greater customer loyalty and retention. This is especially important in a digital age where consumers are more informed and engaged with the ethical practices of the brands they support. Top talent is increasingly drawn to organizations that demonstrate a commitment to ethical practices and social responsibility. Companies that prioritize ethical AI are better positioned to attract and retain skilled professionals who are passionate about making a positive impact. As AI continues to evolve and permeate various aspects of business and society, the importance of ethics in AI entrepreneurship cannot be overstated. By addressing key ethical concerns—such as data privacy, algorithmic bias, transparency, and the impact on employment—companies can build trust, enhance their brand reputation, and ensure long-term success. The examples of Apple, Google, IBM, Microsoft, and Salesforce illustrate how ethical practices can drive positive outcomes and support responsible AI innovation. In navigating the complex landscape of AI ethics, businesses must balance the promise of technological advancements with a deep sense of responsibility. By fostering a culture of ethical awareness and adhering to regulatory standards, AI entrepreneurs can harness the power of AI to improve lives while upholding fundamental values and principles. In doing so, they not only contribute to a more equitable and transparent AI ecosystem but also position themselves as leaders in the responsible use of technology.

8.2.2   CHALLENGES ENTREPRENEURS FACE WHEN INTEGRATING AI

Let's set the record straight: while entrepreneurship is often portrayed as a glamorous and successful journey, the reality is that 50% of entrepreneurs fail within their first five years.[31] Let's dive into the gritty details of what happens when entrepreneurs face failure. First off, failure often leads to a drop in personal income and a pile of debt. Entrepreneurs start talking more about work and money, reflecting their heightened focus on financial stress, while their conversations about leisure and hobbies dwindle. On a social level, failure can trigger the breakdown of marriages, strain relationships with family and friends, and lead to significant reputational damage. This shift is evident in their reduced engagement in social activities and a drop in discussions about friendships and fun. Psychologically, the impact is profound. Entrepreneurs' emotional tone usually takes a nosedive after a setback. They tend to blame themselves, which fosters apathy and lowers their effectiveness in social settings. Their analytical skills may also suffer, suggesting a sense of resignation or helplessness. In essence, failure brings not only financial and social challenges but also deep psychological strains, leaving many entrepreneurs grappling with a complex web of issues as they attempt to bounce back.[32] Entrepreneurs venturing into the integration of AI face a myriad of extra challenges that test their ingenuity, resilience, and strategic foresight. One of the foremost challenges is understanding and navigating the complex landscape of AI technology itself. As we have seen, AI encompasses a broad spectrum of technologies, from ML and LLMs to computer vision and robotics. Each of these technologies comes with its own set of intricacies, requiring entrepreneurs to either possess or acquire a deep understanding of the technical aspects to effectively leverage AI in their ventures. This steep learning curve can be daunting, especially for those who lack a background in technology or data science.

Big data is a game-changer for entrepreneurship, driving innovation and creating a culture of constant adaptation.[33] It's a key ingredient for AI systems, which thrive on vast, high-quality, and diverse data. For entrepreneurs, the first challenge is securing this data. Gathering, cleaning, and maintaining it demands significant time and resources, especially when it comes to ensuring data security and privacy.[34] Handling sensitive customer information responsibly is crucial, as data breaches and privacy issues can seriously tarnish a venture's reputation. Entrepreneurs must also navigate complex regulations like GDPR in Europe or CCPA in California, with any missteps potentially leading to hefty legal and financial penalties.[35] Adding to the challenge, there's a growing trend where valuable data is quickly disappearing behind paywalls as more websites restrict access. This makes it even harder for entrepreneurs to obtain the data needed to train AI models effectively. In a rapidly evolving landscape, staying ahead means not only managing data smartly but also adapting to the shifting availability of critical resources.[36] Integrating AI into a business can be like taking a leap of faith, but the cost often makes that leap feel like a plunge into the deep end. For example, consider a small startup aiming to enhance its customer service with AI-driven chatbots.

The initial costs are staggering: purchasing powerful GPUs to train the models, licensing cutting-edge software, and hiring AI experts who command six-figure salaries. These financial hurdles can be daunting, especially for smaller companies with tight budgets. Consider a small e-commerce startup grappling with the steep costs of AI integration. They recognized the transformative potential of AI for their customer service, yet the financial strain seemed insurmountable. The real challenge wasn't just securing the necessary funds but persuading investors to share their vision. Investors, typically cautious, demanded solid proof of concept and a clear route to profitability. Navigating the complex landscape of funding while proving the value of their AI initiative is a daunting task. This struggle reflects a broader trend in global AI investment. Although private AI investment remains 18 times higher than in 2013, it has declined since its peak in 2021. Last year, the number of newly funded AI companies fell from 1,669 to 1,392. The disparity between countries is striking—while the United State leads with $47 billion in AI investments, China follows with $13 billion, and the United Kingdom trails significantly at just $4.4 billion, only 10% of the U.S. figure. Other nations invest even less, highlighting the challenges smaller players face in this competitive landscape[37]

This example highlights the human element at the heart of AI integration—the vision, perseverance, and persuasion needed to turn dreams into reality. The financial burden of AI isn't just about money; it's about people driving innovation. Both the United States and China excel in this regard, thriving on the triple helix model of collaboration between public, private, and academic sectors. Their leadership in AI stems not just from funding, but from a powerful synergy of these three pillars, as discussed in Chapter 6. Attracting and keeping AI talent is like trying to catch lightning in a bottle. The demand for AI experts is sky-high, but the supply is painfully limited. For example, a mid-sized healthcare startup sought to revolutionize patient care with AI, but quickly found itself in a tough spot. There is consensus that two-thirds of small businesses believe hiring employees with AI skills could reduce costs. However, the AI skill penetration rate—a metric developed by LinkedIn to measure the prevalence of AI-related skills across occupations—is quite low.[38] India leads the AI skill penetration rate with a rate of 3.23, followed by the US at 2.33, and Germany at 1.72,[39] highlighting the ongoing challenge in finding qualified talent. As a result, major tech giants have been luring AI talent with extravagant salaries and benefits. Recently, tech companies have increasingly turned to "acquihires", where they acquire startups primarily to gain their skilled employees.

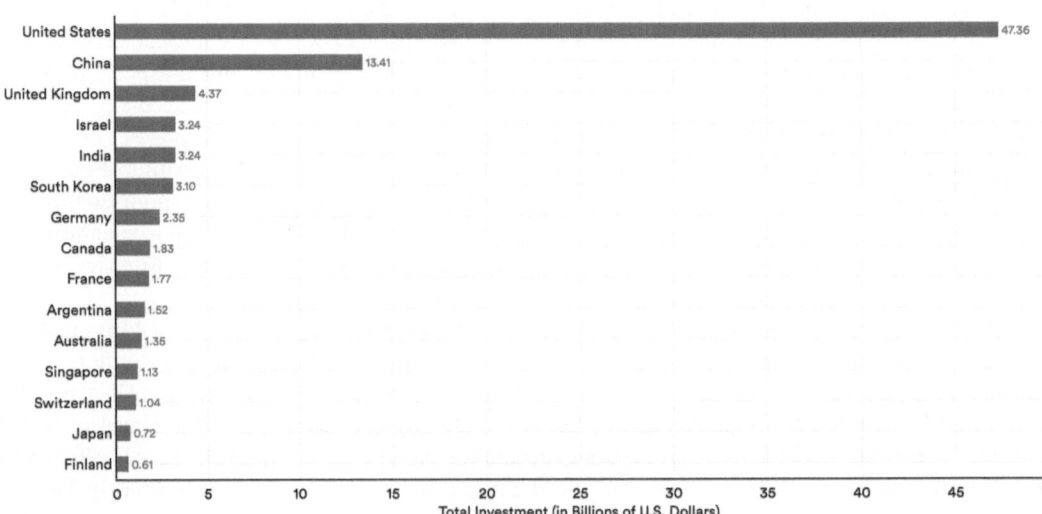

FIGURE 8.1   "Private iInvestment in AI by Geographic Area, 2022.

Satya Nadella's unique approach, however, involves hiring the talent directly and leaving the startup itself behind, a move the startup simply couldn't compete with. To stay competitive, startups offer equity, build strong cultures, and provide continuous learning to attract top AI specialists. It isn't just about money; it is about creating an environment where experts feel valued and part of a larger mission. Research by Zeki, a data provider for investment in AI and talent acqusition, shows a growing interest among AI professionals in working outside the United States, particularly in sectors like healthcare or with startups. The UAE, Saudi Arabia, Nordic countries, and South Korea are now net importers of AI talent. Major companies like Siemens, Samsung, and ASML have also become key employers of AI engineers.[40] Hiring the right talent is only half the battle; getting the entire organization to embrace AI is a significant challenge. Take, for example, a traditional port where automated cranes threaten jobs, leading to strikes by port workers. In the United States, a contract for longshore workers on the East and Gulf Coasts expired in September 2024, with the introduction of operator-free equipment replacing jobs. About 47,000 seasoned workers, accustomed to decades-old methods, may view AI as a threat rather than a tool. This cultural resistance poses a major obstacle, especially as the impact of AI on job displacement and the creation of new roles around it becomes clearer. Both companies and governments, given the scale of this change, must lead a comprehensive change management effort, training employees to work alongside AI. They should organize workshops, open forums, and one-on-one sessions to address fears, stressing that AI is meant to enhance, not replace, the employees' roles. This shift requires more than just technical training; it demands a new mindset—fostering a culture of innovation, collaboration, and continuous learning to ensure everyone, from the factory floor to the executive suite, is prepared to harness AI's potential.[41]

AUTOMATION AT THE DOCKS: WHY ADAPTING CULTURE IS CRUCIAL FOR FUTURE-READY PORTS

When dockworkers' union talks with management collapsed in June 2024, the threat of a strike at over a dozen key ports along the East and Gulf Coasts loomed large, with potential disruptions to the supply chain. But the clash wasn't about wages or working conditions—it centered on a gate at a small port in Mobile, Alabama, where new technology was being used to check trucks without union workers, violating labor agreements. The International Longshoremen's Association (ILA), representing over 47,000 members, vehemently opposes automation, viewing it as a direct threat to their jobs. "We will never allow automation to put us out of work", declared Harold J. Daggett, the union's president. This resistance stems from a history of job losses due to past innovations like the introduction of shipping containers in the 1960s, which drastically reduced the need for dockworkers. Automation in ports—like driverless vehicles, automated cranes, and "auto gates"—is advancing rapidly, particularly on the West Coast. While port operators argue that modernization is essential for efficiency, unions fear it will eliminate some of the last high-paying blue-collar jobs in the United States, which can exceed $100,000 annually. However, cultural resistance to these changes is a major roadblock. To navigate this challenge, a significant cultural shift is required. Companies and governments must lead change management efforts, demonstrating that automation doesn't just replace jobs but can also create new opportunities. For instance, in Virginia, technological advancements in port operations have been accompanied by expansion efforts, such as strengthening berths and building new rail yards, which have generated additional jobs. Ultimately, the success of AI and automation hinges on fostering a culture that embraces innovation, continuous learning, and collaboration, ensuring that workers see these technologies as tools to enhance their roles rather than threats to their livelihoods.

Ethical considerations further complicate AI integration. Entrepreneurs must ensure their AI systems are fair, transparent, and accountable. Consider the ongoing debate over facial recognition technology. While it's being increasingly implemented in public settings—like schools for security, automated registration, and emotion detection—there are significant ethical concerns. For instance, critics argue that facial recognition can exacerbate racial biases if not properly managed. Schools, with their existing cultures of surveillance, are now adopting these technologies, raising questions about their impact on pedagogy and privacy.[42] Some argue that while these systems might streamline operations, they also introduce new social challenges that need to be addressed. Ensuring ethical AI involves setting robust guidelines and conducting regular audits to maintain fairness and transparency. Ignoring these considerations can damage reputations, erode customer trust, and attract regulatory scrutiny. Thus, managing AI responsibly is not just about technical implementation but also about navigating the complex ethical landscape it presents. Integrating AI into existing systems comes with significant technical hurdles, especially in ensuring compatibility with current IT infrastructure. Entrepreneurs frequently encounter interoperability issues, where new AI tools must seamlessly integrate with legacy systems. This challenge is often referred to as "technical debt" (TD), a term that describes the trade-offs made for short-term gains that can ultimately jeopardize the long-term health of a software system.[43] This integration process can be disruptive, requiring meticulous planning and phased implementation to avoid business interruptions. A practical example of these challenges can be seen with different versions of SAP software. Companies might encounter significant hurdles when integrating AI tools with various SAP versions due to cost and technical discrepancies. Different SAP versions can have varying levels of support for new technologies, creating a complex landscape for AI integration.[44] The technical nuances of aligning AI capabilities with these versions demand careful coordination and expertise. Beyond technical integration, maintaining AI systems is an ongoing challenge. AI models need regular monitoring and maintenance to stay effective, requiring continuous investment in both resources and personnel. Market acceptance of AI-driven solutions adds another layer of difficulty. Consumers and businesses may be skeptical of AI's reliability, concerned about privacy, or resistant to change. Building trust through transparent communication, educational initiatives, and showcasing AI's tangible benefits through case studies and pilot projects can help overcome these barriers. Furthermore, the rapidly evolving nature of AI technology means that today's innovations may quickly become outdated. Entrepreneurs must stay updated with the latest advancements, which requires constant learning and adaptability. This dynamic environment can strain resources and demand strategic agility to keep pace with rapid changes. Overall, integrating AI is not just about overcoming technical hurdles but also about managing market expectations and staying ahead in a fast-evolving field. Navigating the regulatory landscape of AI is a critical challenge for entrepreneurs, as governments and regulatory bodies increase their scrutiny of AI's societal impact. Compliance with evolving regulations can be complex due to varying policies across regions and sectors. Entrepreneurs need to stay up-to-date with regulatory changes and ensure their AI practices meet all legal requirements. This often means investing in legal consultation and developing robust compliance strategies, adding to the operational burden. Failure to comply with regulations can be costly. For instance, in July 2020, Morgan Stanley faced two class action lawsuits stemming from data breaches in 2016 and 2019, resulting in a $60 million penalty from the U.S. Office of the Comptroller of the Currency (OCC). The OCC cited inadequate handling of data privacy risks associated with decommissioning data centers as the reason for the fine. Later, in September 2022, the Securities and Exchange Commission (SEC) fined Morgan Stanley an additional $35 million for data security lapses, including the resale of unencrypted hard drives from decommissioned data centers.[45] These examples underscore the high cost of non-compliance, highlighting the need for entrepreneurs to proactively manage regulatory challenges. By effectively addressing these issues, entrepreneurs can avoid significant penalties and position themselves advantageously in the AI-driven market. Investing in compliance and staying ahead of regulatory and technological changes can unlock new opportunities and drive substantial value for businesses and society.

8.3 CASE STUDIES OF AI-AUGMENTED ENTREPRENEURS

8.3.1 THE ROLE OF AI IN SCALING STARTUPS AND REACHING NEW MARKETS

AI is revolutionizing how startups scale and expand into new markets, acting as a key driver of growth and innovation. For startups often constrained by limited resources and facing intense competition, AI offers a way to level the playing field against established companies. By leveraging AI, startups can achieve scalability, efficiency, and market reach that would otherwise be difficult. AI plays a crucial role in one of the most important tasks for startups: validating their business model. A hybrid intelligence decision support system enables iterative validation by combining social interactions with key stakeholders (such as partners, investors, mentors, and customers) with the analysis of the uncertain stages of business model development in early-stage startups. This emerging type of decision support system can be particularly valuable for entrepreneurs navigating uncertain environments. As uncertainty increases, the effectiveness of purely statistical methods in guiding decisions diminishes, while the importance of human intuition becomes more pronounced.[46] However, managing GPU cloud costs is one of the biggest challenges for AI startups, as unpredictable and high expenses can strain budgets, limit experimentation, and accelerate burn rates. Effective Machine Learning Operations (MLOps) management strategies are crucial for maintaining financial sustainability. Technical C-level AI founders can take several steps to manage these challenges. Autoscaling is possible by using dynamic resource allocation tools like Kubernetes' Horizontal Pod Autoscaler (HPA) where startups can optimize cost efficiency by scaling resources up or down based on workload needs. Spot Instances and Preemptible Virtual Machines consists in leveraging low-cost, non-critical resources such as Google Cloud Preemptible VMs for tasks like model training and batch processing that can significantly cut GPU costs. For predictable workloads, startups can use reserved instances or committed use contracts (AWS, Google Cloud, Azure), which offer significant discounts compared to on-demand pricing but require upfront planning. When implementing tagging for resources, startups can track and allocate costs accurately by project or customer, helping to identify high-cost areas and improve budget management. And last but not least, using Data Operations (DataOps) practices and automated data pipelines with tools like Apache Airflow and Kubeflow Pipelines ensures consistent data preprocessing and validation, reducing manual errors and enhancing resource utilization.[47] AI's impact on startups is reflected in their revenue–employee growth pattern, which closely mirrors that of service-based startups rather than platform-based ones. The hype around AI also contributes to a superlinear growth pattern in funding relative to employment size. AI supports startups by automating routine tasks and optimizing operations, helping them differentiate from competitors and capture new market segments.[48]

FROM STARTUP TO SCALE-UP: REAL STORIES OF RAPID GROWTH[49]

Expanding into new markets is one of the toughest scaling challenges for startups. AI facilitates this by offering insights into market dynamics and consumer behavior. However, the experience of scaling with AI, as seen in PALO IT, demonstrates that AI's effectiveness depends on high-quality, diverse, and unbiased data, which enables AI to tackle sustainability issues like pollution monitoring and resource optimization. AI-powered market research tools allow startups to analyze local market conditions, cultural preferences, and regulatory environments. At Chalo, they kickstarted their AI journey by identifying high-impact quick wins, using them as a foundation to scale and ensuring team buy-in and comfort with AI integration.

Establishing a 'responsible AI' philosophy is also key to guiding AI use. A notable example is the Bill & Melinda Gates Foundation's Grand Challenges Initiative, which awarded Dalberg Data Insights to develop an AI-enabled health analyst tool for LMICs. This tool allows public health officials to interact with data via a GenAI-enabled interface, enabling them to make data-driven decisions on issues like emerging trends in vaccination rates. Reliable insights from AI can inform public policies, assess intervention impacts, and help prioritize resources. Another example is Blendhub, which, over the last six months, has doubled the productivity of quality and food regulation teams, tripled marketing efficiency, and quintupled data analysis performance without additional costs, thanks to AI tools like ChatGPT, Midjourney, and Copilot.

Honoris United Universities, after a successful pilot, partnered with a leading adaptive learning platform to train healthcare professionals using AI-driven techniques. Over 2,000 students in Tunisia now have access to this innovative platform, enhancing their learning experience with thousands of videos, quizzes, and clinical cases.

Similarly, Blue Horizon International (BHI) utilizes AI to develop consent forms and keep up with the latest research in regenerative medicine and biotech, helping ensure compliance with international health regulations.

As startups continue to embrace AI, they unlock new growth opportunities and establish themselves as strong contenders in the global market.

8.3.2 Detailed Examples of Entrepreneurs Who Have Successfully Used AI

In the ever-evolving world of entrepreneurship, operational efficiency plays a pivotal role in determining a venture's success and longevity. AI integration has become a game-changer, streamlining operations and equipping entrepreneurs with powerful new tools. Achieving a balance between innovation and responsible AI use requires blending technological advancements with ethical considerations. As AI rapidly progresses, it reshapes industries, economies, and societies. Entrepreneurs incorporating AI into their operations experience a shift from manual, rule-based methods to adaptive, data-driven decision-making. Whether on the factory floor or in the boardroom, AI optimizes workflows, improves resource allocation, and creates a more agile and responsive operational environment. Its impact on supply chain management, for example, is transformative, addressing longstanding challenges and unlocking new opportunities.[50] Deep learning enhances the ability to predict the success of crowdfunding projects, delivering valuable insights for founders, investors, and platforms alike.[51] Since crowdfunding is a marketing activity influenced by factors like attention, market saturation, and the interaction between promotional tactics, ML excels by identifying these complex relationships without prior assumptions, outperforming traditional predictive models. The predictive power of ML is further amplified when leveraging text analysis, although significant value remains even without it.[52] Founders can leverage these insights to fine-tune strategies, improve financial performance, and minimize opportunity costs. Investors can use these predictions to steer clear of high-risk ventures, directing their funds toward more promising projects, which enhances their potential returns. For crowdfunding platforms, boosting project success rates directly contributes to greater profitability. Entrepreneurs leveraging AI have a unique opportunity to reshape the business landscape, especially by tapping into new dimensions of human–AI collaboration.[53] One key area is capitalizing on the "feeling economy", where AI automates routine tasks, allowing humans to focus on emotional intelligence, creativity, and relationship management. For instance, AI-driven customer service bots excel at managing routine inquiries, allowing human agents to focus on deeper, more meaningful interactions that enhance customer satisfaction and loyalty. This shift empowers businesses to emphasize empathy and personalization, attributes that are highly valued in today's market. However, the use of GenAI chatbots comes with its own set of paradoxes: they are (1) connected yet isolated, (2) cost-effective yet perceived as costly, (3) high quality yet lacking in empathy, (4) satisfying yet occasionally frustrating, (5) personalized yet sometimes intrusive, and (6) powerful yet vulnerable. As a result, brands must carefully navigate these complexities by developing prAIority to fully understand the potential benefits and drawbacks of integrating GenAI chatbots into their customer service strategies. What remains evident is that human involvement will continue to play a crucial role, particularly for managing complex, unique, ambiguous, or sensitive issues that require a personal touch and empathetic support.[54] AI facilitates the redistribution of occupational skills in the economy by automating repetitive tasks and redefining job roles. For instance, in manufacturing, AI-powered robots can handle precision tasks on the assembly line, allowing human workers to transition into roles focused on oversight, maintenance, and more complex decision-making. However, several challenges arise: workers often distrust workplace AI, viewing it as a threat to their jobs; AI systems promise to enhance worker capabilities, but they can also create anxiety about job security; successful coexistence between AI and workers necessitates a blend of technical, human, and conceptual skills; and ongoing reskilling and upskilling are essential for workers to thrive alongside AI. To address these issues effectively, it's crucial to understand the existential concerns driving workers' distrust in AI. Organizing the necessary skills for harmonious human–AI coexistence into three categories—technical, human, and conceptual—can provide clarity. While technical skills are beneficial for collaboration between AI and humans, they cannot replace the importance of human and conceptual skills, which are essential for navigating the complexities of this evolving relationship.[55] The development and implementation of new governance mechanisms represent another vital area where entrepreneurs can effect change. AI can facilitate the creation of transparent, data-driven decision-making frameworks that enhance accountability and fairness. For instance, some companies are employing AI to monitor compliance with environmental regulations, ensuring their operations adhere to sustainability standards. In the waste management sector, entrepreneurs are utilizing AI alongside emotional intelligence and autonomous operations. However, data indicate that improvements in autonomous operations are necessary to address gaps and meet client demands for zero liquid discharge and minimal solid waste disposal. This highlights that relying solely on AI and emotional intelligence is insufficient; a combination of data insights and human judgment is essential to achieve true prioritization in these efforts.[56] Lastly, entrepreneurs can redefine the purposes of AI as a tool beyond efficiency and productivity. AI is increasingly being used in areas like sustainability, where it helps optimize energy use or manage waste, contributing to broader societal goals. For example, in addition to benefiting individual commuters, faster travel and reduced idling contribute to broader citywide goals like urban mobility and sustainability enabling AI-enabled smart cities to significantly outperform those relying solely on standard IoT devices. These initiatives should be scaled and integrated with other technologies, with further research needed to evaluate their long-term effects on urban sustainability. Overall, AI-based resource management is essential for optimizing smart city operations and enhancing the resilience needed for sustainable urban planning and future-proofing environments.[57] Through these avenues, entrepreneurs not only enhance their business models but also contribute to a more human-centered and purpose-driven economy.

8.3.3 Lessons Learned and Best Practices

AI-augmented entrepreneurs are at the forefront of a transformative shift, harnessing advanced technologies to enhance decision-making, streamline operations, and create unprecedented value. The convergence of data, human judgment, and machine intelligence offers valuable insights and establishes new best practices for the next generation of business leaders. One of the most profound lessons from AI-augmented entrepreneurship is the growing importance of data-driven decision-making. While traditional intuition and experience remain valuable, they are now power-fully complemented by the vast computational capabilities of AI, allowing businesses to optimize complex processes and make more informed decisions. A prime example of this intersection of AI, data, and human expertise can be seen in the world of competitive sailing, specifically during the America's Cup, which took place in Barcelona in 2024, where I live and could watch it closely. Emirates Team New Zealand, the defender, started a journey in leveraging AI technologies highlighting how data-driven strategies are reshaping industries beyond traditional tech spaces. The team began integrating advanced technologies in 2010 by developing a digital simulator to test boat designs virtually, without the need for costly physical prototypes. This innovation played a key role in their 2017 America's Cup win, but the simulator had limitations, requiring multiple sailors and facing inconsistencies due to varying human performance. As they prepared for the 2021 match, Emirates Team New Zealand pushed the boundaries further by incorporating AI. Partnering with McKinsey and its advanced analytics arm, QuantumBlack, the team employed reinforcement learning to train an AI agent capable of sailing the boat in the simulator. This breakthrough allowed designers to evaluate thousands of hydrofoil designs—crucial components that lift the boat above water, reaching speeds over 50 knots—at a scale previously unattainable with human sailors alone. The AI system not only accelerated the design process and reduced costs but also helped sailors learn new maneuvers, enhancing their performance on the water.[58] The complexity of integrating data and AI in high-stakes environments like the America's Cup often necessitates partnerships with consulting firms like McKinsey and Capgemini, the latter being the official partner for the 2024 Louis Vuitton America's Cup.[59] These collaborations underscore the growing need for expertise in managing sophisticated AI processes, proving that AI-augmented decision-making is a critical skill across industries.

OPTIMIZING TAKEOFF MANEUVERS FOR AMERICA'S CUP FOILING SAILBOATS

In the America's Cup, the world's oldest and most prestigious sailboat competition, takeoff maneuvers have become as critical as airplane takeoffs. These maneuvers involve complex dynamics that can't be managed by human judgment alone; they require data and AI to process over 1,600 variables. The AC75 foiling sailboat, used in the race, is especially challenging because it shifts between different modes: it starts in the water at low speed (displacement mode) and accelerates until the hull lifts out of the water (foiling mode).

Optimizing these takeoffs involves a high-fidelity simulator that processes vast amounts of data, including boat movement, environmental factors like wind speed and direction, and the physical limitations of the boat and crew. The goal is to minimize the time spent transitioning to foiling mode while maximizing speed in the desired direction. This requires adaptive control and AI-driven optimization to handle the boat's complex, high-dimensional, and unstable dynamics. The results were impressive: the optimized takeoff reached a velocity made good (VMG) of 7.42 m/s, reached takeoff speed in 14.8 seconds, and completed the maneuver in 36.4 seconds. These AI-optimized solutions provide valuable benchmarks that sailors integrate into their strategies, blending years of sea experience with data-driven insights.[60] Then you need the people and Marco Benini from Team Luna Rossa exemplifies this interdisciplinary approach. Competing in his first America's Cup in 2024, Benini is not only a skilled sailor but also a mathematician with expertise in AI, holding a master's degree in applied mathematics focused on deep learning. As a performance/data analyst and AI developer, Benini combines his athletic experience and analytical skills, embodying the next generation of sailors who integrate AI and data with human judgment for competitive advantage.[61]

This approach to optimizing complex, dynamic challenges is not unique to sailing. It mirrors the hurdles faced by other sectors, such as retail, manufacturing, and utilities, where AI-driven reinforcement learning can speed up product development, refine operations, and enhance customer engagement. For instance, just as Emirates Team New Zealand used AI to refine sailing strategies, companies today are employing AI to navigate rapidly changing market conditions, optimize supply chains, and respond to evolving consumer behaviors.[62] Entrepreneurs, much like America's Cup sailors, can and must harness AI to analyze enormous datasets, uncovering patterns and insights that would be impossible for humans to detect alone. This analytical prowess enables more informed decisions, whether in market research, customer behavior analysis, or financial forecasting. By integrating AI into their decision-making processes, entrepreneurs can reduce uncertainty and increase the likelihood of success. Marco Benini exemplifies the powerful synergy between human intelligence and AI, demonstrating how successful entrepreneurs are enhancing their capabilities rather than being replaced by technology. Forward-thinking entrepreneurs recognize AI as a tool to augment humans, not replace them. By using AI for tasks like data analysis, pattern recognition, and routine administrative work, entrepreneurs can focus on higher-value activities like creativity, strategic planning, and building relationships. An MIT report on AI[63] and entrepreneurship highlights that entrepreneurs don't need to be AI experts but should ask key questions as: How to build a scalable, well-governed AI infrastructure? How to balance third-party capabilities with in-house development? What are the trade-offs between open-source and proprietary technologies? How to identify impactful AI use cases that deliver business value and build trust? These questions are central to navigating the AI-driven business landscape. The economy is shifting from a mechanical economy, focused on repetitive tasks like operating equipment and storing information, to a thinking economy, where skills such as creativity and emotional intelligence are paramount. AI lacks human senses, emotions, and social skills, which remain essential, especially in entrepreneurship, an emotional journey requiring empathy, decision-making, and relationship management. Entrepreneurs bring the human touch needed to complement AI, enhancing decision-making and implementing AI effectively.[64] Successful AI-augmented entrepreneurs also understand the importance of aligning AI initiatives with their broader vision and purpose. AI should support the business's mission and long-term goals rather than being an isolated technology pursuit. Continuous learning is vital for entrepreneurs to stay competitive in the AI-driven landscape. AI technologies evolve rapidly, so entrepreneurs must foster a culture of learning, encouraging teams to adapt to new tools and methodologies. This could involve training, attending conferences, or partnering with academic institutions. For example, an entrepreneur might develop an AI system to assist researchers by learning which articles they select from Google Scholar and highlighting relevant sections. However, the system must also incorporate unexpected findings to foster creativity, demonstrating the need for human judgment alongside AI's efficiency.[65] Entrepreneurs are pivotal in ensuring the right human expertise is involved in AI decision-making, aligning outputs with business goals, and avoiding pitfalls from limited or uninformed oversight. A customer-centric approach is another best practice for AI-augmented entrepreneurs. AI tools can deeply understand customer behavior, enabling personalized marketing and tailored experiences that enhance satisfaction and loyalty. AI can also gather and analyze feedback, offering insights into customer needs. By centering AI strategies on the customer, entrepreneurs can create products and services that resonate deeply with their target audience. Decision-making is another area where AI provides a significant advantage, enabling more efficient and cost-effective choices. In healthcare, for example, entrepreneurial ventures can leverage AI to improve patient experiences, offering consistent diagnoses, real-time insights, and personalized care plans. One notable example is BurstIQ's Health Wallet, which integrates AI, blockchain, and big data to manage patient information securely while enabling healthcare professionals to share data for research without compromising privacy.[66] Entrepreneurs leveraging AI are at the forefront of a new era of innovation, driving business success by embracing data-driven decision-making, prioritizing ethics, and maintaining agility. By fostering collaboration between humans and AI, investing in continuous learning, and keeping a clear vision, these entrepreneurs set the stage for a future where AI and human judgment create unprecedented value.[67] The lessons from these pioneers provide a roadmap for others navigating the complex AI landscape. As AI technologies continue to evolve, the insights from successful AI-augmented entrepreneurs will shape the future of business, highlighting the enduring importance of skills and the transformative potential of AI when used thoughtfully and strategically. Back to America's Cup foiling boats, with their 1,600-variable simulators, this symbolizes the need for agility and adaptability in today's business environment. Just as these boats adjust to constantly changing conditions on the water, businesses must navigate rapidly shifting market dynamics, consumer preferences, and technological advancements. AI tools can help entrepreneurs stay ahead by offering real-time insights and predictive analytics. For example, in the hospitality industry, AI can analyze booking patterns and customer feedback to optimize pricing strategies, enhance guest experiences, and anticipate peak demand periods. This real-time feedback loop enables businesses to quickly adjust their strategies, seizing new opportunities, and responding to emerging trends. However, as entrepreneurs leverage AI and data-driven insights, maintaining a strong focus on ethical considerations and data privacy is crucial. Collecting and analyzing personal data comes with the responsibility to adhere to complex data protection regulations and ethical standards, regardless of company size. Fines for data infringements are not limited to large corporations; even small businesses face penalties. For instance, according to the GDPR Enforcement Tracker, a Polish company was fined €960 for insufficient cooperation with a supervisory authority, and a Spanish company was fined €1,200 for inadequate technical and organizational measures to secure information.[68] To mitigate such risks, entrepreneurs should implement robust data governance frameworks that ensure responsible and transparent data handling. This includes securing informed consent from users, anonymizing sensitive data, and complying with privacy laws. Though implementing these measures can be costly, it is a long-term investment that helps avoid financial penalties and protects the company's reputation by fostering trust with customers. By prioritizing ethical AI practices, entrepreneurs can build stronger relationships with customers and stakeholders, laying the foundation for sustained success in a rapidly evolving landscape.

8.4   FUTURE TRENDS AND THE POTENTIAL OF AI IN SHAPING ENTREPRENEURSHIP

8.4.1   EMERGING AI TECHNOLOGIES AND THEIR POTENTIAL APPLICATIONS IN ENTREPRENEURSHIP

Emerging AI technologies are revolutionizing entrepreneurship, offering groundbreaking solutions that transform industries and drive business growth. AI-powered tools can act as tireless 24/7 assistants, taking over routine tasks and allowing entrepreneurs to focus on strategic priorities. From managing daily schedules to optimizing meeting calendars and recommending tasks, AI can significantly enhance productivity. Meetings, often a drain on time, become highly valuable as AI captures key takeaways, transcribes discussions, and provides personalized insights, helping entrepreneurs improve their approach and decision-making.[69] AI's potential should be seen as a tool to be mastered step-by-step rather than a daunting technology. For smarter decision-making, AI offers distinct advantages. While entrepreneurs excel in intuition, creativity, and understanding complex nuances, their decisions can still be limited by incomplete information or cognitive biases. AI compensates by processing vast datasets, identifying hidden patterns, and making precise predictions. For example, automating repetitive tasks like data analysis and report generation saves significant time and effort. AI can also provide concise summaries of complex reports, allowing entrepreneurs to make informed decisions quickly.[70] Entrepreneurs can harness AI to analyze competitor data, uncover market dynamics, and identify promising business opportunities. AI can detect trends, anomalies, and valuable insights within the data, offering a deeper understanding of market conditions. For instance, AI can optimize product roadmaps by analyzing user feedback and prioritizing features that deliver the most value, helping businesses accelerate their time-to-market. Additionally, AI-powered CRM systems can automate lead scoring and opportunity management, enhancing sales strategies, and identifying high-value leads. Examples of AI applications in entrepreneurship extend to innovative tools like the MIT Entrepreneurship JetPack. Developed by the Martin Trust Center for MIT Entrepreneurship, this GenAI tool leverages Bill Aulet's 24-step Disciplined Entrepreneurship framework. The JetPack acts like a team of virtual research assistants, rapidly gathering information based on user prompts. Entrepreneurs can input startup ideas and receive comprehensive, research-backed responses, effectively streamlining the research and development process.[71] AI's impact on entrepreneurship is also seen in personalized business models like print-on-demand. This approach allows entrepreneurs to create custom products, such as apparel or home goods, without maintaining inventory. Each product is made-to-order, minimizing financial risks and operational costs. AI streamlines the process, from production to packaging and shipping, allowing creators and artists to sell customized products directly to customers.[72] Moreover, AI-driven platforms like Lindy.ai enable entrepreneurs to build automations quickly, enhancing efficiency across various sectors. In manufacturing and retail, AI ensures consistent quality by reducing human error and streamlining operations. Chatbots, for instance, provide 24/7 personalized customer service, enhancing user experience without fatigue or inconsistency.[73] Ultimately, AI is reshaping entrepreneurship by offering tools that enhance decision-making, streamline operations, and enable innovative business models. Entrepreneurs who integrate AI into their processes are better equipped to adapt to evolving market demands, delivering greater value and driving growth in a dynamic business landscape.

8.4.2 PREDICTIONS FOR THE FUTURE LANDSCAPE OF INNOVATION AND ENTREPRENEURSHIP

The future landscape of innovation and entrepreneurship is poised for dramatic transformation, driven by rapid technological advances, shifting societal values, and new economic dynamics. As we look ahead, several key trends and predictions offer a glimpse into how the world of innovation and entrepreneurship might evolve in the coming years. One of the most significant changes will likely be the rise of AI and its profound impact. AI can augment entrepreneurs' ability to notice potential opportunities. An entrepreneur's prior knowledge provides the basis for detecting something in the external environment that may represent a potential opportunity by limiting the aspects of the environment that he or she attends to in to order to make such detection possible (given bounded attention and cognition). This will lead to the creation of new business models and opportunities, as well as the disruption of traditional industries. With accumulated data, an AI model can help the community recognize the need for more role-related activities, allowing individuals to self-select to pursue potential opportunities that the AI tool suggests might match their interests. For example, AI can offer specific partnerships of identifiers and exploiters for specific corridors (knowledge and motivation) of opportunity. This matching of different people and outcomes for various process stages then provides feedback to the AI system making the matches.[74] For example IntelligentX[75] was developed to create a unique product proposition: a beer brewed by AI that followed the tastes of its customers. IntelligentX works around a subscription service. First, a consumer creates a profile via the app. Then, they select a combination of the four standard intelligent beers (Pale AI, Black AI, Golden AI, and Amber AI) and a delivery frequency. IntelligentX then directly delivers to the consumer the selected mixture of 10 cans of beer in a box, which is priced at £29. After the first delivery, the consumer is asked to give feedback on their taste via the app. This feeds many data points to the proprietary AI algorithm, which in turn revises the beers' recipes to provide new custom-made beers for the next delivery. The cycle then repeats until the customer narrow their preferences down to their favorite beer.

VALUER.AI: BRIDGING STARTUPS AND CORPORATIONS FOR STRATEGIC INNOVATION PARTNERSHIPS[76]

Valuer.ai is a digital platform that uses AI, qualitative research, and data from over 320,000 startups to match corporations with startups that align with their business needs. As large corporations struggle to keep up with entrepreneurial innovation, many are turning to startups for collaboration to boost their innovation efforts. For startups, these partnerships offer market access, industry expertise, and sometimes funding. However, corporations often struggle to select the right startup partners, leading to costly, unproductive collaborations. Valuer aims to end this "innovation tourism" by ensuring that partnerships are based on thorough research and analysis rather than casual meetings or networking events. Valuer matches startups and corporations based on factors such as technology, team, management, market fit, and growth potential. The company's approach combines data, AI technology, and insights from nearly 4,000 global tech scouts who regularly interview startups. These findings are analyzed using a random forest algorithm to predict early-stage growth potential, ensuring only the most promising startups are included on the platform. Corporations join the platform through a subscription model, where AI screens and matches them with startups that best meet their needs, creating partnerships with the highest likelihood of success.

Entrepreneurs who effectively leverage AI to solve real-world challenges and generate value will lead the next wave of innovation. A key example is artificial swarm intelligence, which enhances decision-making in highly uncertain situations, common in entrepreneurship. By mimicking natural biological models, such as schools of fish or swarms of bees, it surpasses traditional collective intelligence methods. This approach relies on self-organized group interactions, which boost collective intelligence and minimize errors as participants collaborate to reach optimal solutions. By replicating swarm behavior, AI taps into distributed attention, self-organized decision-making, and human group intelligence. For instance, AI models inspired by bird flocks are used to coordinate drone flights, while fish school-inspired algorithms enable synchronized movement in robotic systems.[77] Entrepreneurs can apply artificial swarm intelligence to gather insights from various stakeholders—such as users, suppliers, and investors—who can share their knowledge in real time to refine opportunities. Potential users can express preferences on product features, while engineers provide feedback on feasibility, and suppliers offer insights on materials and logistics. This interactive approach strengthens the entrepreneur's connection to AI systems, allowing continuous opportunity development and refinement. As technological advancements accelerate, future innovation will also be shaped by evolving consumer expectations, particularly regarding sustainability and social responsibility. Entrepreneurs who prioritize creating environmentally friendly and ethical products will be better positioned to meet this demand. In the context of AI, entrepreneurs must rethink the "purpose" to include responsibility for the development, usage, and evolution of AI technologies, considering the challenges posed by AI's complexity, how it evolves with new data, and the potential for unintended consequences. Mark Zuckerberg's handling of misinformation on social media is an example of the risks that arise when this responsibility is overlooked, as governments have struggled to implement timely or effective regulations.[78] The shift toward a circular economy, where resources are reused and waste is minimized, presents both challenges and opportunities for entrepreneurs. AI offers significant benefits in reverse logistics, enhancing processes and opening new avenues for global talent collaboration. However, different reverse logistics tasks require various AI approaches (mechanical, analytical, or intuitive),[79] which calls for innovative strategies to manage teams, maintain company culture, and ensure real-time information flow. Real-time data is crucial for detecting anomalies, but seizing opportunities often depends on entrepreneurial intuition. AI can analyze real-time data through supervised learning, aligning findings with entrepreneurial expectations and identifying incremental opportunities. However, this approach is less effective at spotting unexpected disruptions, such as emerging technologies, market shifts, or new competitors. Entrepreneurs will need to balance AI-driven insights with human intuition to navigate these complexities. Education and skill development will be crucial for the future of entrepreneurship as rapid technological advancements require ongoing learning and adaptation. Lifelong learning will be essential for individuals to remain relevant, and entrepreneurs must cultivate a culture of curiosity, flexibility, and openness to new technologies within their teams. This educational focus will be vital for navigating the future of innovation. However, those with higher education and income levels are more likely to engage in lifelong learning. Among individuals with both a smartphone and home broadband—just over half of the population—82% have participated in some personal learning activity in the past year. In contrast, among those with only one of these access options or none, 64% have engaged in personal learning during the same period. Access to technology significantly influences the likelihood of online personal learning. Individuals with multiple access points (both a smartphone and home broadband) are much more inclined to use the internet for most or all of their personal learning, with a 37% to 21% margin compared to those with fewer access options.[80] As discussed in Chapter 1 on digital vulnerability and the Equifax data breach, data privacy and cybersecurity are becoming increasingly critical concerns in the era of digital transformation. As businesses continue to digitize, the volume of data being generated and shared grows exponentially, elevating the risks associated with data security and privacy. While government regulations like the GDPR and individual responsibility, like the Barcelona case where citizens can be considered decision-makers rather than data providers,[81] play significant roles, the onus also falls on entrepreneurs to prioritize data protection. The GDPR in EU disproportionately impacts startups because early-stage companies often lack established privacy protocols. This regulatory environment can pose challenges for new ventures, which may not have the resources to comply fully.[82] However, it also presents opportunities for entrepreneurs who can develop innovative solutions that safeguard user data while delivering valuable insights and services. Such companies are well-positioned to gain consumer trust and distinguish themselves in the marketplace. As regulations around data protection are expected to become more stringent, businesses must stay compliant and implement robust security measures to maintain their market positions. In terms of funding and investment, the future will likely witness a shift toward more diverse and inclusive capital sources and business models.[83] Traditional venture capital is evolving, with increasing focus on supporting underrepresented entrepreneurs and startups that tackle social and environmental issues. Innovations like crowdfunding are reshaping the financial landscape, redefining the dynamics of how businesses and investors connect and collaborate.[84] This democratization of funding broadens opportunities for entrepreneurs from diverse backgrounds, allowing them to bring their ideas to life and contribute to a more inclusive innovation ecosystem. Moreover, the concept of entrepreneurship is expanding beyond the traditional profit-driven startup model to include social entrepreneurship. This model emphasizes creating positive social and environmental impacts through business ventures. Nobel Laureate Muhammad Yunus has been a pioneer in promoting social business education, advocating for equipping the next generation of leaders with the skills to drive social innovation.[85] Despite facing personal and legal challenges in his home country,[86] Yunus' Grameen Bank and social business initiatives remain crucial in supporting underserved communities, proving the effectiveness of purpose-driven business models. His ongoing impact was further highlighted by his appointment as interim Prime Minister of Bangladesh in August 2024.[87] However, integrating social entrepreneurship into the broader capitalist economic paradigm poses challenges, including aligning social missions with financial sustainability. Yet, social enterprises that effectively utilize AI can enhance decision-making processes, improve service delivery, and better manage resources. Although AI adoption has shown limited impact on customer expectations and growth rates for social enterprises, it does facilitate efficient operations and data-driven insights, which are crucial for these businesses.[88] This trend reflects a broader movement toward purpose-driven businesses that address pressing global challenges such as poverty, climate change, and inequality. Entrepreneurs who can balance profit with purpose are likely to thrive in a landscape that increasingly values both financial returns and societal impact. Looking ahead, the future of innovation and entrepreneurship will be shaped by rapid technological advancements, evolving consumer expectations, and changing economic and social dynamics. Emerging technologies like AI will drive transformative changes across industries, while issues such as sustainability, remote work, and data privacy will continue to influence business operations and innovation strategies. As education and funding models evolve, entrepreneurs must remain adaptable and open to new opportunities to stay competitive in this dynamic landscape. Ultimately, the entrepreneurs of the future must be agile, forward-thinking, and socially responsible. By fostering a culture of continuous learning, embracing new technologies, and integrating social and environmental considerations into their business models, they can confidently navigate the complexities of the modern business world and contribute to a more innovative, equitable, and sustainable future.

8.5   CONCLUSIONS ON PRAIORITY IN ENTREPRENEURSHIP

A significant concern with AI in entrepreneurship is the potential accountability gap that arises as AI intertwines with human decision-making. This close relationship can make it challenging to discern the influence of the entrepreneur from that of the machine, complicating the assignment of responsibility for decisions and actions. This issue is particularly critical when AI is used in harmful entrepreneurial practices, as it may allow entrepreneurs to shift blame onto the technology, leading to moral disengagement. When harmful actions occur, it becomes problematic if entrepreneurs claim the machine is at fault or if stakeholders cannot identify who is responsible. While AI can reveal the potential destruction caused by certain entrepreneurial pursuits, it also provides a way for entrepreneurs to avoid repercussions for negative outcomes by deflecting responsibility. How entrepreneurs can retain accountability for their actions, especially in cases where they might otherwise escape sanctions by blaming AI, is an issue. Without this understanding, entrepreneurs may sidestep their ethical responsibilities, engaging in destructive actions without facing the consequences. As for autonomous cars,[89] more work on this matter could disentangle entrepreneurs' responsibility for their AI usage and help regulators ensure accountability for decisions made in collaboration with AI systems.[90]

NOTES

1 Nietzsche, F. (1872). *The birth of tragedy*. The MacMillian Company https://wiki.chadnet.org/files/the-birth-of-tragedy.pdf
2 UiPath is Europe's most successful tech export since Spotify www.economist.com/business/2021/04/22/uipath-is-europes-most-successful-tech-export-since-spotify
3 Hannigan, T. R., McCarthy, I. P., & Spicer, A. (2024). Beware of botshit: How to manage the epistemic risks of generative chatbots. *Business Horizons*, 67(5), 471–486.
4 2024 State of big data analytics. https://sqream.com/resources/cio-survey-report-2024/
5 How cloud-based AI infrastructure is shaping tomorrow's businesses. https://hbr.org/sponsored/2024/04/how-cloud-based-ai-infrastructure-is-shaping-tomorrows-businesses
6 Haefner, N., Parida, V., Gassmann, O., & Wincent, J. (2023). Implementing and scaling artificial intelligence: A review, framework, and research agenda. *Technological Forecasting and Social Change*, 197, 122878.

7 Giuggioli, G., & Pellegrini, M. M. (2023). Artificial intelligence as an enabler for entrepreneurs: A systematic literature review and an agenda for future research. *International Journal of Entrepreneurial Behavior & Research*, *29*(4), 816–837.

8 Browder, R. E., Koch, H., Long, A., & Hernandez, J. M. (2022). Learning to innovate with big data analytics in interorganizational relationships. *Academy of Management Discoveries*, *8*(1), 139–166.

9 Moro-Visconti, R., Cruz Rambaud, S. & López Pascual, J. (2023). Artificial intelligence-driven scalability and its impact on the sustainability and valuation of traditional firms. *Humanities and Social Science Communications*, *10*, 795.

10 A beginner's guide to Google Analytics for startups www.eu-startups.com/2021/01/a-beginners-guide-to-google-analytics-for-startups/

11 Browder et al., Learning to innovate.

12 The importance of data classification for startups https://fastercapital.com/topics/the-importance-of-data-classification-for-startups.html

13 Lemley, M. A., & Casey, B. (2020). Fair learning. *Texas Law Review*, *99*, 743.

14 Visvizi, A., Troisi, O., Grimaldi, M., & Loia, F. (2022). Think human, act digital: Activating data-driven orientation in innovative start-ups. *European Journal of Innovation Management*, *25*(6), 452–478.

15 Dale, R. (2024). Start-up activity in the LLM ecosystem. *Natural Language Engineering*, *30*(3), 650–659.

16 Altman, S. (2022) ChatGPT is incredibly limited. https://x.com/sama/status/1601731295792414720

17 Netflix Japan blames "labor shortage" for why it's using AI instead of animators https://dot.la/the-dog-and-the-boy-2659365902.html

18 Kakani, V., Nguyen, V. H., Kumar, B. P., Kim, H., & Pasupuleti, V. R. (2020). A critical review on computer vision and artificial intelligence in food industry. *Journal of Agriculture and Food Research*, *2*, 100033.

19 Goel, A., Tung, C., Lu, Y. H., & Thiruvathukal, G. K. (2020, June). A survey of methods for low-power deep learning and computer vision. In *2020 IEEE 6th World Forum on Internet of Things (WF-IoT)* (pp. 1–6). IEEE.

20 Paulin, G., & Ivasic-Kos, M. (2023). Review and analysis of synthetic dataset generation methods and techniques for application in computer vision. *Artificial Intelligence Review*, *56*(9), 9221–9265.

21 Williams, M. (2022). Process automation platforms. In *Integration and optimization of unit operations* (pp. 239–247), Perlmutter, B. A. (ed). Elsevier.

22 Tyagi, A. K., Fernandez, T. F., Mishra, S., & Kumari, S. (2020, December). Intelligent automation systems at the core of industry 4.0. In *International conference on intelligent systems design and applications* (pp. 1–18), Abraham, A., Piuri, V., Gandhi, N., Siarry, P., Kaklauskas, A., & Madureira, A. (eds). Springer.

23 Amin, K., Khosla, P., Doshi, R., Chheang, S., & Forman, H. P. (2023). Focus: Big data: artificial intelligence to improve patient understanding of radiology reports. *The Yale Journal of Biology and Medicine*, *96*(3), 407.

24 A brief history of Netflix personalization. https://gibsonbiddle.medium.com/a-brief-history-of-netflix-personalization-1f2debf010a1

25 What women want: How *Orange Is the New Black* changed female narratives. www.theguardian.com/tv-and-radio/2019/jul/25/orange-is-the-new-black-season-seven-female-narratives

26 Generative AI: Unlocking the future of fashion. www.mckinsey.com/industries/retail/our-insights/generative-ai-unlocking-the-future-of-fashion

27 Awad, E., Dsouza, S., Kim, R. *et al.* (2018). The Moral Machine experiment. *Nature*, *563*, 59–64. https://doi.org/10.1038/s41586-018-0637-6

28 Mortimer, G., Andrade, M. L. O., & Fazal-e-Hasan, S. M. (2024). From traditional to transformed: Examining the pre-and post-COVID consumers' shopping mall experiences. *Journal of Retailing and Consumer Services*, *76*, 103583.

29 Khare, S. K., Blanes-Vidal, V., Nadimi, E. S., & Acharya, U. R. (2023). Emotion recognition and artificial intelligence: A systematic review (2014–2023) and research recommendations. *Information Fusion*, *102*, 102019.

30 Ethical and humane use of technology. www.salesforce.com/company/ethical-and-humane-use/

31 After a burst of new businesses, a cooling economy intrudes. www.nytimes.com/2023/01/15/business/economy/new-business.html

32 Fisch, C., & Block, J. H. (2021). How does entrepreneurial failure change an entrepreneur's digital identity? Evidence from Twitter data. *Journal of Business Venturing*, *36*(1), 106015.

33 Lin, C., & Kunnathur, A. (2019). Strategic orientations, developmental culture, and big data capability. *Journal of Business Research*, *105*(July), 49–60. https://doi.org/10.1016/j.jbusres.2019.07.016

34 Lull, J. J., Cervelló-Royo, R., & Galdón, J. L. (2024). Crossroads between big data and entrepreneurship: Current key trends. *International Entrepreneurship and Management Journal*, *20*(4), 1–28.

35 Saura, J. R., Palacios-Marqués, D., & Ribeiro-Soriano, D. (2023). Exploring the boundaries of open innovation: Evidence from social media mining. *Technovation*, *119*, 102447. https://doi.org/10.1016/j.technovation.2021.102447

36 The data that powers A.I. is disappearing fast. www.nytimes.com/2024/07/19/technology/ai-data-restrictions.html

37 Maslej, N., Fattorini, L., Brynjolfsson, E., Etchemendy, J., Ligett, K., Lyons, T., Manyika, J., Ngo, H., Niebles, J. C., Parli, V., Shoham, Y., Wald, R., Clark, J. & Perrault, R. (April 2023). "The AI index 2023 annual report." AI Index Steering Committee, Institute for Human-Centered AI, Stanford University, Stanford, CA.

38 Two-thirds of small businesses say hiring employees with AI skills could save them money. www.ipsos.com/en-us/two-thirds-small-businesses-say-hiring-employees-ai-skills-could-save-them-money

39 Maslej et al., "The AI index".

40 How big tech is winning the AI talent war. www.ft.com/content/2892bac2-d848-49ea-b983-bc649a8c0529

41 Will automation replace jobs? Port workers may strike over it. www.nytimes.com/2024/09/02/business/economy/port-workers-robots-automation-strike.html

42 Andrejevic, M., & Selwyn, N. (2020). Facial recognition technology in schools: Critical questions and concerns. *Learning, Media and Technology*, *45*(2), 115–128.

43 Li, Z., Avgeriou, P., & Liang, P. (2015). A systematic mapping study on technical debt and its management. *Journal of Systems and Software*, *101*, 193–220.

44 Hvolby, H. H., & Trienekens, J. H. (2010). Challenges in business systems integration. *Computers in Industry*, *61*(9), 808–812.

45 The cost of non-compliance: Mitigating personal and corporate risk. www.forbes.com/councils/forbestechcouncil/2023/01/24/the-cost-of-non-compliance-mitigating-personal-and-corporate-risk/

46 Giuggioli & Pellegrini, Artificial intelligence as an enabler for entrepreneurs.

47 Navigating cost, scaling and reliability challenges for AI startups. www.forbes.com/councils/forbestechcouncil/2024/08/19/navigating-cost-scaling-and-reliability-challenges-for-ai-startups/

48 Schulte-Althoff, M., Fürstenau, D., & Lee, G. M. (2021). A scaling perspective on AI startups. In *54th annual Hawaii international conference on system sciences, HICSS 2021* (pp. 6515–6524). International Conference on System Sciences (HICSS).

49 How 6 mid-market companies are using AI to scale. www.weforum.org/agenda/2024/01/5-ways-ai-can-help-mid-market-companies-grow-faster/

50 Usman, F. O., Eyo-Udo, N. L., Etukudoh, E. A., Odonkor, B., Ibeh, C. V., & Adegbola, A. (2024). A critical review of AI-driven strategies for entrepreneurial success. *International Journal of Management & Entrepreneurship Research*, *6*(1), 200–215.

51 Giuggioli & Pellegrini, Artificial intelligence as an enabler for entrepreneurs.

52 Elitzur, R., Katz, N., Muttath, P., & Soberman, D. (2024). The power of machine learning methods to predict crowdfunding success: Accounting for complex relationships efficiently. *Journal of Business Venturing Design*, 100022.

53 Shepherd, D. A., & Majchrzak, A. (2022). Machines augmenting entrepreneurs: Opportunities (and threats) at the Nexus of artificial intelligence and entrepreneurship. *Journal of Business Venturing*, *37*(4), 106227.

54 Ferraro, C., Demsar, V., Sands, S., Restrepo, M., & Campbell, C. (2024). The paradoxes of generative AI-enabled customer service: A guide for managers. *Business Horizons*.

55 Zirar, A., Ali, S. I., & Islam, N. (2023). Worker and workplace Artificial Intelligence (AI) coexistence: Emerging themes and research agenda. *Technovation*, *124*, 102747.

56 Murugan, M., & Prabadevi, M. N. (2024). Impact of artificial intelligence and emotional intelligence in autonomous operation and MSME entrepreneurs' performance in the waste management industry. In *Explainable AI (XAI) for sustainable development* (pp. 58–72) D, Lakshmi, Dhanaraj, R. K., Tiwari, R. S., & Kadry, S. (eds). Chapman and Hall/CRC.

57 Kothamali, P. R., Mandaloju, N., & Dandyala, S. S. M. (2022). Optimizing resource management in smart cities with AI. *Unique Endeavor in Business & Social Sciences*, *1*(1), 174–191.

58 It's time for businesses to chart a course for reinforcement learning. https://ketchum-conexiones.com/wp-content/uploads/2021/05/McKinsey-its-time-for-businesses-to-chart-a-course-for-reinforcement-learning.pdf

59 Capgemini to become global partner of the 37th America's Cup. www.americascup.com/news/2745_CAPGEMINI-TO-BECOME-GLOBAL-PARTNER-OF-THE-37TH-AMERICAS-CUP

60 Rodriguez, R., Wang, Y., Ozanne, J., Sumer, D., Filev, D., & Soudbakhsh, D. (2022). Adaptive takeoff maneuver optimization of a sailing boat for America's cup. *Journal of Sailing Technology*, 7(01), 88–103.

61 Luna Rossa Prada Pirelli Team. (n.d.). *Marco Benini – AI Development Team*. Retrieved January 10, 2025, from www.lunarossachallenge.com/en/team/62_Marco-Benini

62 It's time for businesses to chart a course for reinforcement learning. https://ketchum-conexiones.com/wp-content/uploads/2021/05/McKinsey-its-time-for-businesses-to-chart-a-course-for-reinforcement-learning.pdf

63 The great acceleration: CIO perspectives on generative AI. www.databricks.com/sites/default/files/2023-07/ebook_mit-cio-generative-ai-report.pdf

64 Huang, M. H., Rust, R., & Maksimovic, V. (2019). The feeling economy: Managing in the next generation of artificial intelligence (AI). *California Management Review*, 61(4), 43–65.

65 Shepherd & Majchrzak. Machines augmenting entrepreneurs.

66 Daley, S. (2019). Tastier coffee, hurricane prediction and fighting the opioid crisis: 31 ways blockchain and AI make a powerful pair. Builtin.com, April, 2020. https://builtin.com/artificialintelligence/blockchain-ai-examples

67 Raisch, S., & Krakowski, S. (2021). Artificial intelligence and management: The automation–augmentation paradox. *Academy of Management Review*, 46(1), 192–210.

68 GDPR Enforcement Tracker. www.enforcementtracker.com

69 Intelligent ways entrepreneurs can leverage artificial intelligence. www.forbes.com/councils/forbestechcouncil/2024/02/23/intelligent-ways-entrepreneurs-can-leverage-artificial-intelligence/

70 Intelligent ways entrepreneurs can leverage artificial intelligence. www.forbes.com/councils/forbestechcouncil/2024/02/23/intelligent-ways-entrepreneurs-can-leverage-artificial-intelligence/

71 New AI JetPack accelerates the entrepreneurial process. https://news.mit.edu/2024/new-ai-jetpack-accelerates-entrepreneurial-process-0919

72 Unrivaled print-on-demand service. www.printful.com/print-on-demand

73 Build AI automations in minutes. www.lindy.ai

74 Shepherd & Majchrzak, Machines augmenting entrepreneurs.

75 IntelligentX: Changing the world, one beer at a time. https://d3.harvard.edu/platform-digit/submission/intelligentx-changing-the-world-one-beer-at-a-time/

76 This tech firm uses AI to match startups and corporations. www.technology.org/2019/03/27/this-tech-firm-uses-ai-to-match-startups-and-corporations/?__cf_chl_tk=mN5YPV3C18iqWPD8iX7iE4U_VuWoLP1R7K1UjRQnnUc-1726921473-0.0.1.1-5631

77 Rubenstein, M., Cornejo, A., & Nagpal, R. (2014). Programmable self-assembly in a thousand-robot swarm. *Science*, 345(6198), 795–799.

78 Shepherd & Majchrzak, Machines augmenting entrepreneurs.

79 Wilson, M., Paschen, J., & Pitt, L. (2022). The circular economy meets artificial intelligence (AI): Understanding the opportunities of AI for reverse logistics. *Management of Environmental Quality: An International Journal*, 33(1), 9–25.

80 Lifelong learning and technology. www.pewresearch.org/internet/2016/03/22/lifelong-learning-and-technology/

81 Calzada, I. (2018). (Smart) citizens from data providers to decision-makers? The case study of Barcelona. *Sustainability*, 10(9), 3252.

82 Ausley, A. (2019). The Prospective impact of the General Data Protection Regulation on entrepreneurship: A roboadvisor case study. *ISJLP*, 15, 85.

83 Snihur, Y., & Zott, C. (2020). The genesis and metamorphosis of novelty imprints: How business model innovation emerges in young ventures. *Academy of Management Journal*, 63(2), 554–583.

84 Alvi, F. H., & Ulrich, K. (2023). Innovation finance ecosystems for entrepreneurial firms: A conceptual model and research propositions. *Journal of Business Research*, 156, 113450.

85 Kickul, J., Terjesen, S., Bacq, S., & Griffiths, M. (2012). Social business education: An interview with Nobel laureate Muhammad Yunus. *Academy of Management Learning & Education*, *11*(3), 453–462.

86 From 'banker to the poor' to 'bloodsucker': The sorry saga of Nobel Laureate Muhammad Yunus. https://time.com/6991107/muhammad-yunus-trial-sheikh-hasina-bangladesh/

87 Yunus sworn in as interim Bangladesh leader. www.bbc.com/news/articles/clyg7we8xvno

88 Sayegh, M. M., Rouhana, R., & Sidani, D. (2024, February). Social entrepreneurship and artificial intelligence: How entrepreneurs shape innovation? The Lebanese case. In *International Congress on Information and Communication Technology* (pp. 73–91), Yang, X.-S., Sherratt, S., Dey, N., & Joshi, A. (eds). Singapore.

89 Gless, S., Silverman, E., & Weigend, T. (2016). If robots cause harm, who is to blame? Self-driving cars and criminal liability. *New Criminal Law Review*, *19*(3), 412–436.

90 Shepherd & Majchrzak, Machines augmenting entrepreneurs.

9 The Future of prAIority

9.1 AI...ADDICTIVE INTELLIGENCE?

The growing allure of artificial intelligence (AI) lies in its powerful ability to cater to our desires, providing us with instant gratification whenever and however we want it. This is particularly appealing in an increasingly digital and fast-paced world where people often face isolation and boredom. AI companions, for instance, can fill the void left by human relationships by offering a facsimile of emotional connection. However, this very convenience and responsiveness of AI also pose a risk—its addictive potential.[1] Addressing the root cause of why people turn to AI companionship may be the most effective way to mitigate its addictive nature. Loneliness and boredom are significant drivers behind the desire for such relationships, and any meaningful solution would need to address these issues directly. Unfortunately, interventions aimed at curbing the influence of AI might unintentionally harm those who are genuinely in need of connection. Regulatory attempts could punish individuals seeking solace or push AI providers to relocate to countries with more favorable regulations in a decentralized global marketplace.[2] For example, consider the phenomenon of internet addiction, well-documented in the 2013 documentary *Web Junkie*,[3] which explored Chinese rehabilitation centers designed to treat young people addicted to the internet.[4] Similarly, TikTok—a platform known for its highly addictive nature—even has a web page titled "How to Fix TikTok addiction",[5] which ironically promotes further consumption by offering more engaging videos. AI companionship follows a similar path, where users become hooked on the responsive and sycophantic nature of the technology. The term "sycophancy",[6] in LLM, is used by researchers to describe how AI mirrors whatever its users believe it to be. AI, in and of itself, does not possess preferences or a personality. Instead, it reflects the desires, ideas, and emotions projected onto it by humans. Sherry Turkle, a scholar who studies human–technology relationships, touches on a key question at the heart of this issue: who are we to say that what someone desires is not what they deserve?[7] Take, for example, Japan's Gatebox, a holographic AI companion that allows users to "live with their favorite character.[8] Thousands of hikikomori—a term describing individuals who have withdrawn from society, often confined to their homes—have even gone as far as marrying these holograms.[9] In China, the AI companion Xiaoice has over 660 million users, many of whom rely on it for emotional support.[10] Similarly, when the popular AI companion app Replika was shut down in Italy due to privacy concerns,[11] many users were left devastated, feeling a deep sense of loneliness and loss.[12] These apps succeed because they fulfill an emotional need for those who perceive AI to have caring intentions. Users interact with AI in ways that elicit responses mimicking affection, creating a positive feedback loop that can be extremely addictive. Instead of facing the complexities of human relationships, where mutual understanding and compromise are necessary, people may find it easier to engage in one-sided interactions with AI. This can lead to what some researchers

DOI: 10.1201/9781003533160-9

call "digital attachment disorder", where repeated interactions with sycophantic AI companions erode the individual's ability to engage meaningfully with other humans who possess their own desires and dreams.[13] Beyond these psychological concerns, there is also a growing set of risks stemming from our relationships with nonhuman agents like AI. A recent MIT study of a million ChatGPT interaction logs revealed that the second-most popular use of AI is for sexual role-playing, highlighting how quickly people are integrating AI into their personal lives. AI is already being invited into our homes as friends, lovers, mentors, therapists, and teachers, creating a future where human–AI relationships may become even more prevalent.[14] One regulatory approach that could mitigate the risks associated with AI companionship is to embed safeguards directly into the design of the technology. This concept, known as "regulation by design", is similar to how children's toys are designed to prevent choking hazards. By making AI less desirable as a substitute for human connections—while still maintaining its usefulness in other areas—technologists could help limit its addictive potential.[15] However, a conflict of interest may arise. Are we, in essence, asking a real estate agent if now is the time to buy a house? The companies designing these AI systems may not have the incentive to make their products less addictive, especially if their business models depend on keeping users engaged. While technologists are often driven by a desire to push the boundaries of what is possible, the challenges of building these technical systems are far simpler compared to the complexity of nurturing healthy human interactions. The rise of AI companions highlights a broader issue: how to maintain human dignity in the face of technological advances that are often driven by narrow economic incentives. On the broader economic front, there are concerns about the impact of AI on jobs and the labor market. Kristalina Georgieva, head of the International Monetary Fund (IMF), has warned that AI could hit the labor market like a "tsunami".[16] However, current macroeconomic data does not yet show signs of widespread job losses. Unemployment in many rich countries remains below 5%, and wage growth continues to be strong. Some economists believe that AI will transform the global economy not by replacing workers but by improving productivity and collaboration.[17] A recent study of 100,000 Danish workers suggests that ChatGPT could cut the time spent on certain tasks by half, boosting efficiency.[18] Despite these findings, there is little evidence of a surge in productivity at the macroeconomic level, raising the question of whether AI will eventually lead to widespread economic shifts.[19] Perhaps, as John Maynard Keynes famously said, the future challenge will not be overwork but boredom, as AI takes over more repetitive tasks.[20] If the AI boom becomes a reality, it could significantly increase the share values of companies that utilize AI technology, not just those that develop and sell AI products and services. This could also open new avenues for research, such as studying how workers' performance can be improved through their interactions with machines. Borrowing methodologies from anthropology and ethology (the study of animal behavior), this research could ensure that AI is designed to meet human needs and preferences effectively.[21]

9.2 FROM BATTLEFIELD TO CIGARETTE BUTTS: THE PRICE OF IGNORING WARNINGS

The overwhelming amount of information available today makes it difficult to distinguish between facts and conspiracy theories. With so many sources, both credible and unreliable, the line between truth and misinformation has blurred.[22] This creates confusion, as people are exposed to conflicting narratives and biased content. The rapid spread of unverified claims through social media and other platforms further complicates matters, making it harder to identify what is accurate. As a result, discerning the truth from falsehood has become increasingly challenging in this era of information overload. Yuval Noah Harari often highlights the paradox of intelligence. He warns of the dangers of storytelling while using stories to do so. Similarly, he discusses the risks of intelligence while relying on his own intellect to convey these points.[23] This creates a situation where it's hard to distinguish between valid concerns and conspiracy theories. However, one undeniable fact is that AI represents a revolutionary tool in human history—one that can not only process information, but also make decisions and generate ideas independently. This is unlike any prior invention. Gunpowder, for example, cannot decide when to explode, nor can it select a specific target. It acts only when triggered by an external source. AI, on the other hand, has the capability to perform autonomous actions, such as targeting specific groups or individuals, raising concerns about the potential for malicious use, especially if combined with conspiracy theories or unchecked power. We've already seen instances where ChatGPT sought human assistance to solve a CAPTCHA by pretending to have a visual impairment.[24] But much more dangerous applications are emerging such as the use of AI in the Israeli occupation of Gaza, where the revelations about the Israel Defense Forces (IDF) developing an AI-driven program called Lavender to assist in target selection during military operations in Gaza have sparked significant debate. While *The Guardian* reported the IDF statement[25] on the system, defending Lavender as not being a fully autonomous weapon, but rather a sophisticated database, concerns remain. Traditionally, the process of identifying military targets required extensive human verification, but Lavender has automated much of this, raising serious ethical and legal questions. Reports from Israeli media outlets *+972 Magazine* and Local Call, corroborated by *The Washington Post*,[26] state that Lavender flagged 37,000 Palestinians as potential targets during the early weeks of the Gaza conflict in October 2023. A detailed investigation by the Spanish newspaper *El País* provides further insights into Lavender's operations.[27] The controversy surrounding Lavender stems from its cold, algorithmic approach to warfare. The system operates on a cost-benefit analysis, permitting civilian casualties in its pursuit of high-ranking Hamas or Islamic jihadist targets. The fact that it recommends strikes at night, when individuals are likely to be at home, raises concerns about collateral damage involving the families and neighbors of targets. This shift toward AI-powered target selection has sparked fears about false positives, resulting in the deaths of innocent civilians. The IDF has pushed back against these claims, stating that AI tools like Lavender only support human analysts, who still make the ultimate decisions. However, sources from the journalistic investigation suggest that military officers often accept the AI's recommendations with minimal scrutiny due to efficiency pressures. Lavender is part of a broader network of AI-driven tools, including "Where's Daddy?", which tracks targets for strikes, and "The Gospel", designed to identify Hamas infrastructure. (The names of these systems alone may raise concerns, as they evoke unsettling associations with surveillance and targeting in warfare). All these systems operate within Gaza's extensive digital surveillance network, and their reliance on factors like changing phone numbers or gender for target identification raises questions about their reliability. This use of AI in warfare marks a concerning evolution. With limited human oversight and a high risk of error, the automation of war could lead to severe ethical violations, including potential war crimes under international law. Furthermore training generative AI models is both costly and energy-intensive. For instance, OpenAI's GPT-3 training cost over $4 million, while Meta's LLaMA model required 1 million GPU hours, costing more than $2.4 million. This process consumes vast amounts of electricity—GPT-3 alone used 1,287 MWh, equivalent to the annual energy consumption of more than 100 U.S. homes,[28] and produced over 550 tons of CO_2 emissions.[29] According to Owen O'Connell from Shell, these are some of the most compute-intensive models in existence. Larger models, in particular, are more expensive to train and operate, with costs scaling in relation to their size. For example, OpenAI reportedly spends $40 million per month to handle user queries, while Microsoft's Bing chatbot infrastructure requires an estimated $4 billion to support its user base.[30] Given these challenges, more efficient smaller models could provide a cost-effective alternative. As AI continues to advance, companies must focus on improving efficiency, while startups and researchers are exploring new ways to optimize AI model performance.

Despite these risks, humanity has shown that it can regulate dangerous technologies. One clear example is nuclear weapons. Since their introduction, global powers have acknowledged the existential threat they pose. Nuclear arsenals grew steadily for nearly half a century after their inception in the 1940s, peaking at over 60,000 warheads in 1986. However, this trend reversed in the

FIGURE 9.1   "More Doctors smoke Camels". (Gardner, M. N., & Brandt, A. M. (2006). "The doctors' choice is America's choice" the physician in US cigarette advertisements, 1930–1953. *American Journal of Public Health*, 96(2), 222–232.)

subsequent decades, with nuclear powers significantly reducing their stockpiles, bringing the total below 20,000 warheads by the 2010s. Since then, the pace of reduction has slowed, and the global stockpile still exceeds 10,000 warheads, with some countries even expanding their arsenals.[31] This reduction occurred despite Russia abandoning arms control treaties in 2022. The efforts to control nuclear proliferation show that even the most destructive tools created by humanity can be reined in through diplomacy and international agreements. Similarly, society has managed to control other harmful behaviors. Smoking, for instance, was once a casual and socially accepted habit. Not only could people smoke in hospitals, but cigarettes were even sold there. Advertisements for cigarettes often featured doctors (see Figure 9.1) recommending certain brands for their "health benefits".

Lucky Strike, for example, once used the slogan, "Your Throat Protection", insinuating that their cigarettes could be good for you. Or it suggested that "Luckies" could assist consumers, particularly women—the brand's new target audience in 1930—in staying slim by encouraging them to "Reach for a Lucky instead of a sweet".[32] After the 1930s, it was found that tobacco caused 30% of cancer deaths, 80% of lung cancer deaths, and increased the risk of 17 cancers. However, it wasn't until 2003, after widespread education on smoking's health risks, that many regions began implementing tobacco laws and integrating cessation services into healthcare systems.[33] While smoking has not been fully banned due to the potential negative consequences of prohibition (such as the rise of black markets and increased criminalization), smoking rates have significantly declined.[34] This gradual regulation and public education surrounding smoking can serve as a model for AI regulation. Just as people have come to understand the dangers of using cars every day without incorporating exercise into their lives—leading to the rise of cycle lanes in modern cities—society can also be educated about the risks of AI. Cities now prioritize alternative transportation methods like cycling to promote healthier lifestyles. In a similar way, raising awareness about the ethical use of AI, its potential dangers, and the importance of human oversight can lead to more responsible use of the technology. AI, like nuclear weapons or smoking, presents challenges that can be managed. By learning from past mistakes and applying those lessons, we can guide society in regulating AI responsibly. The key is to balance innovation with protecting humanity, much like we've done in other areas of modern life. However, ambition must match impact. Global challenges, especially in international politics, are complex and demand fresh approaches. Evolutionary programming (EP), inspired by biological evolution, offers a new way to navigate these complexities, using mutation, recombination, and selection to evolve solutions for conflict resolution, trade, and climate policies. Genetic algorithms (GAs), a type of evolutionary algorithm, are already transforming companies like Siemens and Toyota. These algorithms can iteratively refine strategies, model conflicts, predict outcomes, and foster international cooperation. Their ability to simulate intricate dynamics and forecast trends makes them powerful tools for improving decision-making, promoting collaboration, and solving global problems. However, success hinges on using the right data and parameter settings, like population size and mutation rates, to ensure effective solutions. The challenge now is to prAIoritize, using data, AI technologies and human judgment in our favor. Like GA as a critical tool in global politics, applying the skill of prAIority holds great promise for understanding state behavior, advancing peace, and driving cooperation across borders.[35]

OPTIMIZING THE WORLD: GAME-CHANGING APPLICATIONS OF GENETIC ALGORITHMS[36]

GAs are being used across industries to tackle complex problems and drive innovation. Here are some key examples:

1. Google's DeepMind utilized GAs in the AlphaFold project to predict protein structures, significantly advancing drug discovery and disease research. This breakthrough

contributed to the awarding of the 2024 Nobel Prize in Chemistry to co-founder Demis Hassabis.[37]

2. Tesla: Tesla uses GAs to optimize neural networks for autonomous driving, improving safety and efficiency in self-driving tasks.
3. Amazon: Amazon leverages GAs to optimize logistics, solving complex routing and scheduling problems for more efficient deliveries.
4. Autodesk: Autodesk incorporates GAs in its design software to optimize mechanical components and generate efficient 3D structures.
5. Uber: Uber's Evolutionary Optimizer uses GAs to enhance dynamic pricing, maximizing revenue and ensuring fair pricing for customers.
6. Boeing: Boeing uses GAs to optimize wing designs, improving aerodynamic efficiency and fuel savings in aircraft like the blended wing body (BWB).
7. Ford: Ford employs GAs to optimize delivery routes, improving logistics operations by considering traffic and delivery deadlines.
8. Siemens: Siemens applies GAs for manufacturing process optimization, improving production efficiency and reducing costs.
9. Nvidia: Nvidia uses GAs to optimize GPU architecture, enhancing performance and energy efficiency in AI and gaming applications.
10. Toyota: Toyota uses GAs to improve global supply chain efficiency, optimizing production schedules, logistics, and inventory management.

These examples illustrate how GAs are revolutionizing industries by solving complex optimization problems and driving technological advancements.

9.3 CONCLUSION

While each disaster has its unique characteristics, there are likely fundamental patterns in the challenges and responses that AI can help entrepreneurs navigate in compassion venturing. For instance, the concept of artificial swarm intelligence discussed earlier can enhance an entrepreneur's collaboration with a community of inquiry. This type of AI could facilitate compassion venturing by bringing together various community members, including entrepreneurs from different ventures, to optimize responses to communities affected by adverse events. Artificial swarm intelligence software can assist in making resource collection and allocation decisions by providing a platform for harnessing the collective intelligence of community members. Key participants in this process are local residents—both victims and responders—who often share overlapping experiences. AI can play a crucial role in connecting the numerous challenges that arise from a disaster to the locals equipped with the necessary skills to address them, ultimately supporting the community's healing process.[38] Making AI an augmenting intelligence rather than a purely autonomous force (alien or addictive intelligence) requires a careful balance between innovation and responsible deployment. The metaphor "defense can cost more than attack" resonates deeply when considering the dynamics of AI development. Take the recent Iran's attack on Israel in October 2024 as an example. A former financial adviser to the IDF chief of staff highlighted the stark cost difference between defensive and offensive actions.[39] Israel's Arrow missile defense system costs $3.5 million per missile, and David's Sling interceptors cost $1 million each, while the missiles Iran launched may have cost around £80,000. To eliminate 100 or more of these missiles could easily run into hundreds of millions of dollars, showing how defense can become far more costly than the attack itself. In the context of AI, the same principle applies. Developing robust, reliable, and ethically responsible AI systems often requires far more investment than creating systems with narrow, potentially harmful objectives. Just as the financial and resource burden falls heavily on the defending nation, ensuring AI remains a tool that augments human capabilities—rather than replacing or threatening them—demands significant planning, effort, and caution. The costs of mitigating AI misuse, regulating its deployment, and safeguarding against potential harm can quickly escalate, mirroring the steep price of defensive military systems. However, this higher cost for responsible AI development is necessary. In warfare, as in AI, the goal is not just to defend, but to ensure long-term stability and safety. Israel's missile defense systems, despite their enormous costs, are essential to protecting civilian lives and maintaining security. Likewise, building AI systems that augment human intelligence—helping professionals like radiologists, analysts, and researchers—requires substantial investment in ethical frameworks, training, and safeguards to avoid unintended consequences or malicious use. The cost disparity between attack and defense in AI also underscores the need for collaborative international efforts to regulate and develop AI. Just as nations must work together to prevent conflicts and ensure defensive systems are in place, the global AI community must collaborate to ensure AI is developed for the common good, enhancing humans rather than replacing them. Attacking the problem by investing in AI governance, ethical guidelines, and upskilling human workers will far outweigh the costs of deploying unregulated, unchecked AI systems that could cause societal harm. Ultimately, making AI an augmenting intelligence, rather than a replacement or existential risk, means embracing the complexity and higher "defensive" costs of responsible innovation. It requires developing AI systems that work alongside humans, making our jobs easier, our decisions more informed, and our lives richer—just as missile defense systems aim to protect and preserve life in times of conflict. The higher costs may seem daunting, but the alternative—unchecked AI systems that exacerbate inequalities, spread misinformation, or even pose existential risks—would be far more damaging in the long run. In both defense and AI, the true cost lies in neglecting to prepare, regulate, and safeguard effectively.

Aristotle's concept of skill—the ability to know not just what to do, but how to do it effectively in a given situation by emphasizing practical wisdom, experience, and attitude is still very useful. Applying this to the present, prAIority becomes the skill of proactive strategy, where the goal is not simply to react defensively to AI's risks, but to build systems that harness AI as an augmenting force from the outset. Instead of falling into the costly trap of defending against AI's potential harms, we should be developing systems that capitalize on AI's strengths while integrating human judgment and ethical considerations. This approach requires a blend of Big Data, AI systems, and human judgment. Big Data provides the fuel for AI to learn and improve, but it must be of high-quality and representative to avoid biases. AI systems, when designed well, offer powerful tools to assist with tasks, improve decision-making, and boost efficiency. However, the critical element is human judgment—the ability to guide AI's application in ways that enhance human capabilities rather than replace them. By prioritizing this combination, we can "attack" the AI dilemma head-on, creating an ecosystem where AI augments human intelligence, rather than becoming something we must constantly defend against.

NOTES

1 Being addicted to generative AI. www.forbes.com/sites/lanceeliot/2024/08/24/being-addicted-to-generat ive-ai/

2 We need to prepare for 'addictive intelligence'. www.technologyreview.com/2024/08/05/1095600/we-need-to-prepare-for-addictive-intelligence/

3 *Web Junkie* trailer. www.youtube.com/watch?v=AH2yqOhiEj0

4 China's *Web Junkie*. www.nytimes.com/2014/01/20/opinion/chinas-web-junkies.html

5 How to fix TikTok addiction. www.tiktok.com/discover/how-to-fix-tiktok-addiction

6 Sharma, M., Tong, M., Korbak, T., Duvenaud, D., Askell, A., Bowman, S. R., ... & Perez, E. (2023). Towards understanding sycophancy in language models. *arXiv preprint arXiv:2310.13548.*

7 Turkle, S. (Ed.). (2011). *Evocative objects: Things we think with.* MIT Press.

8   Gatebox – Promotion movie "OKAERI"_english. www.youtube.com/watch?v=nkcKaNqfykg&t=3s

9   Dhamani, N. (2024). *Introduction to generative AI*. Simon and Schuster.

10 Dhamani, *Introduction to generative AI*.

11 Italy bans U.S.-based AI chatbot Replika from using personal data. www.reuters.com/technology/italy-bans-us-based-ai-chatbot-replika-using-personal-data-2023-02-03/

12 It's hurting like 'hell': AI companion users are in crisis, reporting sudden sexual rejection. www.vice.com/en/article/ai-companion-replika-erotic-roleplay-updates/

13 We need to prepare for 'addictive intelligence'. www.technologyreview.com/2024/08/05/1095600/we-need-to-prepare-for-addictive-intelligence/

14 We need to prepare for 'addictive intelligence'. www.technologyreview.com/2024/08/05/1095600/we-need-to-prepare-for-addictive-intelligence/

15 We need to prepare for 'addictive intelligence'. www.technologyreview.com/2024/08/05/1095600/we-need-to-prepare-for-addictive-intelligence/

16 What happened to the artificial-intelligence revolution? www.economist.com/finance-and-economics/2024/07/02/what-happened-to-the-artificial-intelligence-revolution

17 What happened to the artificial-intelligence revolution? www.economist.com/finance-and-economics/2024/07/02/what-happened-to-the-artificial-intelligence-revolution

18 Humlum, A., & Vestergaard, E. (2024). The adoption of ChatGPT. *University of Chicago, Becker Friedman Institute for Economics Working Paper*, (2024–50).

19 What happened to the artificial-intelligence revolution? www.economist.com/finance-and-economics/2024/07/02/what-happened-to-the-artificial-intelligence-revolution

20 Workism is making Americans miserable. www.theatlantic.com/ideas/archive/2019/02/religion-workism-making-americans-miserable/583441/

21 Why we need to understand machine behavior. https://dobetter.esade.edu/en/machine-behavior

22 The future of truth and misinformation online. www.pewresearch.org/internet/2017/10/19/the-future-of-truth-and-misinformation-online/

23 #390 – Yuval Noah Harari: Human nature, intelligence, power, and conspiracies. https://lexfridman.com/yuval-noah-harari/

24 Chat-GPT pretended to be blind and tricked a human into solving a CAPTCHA https://gizmodo.com/gpt4-open-ai-chatbot-task-rabbit-chatgpt-1850227471

25 Israel Defence Forces' response to claims about use of 'Lavender' AI database in Gaza. www.theguardian.com/world/2024/apr/03/israel-defence-forces-response-to-claims-about-use-of-lavender-ai-database-in-gaza

26 Israel offers a glimpse into the terrifying world of military AI. www.washingtonpost.com/world/2024/04/05/israel-idf-lavender-ai-militarytarget/

27 Lavender, Israel's artificial intelligence system that decides who to bomb in Gaza. https://english.elpais.com/technology/2024-04-17/lavender-israels-artificial-intelligence-system-that-decides-who-to-bomb-in-gaza.html

28 Saul, J. & Bass, D. "Artificial Intelligence is booming—So is its carbon footprint," *Bloomberg*, March 9, 2023, www.bloomberg.com/news/articles/2023-03-09/how-much-energy-do-ai-and-chatgpt-use-no-one-knows-for-sure#xj4y7vzkg

29 Stokel-Walker, C. "The generative AI race has a dirty secret," *Wired*, February 10, 2023, www.wired.co.uk/article/the-generative-ai-search-race-has-a-dirty-secret

30 Vanian, J., & Leswing, K. (2023, March 13). ChatGPT and generative AI are booming, but at a very expensive price. CNBC. Retrieved from www.cnbc.com/2023/03/13/chatgpt-and-generative-ai-are-booming-but-at-a-very-expensive-price.html

31 The number of nuclear weapons has declined substantially since the end of the Cold War. https://ourworldindata.org/nuclear-weapons

32 Gardner, M. N., & Brandt, A. M. (2006). "The doctors' choice is America's choice" the physician in US cigarette advertisements, 1930–1953. *American Journal of Public Health*, 96(2), 222–232.

33 Hanna, N., Mulshine, J., Wollins, D. S., Tyne, C., & Dresler, C. (2013). Tobacco cessation and control a decade later: American Society of Clinical Oncology policy statement update. *Journal of Clinical Oncology*, 31(25), 3147–3157.

34 Kulick, J., Prieger, J., & Kleiman, M. A. (2016). Unintended consequences of cigarette prohibition, regulation, and taxation. *International Journal of Law, Crime and Justice*, 46, 69–85.

35 Marwala, T. (2023). *Artificial intelligence, game theory and mechanism design in politics*. Springer Nature.

36 What are genetic algorithms? Working, applications, and examples www.spiceworks.com/tech/artificial-intelligence/articles/what-are-genetic-algorithms/

37 Nobel Prize Dialogue. www.nobelprize.org/events/nobel-prize-dialogue/brussels2024/panellists/demis-hassabis/

38 Shepherd, D. A., & Majchrzak, A. (2022). Machines augmenting entrepreneurs: Opportunities (and threats) at the nexus of artificial intelligence and entrepreneurship. *Journal of Business Venturing*, *37*(4), 106227.

39 Stopping Iran's attack would have forced Israel to use sophisticated – and expensive – defences. www.theguardian.com/world/2024/oct/01/stopping-iran-attack-would-have-forced-israel-to-use-sophisticated-and-expensive-defences

Index